THE SOUL
OF THE
TORAH

THE SOUL
OF THE
TORAH

**Insights of the Chasidic Masters
on the Weekly Torah Portions**

Victor Cohen

JASON ARONSON INC.
Northvale, New Jersey
Jerusalem

This book was set in 11 pt. Granjon by Alabama Book Composition of Deatsville, AL, and printed and bound by Book-mart Press, Inc. of North Bergen, NJ.

10 9 8 7 6 5 4 3 2 1

Library of Congress Cataloguing-in-Publication Data

The soul of the Torah: insights of the chasidic masters on the weekly Torah
    portions/ [compiled by] Victor Cohen
        p. cm.
    Includes bibliographical references and index.
    ISBN 0–7657–6141–6
    1. Bible. O.T. Pentateuch—Commentaries. 2. Hasidism.   I. Cohen,
    Victor, 1930–
BS1225.3 .F76   2000
222'.107—dc21   00–462237

Printed in the United States of America. Jason Aronson Inc. offers books and cassettes. For information and catalog write to Jason Aronson Inc., 230 Livingston Street, Northvale, NJ 07647-1726, or visit our website: http://www.aronson.com

To My Grandchildren

CONTENTS

The following is a list of abbreviations used throughout the citations of this text. Detailed information can be found in the bibliography.

Ch.B.	*Chachimah Birmizah*
D.Z.	*Derech Tzadikim*
F.C.O.	*Fun di ChasidisheOtsros*
F.U.A.O.	*Fun Unzer Alten Oitzer*
G.O.T.	*In the Garden of the Torah*
H.A.	*Hasidic Anthology*
M.D.	*Milei D'Chasida*
M.T.	*M'einah Shel Torah*
M.Tz.	*Menachem Tzion*
S.S.K.	*Siach Sarfei Kodesh*
T.D.H.T.R.	*The Torah Discourses of the Holy Tzaddik*
T.S.	*Tiferet Shlomo*

ACKNOWLEDGMENTS

First and foremost, I would like to thank Hashem for instilling within me the desire to understand the meaning of the soul of the Torah. I would like to thank Arthur Kurzweil for recognizing the need for this work and its implications. To Rob Crowner, for his painstaking editing, a *Yasher Koach*. To Ms. Hope Breeman and staff for their concern in seeing this book through production and publication, my sincere gratitude. My deepest appreciation to the members of my family for their concern and encouragement. And last and definitely not least, it is very difficult to express fully to my best friend, my wife, my appreciation for her diligence in editing the book. Her persistence, sincerity, and thoughtfulness are what made the book a reality. A true *eishet chayil*.

INTRODUCTION

The Chasidic movement of the eighteenth century is one of the most inspiring manifestations of spiritual development in the history of the Jews. Its genesis came at a time of spiritual depression caused by persecution from the outside and elitism on the inside. Jewish life had declined and education left much to be desired. There was economic depression and spiritual darkness. The intention of the Baal Shem Tov (1698–1760), founder of Chasidism, was to create an atmosphere of closeness to Hashem for all—learned and unlearned—and a consolidation leading to the brotherhood of Jews. Chasidism did not introduce anything new. It adhered to the Code of Law and the *mitzvot* incumbent upon a Jew. However, it emphasized the essence of the mitzvah by asking that one should perform the mitzvah by going beyond the letter of the Law—*Lifnim m'shurat hadin*.

Chasidism, with its emphasis on the mystical, looks for a meaning beyond the immediate. Its focus is upon the spiritual aspect of *devekut*, the communion of Hashem and the inner self. It insists that the joyful affirmation of life is the quintessence of a positive existence. Chasidism teaches the simplicity of uprightness while realizing that human nature is complex and vulnerable. Through brotherhood, deep association with the Tzaddik, and constant meditation leading to communion with Hashem for *tikkun*—rectification of the soul—the Chasid works at constantly striving for the sanctification of life. He yearns for a world that is good, for the untainted truth, and for a generation that is wholly pure. He attempts to live with an ideal, with a prayer that it will become real and pragmatic. The Chasid has the following on his lips: Blessed is the man that makes Hashem his trust, and respects not the proud, nor such that turn to lies.

We can see the development of the chasidic movement through the teachings of the Baal Shem Tov and his followers to this very day. The Besht's pupils listened to him in conversations, at discourses at the Sabbath third meal, as he expounded portions of the Torah, and as he clarified the human condition. In his day and the decades that followed, Chasidic interpretations were applied to the problems of the universe, Hashem, interrelationships, and personal development in holiness by many Tzaddikim. They taught that Godliness is everywhere and in everything and that He should be served in an atmosphere of joy, for one should worship Hashem with awe and with joy. Both are necessary and cannot be separated, for awe without joy is fear. One need only remove the accent on material needs to find Hashem. One need only pray with *kavannah* (sincere concentration) and *hitlahavut* (a burning sense of enthusiasm) to obtain a sense of *devekut* (attachment to the Almighty).

The Tzaddik devotes his days and nights to meditation and study to obtain an in-depth knowledge and understanding of what Hashem requires of us to lead a positive spiritual life. The Tzaddikim conveyed their messages to small groups of adherents who in turn transmitted the significance of the message to a larger sphere.

The Baal Shem Tov showed the importance of the *mashal* (allegory) by giving the example of a prince who stored coarse food in the fortress against his enemies' siege. He explained that one should store simple as well as profound tales in one's memory, for in disseminating the Chasidic viewpoint one may need to make use of either one. In the same light, a Rebbe asked another if any writings had been left by his Rebbe. The answer was that the writings were imprinted in the hearts of all the disciples.

The nineteenth-century philosopher Henri Bergson, in his book *The Two Sources of Morality and Religion*, states:

"Just as there have been men of genius to thrust back the bounds of intelligence . . . so exceptional souls have appeared who sensed their kinship with the soul of Everyman, who thus, instead of remaining within the limits of the group and going no further than the solidarity laid down by nature, were on a great surge of love toward humanity in general. The appearance of each one of them was like a creation of a new species, composed of one individual. . . . Each of these souls marked then a certain point attained by the evolution of life; and each of them was a manifestation, in an original form, of a love which seems to be the very essence of the creative effort. The creative emotion which exalted these exceptional souls, and which was an overflowing of vitality, has spread far and wide about them; enthusiasts themselves, they radiated enthusiasm which can be readily fanned into flame again. . . . When we listen to their words and see them at work, we feel that they can communicate to us something of their fervor. . . . True mystics simply open their souls to the oncoming wave. Sure of themselves, because they feel within them something better than themselves, they prove to be great men of action . . . the necessity to spread around them what they have received affects them like an onslaught of love . . . a love which can be just as well passed on through the medium of a person who has attached himself to them or to their evergreen memory and formed his life on that pattern."

The Gerer Rebbe (1799–1866) noted that it is imperative to bear in mind that it becomes our duty, as members of the people of Israel, to perform any act that may make the world a better place to live. Thus, there is a regard for the Jew as a person, a creation of Hashem, and there is a spark of the Divine within us that must be nurtured. This perspective is seen through the interpretations of the various *Pasukim* in the Torah. The Rebbe's insight into the words of the Torah permits us to integrate the word of Hashem into our souls and show our relationship to Him and to our fellow man. Each interpretation helps create in us a sense of appreciation for life with the understanding of Who created it. Taking the Rebbe's explanation of each *Pasuk* to heart brings a sense of *devekut*, an attachment to the Divine, permitting Him to enter all facets of life. The Rebbe draws from the "upper worlds" to instruct (*Sichot*

Haran). He gives each person an understanding of what Hashem requires for his needs to be met or his problems to be solved.

The *Pasukim* of the Torah are not purely academic, nor to be studied as a separate subject, but to help us to comprehend the dynamics of life as created by Hashem. As Rabbi Isaiah Horowitz, the HaShelah HaKadosh, states, "Who is a Chasid? He who acts with love of his Creator, striving to give Him pleasure, and whose whole intention is to cleave to Him in *devekut* for the sake of His great name, becoming thereby a chariot for Hashem." (*Kitzur Shnei Luchot haBrit, Sh'ar ha-Ahavah*, p. 11)

> "Our Father, the merciful Father, Who acts mercifully, have mercy upon us; instill in our hearts to understand and elucidate; to listen, learn, teach, safeguard, perform, and fulfill all the words of Your Torah's teaching with love; enlighten our eyes in Your Torah, attach our hearts to Your commandments, and unify our hearts to love and fear Your name. . . . You have brought us close to Your great name forever in truth, to offer praiseful thanks to You, and proclaim Your Oneness with love."
>
> (*Ahavah Rabbah*—Prayer Book)

WEEKLY PORTIONS OF BERESHIT/GENESIS

BERESHIT
"IN THE BEGINNING"

The Sassover explained why the Torah begins with the words "In the beginning, God created." (Gen. 1:1) This is to inform us that the basis of all knowledge is that God is the sole creator of everything. (M.T., vol. 1, p. 7)

The Midrash (*Bereshit Rabbah* 1:6) comments that Israel is called "first" in the Torah. The Gerer Rebbe said that the word "first" is used rather than "beginning" to show that the Creation came for the sake of Israel. It is imperative to bear in mind that it becomes our duty, as Jews, to perform any act that may make the world a better place in which to live. (H.A., p. 200)

The Lubavitcher Rebbe, Rabbi Menachem Mendel Schneerson, commented that it is a known fact that God, the Torah, and the Jewish People are one. Therefore, observance of the *mitzvot* expresses the purpose of creation. The words "In the beginning" indicate that creation is only the first phase in an ongoing process, for man is intended to be God's "partner in creation" (*Shabbat* 10a), helping God realize His desire for a dwelling. God created the material world but left to man the task of revealing the spiritual within it. The Zohar states that "God looked into the Torah and created the world. Man looks into the Torah and maintains the world." (G.O.T., p. 1–5)

⮌

The Yid HaKadosh commented that when a Jew feels depressed and worried because of difficult times, let him remember how the world was created. The world was created with ten (*yid*) sayings. The world was created for the sake of the Jew (*Yid*). This outlook would give solace to the Jew and lighten his burden. (F.C.O., p. 2)

⮌

The Strikover Rebbe finds character implications in the letters of the word *Bereshit*, namely: *bitachon*, trust; *ratson*, will; *ahavah*, love; *shetikah*, silence; *yirah*, fear; Torah, learning. The word *barah* (created) reminds us of our material needs, namely: *bar*, children; *bari*, health; and *bar*, grain. The last letters of the words *Bereshit Barah Elokim Et* (In the beginning God created) spell *emet*, truth. (H.A., p. 62)

⮌

R' Bunim commented that Hashem created the world in a state of beginning so as to always be in a creative state. It is not like an object formed and completed by a craftsman. The universe needs continual labor and renewal. If this process were to stop then the universe would revert to its original chaos. (H.A., p. 62)

⮌

The Bratzlaver said, "Declare at all times: The world was created for my sake. Do not declare: Of what concern is this to me? But do your share to add some improvement, to supply something that is missing, and to leave the world a little better than when you first came into it." (*Kitzur Likkutei Maharan*)

⮌

The Lechivitzer translated the word *Bereshis* as "For the sake of the first." He said that Hashem demands that man make a beginning in the right direction and after, He will assist him to continue on the right path. Therefore, He ordained that we should dedicate the first fruits, the first stalks of grain, the first cattle to Him, and the Law of Tradition commands us to devote the first part of the day to prayer. (H.A., p. 61)

～～

R' Aharon Karliner noted that just as the Almighty renews creation everyday so must each individual be an innovator everyday. (F.C.O., p. 1)

～～

The Lenchener commented that if a person reminds himself everyday that Hashem created the heavens and the earth then he will recognize that all material needs are as nothing. (F.C.O., p. 1)

～～

The Berditchever said that the reason we say "He creates light and creates darkness" (Prayer Book) in the present rather than the past tense is that the process of creation is a continuous one. Thus it says, "He is constantly renewing, with His goodness, creation everyday." (F.C.O., p. 1)

～～

Tzemach Tzedek of Lubavitch commented on the *Pasuk* "Let there be light." (Gen. 1:3) He said that God wanted that there should be a "lower realm," otherwise He would have created a world that would recognize Him effortlessly. God wanted a universe in which the creation was separated from its Creator; that man should realize the connection for himself and develop it until the world would proceed to the state of ultimate fulfillment. For man to reach such heights requires a fusion of opposites, and it is in such a fusion that God's essence is revealed. "Israel, the Torah, and the Holy One, blessed be He, are all one." (Zohar, vol. 3) Every Jew's soul is "an actual part of God" (*Tanya*), and the Torah is God's will and wisdom. Since the Torah and the Jewish people are one with God, the observance of the *mitzvot* expresses the purpose of creation. (G.O.T., vol. 1, pp. 1–5)

〜

Rabbi Schneur Zalman, with great passion and enthusiasm, exclaimed, "Almighty, I have no need for your *Gan-Eden* and I forgive you for your Creation. All I want is You, Your sense of Holiness, and to become attached to You." (F.C.O., p. 2)

〜

The Baal Shem Tov stated, "The word with which the Almighty established the world remains and thus sustains and preserves its existence." (F.C.O., p. 2)

〜

Reb Simcha Bunim, in contemplating the creation, remarked, "When I look deeply at the world I see a vast desert. The people are as trees. Yet the only one I really see is the proprietor of all, namely, the Almighty Himself." (F.C.O., p. 3)

〜

On the *Pasuk* "And there was evening and there was morning" (Gen. 1:5), the Imrei Shefer commented that the Jews start the day on the night before and the evening becomes part of the next day. The night is laden with trepidation and fear. However, when daytime comes, there is light and salvation. As is known, "the righteous begin with affliction and end with salvation. The wicked begin with salvation and end with affliction." (M.T., vol. 1, p. 10)

〜

On the biblical statement "Let there be a division between the waters" (Gen. 1:6), R' Aharon Karliner said that the Torah is known as "waters" for it is written: "All who are thirsty, go to the waters." Therefore, we must learn to differentiate between the waters as between the Torah and any other knowledge. (F.C.O., p. 4)

R' Bunim interpreted the phrase "to differentiate between the light and the darkness" (Gen. 1:18) as follows: "As there is light and darkness in the world, so there is light and darkness in our daily lives and in our intellectual life." (F.C.O., p. 4)

There is a Midrash on the biblical statement "And God said, Let Us make Man." (Gen. 1:26)

> At the time that the Almighty was about to create Man, *Chesed* (kindness) said, "Create." *Emes* (truth) said, "Do not create." *Tzedek* (righteousness) said, "Create." *Shalom* (peace) said, "Do not create." What did God Almighty do? He threw Truth to the earth.

The Kotzker Rebbe, commenting on this Midrash, said that this is somewhat difficult to understand. Both *Shalom* and Truth requested that Man not be created. Then why did God throw Truth downward? It shows that when we deny truth, we think that there is peace, because most arguments are carried on for the sake of peace and not for truth. So, in the course of arguing truth is overlooked and peace, we assume, is restored. (F.C.O., p. 9)

The following interpretation was given by the Strikover Rebbe: "And it was evening" (Gen. 1:5) signifies the persecutions of the Diaspora; "And it was morning" signifies the Redemption. "It was one day" lets us know that when the Jews will act as one, there will peace and harmony among them. (F.U.A.O., p. 9)

"The Angels are greater than the Human Being," said the Chidushei Harim. "In the world of Mankind, there are disagreements because Man has free choice but the Angels are of one mind for they have no choice. When the Almighty was ready to create Man, the Midrash relates that the Angels took sides. One group suggested that Man should be created and the other group opposed his creation. When God saw that there was a disagreement among the Angels, He saw no difference, so He created Man." (F.C.O., p. 9)

⸺⸺

The Kotzker asked a Chasid, "Did you ever see a live wolf?" "Of course I did, " answered the Chasid. "Were you scared of him?" asked the Kotzker. "Without a doubt I was scared," noted the Chasid. "Did you know that you were scared?" questioned the Kotzker. "No! At the time of extreme fear, I had no inkling that I was scared," was his answer. "That is 'true fear of Heaven,'" said the Kotzker, "to fear and not know it." (F.C.O., p. 7)

⸺⸺

The S'fas Emes commented on the verse "And God had finished on the seventh day." (Gen. 2:2) Although the creation was finished by the seventh day, God felt that rest was missing—so God gave the Sabbath. God created the world out of chaos and ended with rest. This is why the Jew who works on the Sabbath is called a *m'chalel Shabbos*—because he degrades rest and makes it appear as if the world is still in chaos as at the beginning. (F.C.O., p. 13)

⸺⸺

On the *Pasuk* "God blessed them and God said to them" (Gen. 1:28), the Koznitzer commented that the soul of each individual has a spark of the Divine within him, as it is written, "For the portion of Hashem is His people; Jacob is the lot of His inheritance." (Deut. 32:9) Its essence is that one should become holy and pure according to his ability. He should be like a spotless container to guard the Divine that is within him. As it is written, "And they shall make Me a sanctuary; and I will dwell in it." (Ex. 25:8) Then one will be worthy to be as one with the Almighty. Hashem blessed them to continue the Divinity within, so that Hashem, so to speak, will be able to converse personally. (M.D., p. 11)

On Rashi's statement "It is the nature of Man to conquer" (Gen. 1:28), the Zitomer Rebbe said that it is only when the individual conquers his evil inclination can he call himself "Man." (F.C.O., p. 15)

The Vorker Rebbe commented that Adam's transgression was that his main concern was for the morrow. The serpent prodded him by telling him that he was a servant who was unable to tell the difference between good and evil. He was told to eat the fruit so he could choose good and receive a reward. And Adam, worried about the morrow, listened and did evil. He would not have done so if he would have been grateful for the present. He would have listened to God's commandments and resisted. The morrow would have taken care of itself. (H.A., p. 95)

The snake said to Eve, "Why is it necessary to listen to God's command not to eat from the fruit of the Garden and why is one obligated to obey every single command?" (Gen. 3:1) The Chidushei Harim said that the question the snake asked is utilized by all who wish to disobey the commandments of God. (F.C.O., p. 17)

A pious individual complained to the Baal Shem Tov that he worked very hard in his observances and yet found no improvement in that he was still an ordinary and ignorant man. "Not true," said the Baal Shem Tov. "You now realize that you are an ordinary and ignorant man and that is an improvement." (H.A., p. 429)

NOACH

"And Noach found favor in God's eyes." (Gen. 6:8) The question posed is why favor in God's eyes rather than in the eyes of man. The Rimanover understood from this *Pasuk* that since Noach was a righteous person in his time, he did admonish the people for their wrongdoing. However, because it is the nature of people to deny wrongdoing, they reject moral rebuke. Therefore, while the people rejected Noach, nevertheless he "found favor in God's eyes." (M.Tz., p. 125)

The Ostrovitzer made the following observation on the *Sidra* "These are the generations of Noach." (Gen. 6:9) He said that there is spiritual Noach and the Noach who has concern for his fellow man. As a spiritual person, he was a God-fearing individual and a wholesome pure person, yet he lived in peace with his neighbors and tried to overlook their poor behavior and justify them. Therefore, we find that some praise him and some find fault with him. (F.C.O., p. 29)

The Yid HaKadosh noted that fathers strive to help their children become learned and pious Jews. In turn, their children train their own children to follow in their footsteps. However, he asked, "When will the time come when the father will strive to be on a high level and not leave the task to his children?" He said that is why it is stated: "These are the sons (or generations) of Noach. Noach was a just, wholehearted man." (Gen. 6:9) "Noach himself was what he wanted his sons to be," explained the Yid HaKadosh. (F.C.O., p. 31)

The Lizensker commented on the same *Pasuk*. He said that the fact that Noach thought of himself as righteous made him a good man but of a lesser degree. The man who continues to labor in search of Hashem never stands still. The Tzaddik seeks to purify that which necessitates change for all generations. Every change marks a different "generation" in his life. It is in this way that a man lives in many generations, as it is written of Noah "in his generation." (Gen. 6:9) (*Noam Elimelech*, p. 3)

Rabbi Menachem Mendel Schneerson, the Lubavitcher Rebbe, noted that the Maggid of Mezritch interpreted the statement "Know what is above you" as "Know that everything 'above'—all that transpires in the spiritual realms—is from you, dependent on your conduct. Each of us has a potential to influence even the most elevated spiritual realms." The Rebbe commented that the Torah alludes to this potential in the *Pasuk* "These are the generations of Noach. Noach was a righteous man." (Gen. 6:9) The name "Noach" refers to satisfaction and tranquillity. The Hebrew word *Noach* means "rest" and suggests the word *nachas*, pleasure. (*Bereshit Rabbah* 30:5 and the Zohar) The Torah implies that Noach and his descendants implanted these two qualities among their fellow men and the spiritual world above. Every person affects his environment. Therefore, our thoughts, words, and deeds can inspire peace and tranquillity by helping create meaningful pleasure. (G.O.T., pp. 7–8)

The Berditchever noted that there are two types of Tzaddikim. There is the Tzaddik who is concerned only for himself and does not get involved with others, who therefore does not influence others in developing spiritual heights. Then, there is the Tzaddik who is very much concerned for his fellow man. He is the one who tries to bring people closer to God and so helps people reach transpersonal heights. Noach exemplified the first type of Tzaddik. (F.C.O., p. 30)

Commenting on the *Pasuk* "Noach was a righteous person; he was pure in his generation" (Gen. 6:9), the Amshinover said that the people in Noach's generation considered him a righteous person because he did not admonish them. He let them go about their wicked ways. People accept this type of a Tzaddik. (F.C.O., p. 32)

On the same *Pasuk*, Rashi comments that there are rabbis who interpret the words "in his generations" as praise of Noach, and there are rabbis who interpret the words to the detriment of Noach. The Primishlaner noted that Rashi was teaching us that no one is exempt from gossip, even the leader of a generation. All one can do is deal with the situation. There were those in Noach's generation who spoke against Noach, even though the Torah is witness to the fact that he was "righteous in his generation." (F.U.A.O., p. 31)

"These are the generations of Noach. Noach was a righteous man." (Gen. 6:9) Rashi comments: "To teach you that the main offspring of the righteous are good deeds." R' Yaacov Aaron of Alexander noted that the Yid HaKadosh said that one works very hard for the sake of his children so that they should grow up to be good people—and when they have grown up, they, too, will forget about themselves and work hard on behalf of their children. Noach did not only work for his children but he also considered himself a child. Therefore, he worked on his own development. He realized that his good deeds were the offspring of serving Hashem. This is what is meant by "The main offspring of the righteous are good deeds." (M.T., vol. 1, p. 36)

The Lubliner asked a very interesting question on the *Pasuk* "Noach was a righteous man and a *tammim* in his generation." (Gen. 6:9) "Who is of a higher status, a *tammim* (a wholesome person) or a *gadol* (a great person)?" The Lubliner reasoned as follows: "We put two *challot* on the table. One is big but part of it is gone and the other is small but complete. The question is, over which one do we recite the *Motzei*? Obviously, the completed one." From this we see that a *tammim* is preferable to a *gadol*. (F.C.O., p. 33)

‿‿

The Yid HaKadosh, interpreting the spirituality of Noach, said that there are three categories in the service of God:

1. In the highest category are those who are constantly involved with *mitzvot* and good deeds. They feel that what they are doing is necessary and they do not look for any reward.
2. There are those who are aware that they do not perform many *mitzvot* and do not do many good deeds. For these people there is hope that they will begin to perform more *mitzvot* and good deeds.
3. There are those who think of themselves as Tzaddikim and therefore feel no need for self-improvement. They will never reach any great spiritual heights. (F.C.O., p. 33)

‿‿

When asked why a Tzaddik is called a "good Jew," R' Bunim answered that if he prays well, he should be called a "good worshipper"; if he learns well, a "good learner." However, when a Jew thinks, eats, sleeps, and intends goodness, he is a "good Jew." (H.A., p. 531)

‿‿

There is a story told about a time when a group of Chasidim were discussing their noble heritage in front of the Ropshitzer Rebbe. At one point, one of the Chasidim called out that he was a greater person than any. Upon quieting the group, the Rebbe asked why he felt that way. "I want you to know," he said, "that I am the only one in my family observing the *mitzvot*." The Rebbe replied that he was definitely a much greater person. (F.C.O., p. 35)

~

On the *Pasuk* "And Noach had begotten three sons: Shem, Ham, and Yaphet" (Gen. 6:10), the Noam Elimelech gave the following symbolic interpretation. Noach had three sons, three degrees of perfection. Shem (the name) stands for the first degree, which is to sanctify the Holy Name within us and to do repentance for our flaws. Ham, meaning "warmth," the second degree, represents the warmth in our prayers needed to do battle against the return of our former faults. The third degree, Yaphet, meaning "beautifying" or "perfecting," offers Hashem perfect devotion, a devotion that should burn within us. (*Noam Elimelech*, pp. 3–4)

~

On the *Pasuk* "And God saw that the wickedness of man was great upon the earth" (Gen. 6:12), the Radamsker noted that in the Midrash we are told that Abraham asked Noach's son Shem how they were saved from the flood. He answered that they had mercy on the animals and birds, so Hashem had mercy on them. The Radamsker commented that if the people would have had mercy on each other, they would have awakened the mercy above and they, too, would have been saved. However, they were wicked and petty to each other and had no mercy, "And God saw the earth and behold it was corrupted" (Gen. 6:12), so God had no mercy on all their wickedness. (M.T., vol. 1, p. 40)

~

On the *Pasuk* "With bottom, second, and third stories you shall make it [the ark]" (Gen. 6:16), the Lizensker said that these words can be explained in two ways. In the first, he said that there are three types of people: the perfect, the moderately good, and the wicked. The second meaning is that there are three periods in a person's life. When he is young, he is most vulnerable to transgressions. In his middle age, he is too involved with making a livelihood to sin. In his old age, he is able to work for self-improvement and to repair the injuries to his soul that he had caused until then. It is for this reason that the Torah says "Thou shall make it" near the "third story." (H.A., p. 527)

On the *Pasuk* "You shall make a window for your *teyvah*" (Gen. 6:16) (*teyvah* can mean "ark" or "word"), the S'fas Emes commented that one should bring light to the word, for the words of the Torah and one's prayers should be bright and clear. (F.C.O., p. 37)

On the same *Pasuk*, the Baal Shem Tov commented that one should make sure that what emanates from the mouth will enlighten others. The word is the life of the individual and of the Almighty. If a person says something positive and worthwhile, the word will ascend heavenward and will awaken the heavenly words to do good. If the words are evil than the life leaves the word and it will not ascend heavenward but will remain as an evil force on earth. (F.C.O., p. 37)

On the *Pasuk* "And you shall take all kinds of food to eat" (Gen. 6:21), the Koznitzer noted that from this we learn that when one eats food and does not derive any pleasure from it, he must say that he is not an expert on food. Food is like a human being, and one is not permitted to degrade it. (F.C.O., p. 37)

On the *Pasuk* "Noach and his sons . . . went into the ark because of the waters of the Flood" (Gen. 7:7), Rashi comments that Noach, too, was one of little faith. Though he believed, he did not enter the ark until the waters compelled him. The Vorker queried how Noach could be called a "righteous man, perfect" (Gen. 6:9) if he was not a complete believer. The Vorker answered that Noach still believed that the people would repent and the flood would not come and the decree would be averted. (M.T., vol. 1, p. 44)

It is interesting to note that on the *Pasuk* "Man and woman shall come into the *teyvah*" (Gen. 7:9), based on the double meaning of the word ("ark" and "word"), the Baal Shem Tov said that each word in the Torah has two meanings, the hidden and the revealed. (F.C.O., p. 38)

The Yismach Moshe commented on Rashi's interpretation of the word *vayitzer*, spelled with two *yids*, meaning "and He formed." This informs us that each individual has a *yetzer tov* and a *yetzer harah*, bad and good inclinations. Whichever *yetzer* is permitted in through the window will dictate all actions. (F.C.O., p. 39)

There are two interesting interpretations on the *Pasuk* "Whoever sheds the blood of man, among man his blood shall be shed; for in the image of God He made man." (Gen. 9:6) First is a comment made by the Yid HaKadosh: "The Sages tell us, 'Anyone who embarrasses another in public, it is as if he has shed blood.' If we are not absolutely sure that it will cause him to mend his ways, then it is an obvious embarrassment and that is definitely not permitted." (F.C.O., p. 42) The other is a story told about the Lubliner, who strongly admonished a Chasid of his to the extent that the Chasid became ill. The Chasid asked the Rebbe, "How come that the Rebbe should embarrass one to such an extent?" The Rebbe answered, "You are correct, my son. Please forgive me! I sincerely thought that my words would be a healing for your sick soul and that my words would be like a medicine and heal you. It appears that you do not consider me as a physician to understand illness; therefore my medicine was not appropriate for you. Since I did not cure you, I beg for your forgiveness for I did embarrass you." (F.C.O., p. 42)

On the *Pasuk* "Cursed be Canaan; a servant of servants shall he be to his brethren" (Gen. 9:25), the S'fas Emes commented that the worst curse is slavery and the greatest blessing is freedom. (F.C.O., p. 42)

LECH L'CHAH
"GO TO YOUR BIRTHPLACE"

The Lizensker explained the words of the *Pasuk* "Go out of the country, from your birthplace, and out of your father's house to the land that I will show you." (Gen. 12:1) "Get out of your country"—do not hesitate to leave your country because famous people live there. "And out of your birthplace"—out of the place where they generate only intellectuals. "And from your father's house"—from where you are a respected member of your family. "Go to the land that I will show you"—to establish there a center of culture, learning, and nobility made by your own labors. (F.C.O., p. 46)

Rabbi Menachem Mendel Schneerson, the Lubavitcher Rebbe, commented that *lech* means "proceed," referring to the beginning of a journey. Real spiritual progress requires that one leaves one's current state behind. Yet as long as an individual's growth depends entirely on his own power, his progress will be limited; nobody can exceed the bounds of his own understanding. "Go out of your land, your native land, and your father's house" is an instruction to abandon one's ordinary way of thinking, to go to levels beyond and to transcend one's own limits. With progress that is guided by God, there are no limits to the potential of growth. The Torah and its *mitzvot* can take a person far beyond his natural horizons. Thus Hashem's statement to Abraham: "To the land that I will show you." (G.O.T., pp. 15–17)

On the same *Pasuk*, the Noam Elimelech commented that one should pave his own path, show pride in his performance of the *mitzvot*, and not be dependent on the behavior of his ancestry. (F.C.O., p. 44)

Lech l'chah means that one should always go forward to reach greater heights, advised the S'fas Emes. (F.C.O., p. 44)

Commenting on the *Pasuk* "To the land that I will show you" (Gen. 12:1), the S'fas Emes asked the question, "Why didn't the Almighty show Abraham the land immediately?" The answer was that the Almighty wanted Abraham to have the desire to look to the future for fulfillment of inner striving. (F.C.O., p. 44)

On the *Pasuk* "And I will bless those that bless you, and he that curses you, I will curse; and in you shall all the families of the earth be blessed" (Gen. 12:3), the Berditchever commented that Hashem would bless immediately those who had thoughts of blessing Abraham. The people who would verbally curse would be treated in kind. (F.C.O., p. 48)

On the *Pasuk* "And the souls they made in Haran" (Gen. 12:5), Rashi comments that Abraham would convert the men. The Chidushei Harim noted that one should not think that only a good generation deserves a strong Rebbe while a mediocre generation does not. Just the opposite, the Chidushei Harim commented that the mediocre generation needs a stronger Rebbe, for as in an illness, the worse the illness, the greater the need for a specialist. (F.C.O., p. 49)

Concerning the *Pasuk* "Let there not be a quarrel between you and me" (Gen. 13:8), the Ollelut Ephraim said that Abraham pleaded with Lot that they should not quarrel between themselves because of the Canaanites and the Peruzim who lived in their midst. When two people have a dispute, the third party wins. (F.C.O., p. 50)

On the *Pasuk* "Fear not, Abram, I am a shield for you" (Gen. 15:1), the Osrovitzer said that Hashem guaranteed Abram, since he brought the idea of monotheism and faith to the world, that He would protect him under all difficult circumstances. (F.C.O., p. 51)

On the same *Pasuk*, the Yid HaKadosh commented that in every Jewish heart there is a spark of the Divine that protects so that it can never be extinguished. (F.C.O., p. 52)

"And He took him outside, and said, 'Gaze, now, toward the Heavens and count the stars, if you are able to count them!' And He said to him, 'So shall your offspring be!'" (Gen. 15:5) Rashi comments that God took Abram out of the space of the world and raised him above the stars. The S'fas Emes explained that Hashem raised Abram to a high spiritual state beyond the natural. Hashem promised him that the future generations, "your offspring," would live above the norm and would be on a high spiritual level. (F.U.A.O., vol. 1, p. 68)

On the same *Pasuk*, Rashi quotes the midrashic interpretation, "Go out of your astrology that you have seen in the Zodiac." The Chidushei Harim said that Hashem promised Abraham that his life activities would be beyond the natural and the signs of the constellations. Though he would not be able to have children, Hashem put him above the natural. "So will be your children"—they, too, will be beyond the natural and their behavior will be extraordinary. They will be under Divine supervision in a miraculous manner, as our Sages have said: "The signs of the constellation will hold no sway over Israel." (Talmud *Shabbat* 166) (M.T., vol. 1, p. 67)

~~~

On the same *Pasuk*, the Baal Shem Tov explained that when one looks at the stars, they appear very small. In actuality, they are very large. So will it be with the Jews: They will seem small and insignificant but in the Heavens they will be large and they will build the foundation of all existence. (M.T., vol. 1, p. 66)

~~~

On the *Pasuk* "And he trusted in Hashem, and He reckoned it to him as righteousness" (Gen. 15:6), R' Moshe Kobriner commented that Abraham, our father, was thankful to Hashem that he merited becoming a firm and perfect believer. Abraham considered this to be Divine charity. (F.C.O., p. 53)

~~~

On the *Pasuk* "He said, My Lord God, whereby shall I know that I shall inherit it?" (Gen. 15:8), R' Elimelech Grodzisker wondered how was it possible that Abraham, who was a sincere and wholehearted believer, should ask, "Whereby shall I know?" His answer was that Abraham was asking about his children. He was a believer but his concern was for his children and all future generations. How would they inherit his deep beliefs? (F.C.O., p. 52)

~~~

On the *Pasuk* "Know with certainty that your offspring shall be sojourners in a land not their own" (Gen. 15:13), the Kotzker commented that Jews should always feel that they are in a land that is not their own rather than have an emancipated attitude. The latter attitude causes a feeling of equality that might jeopardize their behavior as Jews. (F.C.O., p. 54)

~~~

In the same *Pasuk*, though we find two diverse attitudes toward Hashem's relationship with His people, there is a deep Chasidic philosophy of Hashem's love for His people in spite of their behavior. The

Shpolyer Zayde complained to God, "Why do You continue to argue with Your people to prove Your conquest and withhold redemption? We say, 'Return to us and we will return,' and You say, 'Return unto Me and I will return.' Are You really waiting for us to repent and You will redeem us? I swear to You by all that is Holy that the Jews will not repent for the sake of redemption." However, R' Yisroel Riziner said that he would swear and guarantee that the Jews would definitely repent when the Messiah will come, for the Jews have a good argument: "But because of our sins, we have been exiled from our land and sent far from our soil." (High Holy Days Prayer Book) Before we transgressed, You guaranteed Abraham that "Your offspring shall be sojourners in a land not their own." (Gen. 15:13) Therefore, You must first redeem us and then we will repent. (F.C.O., p. 54)

On the *Pasuk* "And He said to Abram" (Gen. 15:13), the Radamsker noted that in the entire *parsha* (portion), we find phrases like "And Hashem said to him" and "Hashem said to Abraham." However, here we note that it says "And He said to Abram." It is a known concept of our Sages that "The Divine Presence will not dwell in the midst of sadness." (*Shabbat* 30b) "And He said to Abram, 'Take to Me three heifers, and three goats, etc.'" (Gen. 15:9). Because this was meant to be a sacrifice of repentance, Hashem is not mentioned. The statement "He said to Abram, 'You will certainly know'" (Gen. 15:13), was a hint that the Israelites would be in exile. Therefore, Hashem did not want the Divine Presence to be associated with the sad tidings. Once Abraham brought the sacrifice, Hashem was able to dwell in the midst of happiness and promise wealth. (M.D., p. 31)

On the *Pasuk* "And you (Abraham) shall come to your ancestors in peace" (Gen. 15:15), Rashi comments: "This has taught you that Terach repented." The Chidushei Harim wondered how Rashi knew that Terach (Abraham's father) had repented. Terach may have merited being buried with his son, for it is known that a son brings merit to a father. However, it would not have mentioned "ancestors" if Terach's

father had not also been included. Terach's repentance enabled his
father to be buried with his son. (F.U.A.O., vol. 1, p. 72)

⌇⌇

"Therefore he called the well (*lab'er*) 'The Well of the Living One
Appearing to Me.'" (Gen. 16:14) In his *sefer*, *Razin D'Oraisa*, R' Zev Tzvi
of Zbariz said that a basic principle of the Torah is that it is everlasting and not a series of stories. It teaches us to be vigilant of the evil
inclination and offers us the means of repentance. Being of a devious
nature, the evil inclination begins by telling a person that everything is
good. That is why one should be diligent at all times to study, do
repentance, and do good deeds. The word *b'er* is analogous to a person
who is like a "bubbling spring" and does good deeds from the depths of
his essence. He is like a fountain that derives all from its source. Therefore, if a person wishes to be called a *b'er*—a fountain—he must
constantly be absorbed in learning Torah, performing *mitzvot*, and
being penitent. He should be as a "Well of the Living One." He should
try to bring others to repentance while he, too, is examining himself.
Thus he will become like a living well drawing from his inner source.
(M.D., p. 31)

⌇⌇

On the *Pasuk* "Walk before Me and be perfect" (Gen. 17:1), the Strikover
noted that to be truly "perfect" is to be with the Almighty. However, he
said that to get along with other people and be "perfect" is very difficult.
(F.U.A.O., vol. 1, p. 74)

⌇⌇

R' Mordechai of Nadburna made the following comment on the same
Pasuk. He said that every person finds it difficult to reach beyond his
level. When it comes to becoming wholesome in faith, one needs to be
close to the Almighty, as it is written: "Wholehearted shall you be with
the Lord, your God." (Deut. 18:13) This would permit him to reach
higher levels. This is why the Torah says, "Walk before Me," and thus
you will become perfect in faith. (M.D., p. 32)

On the *Pasuk* "And as for you, you shall keep My covenant" (Gen. 17:9), R' Yosef Moshe of Z'barov commented that if one wishes to merit being with the Almighty, one must first "keep My covenant." (M.D., p. 32)

On the *Pasuk* "For every male among you to be circumcised" (Gen. 17:10), R' Heschel Apter said that it is interesting to note that our Sages tell us that Abraham observed all the *mitzvot*, even the mitzvah of *eruv tavshilin* (permitting one to cook on a holiday in preparation for the Shabbat). Therefore, it seems almost impossible that Abraham did not observe the mitzvah of circumcision. Why did Hashem have to command him to observe this mitzvah? The Apter explained that there are certain *mitzvot* that necessitate a specific command and circumcision is one of them. This is based on the talmudic injunction "A person is not permitted to bring pain upon himself." (*Babba Kamma* 91b) (F.U.A.O., vol. 1, p. 75)

VAYEIRA
"AND HASHEM APPEARED"

The S'fas Emes, on the *Pasuk* "Hashem appeared to him [Abraham]" (Gen. 18:1), commented that everything in the universe has a Divine aspect within it. All we have to do is peel away the shell, the material parts, and the Divine within it will appear. (F.C.O., p. 55)

⸻

"And Hashem appeared unto him, and he, Abraham, was sitting at the open door of his tent." (Gen. 18:1) The Gerer Rebbe commented that the reason Abraham kept an open door was to invite people to learn the true nature of God. He sat by the door to personally greet the passersby and teach that one should be free from pride, aloofness, and envy, for that would be the path to spiritual perfection. (H.A., p. 182)

⸻

"He was sitting at the entrance of the tent." (Gen. 18:1) R' Yaakov Yosef of Polnoye commented that it is the sign of a truly righteous person that he is always "at the entrance." This means that he is aware that he has much to do and much to accomplish. (F.U.A.O., p. 78)

⸻

"Please pass not from before your servant." (Gen. 18:3) Based on this *Pasuk*, the Talmud (*Shabbat* 127a) states that "Greater is hospitality than accepting the Divine Countenance." The Primishlaner commented that the very being of Abraham, our father, was so holy to the extent that every part of his body performed the mitzvah, which was the Divine Will. When Abraham felt that his feet ran by themselves to greet the guests, he understood that "greater is hospitality than accepting the Divine Countenance." (M.T., vol. 1, p. 75)

～～

The Baal Shem Tov explained, according to Jewish Law, why there should be a difference to us that "greater is hospitality than accepting the Divine Countenance." We can say that there is a possibility that while being hospitable, we may miss chances of learning Torah or we may get involved in slanderous gossip. However, we learn that we overlook these and perform the mitzvah of hospitality. (M.T., vol. 1, p. 75)

～～

"Let some water be brought, please, and wash your feet." (Gen. 18:4) Rashi comments: "He was under the impression that they were wilderness dwellers, who bow to the dust of their feet." Rabbi Nachum Mordechai Perlow, the Novominsker Rebbe, said that from this we learn that each goal reveals the intention of an individual. To reach that goal there is much labor and strain, for as one approaches his goal, there are many compelling forces that challenge him. The language of our Sages calls these the "dust" of the ways. The Talmud states that indirect interest is called the "dust of interest" (*Baba Metzia* 61b) and slander is the "dust of an evil tongue" (*Baba Batra* 165a). We were created to attain a spiritual life; therefore, Abraham performed the mitzvah of hospitality to achieve his goal. He wanted to bring his guests under the "Wings of the Presence." First, he taught them that they must cease the worship of the dust on their feet, the material aspects of their lives. To reach spiritual goals, one should not give credence to earthly endeavors or indirect goals, nor submit to compelling behavior. Once the "dust" is wiped away then the goal of service to Hashem can be reached. As King David says in Psalms 119:59–61, "I considered my ways and returned my feet to Your testimonies. I hastened and I did not delay to keep Your commandments. Bands of wicked men plundered me, but I did not forget Your Torah." (*Pe'er Nachum*, p. 28)

⸺

"'I will fetch a morsel of bread that you may nourish your heart. After, you shall pass, inasmuch as you have passed your servant's way.' They said, 'So shall you do, just as you have said.'" (Gen. 18:5) The Midrash 48:11 comments that because the angels do not need food, therefore they said, "You do for yourself as you do but not for us. Hashem will permit you to merit to make another feast for the son that will be born to Sarah." The Novominsker Rebbe explained that when the angels saw that through Abraham's hospitality of serving food he brought people closer to serving Hashem, they were impressed. They knew that with all their greatness, they could only relate to perfect people but could not lower themselves to lift ordinary people to perfection. Therefore, they said to Abraham that since he gave food and drink and brought people closer to the service of Hashem, "So shall you do, just as you have said." Therefore, he will merit to make another feast in honor of his son. To this day on Shabbat and holidays, the Chasidim of the Baal Shem Tov put food on the "table of Hashem" to warm the hearts of people to the Father in Heaven. (*Pe'er Nachum*, p. 30)

⸺

"He took cream and milk and the calf that he made, and placed it before them." (Gen. 18:8) The Chidushei Harim commented that one should learn from Abraham the meaning of hospitality. We know that Abraham was a prophet, a hundred years old, and he was ill because it was only three days after his circumcision—yet he insisted on serving his guests himself. (F.C.O., p. 57)

⸺

On the *Pasuk* "He stood by them beneath the tree" (Gen. 18:8), the Kedushas Levi commented that part of the observance of the mitzvah of hospitality is that the guest should be made to feel comfortable. A righteous person strives to greater heights; an angel stands and remains on one level, as is written in the book of Zechariah (3:7): "Then I will give you free access among those that stand by [the angels that stand by to serve Hashem]." Therefore, we can understand why Abraham "stood by them"; he did not want to be on a higher level than the angels so he "stood by them." (M.T., vol. 1, p. 79)

～～

The Trisker Maggid commented that he never understood the saying of our Sages, "Greater is hospitality than accepting the Divine Countenance." (*Shabbat* 127a) There was one incident that made him see its significance. He was traveling on an extremely cold day so that he could not wait until he came to a Jewish inn. His *gabbai* knocked on the door of th inn. The innkeeper refused to let them in until he knew who they were. Upon entering the warmth of the inn, the Maggid realized the significance of the words of our Sages. The mitzvah of hospitality can save a human being from danger; however, the Divine Spirit is never in danger. (F.C.O., p. 59)

～～

On the *Pasukim* "And Sarah laughed inside, saying, 'After I have withered shall I again have clear skin? And my husband is old!' . . . Sarah denied, saying, 'I did not laugh, for I was frightened'; and he said, 'No, but you laughed.'" (Gen. 18:12,15). The Noam Elimelech commented that Sarah's laughter was a sign of joy, not of disbelief. When the angel told her the news that she would have a child she was happy, but an impious thought entered her mind. She tried to dispel the thought for it implied disbelief in God's power. Since she dismissed the thought immediately, she felt that she had not sinned. However, God explained to her that, nevertheless, it was derision. Therefore, the Noam Elimelech said, "The truly good person must discipline himself so that he will be unable to think impure and unworthy thoughts." (*Noam Elimelech*, p. 8)

～～

On the same *Pasuk*, the S'fas Emes commented that Sarah repented immediately so that the transgression was as if it were null and void, for she said, "I did not laugh." However, the Torah calls it a denial, for her repentance was out of fear, as it is stated: "She feared." After such repentance there always remains a trace of the sin. Therefore, Abraham said to her, "You did laugh," for one must repent out of love so that the laughter itself should become a merit. And so it was that from the laughter Isaac ("Yitzchok," meaning "laughter") was born. Sarah later said, "God has made laughter for me." (Gen. 21:6) Thus the laughter turned into a meritorious act. (M.T., vol. 1, p. 94)

Based on a statement in *Orchot Tzaddikim*, the S'fas Emes commented, "Because of too much laughter, fear of Heaven is diminished." He said that while one is full of folly, he cannot have the fear of Heaven. That is why Sarah said, "I did not laugh, for I feared." (Gen. 18:15) It would not have been meant as a jest if she had feared when she laughted. Therefore, it must have been an uncompleted, unconscious, and latent thought. (M.T., vol. 1, p. 81)

On the *Pasuk* "For I have cherished him, because he commands his children" (Gen. 18:19), the Ostrovitzer commented that he commanded his children that they continue to maintain the values of humility. As Abraham says, "I am but dust and ashes." (Gen. 18:27) (F.C.O., p. 65)

"Because the outcry of Sodom and Gomorrah has become great, and because their sin has been very grave. . . ." (Gen. 18:20) The Vorker Rebbe said that the character of the people of Sodom can be compared to one who says, "What is mine is mine." (*Ethics* 5:13) One who is of a better nature helps strangers as well. Those who promise to give charity but in actuality give nothing can also be compared with the people of Sodom. (H.A., p. 111)

The Lubliner commented that Abraham was very modest, for he said, "I am but dust and ashes." (Gen. 18:27) Moses and Aharon said, "What are we?" King David had more modesty for he said, "And I am but a worm not a person." But the highest level of modesty is for someone not to say anything. (F.C.O., p. 65)

On the same *Pasuk*, the R' Henoch Alexander commented that a person should have two pockets. In one pocket he should carry a note saying, "The world was created because of me." In the other pocket, he should carry a note saying, "I am but dust and ashes." (F.C.O., p. 65)

On the same *Pasuk*, the Riziner commented that in Psalms 121 we read, "I will lift my eyes to the mountains; from where shall come my help. My help is from Hashem." Our Sages interpret it to mean that one should look to our forefathers to comprehend the meaning of greatness so that one may feel humility. Therefore, because he will feel that he is "but dust and ashes," with a broken heart, he will plead to the Almighty that He should send His help. (F.C.O., p. 66)

R' Mordechai Joseph Leiner, the Izbica Rebbe, based on Abraham's prayer concerning the destruction of Sodom, interpreted the words "I am dust and ashes." He explained that "ashes" is something lost. Therefore, had Abraham's prayer been answered, Sodom would have been saved and would have continued to be wicked, and there would be no power for growth. (*Mei Ha-shiloah*, vol. 1, p. 8)

"Sarah saw the son of Hagar, the Egyptian, whom she had borne to Abraham, mocking." (Gen. 21:9) Rashi comments: "Mocking connotes idolatry . . . it connotes sexual immorality . . . it connotes murder." In the *sefer*, *Avnei Nezer*, the author notes that one may think that witticism, jesting, and playfulness may be insignificant but in reality they may lead to serious transgressions, as Rashi noted. (M.T., vol. 1, p. 87)

R' Bunim of Pshys'cha questioned the statement "And they both made an agreement." (Gen. 21:27) "Is it not obvious that the word 'both' is superfluous, since the agreement was made between two people?" His interpretation was that Abraham had a premonition that in the future the Jewish people would follow the ways of other peoples and become like them. Therefore, he made a political agreement with Avimelech, inwardly understanding that it did not mean a spiritual one. The nations would be "two," not "one." The Jews and the other nations could be a political unit but spiritually they should be "two." (F.C.O., p. 68)

❦

"And He said, 'Please take your son.'" (Gen. 22:2) The S'fas Emes explained that this was not a command but a plea. God pleaded with Abraham that he should take his only son as a sacrifice, even though Abraham would not have another son of such a caliber. Because he brought Isaac as a sacrifice with joy and his own free will, so would the generations to come also bring sacrifices with joy and their own free will. (F.C.O., p. 68)

❦

On the *Pasuk* "They both went together" (Gen. 22:7), R' Simcha Bunim questioned the use of the term "together" as if their tasks were equivalent. It would seem that Isaac's trial was much greater than his father's. After all, Abraham's request had been directly from God, while Isaac understood what was happening only from his father. Abraham went to sacrifice his son but Isaac was to be sacrificed. Walking with his son, Abraham felt that Isaac was on a higher spiritual level for his trial was greater than his. He thought that perhaps Isaac's youth gave him the ability to withstand the trial. Therefore, the *Pasuk* states: "And he took the *shney*," meaning two youths. *Shney* can also mean "years." Therefore, R' Bunim said that Abraham reminded himself of his own youth and he took that strength and that of Isaac with him. Thus "they both went together," father and son, with equal strength and ability to withstand the trial. (F.C.O., p. 69)

❦

"And Abraham returned to the youths." (Gen. 22:19) The Kotzker Rebbe said that it is imperative to maintain a relationship with youth.

We learn this from the effect it had upon Abraham when he saw how Isaac went to be sacrificed with such youthful confidence. (F.C.O., p. 70)

~~

"An offspring shall inherit the gate of his enemies." (Gen. 22:17) The Gerer Rebbe commented that the Talmud (*Yoma* 86) states that for one who sins and then is sincerely repentant, his transgressions will be transformed into virtues. From there it follows that the penitent of the children of Abraham will inherit the riches from his enemies, namely his iniquities. Repentance (*teshuvah*) is the offspring of our enemy (iniquities) when we understand and correct our wrongdoing. (H.A., p. 385, quoted from *Siach Sarfei Kodesh*, p. 43)

CHAYE SARAH
"THE LIFE OF SARAH"

The *Sidra* begins with *Vayihiyu chaye Sarah* . . . "The lifetime of Sarah was. . . ." (Gen. 23:1) The Hebrew letters of *vayihiyu* add up to 37, which is the same number as the abbreviation for *Zachreynu l'chayim*, "May he be remembered for a blessing," which is said of a righteous person who has passed away. That is why the *Pasuk* says, commented the Koznitzer Maggid, *Vayihiyu chaye Sarah*. (F.C.O., p. 72)

⌐~

"Sarah's lifetime was one hundred years, and twenty years, and seven years." (Gen. 23:1) Rabbi Menachem Mendel Schneerson, the Lubavitcher Rebbe, commented on the midrashic interpretation of the Torah statement concerning the years of Sarah. Citing the verse from Psalms, "Just as they are perfect, so their years are perfect," the Midrash explained that Sarah was at one hundred as if she were twenty. Only by perfection of a life comes that state of changelessness that characterized Sarah. The repetition of the word "years" in the *Pasuk* tells us that each age (100, 20, 7) is compared to the others. At one hundred, Sarah was as far from the possibility of sin as she was at twenty or at seven. In other words, she had attained the highest levels of integrity. (T.S., pp. 21–27)

The S'fas Emes made the following comment on Sarah's life. He said that it is a known fact that there are negative and positive factors in one's life. These factors have a direct bearing on one's character and behavior, and they can determine the personality of an individual. Sarah experienced good and bad events in her life. In her early years, she had endured many trials as with Pharoah and Avimelech, and at the end of her life she lived in relative peace. Yet all the events were equal, as Rashi says, "All were of a positive nature" (Gen. 23:1), meaning that when the negatives occurred, she did not become depressed nor did she become arrogant when she prospered. (F.C.O., p. 72)

The Lubavitcher Rebbe noted that Sarah lived a life of Divine service. As Abraham's wife, she nurtured his potential, making sure that it developed in a beneficial manner. Abraham dispensed kindness freely, granting hospitality to wayfarers. Sarah sought to direct it to those recipients who would give it expression in holiness. It was Sarah who demanded that Isaac would inherit all, and not any other member of the household. Sarah understood that only those individuals who would reflect the spirituality of Abraham should be the inheritors. (G.O.T., pp. 31–32)

R' Avraham Eger of Lublin made the following comment concerning Abraham's old age, *bo bayamim* — "advanced in years." (Gen. 24:1) He noted that Abraham started to reflect upon his life and said that all was vanity and gave the rest of his life to prayer and repentance. (F.C.O., p. 74)

It says, "And God blessed Abraham with everything." (Gen. 24:1) The Berditchever said that the Almighty blessed Abraham with everything because he blessed everyone. Every time Abraham blessed someone, it was put into his account. (F.C.O., p. 75)

On the same *Pasuk*, the Kedushas Levi commented that the truly righteous individual does not pray and request for himself alone. Even if he is blessed, his concern is for all. If we desire to ask for a blessing for the righteous, we must ask for a blessing for all. The Almighty blessed Abraham because he blessed everyone else. (M.T., vol. 1, p. 117)

On the *Pasuk* "That you not take for my son from the daughters of the Canaanite, among whom I dwell" (Gen. 24:3), the Sochatchover noted that Abraham's family were also idol worshippers and so what was his objection to the Canaanites? The Canaanites, commented the Chodochover, were so morally deficient that immorality became their children's heritage. However, idol worshippers are conceptually misled and their beliefs need not affect the character of their children. (M.T., vol. 1, p. 98)

On the *Pasuk* "The slave ran toward her [Rebecca]" (Gen. 24:17), Rashi said: "Because he saw that the waters went up toward her." The Kedushas Levi remarked that the Ramban (Nachmanides) notes that later on it states, "And she drew for all the camels." (Gen. 24:20) This proves that in the first instance, the waters went toward her. The Kedushas Levi comments that the essence of a mitzvah is the thought and the intent to do the will of God. The first time, her thought was to take the water for herself, so the waters went toward her and she did not have to exert herself. Afterwards, when she had to get water to perform a mitzvah of righteousness, the waters did not come toward her for it is imperative that one has to strain oneself to perform a mitzvah. In the Heavens, it was decreed that she perform the entire deed. (M.T., vol. 1, p. 102)

The *Pasuk* states that "The man was astonished at her." (Gen. 24:21) Eliezer at first did not want to give the jewelry to Rivkah because he did not want to take away from the charitable act of feeding the camels, noted the S'fas Emes. (F.C.O., p. 75)

~~

There is a very interesting story told about the famous brothers who were known Admurim, R' Zusia, and R' Elimelech. The story is based on the *Pasuk* "And I will prepare the house and a place for the camels." (Gen. 24:31) Before the brothers became know as Tzaddikim, they were wanderers as part of the early Kabbalistic practice known as *galut*, putting oneself in voluntary exile. Traveling everywhere as beggars, they came to the city of Ludmir. Later, after they became known as Tzaddikim, they again traveled to Ludmir. The wealthiest man in town came to greet them and begged them to lodge at his house. He told them that he had a very large house with marble floors and all the necessities to make them comfortable. After giving their consent, they told him to go home and prepare the house and they went to the village inn where they lodged with the peasants. The rich man ran to the inn and wanted to know why they were staying with the poor people. "We want you to know that this is not the first time that we have been in Ludmir. Never did you ask us to lodge in your home. We are the same people. So this time when we came to town with expensive looking horses, we thought that you were preparing the house for them — namely, 'A place for the horses.'" (F.C.O., p. 75)

~~

On the *Pasuk* "I will not eat until I have spoken my words" (Gen. 24:33), the Zighter commented that based on the Zohar (*Miketz* 199b), one is obligated to make a blessing on food before eating. That is why "I have spoken my words" means "making a blessing." (M.D., p. 45)

~~

On the *Pasuk* "Will you go with this man? And she said, I will go" (Gen. 24:58), Rashi commented, "And she said, 'I will go on my own, even if you do not wish.'" The Chernowitzer asked how is it possible that Rebecca should speak to her parents with arrogance and not in a respectful manner. In essence, she was saying that her father, Betuel, who did not agree to the match, had died (*Rashi Pasuk* 55) and the result was that she would have to go by herself even if people would not permit. Heaven will insist on it, so everyone might as well agree. (M.T., p. 106)

TOLDOT
"AND THESE ARE THE GENERATIONS"

On the *Pasuk* "Isaac entreated Hashem on behalf of his wife . . . Hashem allowed Himself to be entreated by him" (Gen. 25:21), Rashi comments: "But not by her, for the prayer of a righteous person who is the child of a wicked person is not comparable to the prayer of a righteous person who is the child of a righteous person. Therefore, 'by him' but not by her." However, the Kedushas Levi maintained that Isaac believed that the Almighty would not accept his prayer on his own merit, so he prayed on her behalf that he should be helped on her merits. When the Torah mentions that "the Almighty allowed Himself," one would assume that Hashem accepted his prayer on Rebecca's merits. That is why Rashi said, "By him, not by her"—for "the prayer of a righteous person who is the child of a righteous person" was accepted because of his merits. (M.T., p. 108)

On the words *V'rav yaavod tza'ir*, "And the elder shall serve the younger," the Stretiner in his *sefer* noted that the word *rav*, generally translated as "elder," can also mean "much." There is *rav* (much) work in the service of Hashem. To be a *tza'ir* one must reach the category of humility. (M.D., p. 50)

⌇

Another interpretation was given by R' Mordechai of Nadburna. He explained that anyone who wishes to gain in Torah knowledge and good deeds must begin to study and work in the service of Hashem while he is still young. (M.D., p. 50)

⌇

On the *Pasuk* "And they called his name Esav" (Gen. 25:25), Rashi comments that everyone called him Esav, but when it came to Jacob, only his father called him Jacob. (Rashi 25:26) R' Bunim of Pshys'cha asked, "Why was everyone so familiar with Esav but only the father knew Jacob?" The reason was that falsehood has a tremendous power. When Esav was born, everyone recognized a part of himself, a child from the world of falsehood. "But it seems," continued R' Bunim, "truth needs experts." The only one who had expertise in truth was Isaac. That is why he was the only one to call him Jacob. (F.C.O., p. 86)

⌇

On the *Pasuk* "And Isaac loved Esav because he was a hunter" (Gen. 25:28), the S'fas Emes commented that the Torah was explaining love. The Torah declared that this was not a true love for it depended on something, namely his being a hunter. (F.C.O., p. 87)

⌇

The Trisker Maggid interpreted the same *Pasuk* differently by explaining that having a skill is a good quality. Esav did not depend on his father, who was wealthy; he earned his own living. (F.C.O., p. 87)

⌇

The Ropshitzer Rebbe, R' Naftali, made an observation on the *Pasuk* "And Rebecca loved Jacob." (Gen. 25:28) He said that from this statement we can learn that innocence by itself is not necessarily a good quality. Isaac was very innocent and naive so that when Esav asked how to give tithes from salt and straw, he thought that it was an honest request. But Rebecca, coming from a home where deceit was prevalent, understood why Esav asked that question. She knew that there was a possibility that one could ask questions as if one were very careful in observance and yet be a wicked person. That is why it says, "And Rebecca loved Jacob." (F.C.O., p. 87)

<hr>

On the *Pasuk* "Jacob said, 'Sell, as this day, your birthright to me'" (Gen. 25:31), the Ropshitzer explained why it was necessary for Jacob to buy the birthright. Esav was concerned with this world and Jacob was looking forward to the World to Come. Jacob understood that to obtain the other world, he must first observe those *mitzvot* that are required for this world. The letters of the word *ka'yom* ("as this day") stand for *kulam yisb'oo v'yisb'oo v'yisangoo mitoovecha*, "They all will be satisfied and delighted with Your goodness." Jacob said, "Sell me a little of this worldly goodness that I will need for the next world." (F.C.O., p. 88)

<hr>

It is stated in the Torah: "And Isaac's servants dug in the valley and found living waters." (Gen. 26:19) The S'fas Emes commented that the Torah is called "water" and is therefore found everywhere. As is true with seeking water, it depends on how deep one wishes to dig and how sincerely one wants to have Torah. Just as water is the elixir of life, so is the Torah. (F.C.O., p. 89)

<hr>

On the *Pasuk* "So that my soul may bless you before I die" (Gen. 27:4), the Vorker asked why Isaac wished specifically to bless the elder son and not both his children as Jacob blessed all his children. The Almighty did not want Jacob to be given the blessing because future generations would assume that in order to receive a blessing one must be on the level of a Jacob. Esav received a blessing to show future generations that no matter what one's status is, he can receive a blessing. (M.T., p. 117)

<hr>

Based on Rebecca's statement to Jacob, "So that he may bless you before his death" (Gen. 27:10), the Lizensker commented that it was Isaac's intention to bless Esav with material riches, and Jacob with spiritual wealth. Rebecca wanted to give Jacob a piece of this world as well. Jacob feared that material riches would take him away from his spiritual growth, and so he said that his brother was not concerned with the spiritual life and liked earthly pleasures and that he had no need for material gain. If he had material gain, God would think of him as a deceiver. Therefore, obtaining material wealth may be more a curse than a blessing. A Divine voice called to Jacob reassuring him that he would be guided in his prosperity and it would be used to fulfill the commandments. (*Noam Elimelech*, p. 12)

━━◦

A *Maskil* (a member of the enlightenment movement) asked R' Shalom Belzer why the people who wear modern clothing are successful in business. He said that we learn the answer from Jacob. When he went for the blessing of material wealth, he dressed as Esav. (F.C.O., p. 91)

━━◦

On the *Pasuk* "The hands are the hands of Esav" (Gen. 27:22), the Mishmeres Itmar noted that Esav used two hands. One he used to befriend and to manipulate. The other hand he used for the kill. (F.C.O., p. 92)

VAYETZE
"AND HE WENT OUT"

The Lubavitcher Rebbe, Rabbi Menachem Mendel Schneerson, noted that the *Sidra Vayetze* shows how a transition from one environment to another affects a person's conduct. The *Sidra* begins with the *Pasuk* "And Jacob departed from Beer-Sheba and went to Haran." (Gen. 28:10) The *Sidra* describes how Jacob went to an alien environment. There he was confronted by a personal challenge. In the company of Lavan and others like him, he had to struggle to maintain his virtue. Despite the influences that prevailed in the community, he infused his family with the spiritual heritage received from Abraham: "To keep the way of Hashem and to implement righteousness and judgment." (*Bereshit* 18:19) In doing so he established a Jewish way of life for all time. Finally, he elevated the environment of Haran. He lifted the Godly sparks from the land's material substance. Thus, although he acquired great wealth, his spiritual life was not affected. (G.O.T., pp. 39–44)

On the *Pasuk Va'yifgah bamakom*, "And he came upon a place" (Gen. 28:11), Rashi comments that our Rabbis explained the word *va'yifgah* as an expression of prayer. The Radamsker commented that Jacob prayed twice. He first made a request for Hashem's honor, Who is called *Makom* — "Place." He also asked about the Temple that would be built on this spot. Later Jacob prayed, "If God will be with me and He will

guard me . . . And He will give me bread to eat and clothes to wear."
(Gen. 28:20) In the same vein, noted the Radamsker, our Sages, in the
High Holiday prayers, first established *Malchiut* in the honor of
Hashem and then *Zichronot* (Remembrances) for personal requests.
(M.T., p. 123)

~~~

On the same *Pasuk*, "And he came upon a place" (Gen. 28:11), R' Aharon
Karliner commented on the word *va'yifgah* ("came upon"). Jacob asked
God that no matter where one prayed, God should listen to his prayers.
When one says that this place is not conducive to prayer, it is really an
empty excuse. (F.C.O., p. 96)

~~~

The S'fas Emes noted that the meaning of the *Pasuk* "A ladder was set
earthward and its top reached heavenward" (Gen. 28:12) is that the
material aspects of the human being dwell earthward but his spirituality is heavenward. (F.C.O., p. 98)

~~~

R' Baruch Mezbitzer gave another interpretation of that *Pasuk*. He
remarked that when one is confident that he is fully secure here on
earth, eventually he will gear his thoughts heavenward. (F.C.O., p. 98)

~~~

The significance of "And behold Hashem was standing over him" (Gen.
28:12) is that one's ideals are shown by one's behavior. "Of the individual
who is a person of high ideals, and whose concepts of life are spiritual
and of a holy nature, we know that 'Behold Hashem was standing over
him,'" said R' Tzadok HaKohen. (F.C.O., p. 99)

~~~

Commenting on the *Pasuk* "Your offspring shall be as the dust of the
earth" (Gen. 28:14), R' Zev Tzvi Zbarisher said that there will be times
when the Jews will be at a low ebb because they will be considered as
nothing by other nations. (F.C.O., p. 99)

An interesting story is told about the Kotzker Rebbe concerning prayer. A Kotzker Chasid overheard another Chasid during prayer constantly screaming *Tate*!!!! ("Father"). Hearing this outburst, the Chasid admonished him, saying, "Perhaps the Almighty is not your father, for does it not say: 'At times that Israel does not do the will of God, we are called servants and not children.'" Upon hearing this angry response, the Kotzker rebuked the Chasid, saying, "Perhaps if he keeps on screaming 'Father' long enough, He will become our Father." (F.C.O., p. 96)

The Primishlaner commented on the *Pasuk* "And Jacob awoke from his sleep and said, 'Surely Hashem is in this place.'" (Gen. 28:16) As soon as Jacob awoke, he proceeded to serve Hashem. Pharoah, as we know, awoke, turned on his side, and went back to sleep. Herein lies the difference: Jacob immediately started to serve Hashem. (M.T., p. 126)

On the *Pasuk* "Jacob awoke from his sleep and said, 'Surely Hashem is in this place and I did not know'" (Gen. 28:16), the Ohev Yisroel commented that while Jacob was in the yeshivah of Shem V'Ever, he never slept while he studied so as not to disturb or waste time in his service to Hashem. However, Jacob did fall asleep during his journey and he had a dream. He dreamt that the "Angels were ascending and descending." (Gen. 28:12) Jacob awoke from his sleep and noted that "Hashem is in this place" and even when one sleeps one can worship Hashem, and "I did not know" this the entire time that I was at the yeshivah. (F.C.O., p. 100)

"Jacob awoke from his sleep . . . And he became frightened." (Gen. 28:16) The S'fas Emes commented that the Torah is telling us how modest Jacob was. When someone has a dream in which Hashem appears to him, he usually develops an arrogant manner, but when Jacob awoke, the Torah tells us, "he became frightened." (F.C.O., p. 99)

≈

On the *Pasuk* "Then Jacob took a vow" (Gen. 28:20), the S'fas Emes commented that Jacob was instructing future generations that if, God forbid, one finds himself in a time of distress, he should give charity. (F.C.O., p. 100)

≈

R' Dovid Lelever noted that Jacob did not ask for more than he needed. It is for this reason that the Torah states: "And give me bread to eat and clothing to wear" (Gen. 28:20)—that and no more. (F.C.O., p. 102)

≈

On the same *Pasuk*, the Sassover said that it is quite obvious that one needs bread to eat and clothing to wear. However, Jacob did not make the request for himself alone. He asked for enough food and clothing so that he might share with others. (F.C.O., p. 102)

≈

Another thought came from the Yid HaKadosh, who considered the request by Jacob, "bread to eat and clothing to wear," as a prophetic request because Jacob knew that there would be difficult economic times ahead, so his request was for the future. (F.C.O., p. 102)

≈

The Koznitzer interpreted the *Pasuk* "Bread to eat and clothes to wear; and I will return in peace (*b'shalom*) to my father's house." (Gen. 28:21) By changing the position of the letters of the word *b'shalom*, the word *malbush* ("clothing") is formed. Jacob, our father, asked not only for spiritual clothing (clothing of holiness) but also for respectable clothing. (F.C.O., p. 102)

On the *Pasuk* "Roll the stone from upon the mouth of the well" (Gen. 29:2), the S'fas Emes commented that when it comes to prayer it seems as if a stone is in a person's mouth. There is very little sincerity and it doesn't seem to be a service from the heart. That is why, before the *Amidah*, we say, "My Lord, open my lips, that my mouth may declare Your praise." Roll the stone from my mouth so that I may praise You with sincerity. (F.C.O., p. 103)

To strengthen that point a story is told about the Chidushei Harim. A Chasid complained that he found it very difficult to concentrate during prayer. It seemed that all sorts of strange thoughts entered his mind and it became impossible for him to concentrate. The Rebbe responded by saying that he should not be the one to complain. "When you get up in the morning, you are concerned about everything possible. Before you begin to pray, you go about your daily tasks and then you decide to pray. No wonder you have strange thoughts. In truth, it should be the Almighty Who should do the complaining." (F.C.O., p. 103)

On the *Pasukim* "Jacob's anger flared up at Rachel" (Gen. 30:2) and "Jacob became angry with Laban" (Gen. 31:36), the Chidushei Harim noted that anger was really not part of Jacob's personality. However, we do read: "Give truth to Jacob." We learn from this that one must know when and how to be angry. It is difficult for a person of truth to stand by and see conniving and not get angry. (F.C.O., p. 106)

R' Chayim Zanzer made the following comment on the *Pasuk* "Then Jacob became angered and he quarreled with Laban; Jacob spoke up and said to Laban, 'What is my transgression? What is my sin, that you have pursued me?'" (Gen. 31:36) It is a known fact that impurity runs after holiness. Jacob noticed that Laban, who is symbolic of impurity, was running after him and Jacob could not free himself. This is why Jacob asked "What is my transgression?"—What did I do wrong that you are pursuing me and not letting me go? (F.C.O., p. 108)

⌇⌇

"But when the sheep were covered (*u'v'ha'atif*) he put them not in; so the covered ones belonged to Laban and the tied-up ones to Jacob." (Gen. 30:42) Rashi comments that the word *u'v'ha'atif* means "delay." The Koznitzer, in his *sefer Binas Moshe*, made the following observation on the *Pasuk*, based on Rashi's interpretation. The latecomers in the service of Hashem feel that they did not fulfill their obligations of the study of Torah and Divine service. However, they do not need support for they are on the right road. Those who are tied to Jacob consider that nothing is missing in their service to Hashem. Therefore, they must go to Jacob, the spiritual leader, to be shown pointedly the proper way to serve Hashem. (M.D., p. 64)

⌇⌇

On the *pasuk* "Jacob went on his way, and angels of God encountered him" (Gen. 32:2), the Kotzker Rebbe commented that for those who follow the ways of Torah even the Angels of Justice ask mercy for them in times of need and trouble. (F.C.O., p. 109)

VAYISHLACH
"AND HE (JACOB) SENT"

The message of *Parshas Vaylishlach* is that everyone of us is a *shaliach*, an agent of Hashem, commented Rabbi Menachem Mendel, the Lubavitcher Rebbe. He said that we are sent "to Esav" to refine and reveal the Godliness within the material existence that is identified with Esav. The word *vayishlach* means "and he sent," implying that our mission includes the empowerment of other *shalichim*. A person must inspire others to shoulder a portion of the endeavor. To borrow an expression from our Sages (*Kiddushin* 41a), "One *shaliach* makes another." (G.O.T., pp. 45–49)

The Kotzker interpreted the *Pasuk* "And Jacob sent away the angels." (Gen. 32:4) Jacob sent them away because he did not need their assistance. He wanted to meet his brother alone. (F.C.O., p. 110)

The Yid HaKadosh explained differently the same *Pasuk* by saying that Jacob sent the angels to Esav. He said that one should not wonder why Jacob sent angels to Esav, for to meet an individual like Esav, it is imperative to call on angels to be your messengers. (F.C.O., p. 110)

The Lechivitzer, in his comment on "Then Jacob was afraid and distressed" (Gen. 32:8), asked the question: Why "distressed?" Jacob rec-

51

ognized that his fear was of man and not of Hashem. This brought him distress. (M.T., p. 141)

～～

On Jacob's statement, "I have been diminished by all the kindness" (Gen. 32:11), the Rebbe of Lublin said that when one begins to understand all the kindnesses that are bestowed upon him, then does the individual begin to appreciate his mundane existence. (F.C.O., p. 112)

～～

On the same *Pasuk*, the S'fas Emes commented that Jacob said that even after all the kindnesses that were bestowed upon him, he did not become arrogant. On the contrary, he became more modest and unpretentious. (F.C.O., p. 113)

～～

On the *Pasuk* "I have sojourned (*garti*) with Laban" (Gen. 32:5), Rashi states a *Bereshit Rabbah* that says: "The numerical value of *garti* is 613 as if to say, I sojourned with Laban, the evil one, yet I kept the 613 *mitzvot* and did not learn from his evil ways." The Rimanover noted that this should not come as a surprise. Jacob lived with Laban for twenty years and yet was a stranger (*ger*). This was because he observed the *mitzvot*. In spite of his environment, he still behaved as a Jew. This shows us that no matter where we live as Jews, we are strangers. (F.C.O., p. 111)

～～

On the *Pasuk* "Rescue me, please, from the hand of my brother Esav, for I fear him" (Gen. 32:12), the Kedushas Levi commented that the Zohar (vol. 3, 185) equates Esav with the "Other Side," that is, the evil inclination. Jacob pleaded not to make the evil inclination "my brother." Often the evil inclination leads one to transgress by making one think that it is a good deed. It is then imperative to conquer the evil inclination. (M.D., p. 68)

R' Yaacov Radamsker said that the reason Jacob said, "I fear him" (Gen. 32:12) is that he remembered that he had pretended to be Esav and had said to his father, "I am Esav, your firstborn." (Gen. 27:19) So now he feared that that act would count as a sin. (F.C.O., p., 113)

Jacob said to God, "And you said, 'I will surely do good with you.'" (Gen. 32:13) R' Moshe Leib Sassover interpreted the words "surely do good" in the following manner: "Almighty God, it is a fact that all that You do is surely good, for it is written, 'Evil does not come from You.' However, we know that good can come from good but good can also come from evil. So I pray and beg of You, give us good that is a wholesome good, as Jacob prayed *Haytiv Aytiv*, good for good, that is 'surely good.'" (F.C.O., p. 114)

There are two interpretations of the *Pasuk* "And he took of that which came to his hand a tribute for Esav, his brother." (Gen. 32:14) The Kotzker Rebbe noted that when a person gives what is convenient and has no thought of its significance, he does not question whether it is for the good. Even if he gives something for a mitzvah but without thought, it is as if he is giving a "tribute to Esav." However, from another perspective, the Yismach Moshe commented that Jacob did not know what to select or give because everything had a spark of the Divine in it. Therefore, he took whatever was at hand with the assumption that it would be proper. (F.C.O., p. 114)

On the *Pasuk* "And he said to his servants, 'Pass on ahead of me and put a space between herd and herd'" (Gen. 32:17), R' Avraham Dovid Butchacher commented that Jacob, our father, begged of the Almighty that when the Jews were in the Diaspora, Hashem would separate the people into two divisions. Therefore, when one section would have to encounter hardships, evil decrees, and all kinds of torments, Hashem would ensure that there would be a saving factor in the other section so that the Jews elsewhere would have peace and quiet. (F.C.O., p. 115)

~~

"And Jacob was left alone." (Gen. 32:25) The Ostrovitzer commented that when Jews gather for worship or learning in public, they reach the level of "Israel," but when one prays by himself his choice is that of "And Jacob was left alone," alone and forlorn. However, with the blessing Hashem gave Jacob, "And your name will be Israel," Israel will be mentioned when Jews gather for prayer or learning as a people. When Jews gather to pray or participate in learning as a people, they reach the much higher standard of "Israel," the standard of unity and brotherly love. (F.C.O., p. 115)

~~

On the same *Pasuk*, Rabbi Avraham Moshe Rabinowitz, the Skoyler Rebbe, noted Rashi's comment that "He [Jacob] had forgotten small jars and went back for them." (Gen. 32:25) The Rebbe also noted a comment by the Birkas Shmuel that the jars that Jacob saved were meant for the miracle of Chanukah. He also noted that in the *sefer Eish Kadosh* the awe of the Almighty overcame him. It is this same awe that was the factor that helped the Hasmoneans to defeat the Greeks. This spiritual attitude permitted the defeat of "the few over the many." This hinted that a miracle would occur with small jars. (Ch. B., p. 118)

~~

The Karliner commented on the *Pasuk* "And he said I will not let you go until you bless me." (Gen. 32:27) He said that Jacob was not concerned for himself but for his children. His request was that of a concerned father who went through the trials and tribulations of raising children. (F.C.O., p. 116)

~~

R' Asher Horowitz noted that Esav's surprise at Jacob's wealth was based on selfish interest and was an omen for future generations. Esav asked, "What was all that in your camp that I met?" (Gen. 33:8) In other words, commented R' Asher, Esav could not understand how his brother had become so wealthy. After all, wealth is the attribute that Esav should have had, not Jacob. Jacob answered, "If it will find favor in your eyes, take this tribute from me." The wealth is yours—take it. That will be the history of the Jewish people as long as the Jews are in the Diaspora: Whatever will be Jacob's achievements, Esav will take. (F.C.O., p. 116)

The Strikover made an interesting comparison between Jacob and Esav based on two *Pasukim*. In *Bereshit* 32:9, Esav said, "I have plenty," and in *Bereshit* 32:11, Jacob said after praising God, "I have everything." To an Esav, no matter how much he has it is not enough. To a Jacob, who is *sameach b'chelko*, a satisfied individual, no matter what he has he has everything. (F.C.O., p. 117)

When Esav said, "Travel on and let us go and I will proceed alongside of you" (Gen. 32:12), R' Yehoshua Belzer noted that Rashi explained "along" to mean "in line with you." Esav wanted that Jacob's children should dress the same as he did. In all other ways they could do as they were accustomed, but not in dress. Jacob answered that the children were tender, meaning vulnerable. Clothing has a great influence on a person. His concern was that if the children made a change in their clothing and dressed like Esav, they would then eventually take on his other customs. (F.C.O., p. 117)

On the *Pasuk* "And Jacob came whole (intact)" (Gen. 32:18), Rashi explained that it meant "Whole in body, whole in his money, whole in his Torah." R' Asher Horowitz commented on Rashi's thought. The normal behavior of an individual, when he travels or finds a new place to live, is to change his habits and his customs to conform to the new environment. This Jacob did not do. Although he wandered and traveled everywhere, he remained intact. The acronym *shalaym* ("whole") stands for *shem* ("name"), *lashon* ("speech"), *malbush* ("dress"). Therefore, the Midrash says that because they did not change their names, their language, and their manner of dress, the generation that was in Egypt was freed. (F.C.O., p. 118)

~~~

On the *Pasuk* "The men were distressed, and were fired deeply with indignation" (Gen. 34:7), R' Yechiel Ichal of Melitz commented that joy leads to peace. Sadness leads to anger and impatience. This we note when Joseph said to his brothers, "And now do not be sad, nor be angry with yourselves." (*Bereshit* 45:5) This is what our Holy Torah teaches us: that one should not be distressed for it will lead to indignation. (M.D., p. 72)

VAYESHEV
"AND HE SETTLED"

Taking the letters of the word *vayeshev*—the *yid*, the *shin*, the *vet*, and the *vav*—R' Asher Horowitz said that the word *vayeshev* stands for *Y'reh shamayim b'seser v'galguy*. A Jew must be a God-fearing person both in the revealed and in the esoteric aspects of life. (F.C.O., p. 119)

～～

Along the same thinking, "A person," said R' Bunim, "must be God-fearing in the revealed law and in the hidden aspects of life, admitting the truth and always acknowledging the truth in his heart. This type of a person can, without doubt, arise in the morning and say with complete sincerity, 'Master of the World.'" (F.C.O., p. 119)

～～

The Chidushei Harim was asked why we say "the fear of heaven" and not "the fear of God." He said that when the world was created the Heavens were weak. At that point, the Creator cried out "Let there be Heaven!" The Heavens immediately became firm. The fear that the Heavens had for the Almighty became a lasting concept. This is the reason why we say "fear of Heaven" and not "fear of God." (F.C.O., p. 119)

~~~

The reason it says, "These are the generations (*toldoseihem*) of Jacob" (Gen. 37:2) is to teach us that a Jew must never be satisfied with his momentary spiritual status but must constantly strive toward higher spiritual goals. The word *toldoseihem* signifies "The generations of the Tzaddikim are their good deeds." The Rimanover said that this *Pasuk* is a lesson for us to reach higher goals in the performance of our deeds. (F.C.O., p. 120)

~~~

"Joseph brought evil reports of them [his brothers] to his father." (Gen. 37:2) R' Mendel Vorker cautioned that it must not be thought that Joseph maligned his brothers. It was that he behaved better than his brothers. This prompted Jacob to notice the behavior of his other children and he reproved them. (D.Z., p. 50)

~~~

The Koznitzer gave an interesting interpretation of the *Pasuk* "His brothers saw that it was he whom their father loved most of all his brothers, so they hated him; and they were not able to speak to him peacefully." (Gen. 37:4) The brothers could not tolerate Joseph's friendly behavior to them. They said to him that if he considered them as sinners because they were doing things incorrectly, then he was obligated to hate them, as it says: "When one see someone commit a sin it is a mitzvah to dislike him." So, if he was being polite and pleasant, it meant that he did not see them committing any sins. Then the only reason he was polite was that he insisted on maligning them—for that "they hated him." (F.C.O., p. 120)

~~~

The *Pasuk* states: *Lech nah r'ey et sh'lom achechah*, "Go see how your brothers are doing"—literally, "Go see the *shalom* (peace) of your brothers." (Gen. 37:14) The S'fas Emes said that Jacob did not intend to make Joseph a messenger to find out how his brothers were doing. He could have sent one of his servants. Jacob used the term *shalom* deliberately. He wanted Joseph to stop looking only at his brothers' faults. He sent him so that he should also notice their good traits and their *shleymut*, their wholesomeness. (F.C.O., p. 121)

have sent one of his servants. Jacob used the term *shalom* deliberately.

The Radamsker gave the following interpretation on the *Pasuk* "Go see how your brothers are faring and how the herd is doing." (Gen. 37:14) He noted that the *Pasuk* teaches us that a true leader must be concerned with how his people earn a living. (F.C.O., p. 121)

"He [Joseph] was wandering in the field; the man asked him, saying, 'What do you seek?' And he said, 'My brothers do I seek.' . . . The man answered, 'They [the brothers] journeyed on from here, for I heard them saying, "Let us go to Dothan.' . . . They [the brothers] saw him from afar; and when he approached them, they conspired to kill him." (Gen. 37:16) The Sassover explained that as soon as Joseph left his father's house, he felt alone and lost. That is why he said, "I am seeking my brothers!" When he was told that they were in Dothan, he understood that it meant Diaspora, for Dothan (*Dosoynah*) numerically is Diaspora. He wondered why the Israelites would be in the Diaspora. "They saw him from afar . . . they conspired to kill him"—he immediately understood that the reason for the Diaspora would be senseless hatred. (F.C.O., p. 121)

On the *Pasuk* "It is my brothers that I am seeking" (Gen. 37:16), the Radamsker commented that it is not enough to have anguish over the fact that the Holy Presence is in exile. He has no need for our pity. It is written: "And You, God, will always exist." He said, "The world is replete with Your Presence. Our pain is based on the attitude that the Almighty has forgotten us for we are not in our home. That is why we are bitter. We are seeking our brothers. We are concerned with the status of our brethren." (F.U.A.O., vol. 1, p. 211)

⌁

On the *Pasuk* "And the pit was empty, no water was in it" (Gen. 37:24), Rashi comments: "There were snakes and scorpions in it." A person that is a boor, who has no understanding of spiritual concepts and is "empty" of Torah education and good deeds, finds fault with Torah based on "enlightened information." "This is a sign," said R' Asher Horowitz, "that 'snakes and scorpions are in it.'" (F.C.O., p. 123)

⌁

"And he [Reuben] returned to his brothers and said, 'The boy is gone and he cried.'" (Gen. 37:30) The S'fas Emes commented that from this *Pasuk* we can see the difference between a righteous individual and a wicked one. When Jacob took the birthright away from Esav, Esav was ready to kill him. Not so in the case of Reuben: Reuben knew that his brother Joseph would take the birthright away from him; nevertheless he wanted to save him. (F.C.O., p. 123)

⌁

R' Moshe Kobriner interpreted the following *Pasuk*, *Vayehee Er b'chor Yehudah rah b'eyneh Hashem*, "And Er, Judah's firstborn, was evil in the eyes of Hashem." (Gen. 38:7) When a *Pasuk* begins with the word *vayehee*, it connotes trouble or pain. *Er* means "enlightment." When a leader, whose task it is to teach and to enlighten his people, does evil in the eyes of God, then much sorrow comes to that generation. (F.C.O., p. 123)

⌁

On the *Pasuk* "And he [Joseph] became a successful man" (Gen. 39:2), R' Moshe Lelever noted that it is a known fact that there is a difference between blessings and success. Blessings come in an unnatural manner and success comes in a natural way. The Torah comes to tell us that in the Diaspora, one can have success but blessings can only come from Zion. The Torah tells us: "From Zion shall come your blessing." (F.C.O., p. 124)

～

R' Bunim of Pshys'cha commented on the *Pasuk* "Hashem was with Joseph, and he was a successful man; and he remained in the house of his Egyptian master." (Gen. 39:2) In success and adversity, Joseph was with God. Whether successful or an Egyptian slave, Joseph remained with God. (*Simchas Yisroel*, p. 74)

～

On the *Pasuk* "And he [Joseph] was in the house of his Egyptian master" (Gen. 39:2), the S'fas Emes remarked that no matter in what circumstances Joseph found himself while in his master's house, he was always himself. He did not change. Thus a Jew must behave—no matter what should happen to him, he should always behave as a Jew. (F.C.O., p. 124)

～

On the *Pasuk* "Now Joseph was handsome of form and handsome of appearance" (Gen. 39:6), Rashi makes the following comment: "Once Joseph saw himself in a position of authority, he began to change his manner of eating and drinking, and started to curl his hair. The Holy One, blessed is He, said, 'Your father is in mourning and you curl your hair?'" The Lenchener wondered how it was possible that Joseph, knowing his father's sorrow, should be concerned with mundane things such as food, clothing, and his hairdo. The Letchener explained that when Joseph tried to teach the ways of God to the Egyptians dressed as a Jew—that is, as a foreigner—no one would listen to him. Therefore, he decided to change his clothing and his hairdo, hoping the Egyptians would listen to him. Instead, Zlichah, Potiphar's wife, tried to seduce him. The *Pasuk* continues, "And she caught hold of him by his garment, saying, 'Lie with me!' But he left his garment in her hand, and he fled and went outside." Joseph went home and started to reflect on his behavior. He came to the conclusion that because he was dressed as an Egyptian, Potiphar's wife wanted to take advantage of him. At that point did he "leave his garment and fled." He resumed his original behavior. (F.C.O., p. 124)

"But he refused; he said to his master's wife, '. . . There is no one greater in this house than I, and he has denied me nothing but you, since you are his wife; how then can I perpetrate this great evil?'" (Gen. 39:9) The S'fas Emes noted that this is the method one should use when told to perform an evil act. First, give an unqualified refusal and then give the reasons for the refusal. (F.C.O., p. 125)

The Primishlaner noted Rashi's comment on the Pasuk "And it was on that day that he entered the house to do his work." (Gen. 39:11) Rashi comments that Joseph had intended to have relations with Potiphar's wife but "the image of his father appeared to him," as stated in tractate *Sotah*. The Primishlaner said that in order to be like the Egyptians, Joseph started to dress like them and took on their mannerisms. Noticing this behavior, Potiphar's wife thought that there would be nothing wrong with enticing Joseph since he would most likely react as any other Egyptian. Upon her request, "Come lie with me," the image of his father appeared. He realized that it was his modern dress and mannerisms that put him in this position. He began to realize that if he had kept the traditions of his ancestors, he never would have been placed in this predicament. (M.T., vol. 1, p. 172)

On the *Pasuk* "But he left his garment in her hand, and he fled, and went outside" (Gen. 39:12), the S'fas Emes commented that Joseph left his worldly habits and fled from those desires and "went outside" of this worldly behavior. (F.C.O., p. 126)

MIKEITZ
"IT CAME TO PASS AT THE END"

The Lubavitcher Rebbe commented, based on Kabbalistic thought, that the Torah speaks about the upper realm, the Divine or spiritual world, and alludes to the lower realm, the materialistic world. The entire *parsha* speaks about the release of Joseph from prison. The name "Joseph" means "to increase," namely, the unbounded potential for growth. This growth we find in the soul, "the actual part of God from above." (*Tanya*, ch. 2) The prison in which Joseph was held refers to the body, and to the material existence as a whole. These tend to confine the power of the soul and deny it expression. Although God gave us the Torah, the Torah is also affected by the limits of material life, and the Godly source is not always evident. The Jew was sent into this world to reveal Godliness. The material nature of worldly existence may initially restrict the Jewish nature; however, the constraints are temporary. Just as Joseph became the ruler of Egypt, every Jew should become a source of influence showing how the potential of the soul can overcome complete materialistic dominance. (T.S., pp. 60–65)

Mikeitz ("in the end") refers to the days that call for the Messiah. The Shinover noted that the Messiah would not come unless we would give from our hearts. This means that we would be concerned for the welfare of others and not only for ourselves. (F.C.O., p. 128)

Taking the word *shnatayim* in the *Pasuk Vayehi mikeitz shnatayim*, "It happened at the end of two years" (Gen. 41:1), the Ostrovitzer noted that the letters of the word stand for *smol* ("left"), *ner* ("light"), *tadlik* ("you shall light"), *yemin* ("the right hand"), *mezuzah*. With the left hand one should light the Sabbath candles and with the right hand one should affix the *mezuzah*. (F.C.O., p. 128)

On the *Pasuk* "And I heard it said about you" (Gen. 41:15), R' Meir Primishlaner said that Pharoah said to Joseph, "I heard some awful things about you, especially your involvement with Potiphar's wife. How can I trust you with interpretation of a dream?" Joseph explained to Pharoah, "What you heard about Potiphar's wife and me is a rumor and is not true. Regarding my ability to interpret dreams, that is true for it says, 'God will respond to Pharoah's welfare.'" (Gen. 41:16) (F.C.O., p. 129)

On the *Pasuk* "Could we find such a one as this, a man in whom the spirit of God is?" (Gen. 41:38) R' Bunim of Pshys'cha commented that it means that it is very difficult to find a person who curls his hair and "in whom the spirit of God is." (F.U.A.O., vol. 1, p. 232)

On the *Pasuk* "There can be no one so discerning and wise as you" (Gen. 41:39), the Baal Shem Tov noted that when a person wishes to examine another, it is obvious that the one testing should know more. Pharoah wanted to know from his advisors if there was someone who was wiser than Joseph, someone who could question Joseph's interpretation of the dream. Once he was told that there was no one greater than Joseph, he knew that Joseph was smarter than all. (F.C.O., p. 129)

The Torah relates the encounter between Joseph and his brothers: "And Joseph's brothers came, and bowed themselves before him with the face to the earth. Joseph saw his brothers and he recognized them, but he acted like a stranger toward them." (Gen. 42:6–7) The Kedushas Levi commented that it is normal for someone who loses a battle to feel defeated and of low esteem. If the brothers, while they bowed, knew that it was their brother, who predicted that they would some day bow to him, they would have become embittered, as one who is defeated. Joseph did not want his brothers to feel pain. The Torah is telling us the greatness of Joseph. Anyone else would take advantage of this occasion for revenge. Joseph did not reveal himself in order to spare his brothers pain and embarrassment. (M.T., vol. 1, p. 184)

"Joseph saw his brothers and he recognized them, but he acted like a stranger toward them and spoke harshly. He said to them, 'From where do you come?' . . . They said to him, 'We are the sons of one man; we are truthful; your servants have never been spies.'" (Gen. 42:7–8) On these *Pasukim*, the Mishmeres Itmar commented that Joseph noticed that there was unity among the brothers but he detected a sense of arrogance and was disappointed. For that he scolded them and asked them why they were so arrogant: "Don't you know where you come from?" The brothers answered, "We are the sons of one father. That is why we are united, and your servants are not spies but servants of God." (F.C.O., p. 130)

On the *Pasuk* "You are spies" (Gen. 42:9), R' Avraham Moshe of Pshys'cha queried as to why Joseph picked "You are spies" as an accusation to his brothers. Joseph was concerned lest his brothers, knowing that he had been sold to the Egyptians, would inquire about him and discover who he was. Having been called spies, they would avoid asking too many questions. (M.T., vol. 1, p. 185)

❧

There is an enlightening dialogue noted between R' Pinchas Horowitz and his brother, R' Shmelke. Knowing of his brother's humility, R' Pinchas was astonished that R' Shmelke said that he was proud that he had reached the status of being God-fearing. However, we learn from the Torah that one should be proud to be God-fearing. Joseph was proud to proclaim that "I fear God." (Gen. 42:18) For the performance of a mitzvah one needs Divine help, so one cannot be proud because it is not entirely his action. But to attain the status of being God-fearing, we are told, "All is in the hands of Heaven except the fear of Heaven." (Talmud *Berachot* 32b) Heaven does not help in this instance, for the person must work by himself to attain that level. If he worked and reached that level, he can be proud. (F.U.A.O., vol. 1, p. 240)

❧

On the same *Pasuk*, the Amshinover commented that it was not in the nature of Joseph to boast of his being God-fearing. However, his intention was to convey this attitude to his brothers, hoping to bring them to repentance. Therefore he said, "I fear God," and they responded, "Indeed, we are guilty concerning our brother." (Gen. 42:21) (M.T., vol. 1, p. 186)

❧

"If you are honest men, let one of your brothers remain imprisoned . . . and you go bring the provisions for the hunger of your household." (Gen. 42:19) The Radamsker commented that this shows the kindness of the Almighty. He remains and does not depart from His people even if they are on a low level, for He dwells in the inner depths of their hearts. The *Pasuk* tells us that wherever we are, the Almighty is in the hidden mode, as it states; "I will hide My face from them." (Deut. 31:17) The Radamsker said, "When you go to the marketplace for your necessities, remember that Hashem is in the inner depths of your heart." (M.T., vol. 1, p. 86)

On the *Pasuk* "They drank and they imbibed with him" (Gen. 43:34), the S'fas Emes commented that they did not drink much, yet they got drunk for they were not in the habit of drinking, so the little bit that they did drink affected them. We find the same occurred with Noach in that he got drunk after the flood. Actually, he drank the same amount as he had previously, but after the flood he did not realize that his body could not take the same amount. (F.C.O., p. 132)

VAYIGASH
"AND HE APPROACHED"

The *Pasuk* states: "Then Judah approached him (Joseph) and said, 'If you please, my lord, may your servant speak a word in my Lord's ears and may your anger not flare up at your servant—for you are like Pharoah.'" (Gen. 44:18) R' Aaron Chernobler gave a lesson on prayer based on the word *vayigash*, in which he noted that *hagashah* (approach) means "prayer." When one is about to pray he should have these words in mind: "If you please, my Lord, in me there is a bit of the Divine. May your servant speak a word in my Lord's ears. I beg of you listen to my prayer. May your anger not flare up at your servant. Do not be disappointed in me and have pity. What Pharoah decreed did not come about. So, too, if you decide an evil decree, may it also not come about." (F.C.O., p. 134)

⟜

The Baal Shem Tov noted that we must worhsip Hashem with awe and with joy. Both are necessary and cannot be separated. Awe without joy is complete fear. (F.C.O., p. 134)

⟜

The Chernobler noted that by rearranging the letters of the word *b'simchah*, meaning "joy," we have the word *Machashavah*, meaning "thought." This points out that in every thought there should be joy. (F.C.O., p. 134)

The Mishmeres Itmar noted a method of prayer based on the *Pasuk* "Then Judah approached him and said, 'If you please, my Lord.'" (Gen. 44:18) When one begins his prayers and wishes that his request be fulfilled, he should say, "Please my Lord, I know that You are the Creator and the All-Knowing," and then present his request. (F.C.O., p. 134)

The Ropshitzer noted that Judah told Joseph to immediately free Benjamin so that everyone could exalt Hashem. An acrostic of the words *Vayigash eylav* (Gen. 44:18) is *Gadlu Lashem iti oonreromemu shmo yachdav*, "Declare the greatness of Hashem with me, and let us exalt His Name together." (F.C.O., p. 135)

The S'fas Emes commented that the reason Judah repeated the entire story to Joseph was to tell him that when the brothers first came they were falsely accused of spying and stealing money. They were absolutely sure of their innocence. At that time, they asked, "What is this that Hashem has done to us?" Now, they were convinced that Hashem had found out their wrongdoing. They were ready to confess and accept their punishment. Judah asked, "Why do you blame our father? For how can I go to my father if the youth is not with me, lest I see the evil that will befall my father." (Gen. 44:34) At that point, Joseph saw that his brothers realized what they had done when they sold him and they did not want to continue to distress their father. The Torah tells us, "Now Joseph could not endure in the presence of all who stood before him." (Gen. 45:1) (F.C.O., p. 134)

The Berditchever gave an interesting psychological interpretation of the *Pasuk* "If your youngest brother does not come down with you, you will not see my face again!" (Gen. 44:23) The Berditchever said that there are people who are very materialistic. They have the necessities of life and are very comfortable and so they have a superior attitude. The same is true on a spiritual level. There are those who learn day and night. Their demeanor is that of people who are servants of God, learned and strict observers of Halachah, whose main purpose is to obtain a place in Heaven. However, some have a superior attitude with little concern for others, sometimes not even for their own children. As long as they can guarantee themselves a place in Heaven, they are happy and satisfied. About these people the Torah says, "If your youngest brother does not come down with you,"—if you are not concerned with your brother, who is not on your level or status—then, the Torah continues, "You will not see my face again." (F.U.A.O., vol. 1, p. 135)

Based on the *Pasuk* "How can I go up to my father if the youth is not with me?" (Gen. 44:32), the Primishlaner said that if the youth do not follow in the spiritual footsteps of their fathers, then how can we approach our Heavenly Father if the youth are not with us? (F.C.O., p. 136)

The Mishmeres Itmer made the following observation on the *Pasuk* "And now, be not distressed; do not reproach yourselves for having sold me here." (Gen. 45:5) He said, "And now that you are repenting your actions on selling me as a slave, do not repent in distress. The highest form of repentance is in happiness, joy, and love." (F.C.O., p. 136)

R' Meir Primishlaner noted an insightful perspective in Joseph's message to his father. The message was: "You will reside in the land of Goshen and you will be close to me." (Gen. 45:10) In essence, Joseph was saying that his father was not going to live with him for if they lived together disputes might erupt. The sense of a united and loving family would no longer exist. Thus, Joseph had the family move to Goshen, thereby assuring that "You will be close to me." (F.C.O., p. 137)

⌇⌇

Joseph said to his family, "It is my mouth that is speaking to you." (Gen. 45:12) Joseph was in substance saying, noted R' Asher Horowitz, that both his mouth and his heart were united. "What I am saying to you with my mouth, I feel with my heart." (F.C.O., p. 138)

⌇⌇

On the same *Pasuk*, R' Aharon Karliner commented that Joseph was saying that the entire time he was speaking to his brothers, through the interpreter, he was speaking in the "Holy Tongue." His words were to be taken not as ordinary words but as laden with deep spiritual connotations. (M.T., vol. 1, p. 201)

⌇⌇

"Tell my father of all my glory (*k'vodi*)." (Gen. 45:13) R' Baruch Mezibozer commented that the word *k'vodi* can also mean "difficult," from the word *kaved*. Joseph asked that his father be told that amidst all the difficulties of being with impure people, he still clung to the Almighty. (M.T., vol. 1, p. 202)

⌇⌇

On the same *Pasuk*, the Kotzker made the following comment: "It is interesting to note that we are told that 'If one runs from honor, honor will follow him.'" (Talmud *Eruvin* 13a) He said that if honor continues to run after him, obviously the necessity for honor is still part of his personality. The need for honor must be eradicated from one's personality so that honor will have nothing to chase. (M.T., vol. 1, p. 202)

⌇⌇

"And he fell upon his brother Benjamin's neck and wept, and Benjamin wept on his neck." (Gen. 45:14) Rashi comments that they wept over the two temples destined to be built in the portion of the tribe of Benjamin and to be destroyed. Benjamin also wept over the Tabernacle of Shiloh destined to be in the portion of Joseph and also to be destroyed. R' Yechezkel Kuzmirer was puzzled by this scenario. Why, in this time of joy, did the brothers bemoan the destruction of the Temples? Further-more, why did they not weep over the destruction of their individual Temples rather than their brother's Temple? It is a known fact, noted the Kuzmirer, that the Temples were destroyed because of unwarranted hatred. When the two brothers were united, they knew that their separation had been caused by unnecessary hatred. They immediately saw that the destruction would come from that hatred. They wept over that behavior that would cause so much grief. Therefore, the solution was to develop a strong sense of love so that the pain of others should hurt one more. Therefore, each wept over the pain of the other to show that the ache of the other was greater. This kind of love acts as a corrective measure for unwarranted hatred. (F.C.O., p. 139)

⌖

On the same *Pasuk*, the Berditchever used to pray that no harm should come to those who did him harm. He also prayed that no one should commit a sin because of him. He noted the Midrash *Bereshit, Vayechi*, which states that the Holy Temple was built because of Benjamin and no other brother. The others had been involved in the sale of Joseph. It seems that Joseph, too, was not worthy, since his brothers had com-mitted transgressions because of him. (F.U.A.O., vol. 1, p. 256)

⌖

The *Pasuk* states: "And they told him, saying, 'Joseph is still alive and he is ruler over the entire land of Egypt.' But he [Jacob] had a turn of heart, for he did not believe them." (Gen. 45:26) The Koznitzer Maggid commented that it is impossible to say that Jacob our father did not believe his own children. He said that Jacob did believe his children when he was told that Joseph was observing all the *mitzvot*. After all, he was Jacob's son. What Jacob did not believe was that his son was ruler over Egypt. For Joseph to be a ruler and not disguise his Jewishness, even though he was Jacob's son, was hard to believe. (F.C.O., p. 139)

⌖

On the *Pasuk* "I shall descend with you to Egypt, and I shall also surely bring you up" (Gen. 46:4), the Berditchever commented that even when a person reaches a high level in his observance, it is still incumbent upon him to continue to strive. (F.C.O., p. 140)

⌒⌒

The Master of the Universe promised the generations beyond Jacob that no matter where His children were dispersed, He would be with them. This promise, the S'fas Emes noted, is based on the *Pasuk* "I will descend with you to Egypt." (Gen. 46:4) (F.C.O., p. 140)

⌒⌒

On the *Pasuk* "I shall descend with you to Egypt, and I shall also surely bring you up" (Gen. 46:4), R' Bunim noted that there are different types of leaders and different methods of leadership. He explained what he meant by means of a parable. A king moved to a tower, and the approach to him was very difficult. There were winding staircases, hidden nooks, and corners. A person wanted to reach the king and started going to the tower. He tried every which way but found it very difficult to reach his destination. Another person tried and each time he made a mistake and took a wrong turn. However, he put a mark so that the mistake should not be made again by him or anyone else who wished to approach the king. (F.U.A.O., p. 264)

⌒⌒

On the *Pasuk* "And he [Joseph] fell on his neck" (Gen. 46:29), Rashi says: "But Jacob did not fall on Joseph's neck and he did not kiss him. Our Rabbis commented that Jacob was saying the *Shmah*. The Yid HaKadosh asked why Joseph did not say the *Shmah*. The answer he gave was that when Jacob met Joseph, his joy was so great that he feared that his joy would lead to a much greater love for his son than his love for Hashem. He said the *Shmah* to remind himself that "You should love the Lord, Thy God with all your heart." Joseph, on the other hand, also had joy but his love was based on the precept of "Honor thy father." The Yid HaKadosh said that it is known that all who are involved in performing one mitzvah are absolved from doing another. (M.T., vol. 1, p. 108)

VAYECHI
"AND HE [JACOB] LIVED"

Menachem Mendel Schneerson, the Lubavitcher Rebbe, commented that although the *Sidra* begins with *Vayechi* ("And he lived"), it really speaks of the death of Jacob. As the reading shows, Jacob's life was one of connection to God that transcended the material world. Since he shared this quality with his descendants, it was perpetuated beyond his mortal lifetime. As our sages say, "Jacob, our ancestor, did not die. As his descendants are alive, he is alive." The vitality we experience in our Divine service today is made possible by the life of Jacob. (G.O.T., pp. 69–74)

～

The *Sidra* begins with the words *Vayechi Yaacov*. (Gen. 47:28) Rashi comments: "Why is this passage 'closed?' Because once our forefather Jacob passed away, the eyes and heart of Israel were closed because of their suffering, for they [the Egyptians] began to enslave them. Alternatively, because he [Jacob] would wish to reveal the end to his sons, it was closed off from him. This comment is found in *Bereshit Rabbah* (96:1).

～

There are a few Chasidic interpretations based on the comment above. The S'fas Emes notes that because Jacob's life in Egypt was a preparation for the redemption, "The eyes and heart of Israel were closed." (Gen. 48:10) On the other hand, R' Simcha Bunim said that Jacob would have wished to reveal the end to his children in order to make their lives in the Diaspora easier. (F.C.O., p. 142)

~~~

The Ropshitzer Rebbe gave yet another interpretation. He commented that when Jacob wanted to reveal the end, the Divine Presence left him. When Jacob saw all the difficulties and persecutions the Israelites would endure before the advent of the Messiah, he became sad and depressed. "It is a noted fact," said the Ropshitzer, "that the Divine Presence does not dwell in the midst of sadness and depression." (F.U.A.O., p 271)

~~~

The Yid HaKadosh noted that there are Tzaddikim who wish to reveal the end of the Diaspora—that is, to hint as to when the Messiah will come. The truth is that the coming of the Messiah is a secret. The one who knows the secret will not reveal it. The one who does reveal the secret does really not know the secret. (F.C.O., p. 142)

~~~

The Kotzker noted that our Sages tried to bring the Messiah, but it did not happen. The *Baalei Tosfot* and the Tzaddikim also did not succeed in having the Messiah come. Our Sages tell us that "The son of David will not come until the mind is occupied with other matters." (*Sanhedrin* 97a) The Kotzker further noted that the statement should be taken literally. The minds of the people will be constantly occupied with worldly matters, such as earning a living, so they will not be concerned with the coming of the Messiah. (F.U.A.O., p. 273)

~~~

There are two interpretations of the statement "Jacob our father did not die." (Tractate *Taanit*). The S'fas Emes noted that when a son continues in his father's footsteps, it cannot be said that the father has died. R' Yisroel Modzitzer remarked that the statement "The House of Jacob is afire" means that in every Jewish heart there is a spark of the Divine. Of this spark, our Sages declared, "Jacob, our father, is not dead." This flame would never be extinguished. (F.C.O., p. 143)

On the *Pasuk* "Please do not bury me in Egypt" (Gen. 47:29), Rashi comments: "Its destiny is that its soil will turn into lice . . . so that the Egyptians should not make a pagan deity of me." The Gerer Rebbe said that Jacob was concerned that because Goshen, the city where the Israelites dwelled during the plague of lice, had not been touched, his place of burial might become a shrine. (F.U.A.O., p. 274)

The *Pasuk* states: "*Anochi* (I) *E'eseh* (I will do) *kidvarecha* (in accordance with your words)." (Gen. 47:30) The Ostrovitzer noted that the "I" is superfluous. But Joseph was promising that he, too, would do the same as his father. Just as Jacob requested that his remains be taken out of Egypt to Canaan, so would Joseph make the same request. (F.C.O., p. 143)

Basing his comment on the *Pasuk* "Now Israel's eyes were heavy with age" (Gen. 48:10), the Toldot Yaacov Yosef made the following observation on leadership. He said that the "eyes of Israel," namely the leaders of the generation, who should lead with open eyes and be aware of everything, are usually "heavy with age" and therefore they do not take notice of the behavior of the people. They do not see the actions of their flock. When they finally realize how far astray the people have become and wish to return them to the correct path, it is too late because no one wants to listen or look at them. (F.C.O., p. 143)

On the *Pasuk* "So he brought them near him and kissed them and hugged them" (Gen. 48:10), R' Simcha Bunim, who in his later years became blind, commented that the Torah notes that when Isaac found it difficult to see he requested, "Bring them closer so that I may kiss them." (*Bereshit* 27:26) Jacob made the same request when he found it difficult to see. Usually, when one wants to get closer to another, it is enough to have eye contact. However, when one loses that ability then he must do it with physical contact, namely, hugs and kisses. (F.A.O., p. 277)

On the *Pasukim* "He blessed Joseph . . . Bless the children," the Zohar noted that the *Pasuk* begins with blessing Joseph and ends with blessing the children. "Bless the children" is really Joseph's blessing. The best blessing for a person is that he should have fine, upright children. (F.A.O., p. 279)

On the *Pasuk* "So he blessed them that day" (Gen. 48:20), the Lenchener commented that Jacob blessed Joseph's children that they ought to bless and thank Hashem for today and never worry about the morrow. (F.C.O., p. 144)

On the *Pasuk* "By you shall Israel bless, saying, 'May God make you like Ephraim and like Menashe'" (Gen. 48:20), R' Tzvi Zolizitzer said that the Jewish people will bless their children that they should grow up like the children of Joseph and not the children of the other tribes. There are two principles in the Torah that we are requested to follow. The first is that we should not feel and behave as though we are greater than another, and secondly that we should not be jealous of another. When Joseph informed his father, "Not so, Father, for this is the firstborn; place your right hand on his head" (Gen. 48:18), Jacob answered, "I know, my son, I know; he, too, will become great; however his younger brother shall become greater than he." (Gen. 48:19) Jacob noticed that although he had promised the younger one greatness, Ephraim did not become arrogant and Menashe did not become jealous. Both brothers were as before—no change in character. That is why Jacob promised, "By you shall Israel bless." The Jewish people will bless their children for the same attributes of Joseph's children: "May God make you like Ephraim and like Menashe." (F.C.O., p. 145)

On Jacob's words, "With my sword and with my bow" (Gen. 48:22), the Koznitzer made the following observation. Esav was gratified by Isaac's blessing that he would live by the sword. By contrast, Jacob inherited Torah and service to God from his father. However, Jacob's inheritance became the sword by which the children of Israel would overpower the sword of Esav. That is the meaning of our Sages' statement: "At the time that the 'voice of Jacob' will be heard in the synagogues and halls of study, the 'hand of Esav' will not rule." (F.C.O., p. 145)

On the words "With my sword and with my bow" (Gen. 48:22), the Kotzker commented that prayer is likened to a bow. The more one stretches the bow, the farther and higher it goes. It is the same with prayer: The more we concentrate with deep feeling, the farther and higher it will reach. (F.C.O., p. 146)

"Then Jacob called for his sons and said, 'Assemble yourselves and I will tell you what will befall you in the end of days.'" (Gen. 49:1) Rashi commented that he wished to reveal the end to them but the *Schechinah* (Immanent Presence of God) departed from him. The Riziner wondered what sin Jacob committed such that the *Schechinah* should depart from him when he wanted to reveal the end. It is known that if the Jews are worthy, redemption will come before its time, and if not, the redemption will come when Hashem decides. Jacob, prophetically, saw that the Jews would not merit early redemption because of their behavior. Therefore, the *Schechinah* departed before Jacob spoke evil against the Jewish people, for to listen to evil talk is not permitted. (F.C.O., p. 146)

Jacob said, "Gather yourselves," and then, "I will tell what will befall you in the end of days." (Gen. 49:1) The Rimanover said that gathering is likened to the binding of the hyssop as in the days of Sukkot, and "I will tell" is likened to coolness and chilling. Jacob, our father, commanded his children to bind themselves in deep love, gather themselves in one association, so that there would be unity, for in the end of days there will be coolness and many hindrances when performing *mitzvot*. (M.D., p. 98)

"Gather yourselves and listen." (Gen. 49:2) The Mishmeres Itmer said that when you will be united and remain close with one another, then Israel your father will listen—that is, Hashem, Israel's Father. (F.C.O., p. 146)

On the words "Shimon and Levi are brothers" (Gen. 49:5), the Ropshitzer noted that the brothers were zealous for the sake of *mitzvot*. They did not fight for vain purposes. They defended the honor of their sister. Even though they were zealous for a good cause, nevertheless Jacob condemned their behavior. Jacob said, "Accursed is their rage for it is mighty, and their wrath for it is harsh." (Gen. 49:7) One must learn to control both anger and zealousness even if one has the best of intentions. (F.U.A.O., p. 284)

On the *Pasuk* "Into their design, may my soul not enter" (Gen. 49:6), the Chidushei Harim commented that the essence of this request was that Jacob's name should not be mentioned in the controversy of Korach and Moses. The disputants would justify their behavior by saying that their quarrel was for the sake of Heaven and bring proof from Jacob's behavior. Jacob did not want his name mentioned because the conflict would not be for the sake of Heaven but primarily against Moses. (F.C.O., p. 147)

On the *Pasuk* "Judah . . . your bothers shall acknowledge your hand" (Gen. 49:8), the S'fas Emes said, "All your brothers will be known by your name, *Yehudim*." (F.C.O., p. 147)

On the *Pasuk* "He [Judah] crouched, lied down like a lion" (Gen. 49:9), the Chidushei Harim commented that this was Judah's personality. Even though he had to kneel, he did so as a lion. He may have to kneel, but he does so with pride. He does not become depressed nor give up hope. He admits his error and repents and stands up. Thus Judah admitted his error with Tamar, and because of this the Messiah will come from his descendents. (M.T., vol. 1, p. 223)

Yitzchok Vorker made an interesting comment on Jacob's blessing to Issacher, "And he saw a resting place, that it was good . . . And he bent his shoulder to bear." (Gen. 49:15) He noted that a person has true peace of mind when he can shoulder a burden. Conversely, a person can bear all sorts of situations when he has peace of mind. (F.C.O., p. 147)

On the same *Pasuk*, the Lubliner Rebbe said that Issacher was able to live in peace and harmony with his neighbors because "He bent his shoulder to bear." He learned to bend his shoulder, to let things go by, and never to get involved with someone else's anger and manipulative behavior. He became known as a very patient individual. (F.C.O., p. 147)

On that same *Pasuk*, R' Bunim commented that when one desires release from worries, he may obtain it by bending his shoulder to anything that might befall him and he will be spiritually satisfied no matter what the outcome. (S.S.K., p. 93)

On the same *Pasuk*, the Vorker commented that one does have true peace of mind when one is patient and tolerant. (M.T., vol. 1, p. 224)

On the *Pasuk* "For your salvation do I long" (Gen. 49:18), R' Yitzchak Shapiro of Neshchiz commented that if one wishes to long for salvation he must be always attached to Hashem, for it is written in Psalms 16: "I have set Hashem before me always." (M.D., p. 102)

Asher's blessing was "His bread is rich, and he will provide kingly delicacies. (Gen. 49:20) R' Zev Stritkover noted that we have a lot to learn from Asher. "His bread is rich"—though Asher's was a plain piece of bread, for others he gave a kingly portion. Such must be the life of a Jew. He should lead a very plain life so that he can give the best to others. (F.C.O., p. 148)

The Yismach Moshe said that Jacob blessed Asher so that he might become wealthy, but not to the extent that he would become arrogant and forget everyone else. (F.C.O., p. 148)

"Each according to his blessing he blessed them." (Gen. 49:28) R' Bunim of Pshys'cha commented that even though Jacob had said, "Accursed is their rage for it is mighty" (Gen. 49:7), for Simeon and Levi it was a blessing. The fact that he took away the characteristic of anger from them by acknowledging it is also a blessing. (M.T., vol. 1, p. 224)

"From the God of your father, and He will help you." (Gen. 49:29) The Mishmeres Itmar commented that if it can be shown that all that is happening to you is from Hashem, then Hashem, your Father, will help you. (F.C.O., p. 149)

"Egypt bewailed him for seventy days." (Gen. 50:3) The Yismach Moshe said that the Egyptians did not go into deep mourning out of love for Israel (Jacob). However, they remembered that when Jacob came to Egypt, the Nile River overflowed into the fields and the hunger ceased. With the death of Jacob, the Egyptians feared that the river would return to its previous state and a period of hunger would again return. (F.C.O., p. 149)

~~

The Kotzker made the following comment on the *Pasuk* "So now, please forgive the spiteful deed of the servants of your father's God." (Gen. 50:17) He said that this is the first time that the term "servants of God" is mentioned. It was not until the tribes accepted the yoke of heaven that they proclaimed, "Hear O' Israel." Not till then were they able to be called "servants of God." (F.C.O., p. 149)

~~

The reason Joseph said, "Do not fear" (Gen. 50:19), the Kosover Rebbe explained, was that he wanted to assure his brothers that he would not do them any harm. In essence, he was telling them: "You always wished me harm but Hashem turned everything for the best. The same thing may come about with me. I may want to do you harm—but do I replace God? Hashem may turn it all to the best. Therefore do not fear." (F.C.O., p. 150)

WEEKLY PORTIONS OF
SHEMOT/EXODUS

SHEMOT
"THESE ARE THE NAMES"

The Lubavitcher Rebbe, Rabbi Menachem Mendel Schneerson, noted that there are two aspects to a person's name. One represents the external as he relates to others and for this he does require a name. As the Alter Rebbe writes in *Tanya*, a name also represents a life-force. It is a channel that allows the inner nature to be expressed. This is not merely a theoretical concept, for it affects a person's daily conduct. This is reflected in the main theme of this *chumash*. In the external dimension of a Jew's name, it is possible for him to be subjugated by worldly powers. But when the essence of Yisroel, a Jewish name, is expressed, there is no potential for domination for the name Yisroel indicates that we "contended with God and the man and prevailed." (*Bereshit* 32:29) (G.O.T., pp. 77–80)

Concerning the exile in Egypt, the Chidushei Harim noted that it lasted two hundred and ten years. The Torah gives us an account of this aspect in our tragic history in one *parsha*, *Parshat Shemot*. However, the preparation for the redemption, which lasted forty years, takes up the entire Torah. We can deduce that the Diaspora, no matter how long it lasts, will be only a small percentage of the essence of our lives. (F.U.A.O., vol. 1, p. 30)

~~~

"And Joseph died, and all his brothers and all that generation. And the children of Israel were fruitful and increased abundantly." (Ex. 1:6–7) The Radamsker noted that a *neshamah* (soul) is afraid that it may easily become corrupted and lose its purity when it descends to earth in a body. However, when they saw that an entire generation of souls returned to Heaven with increased purity and holiness, they requested Hashem's permission to enter bodies and gain the opportunity to become holier. (Ohel Shlomo, quoted in H.A., p. 170)

~~~

"And these are the names." (Ex. 1:1) The Chidushei Harim said that though the people would be in dire straits while in the Diaspora, their existence would always be assured. This guarantee was made because they would keep their Jewish names, as they did in Egypt. (F.C.O., p. 151)

~~~

The reason the Torah says, "And Joseph was in Egypt" (Ex. 1:5), noted the Berditchever, is that though Pharoah gave him an Egyptian name, Tzafnat Parneyach, he maintained his own name, Joseph. (F.C.O., p. 151)

~~~

On the *Pasuk* "And the land became filled with them" (Ex. 1:7), the Ostrovitzer noted that the Israelites had large families and worked very hard and therefore, Egypt was filled with abundance and blessings. (F.C.O., p. 152)

~~~

On the *Pasuk* "And there arose a new king . . . who knew not Joseph" (Ex. 1:8), Rabbi Avraham Moshe Rabinowitz, the Skoyler Rebbe, commented that the evil inclination renews each day with new traps to overpower a person. Even the righteous are not exempt in the fight to conquer the evil inclination, for they, too, do not know the stumbling blocks put forth each day. That is the implication of "And there arose a new king," as noted in the Zohar. The evil inclination is an old, wise king who renews his techniques every day and does not recognize the righteousness of a righteous person. Therefore, it is imperative for all to conquer the evil inclination every day. (Ch. B., p. 159)

～～

On the same *Pasuk*, in his *sefer R'vid Hazahav*, R' Yisroel Dov Gilerenter of Ashinize commented that the evil inclination renews his activities every day, as our Sages noted in the Talmud: "A person's inclination overpowers him every day." (*Sukkah* 52b) Therefore, it is incumbent upon the Jew to increase and renew his intensity in the service of Hashem every day, as is stated in the *Sifri*: "Every day shall be unto you a renewal, for the evil inclination blinds the eyes and makes you lazy." (Deut. 32) The evil inclination renews each day his decrees and attaches himself to the individual. However, he does not know Joseph, the character of Joseph, for he, too, renews his intensity in the "service of Hashem." (M.D., p. 107)

～～

On the *Pasuk* "Behold, the people of the children of Israel are more numerous and mightier than we" (Ex. 1:9), there are two comments. The first, by R' Yisroel Riziner, explained that as long as we remain united as a people, we will always be strong and steadfast. The second comment is based on a question posed to R' Shlomo Belzer. He was asked to explain why on Mondays and Thursdays after the reading of the Torah four paragraphs are read, beginning with "And it shall be Thy will," but the last paragraph begins with the words "Our brothers" (a plea for God's mercy on all suffering Jews). The Belzer answered that when we pray as a united people in times of distress, it automatically becomes a time of God's will. (F.C.O., p. 152)

～～

"And they [the Egyptians] were disgusted because of the Children of Israel." (Ex. 1:12) The S'fas Emes commented that the Egyptians suddenly developed a deep hatred for the Jewish people. The Israelites did not understand why this attitude developed after so many years of neighborliness. Apparently, this occurred because of Divine intervention. The Almighty was afraid that too much familiarity might prevail. The comment of the S'fas Emes is based on a sentence in Psalms that says, "Their hearts will change to hate them." God changed the hearts of the Egyptians to hate them, thus eliminating the possiblity of assimilation. (M.T., vol. 1, p. 10)

———

"The King said to the midwives." (Ex. 1:15) R' Tzvi Hirsh Dinever noted that many times the character of a person can be seen in the name. When a person changes his name, his inner self will also change. The Pharaoh knew that as long as the midwives maintained their Hebrew names, such as Yocheved and Miriam, they would not listen to his edict. He therefore commanded them to change their names to Shifrah and Puah. The Pharaoh was hoping that when they changed their names they would behave as Egyptians—namely, that they would develop a sense of cruelty. They would then have no mercy on the children and would do as they were told. It was not until he told them to change their names that he gave the command to kill the Jewish boys. (M.T., vol. 1, p. 11)

———

The Nikolsberger Rebbe noted that the word *uri'eesen* ("And you shall see") (Ex. 1:16) is mentioned only three times in the Torah. He juxtaposed this word with Akivah Ben Mehallel's statement, "Consider three things and you will not come into the grip of sin. . . ." (*Ethics of Our Fathers*, ch. 3:1); "Know from where you come"—"And you shall see on the birthstool"; "Know where you are going"—"And you shall see the land"; "And before Whom you shall give a reckoning"—"And you shall see them and you shall remember them." (F.C.O., p. 153)

———

R' Asher Horowitz noted that the command of Pharoah, "Every son that will be born, into the river shall you throw him" (Ex. 1:22), was really a clandestine form of anti-Semitism. He thought that the Egyptians would be so concerned with his edict that they would make sure that it pertained only to the Jews. (F.C.O., p. 154)

⟜

"A man went from the house of Levi." (Ex. 2:1) The Mishmeres Itmer noted that the reason for anonymity is that the Torah teaches us that Amram, the father of Moses, though a popular person, was a simple and modest human being. (F.C.O., p. 154)

⟜

"She [Pharaoh's daughter] saw the basket among the reeds and she sent her maidservant and she took it." (Ex. 2:5) The Kotzker Rebbe wondered how was it possible for the maidservant to stretch her hand across such a great distance and retrieve the basket. The Kotzker said that we learn from this that if one wishes to reach a goal, one should not be concerned with stumbling blocks. A person should stretch out his hand and eventually the goal will be reached. (F.C.O., p. 154)

⟜

"She opened it and saw him, the child, and behold! a youth was crying." (Ex. 2:6) On this *Pasuk*, R' Bunim of Otovsk made the following observation: "When Pharaoh's daughter opened the basket she was astonished. She noticed the baby seemed to be crying but no sound was heard. That is why she said that it was a Hebrew child. She knew that only a Jew could cry silently." (M.T., vol. 1, p. 14)

⟜

"He hid him in the sand." (Ex. 2:12) The Toldot Yaacov Yosef wondered why it was necessary after "He [Moses] saw an Egyptian man striking a Hebrew man, of his brethren . . . struck down the Egyptian, he hid him in the sand," to state, "He went out the next day and behold — two Hebrew men were striving. He said to the wicked one, 'Why would you strike your fellow?' He replied, 'Who made you a man, a ruler, and a judge over us? Are you saying that you are going to kill me, as you killed the Egyptian?'" (Ex. 2:13–14) The answer he gave was that just as it is

impossible to make string from sand, so it is difficult to develop a sense
of unity among the Jews. (F.C.O., p. 155)

~~~

"Indeed the matter became known." (Ex. 2:12) The S'fas Emes was
saddened by this *Pasuk*. It made him realize why the Jews were still in
the Diaspora. Jews do not permit redemption as long as they continue to
slander and malign those fellow Jews who fight to obtain justice for
their people. (*S'fas Emes*, p. 10)

~~~

On the *Pasuk* "And it came to pass in this long time, that the King of
Egypt died" (Ex. 2:23), the Noam Elimelech noted that the Zohar calls
the King of Egypt "an evil inclination." When a person's inner being is
awakened, he regrets his deeds and wishes to destroy the evil inclination. There are others who do not intend to correct the core of evil and
purify their thoughts. However, it is only after they think about repenting that they say within their hearts that they will cure themselves by
studying the Torah and praying. That is the essence of "service of the
heart." When a person is in pain, cries out, fasts, and says the penitential
prayers but otherwise does nothing, this is not true repentance. That is
what is meant by "And they groaned." However, Hashem in His mercy
will accept the cry as though they prayed with full intent, for the *Pasuk*
says: "And the children of Israel groaned and God remembered His
covenant with Abraham." (Ex. 2:24) (*Noam Elimelech*, p. 31b)

~~~

The Rebbe of Lublin noted that the reason the Hebrews "groaned" (Ex.
2:23) was that the new King gave them a few days' rest. Under the
Pharaoh, the work was so difficult that eventually they did not even feel
their agony and pain. However, after a few days' rest, they realized their
condition and their outcry went up to God. (F.C.O., p. 155)

~~~

R' Shmelke of Nikolsberg noted that the word *ha'avodah* (Ex. 2:23),
which has the double meaning of "work" as well as "service to God," has

special significance in the *Pasuk* "Their outcry went up to God because of work." The outcry of the Hebrews was not because of the work but because they could not pray (service to God). Therefore, their outcry went up to Heaven and was heard. (M.T., vol. 1, p. 17)

~~

On the same *Pasuk*, R' Avraham Heschel, in his *sefer Ohev Yisroel*, comments that when a person is troubled, he should pray that Hashem should help him because he is being deprived of serving Him. Thus, his prayer will not be for his personal needs but for help to continue to serve the Almighty. This is the reason the Hebrews cried out "because of their work," for the Egyptians were holding them back from worshipping the Almighty. They were not praying for themselves and therefore, "Their outcry went up to God." (M.D., p. 101)

~~

"And God saw the children of Israel." (Ex. 2:25) What did God see to take the Jews out of Egypt? R' Dovid Talner commented that God noticed the attitude and behavior of His people. While in slavery, they did not change their names, nor did they change their mode of dress, and they spoke their own language. So God knew that His people must be redeemed and taken out of slavery. (F.C.O., p. 157)

~~

"Do not come closer to here. . . ." (Ex. 3:5) The Yampoler Rebbe interpreted this *Pasuk* symbolically. He said that Hashem is saying that when one wishes to become a servant of God, one should not rationalize his circumstances. One should know that no matter what the conditions are, he can always worship God and become His servant. This is what Hashem meant when He said to Moses, "Do not come closer to here; take off your shoes from your feet, for the place upon which you stand is holy ground." When you come near, when you wish to be close to God, then do it! Do not seek a way out; "take off your shoes" — remove your excuses. No matter where one is, the ground is always holy. (F.C.O., p. 157)

On the *Pasuk* "Take off your shoes from your feet" (Ex. 3:5), the Kobriner Rebbe taught that God says to man, as he said to Moses, "Remove your covering and you will know that the place where you are now standing is holy ground. When you remove the commonplace, you will know that there is no aspect of life in which the Holiness of God cannot be found everywhere and at all times." (M.T., p. 111)

With a play on the word *tzaakosom* of the *Pasuk* "And I have heard their [the Israelites'] outcry (*tzaakosom*) because of their taskmasters" (Ex. 3:7), the Lubliner said that in truth the Israelites were not ready for redemption because they had not reached the status of purity. Nevertheless, in comparison with their environment and their persecutors, they were Tzaddikim. (F.U.A.O., p. 25)

On the *Pasuk* "And now, go and I will send you to Pharoah and you shall take My people, the Children of Israel, out of Egypt" (Ex. 3:10), the S'fas Emes noted that Hashem said to Moses that the redemption from Egypt was the forerunner of the final redemption. If you do not lead the exodus from Egypt now, then there will be no one to lead them later. You must be the example for redemption. (F.C.O., p. 158)

It is interesting to note, said the Rebbe of Lublin, that although Moses questioned being chosen by God to lead the Israelites out of Egypt, God did not shower him with praise. God said that he chose Moses because he did not hold himself to be superior and recognized his own ability. Therefore, when Moses was chosen, God said to him, "I will be with you." (Ex. 3:12) (F.C.O., p. 158)

"When you take the people out of Egypt, you will worship God on this mountain." (Ex. 3:12) Moses wanted to know on what merit the Israelites would be redeemed. The Chidushei Harim explained that the condition for the redemption was that when the Israelites left Egypt, they would accept the Torah, for that in itself is a merit. He further defined the statement "This month in which salvations follow quickly" (*piyyut* for the *musaf* service for the Sabbath before Passover), saying that the month of Nissan brought the salvation. (M.T., vol. 1, p. 19)

"Behold, when I come to the Children of Israel and say to them, 'The God of your forefathers has sent me to you,' and they say to me, 'What is His Name?' what shall I say to them?" (Ex. 3:13) The Riziner could not understand why Moses had a problem defining God's name to the Israelites. In fact, Moses was sure that some of the Israelites in Egypt already knew His name. After all, there were some people who were on a high spiritual level and understood holiness. What Moses was really asking was what new spiritual information could he give them. Hashem answered Moses, "I Shall Be [EYEHE] What I Shall Be." (Ex. 3:14) The letters of the word *Eyehe* total 21 (one *aleph* = one; two *heys* = ten; one *yid* = ten). Doubling 21, because the *Pasuk* mentions *Eyehe* twice, equals 441. *Emes*, "truth," also adds up to 441. What Hashem said to Moses was that he should tell the Children of Israel that the name of the Almighty is "Truth." (F.C.O., p. 158)

On that same *Pasuk*, R' Tzadok HaKohen commented that Moses asked that question for his own edification. (F.C.O., p. 159)

"This is my name (*shmee*) forever." (Ex. 3:15) The letters of *shmee* stand for *Yom Shabbat menucha*, "The Sabbath day is for rest." The Koznitzer said that this means that if the Jews obeyed the Sabbath, then His name would be remembered forever and it would be the basis for Jewish life. (F.C.O., p. 159)

The S'fas Emes wondered how was it possible that Moses could say to God, "They will not believe me." (Ex. 4:1) Why would Moses want to cast aspersions on the Israelites? Moses knew that the Israelites' exile in Egypt was the beginning of the redemption process. He also understood that when the Jews would be in the Diaspora, there would be times when their faith was not strong. Moses wanted to hear from Hashem that even now while the Israelites had little faith, Hashem would redeem them—and so, too, the same would happen in the future. (F.U.A.O., vol. 1, p. 28)

On the *Pasuk* "Then Hashem said to him, 'Who gave man a mouth?'" (Ex. 4:11), the S'fas Emes commented that Moses knew that would be Hashem's answer to his question, "Who am I?" (Ex. 3:11). Being a modest individual, he feared that he might make a blunder in his task because of his handicap. He wanted assurance that his mission would be completely a Godly mission. (M.T., vol. 1, p. 23)

On the same *Pasuk*, the Bratzlaver noted that one should understand that Hashem "gave to man a mouth" so that when he eats, he should do so with a sense of holiness. If one does not eat with a sense of holiness, meaning that he behaves as an animal, then he cannot say that God gave him a mouth. (*Likutei Maharan*)

On the *Pasuk* "So now, go! I shall be your mouth and teach you what you should say" (Ex. 4:12), R' Tzadok HaKohen commented that Hashem told Moses that whatever he said would become the Halachah—the Law. (F.C.O., p. 161)

On the *Pasuk* "He [Aharon] will see you and he will rejoice in his heart" (Ex. 4:14), the Midrash notes that had Aharon known that the Torah would say about him, "He will rejoice in his heart," he would have greeted Moses with all sorts of instruments and dance. The Chidushei Harim commented that Aharon would have done this not because he wanted or needed praise, but knowing that natural joy would command a *Pasuk* in the Torah, it would have led him to increase the joy. (M.T., vol. 1, p. 44)

~~

R' Aharon Karliner interpreted the *Pasuk* "And the people believed, and they heard that Hashem had remembered the Children of Israel" (Ex. 4:31) as follows: The people believed and with this belief, they heard that Hashem is hidden in each Jew. (F.C.O., p. 162)

~~

On Pharaoh's statement to Moses, "Who is God that I should obey Him?" (Ex. 5:2), R' Bunim commented that even the greatest scoffer among Jews is not a genuine nonbeliever. There are times that he will still offer a prayer. The true nonbeliever is the type like Pharaoh who says, "Who is God that I should obey Him?" (F.C.O., p. 162)

~~

Based on the same *Pasuk*, there is a story told that when R' Bunim was in an inn in Danzig, he entered into a discussion with some nonbelievers. Since they were ridiculing him, his son asked that he stop trying to convince them to believe in God. Agreeing with his son, he asked him to step on his foot if he should get involved in a discussion. However, he did get involved and his son stepped on his foot. "I cannot stop," said R' Bunim, "I just heard one who is in pain scream the *Shma*. He is different from Pharaoh, who said, 'Who is God that I should obey Him?' while he was being afflicted." (S.S.K., p. 53)

~~

"You shall not continue to give stubble to the people to make the bricks as yesterday. . . ." (Ex. 5:7) R' Henoch Alexander commented that Pharaoh did not give stubble to the Israelites to make more bricks because he wanted to torment their thinking and their mental abilities.

He reasoned that mental torment was worse than physical stress. It would have been just as easy to give more stubble and increase the amount of bricks, thus causing more physical strain, but that was not the king's intent. (F.U.A.O., p. 30)

Moses felt very guilty when Pharaoh increased the physical labor for the Israelites. Therefore, commented the Kobriner, Moses questioned God. Moses argued that since he caused the problem, someone else should be sent. God assured Moses that because of his modesty, He would make sure that the Israelites would be redeemed by Moses. (F.C.O., p. 164)

On the *Pasuk* "From the time I came to Pharaoh to speak in Your Name, he harmed this people" (Ex. 5:23), the Berditchever commented that this is the way we must plead with Hashem. All of the hatred of the Jews and all acts of anti-Semitism come from our constant defense of You. We are always speaking in Your Name. That is why it is Your responsibility to help us. (F.U.A.O., vol. 1, p. 32)

VA'EIRA
"AND I APPEARED"

It is a natural tendency for children to depend upon the reputation of their parents. Grandchildren, as well, will be extremely proud of their grandparents. However, there is a problem when children and grandchildren do not try to achieve a higher level on their own. Rashi, on the *Pasuk* "And I appeared to Abraham, to Isaac, and to Jacob," says, "And I appeared to the Patriarchs." (Ex. 6:3) R' Meir Primishlaner noted that Isaac was not dependent on the merits of Abraham; Jacob did not rely on the credits of Isaac. Isaac and Jacob tried to reach their own perfection. They developed their own status as Patriarchs. Therefore, continues the Primishlaner, it says: "And I appeared to Abraham, to Isaac, and to Jacob," not to the children nor the grandchildren. (F.C.O., p. 165)

~~~

The Rimanover commented on our Sages' interpretation of the *Pasuk* "So I have also heard the groaning of the children of Israel . . . And I have remembered My covenant." (Ex. 6:5) Our Sages noted that Hashem said that He saw the affliction and He reminded Himself of the Covenant. The Talmud teaches us that affliction forgives. The word "salt" appears near the word "covenant" and the word "covenant" appears near "affliction." (*Berachot* 5a) This means that just as salt improves the taste of meat, so do afflictions improve the person and take away the transgressions. However, the Rimanover commented that while it is true that salt gives flavor, it depends on the amount used. Too much salt may destroy the taste, making it impossible to eat. Affliction must also have its measure to enable one to withstand it. It then may become possible to cure an individual. Too much affliction may make the situation worse. It may cause one to lose reason. Therefore, it says: "Hashem heard the groaning of the Children of Israel" (Ex. 6:5)—the cry of extreme affliction—and "I remembered My covenant"—I must remember the word "salt" that is near the word "covenant." (*Maor V'Shemesh* in M.T., vol. 1, p. 32)

R' Bunim of Pshys'cha commented on the *Pasuk* "I shall take you out from under the burdens (*savlut*) of Egypt." (Ex. 6:6) He noted that the word *savlut*, meaning a "burden," is used, rather than *avdut*, which means "servitude." When one has become accustomed to a burden, it no longer seems stressful, for habit becomes part of one's nature. When God observed that the Israelites were growing accustomed to their tasks and it was becoming servitude and not a burden, He did not want to wait until they accepted the burden without complaint. He decided to redeem them at that time. (F.U.A.O., vol. 1, p. 34)

On the *Pasuk* "I shall take you to Me for a people and I shall be a God to you; you shall know that I am Hashem your God" (Ex. 6:7), the Kedushas Levi commented that one cannot know the Divinity only through the thought process. Jews can come to know the Light of Hashem only through Torah and the performance of the *mitzvot* that Hashem has given us. This is the meaning of "I shall take you to Me." God has given the Torah and thus "You shall know that I am Hashem your God"—to know the Light from the *Schechinah*. (*Noam Elimelech*, p. 72)

"Moses spoke before Hashem, saying, 'Behold, the children of Israel have not listened to me, so how will Pharaoh listen to me?'" (Ex. 6:12) R' Asher Horowitz noted that when people have problems and are depressed, as the Israelites were, they look to their leader for words of consolation, though he might not be a good speaker. However, Moses saw that the Children of Israel went against the norm for they "have not listened to me." He said, "Had I at least been a forceful speaker perhaps Pharaoh would listen to me. But, I am not a forceful speaker; I am a stutterer. Under these circumstances, I ask You Almighty God, 'How will Pharaoh listen to me?'" The S'fas Emes noted that Moses was trying to defend the Jewish People. It is not that the Jews did not want to listen; they could not, for "I am tongue-tied." (F.C.O., p. 167)

The Bialer Rebbe noted that Moses' hesitancy was based on his previous statement, "Why have You sent me?" (Ex. 5:22) In his *sefer Mevaser Tov*, he noted that Moses' hesitancy to accept Hashem's request that he be the spokesman for the Children of Israel and His messenger to Pharaoh was based on his concern for the failure of his mission. Moses considered that this was a test of faith and his ability to be a leader. The Rebbe referred to the statement by the Ramban (Nachmanides) in his *sefer Emunah Ubitachon*, "Tests are not given unless we can succeed and if we do not succeed, and we fail, we begin to stumble. . . . The greatness of our forefathers is based on their passing tests of faith and not only their observance of the Torah and the *mitzvot*." Moses wanted to succeed in his mission so that he might go to the next level. If he failed, then his leadership and faith would be in jeopardy. This he could not let happen. Therefore, Moses was concerned that since the Israelites had not listened to him, then Pharaoh would also not listen and he would fail in his mission. We note in our *tefillot*, "Do not bring us into the power of challenge." (*Mevaser Tov*, p. 349)

Another interpretation given by the S'fas Emes was that we can learn a lesson concerning leadership from this *Pasuk*. He said that when the Jews will not listen to their leaders, then there is very little that the leaders can do. The strength of leadership is received from the people. If the Israelites would have listened to Moses, then his words, based on Divine instructions, would have been clear to Pharaoh. But Moses said to God, "the Israelites will not listen to me." Moses became tongue-tied and found it impossible to demand, "Let my people go!" (F.C.O., p. 167)

～～

"Hashem spoke to Moses and Aharon and commanded them regarding the Children of Israel and regarding Pharaoh, King of Egypt, to take the Children of Israel out of the land of Egypt." (Ex. 6:13) The Ostrovitzer Rebbe wondered why it was necessary to command that the Israelites be taken out of Egypt. After all, that was the hope and desire of the Israelites. The Rebbe noted that the oppressive work put the Israelites into a state of depression. They no longer found joy in life. They had lost all their desire and hope for freedom. The command was made to restore their confidence in becoming free and therefore put joy back into their lives. This would put them on a higher level and prepare them for redemption. (F.C.O., p. 168)

～～

Being concerned about the depression of the Israelites, R' Henoch Alexander noted that when Chasidim talk about joy, they do not mean the joy in the performance of a mitzvah. This is a level unto itself and thus understood. They stress joy to avoid depression. Depression disturbs the development of a positive attitude toward life. (F.C.O., p. 168)

～～

On the *Pasuk* "These are the heads of their fathers' houses" (Ex. 6:14), R' Henoch Alexander noted that this was really the command: to make the Children of Israel realize that they came from such ancestry that they did not deserve to be in servitude. (F.U.A.O., p. 40)

～～

On the *Pasuk* "Provide a wonder for yourselves; you shall say to Aharon, take your staff . . ." (Ex. 7:9), the Kedushas Levi noted that the Ari Hakadosh, in his *sefer Sha'ar Hayichdim* 2, commented that a person should believe that his speech will bring satisfaction to his Creator. A person should therefore heed his speech and avoid nonsense and vanity. He should use speech that would bring merit to Israel by speaking words of Torah, allowing Hashem to grant what one requests. The *Pasuk* tells us that everyone knows all that Hashem can accomplish. If the person does not have the power of speech to make this known, then the staff has that power. (*Kedushas Levi*, p. 73)

～～

"Moses said to Pharaoh, 'Glorify yourself over me — for when should I entreat on your behalf?'" (Ex. 8:5) "Moses cried out to Hashem." (Ex. 8:8) The Chidushei Harim noted that "entreating" and "crying out" are two terms used for prayer. Our Sages tell us that the Egyptian exile hardened the hearts of the Israelites to prayer. Jewish speech was in exile. The Ten Plagues permitted the opening of the hearts and mouths of the Israelites to pray. That is why the words "entreat" and "cry out" appear at the time of the Ten Plagues. At each plague, the hearts and mouths of the Israelites were opened. (*Otzer P'ninim Al HaTorah*, vol. 2, p. 97)

～～

"I will bring about redemption between My people and your people — tomorrow this sign will come about." (Ex. 8:19) The Belzer Rebbe commented that the word "redemption" appears three times. It explains the three types of exile. The word appears for the first time in this *Pasuk*. Hashem said that He would redeem the Israelites from other nations. The second time, the word appears in Psalms 111: "He will send redemption to His people." This refers to when Jews find themselves in exile among Jews — actually, a worse type of exile. The third time, the word appears in Psalms 130: "And with Him is abundant redemption." This refers to when a person creates his own exile because of his evil characteristics. This is the worst type of exile. For this, one needs "abundant redemption." (F.U.A.O., vol. 1, p. 48)

～～

On the same *Pasuk*, the Skoyler Rebbe relates the word *machar*, "tomorrow," to Rashi's interpretation of *machar* in a later *Pasuk*: "And it shall be when your son will ask you *machar*." (Ex. 13:14) Rashi explains that *machar* need not refer only to the morrow but can mean "after a passage of time." One can understand this, for at times it is difficult to overpower the inclination to do evil at the moment. So the advice is to postpone the action when you are tempted by something that is deceptive. That is what is meant by "I will bring about redemption between My people and your people, for tomorrow there will be this sign"—that is, between My people (*mitzvot*) and your people (transgressions) and the *machar* (the future) will be a sign of your choice and you will know the truth of your deed. (Ch.B., p. 174)

~~~

On the *Pasuk* "Moses left Pharaoh's presence and entreated Hashem" (Ex. 8:26), the Mishmeres Itmar commented that one need not always pray out loud. One can entreat Hashem silently. (F.C.O., p. 170)

~~~

"Arise early in the morning and place yourself before Pharaoh." (Ex. 9:13) The Chernowitzer commented that the plague of "hail" was really a phenomenon, a miracle within a miracle, for there was simultaneous fire and hail upon God's command. All the scoffers and evil people saw the hand of God. Even Pharaoh began to have regrets, for he said, "This time I have sinned; Hashem is the Righteous One, and I and my people are the wicked ones." (Ex. 9:27) Still, his heart remained hardened and as soon as the hail let up, he returned to his wickedness. Heaven did not permit him to completely repent, for it was necessary for Pharaoh to continue to seek to sanctify God's name. That is why Hashem said, "For this time I shall send all My plagues against your heart" (Ex. 9:14)—I will send a series of blows at the heart so that you will not just notice it as a phenomenon and miracle but as punishment. (M.T., vol. 1, p. 42)

Bo
"Come"

The word *bo* (Ex. 10:1) means "come" and the word *leych* means "go." It is interesting to note, said the Kotzker, that the Torah uses the word *bo* and not *leych*. The reason is that the Almighty is everywhere. Therefore, the word *bo* is preferable because it means "Come with me"—"I am with you." In this context, *leych* would mean "Go away from me." (F.C.O., p. 171)

On the *Pasuk* "For I have hardened his heart" (Ex. 10:1), the S'fas Emes noted that many times it says that God would harden the heart of Pharaoh to punish him for tormenting the Israelites. The heart is always mentioned, never the mind. That shows that one cannot appeal to an evil person, for he has no good sense. (F.C.O., p. 171)

In R' Kalimus Kalman Epstein of Krakow's *sefer, Maor V'Shemesh*, there is an interesting comment on the *Pasuk* "I shall place these signs of Mine in his heart; and you may relate in the ears of your son and your son's son." (Ex. 10:1–2) Because of the exodus from Egypt, we were privileged to receive two signs. One is the Sabbath, for it says: "It is a sign between you and Me." The other is the *tefillin*, for it says: "It is a sign upon your hand." That is the meaning of "These signs of Mine in his midst." The Almighty said to Moses that through the miracle of the exodus, He would give His two signs, the Sabbath and *tefillin*. (M.T., p. 48)

—◦—

The Koznitzer Rebbe noted that the word *ulma'an*, "And so that you may," is written twice in the Torah. It is written "And so that you may tell" (Ex. 10:2) and "And so that your days may be lengthened." (Ex. 20:12) He said that this is to inform us that though we may feel secure in our Jewishness, we still have a great obligation. To fulfill the *Pasuk* "And so that you may relate in the ears of your son and son's son the wonders that I have wrought in Egypt" (Ex. 10:2), we must have a long life so that we can tell our children and grandchildren. (F.C.O., p. 172)

—◦—

R' Yehoshuah Belzer said that the *Pasuk* "That you may know that I am Hashem" (Ex. 10:2) means that one must have complete faith. "That you may relate in the ears of your son and your son's son" means that your teaching must be words that come from the depths of your heart so that you will be able to persuade another. (F.C.O., p. 172)

—◦—

The S'fas Emes noted that when Pharaoh's servants told him, "Send out the men so that they may serve God" (Ex. 10:7), they meant to send out only the most prominent among the Israelites. Pharaoh's response was "Which ones shall I send?" for they are all prominent. (F.C.O., p. 172)

—◦—

When Moses was asked, "Which ones are going?" (Ex. 10:8), Moses answered, "With our youngsters and with our elders shall we go." (Ex. 10:9) On this the Rebbe of Satmar commented that Moses was also concerned about future redemptions. He said that we need the elders to teach Torah and the young and innocent to perform the *mitzvot*. The youth will go with the older generation who are not ashamed of their deeds. Together they will bring the redemption. (M.D., p. 122)

On the *Pasuk* "With our youngsters and our elders" (Ex. 10:9), the Noam Elimelech commented that if we are on a proper level when we are young, then when we get older, we can strive to be on a higher level. Then we can say, "because of our children," we are reaching higher levels. (F.C.O., p. 172)

On the *Pasuk* "With our youngsters and with our elders we shall go" (Ex. 10:9), the Koznitzer made the following comment. He said that old age can be a virtue and a blessing. This depends on how we developed as youths and how we matured. When one has had a positive and exemplary youth, then, like wine, life gets better with age. If the beginning is sour, then, like wine, it only becomes more sour. (F.C.O., p. 172)

On the same *pasuk*, the Yismach Moshe's comment was that when our youth and elders go together, then it is a *chag Hashem lanu*—a festival of Hashem for us. (F.C.O., p. 173)

The Chidushei Harim made the following comment on "There was a darkness of gloom throughout Egypt. . . . No man could see his brother nor anyone rise from his place." (Ex. 10:23) He said that this darkness was a serious plague. The reluctance of one to see another or to want to feel his pain or know of his agony is tantamount to "nor anyone rising from his place." The person himself cannot move nor rise from where he is. (F.C.O., p. 173)

On the same *Pasuk*, the Mishmeres Itmar noted that no one could see the humanity of his brother. No one saw the worthiness of the other. No one strove to better himself. As it says: "nor could any one rise from his place," all were arrogant and a sense of hatred and conflict was prevalent. (F.C.O., p. 173)

〜〜

"But for all the Children of Israel there was light in their dwellings."
(Ex. 10:23) R' Baruch Mezritcher said that it was a description of the
Jewish people. "Every Jew," said R' Baruch, "has a Divine spark within
him. This spark shines like a diamond. However, it depends on where
one finds the diamond. In some, the diamond is found in Torah and
prayer; in some, it may be found in food and drink; in some, it may be in
the pocket; and in others, it may be found in the heart." (F.C.O., p. 173)

〜〜

On the same *Pasuk*, the Riziner explained that each one of us possesses a
Holy Spark, yet not everyone shows it to the best of his ability. It is like
a diamond that cannot show its luster because it is buried in the ground.
In a proper setting, it can shine like the light that is in each one of us.
(*Esser Orot*, p. 137)

〜〜

The Chidushei Harim explained that we really do not know the worth
of our service to Hashem and our observance of the *mitzvot*. We will not
know until we are judged at the appropriate time. That is why the *Pasuk*
says, "And we will not know how we shall serve Hashem until we will
arrive there." (Ex. 10:26) (F.C.O., p. 174)

〜〜

The Karliner Rebbe noted that the objective of the *Pasuk* "Let each man
request of his friend and each woman from her friend silver vessels and
gold vessels" (Ex. 11:2) is to teach the mitzvah of kindness of one to
another. (F.U.A.O., vol. 2, p. 60)

〜〜

On the same *Pasuk*, the Ostrovitzer Rebbe commented that when Jews
perform deeds of kindness and help each other, especially in times of
need, then even their enemies will notice the favor that Hashem has
granted them. (M.T., p. 54)

＊～＊

R' Meir Primishlaner made the folliwng comment on the *Pasuk* "But against all the children of Israel, a dog (*keleva*) will not sharpen its tongue." (Ex. 11:7) He said that the word *yecherats* (sharpen) is derived from the word *charitsus* (erudite). A Jew need not be too smart. "Too smart" means talking from both sides of the mouth. A Jew must speak honestly, *k'lev*—from the heart, a play on the word *keleva* (dog). The heart and the mouth must be as one. (F.C.O., p. 174)

＊～＊

There are many Chasidic insights on the words "This month shall be for you the beginning of the months; it shall be for you the first of the months of the year." (Ex. 12:2) The Zolizitzer commented that the month of redemption depends completely on one's own self and not on another. (F.C.O., p. 175)

＊～＊

The Berditchever commented that all occurrences of the month depend upon how one sanctifies the month. He said, "Hashem, Who is called the First, He is to you, He is yours. Just as you will define an act toward the holiness of the month, so will Hashem react to you." (F.C.O., p. 175)

＊～＊

The S'fas Emes commented that Jews count the months according to the moon and non-Jews count according to the sun. The rest of the world assumes that it can only exist when there is light and all goes well. If ever something goes wrong, they are lost, for it is as though a catastrophe has occurred. Jews can exist even when something goes wrong, God forbid, for like the moon, they can shine in the darkness. (F.C.O., p. 175)

＊～＊

R' Chayim Zanzer remarked that we ask twice for the "fear of Heaven" in the blessing for the new month. First, we wish to be granted "a life in which there is fear of Heaven and fear of sin." Then we ask for "a life in which we will have love of Torah and fear of Heaven." From this we learn that the "fear of Heaven" is essential for "fear of sin" and "love of Torah." (F.C.O., p. 175)

On the *Pasuk* "You shall take a bundle of hyssop and dip it into the blood . . . and touch the lintel (Ex. 12:22), the Kozmirer commented that when one is as low as the hyssop, which grows low, and then unites as the hyssop does into a "bundle," he will be ready to "dip it in blood" — to give his entire being for the sake of Judaism, solidarity, and harmony. He will "touch the lintel," and reach the highest pinnacle that is possible. (F.C.O., p. 176)

"And Hashem will skip over the entrance and He will not permit the destroyer to enter your homes to smite." (Ex. 12:23) The Ostrovitzer commented that our Sages said that "the wicked, even when they are at the door of *Gehinom*, they do not repent." (Talmud *Eruvin* 19a) Even so, one should not despair, for even at the entrance, you still have time to repent. (F.C.O., p. 176)

R' Baruch Mezibozer commented on a statement of our Sages: "Open the door as little as the sharp end of a needle and I will open the door as wide as the door of a hall." (*Shir Hashirim Rabbah* 5:3) Heaven will help those who will make a beginning to repent. The repentant must first open the door and Heaven will open it wider. However, in Egypt, the Jews had been influenced and immersed in the impurities of the land. Therefore, it was impossible for them to show any signs of repentance. The Almighty had pity and opened the door for redemption, for as the Torah tells us, "Hashem will skip over the entrance." (F.C.O., p. 177)

On the *Pasuk* "You shall observe this matter (*davar*, "word") as a decree (*chok*) for yourself and for your children forever" (Ex. 12:24), the

Koznitzer made the comment that one should heed his word and guard his tongue. This should be a decree forever. (F.C.O., p. 177)

～～

The *Pasuk* states, "Sanctify to Me every firstborn, the first of each womb (*rechem*)." (Ex. 13:1) Deriving the word *rachmanut* (mercy) from *rechem*, R' Yisroel Riziner commented that "the first of each womb" means that one should have mercy on those who are in need first. If one wishes to rise to spiritual heights and gain the respect of others, then he should consider others older and greater than he so as not to be arrogant! (F.C.O., p. 177)

～～

On the *Pasuk* "Nor may leaven be seen in your possession in all your borders" (Ex. 13:7), the Toldot Yaacov Yosef noted the talmudic comment, "What is yours is impossible to see, but you can see that of others and that which is above." (Tractate *Pesachim*). The Toldot Yaacov Yosef commented that one will never see his own failings but will always see the failings of others and those who are above him. (F.C.O., p. 178)

～～

R' Aharon Karliner commented that the *Pasuk* "So that Hashem's Torah may be in your mouth" (Ex. 13:9) has an ethical lesson. One's learning has no meaning if Hashem's Torah is not in his mouth. If your mouth or your learning does not teach you how to behave, then all that you learned in Torah has not been internalized. Therefore, "watch your mouth and your tongue from speaking evil." (F.C.O., p. 178)

BESHALACH
"HE SENT"

An interesting comment was made about the Exodus of the Israelites from Egypt by R' Elimelech of Lizensk. He said that whenever the Torah speaks about *mitzvot*, it always makes mention of the Exodus and not of the Creation of the world, even though the Creation out of nothing was a much greater miracle. However, it should be understood that the Creation was not really a miracle, for all nature is in God and all are subject to Him. Everything became, at His command, in a natural way. But the Exodus was a wonder, for to deal with the personalities of the Egyptians, Hashem had to divest Himself at that time of His Goodness, and let evil prevail. (H.A., p. 307)

On the *Pasuk* "And God did not lead" (Ex. 13:17), the Vorker Rebbe's comment is based on the exile of the Jews. He said that it is very difficult, with the human mind, to comprehend all the persecutions and other difficulties the Jews had to withstand. It is the faith in God, "Who gives strength to the weary," that sustains the Jews in the Diaspora. (F.C.O., p. 179)

The Kobriner Rebbe, in a play on words, commented on "And they encamped or rested before *pi-hachirot*." (Ex. 14:2) Instead of the name of the place, he defined it as the words *pi* ("mouth") and *hachirot* (or *cherut*, "free"). The Kobriner said that God told Moses to exhort the Jewish people to let their mouths rest and be free from unnecessary talk. (F.C.O., p. 180)

⌐⌐

On the *Pasuk* "And they were very frightened; the Children of Israel cried out to Hashem" (Ex. 14:10), the Chidushei Harim made the observation that when the Israelites realized that their fear of the Egyptians had become greater than their fear of God, they were hurt, so "they cried out to Hashem." (F.C.O., p. 180)

⌐⌐

"Pharaoh brought himself close; the Children of Israel raised their eyes and behold! Egypt was journeying after them, and they were frightened; the Children of Israel cried out to Hashem." (Ex. 14:10) The Zohar notes that when the Jews are in distress, they remind themselves of the existence of Hashem. They cry out to Him in prayer and the Almighty has mercy on them and punishes the enemy. That is what occurred at that time. They stood in front of the sea and saw its waves going higher and higher. They turned around, saw the Egyptian army and its arsenal coming toward them, and became frightened. At that point, they remembered Hashem and "cried out to Him." Who caused them to get close to Hashem? "And Pharaoh brought himself close." (Zohar 47)

⌐⌐

The Berditchever made a profound comment on the *Pasuk* "And the Children of Israel cried out to Hashem." (Ex. 14:10) There are different types of miracles that Hashem performs for the Jews. One type occurs when the Jews cry out in prayer and supplication, as at the Red Sea. Then there are miracles that are performed without the Jews' knowledge. They are not aware of the problem and do not plead or cry out. It is not until after the catastrophe that the realization comes that Hashem has performed a miracle. These miracles are daily occurrences. (F.C.O., p. 180)

On the *Pasuk* "Egypt was journeying after them" (Ex. 14:10), Rashi comments that the Egyptians were "with one heart, as one man." The Chidushei Harim wondered where the Egyptians developed the quality of unity. The nations took the quality of unity from us and we became disunited and splintered. That is the reason we are in exile. (F.U.A.O., p. 78)

On the same *Pasuk*, the Kedushas Levi commented that when the Israelites saw the sacrifices the Egyptians made to pursue them, they cried out to Hashem to grant them the strength of purpose to combat that of the Egyptians. Hashem responded by saying, "Go forth" into the sea and that will show your intent and strength to sacrifice your lives. That in itself will show your power. (*Kedushas Levi*, p. 82)

On the same *Pasuk*, R' Henoch Alexander commented that while the Israelites were in Egypt, they were surrounded by wickedness and disgraceful values. At the sea, they saw a base people coming at them. They had hoped that when Hashem took them out of Egypt, all that had been done away with. However, they realized that that part of their lives might not be over and so they "cried out to God." Moses said to the people, "Do not fear! Stand fast and see the salvation of Hashem that He will perform for you today; for that which you have seen in Egypt today, you shall not see them ever again!" (Ex. 14:13) That means that Hashem would help destroy the baseness that had been carried with them. "Hashem will do battle on your behalf and you shall remain silent." (Ex. 14:14) (F.C.O., p. 181)

Concerning decorum in the synagogue, R' Dovid Cherneboler commented that "Hashem will do battle on your behalf, and you shall remain silent." (Ex. 14:14) God will do battle with Satan for you on the condition that, at the time for prayer, in the synagogue, you will conduct yourselves properly and not speak unnecessarily. (F.C.O., p. 180)

~~~

Said R' Moshe Korischiver: "Whenever Satan wishes to denounce the Jews and says words of derision, Hashem makes him become silent. For example, when Satan calls the Jews drunkards, thieves, and liars, Hashem asks, 'How do you know that if the other nations would have accepted the Torah, they would have behaved differently?' Then Satan complains that the Jews do not show respect nor fear of Heaven at the time that they pray in their synagogues. They discuss mundane things, they argue, and they cause commotions. Other people stand with respect and awe in their places of worship. On this accusation, Hashem has nothing to say." (F.C.O., p. 181)

~~~

Based on the *Pasuk* "Hashem said to Moses, 'Why do you cry out to Me? Speak to the Children of Israel.'" (Ex. 14:15), there is a story told about the Kotzker Rebbe. He asked a disciple of the rabbi of Lentshno why his rabbi cried to God to send Meshiach. He said that the *Pasuk* says, "Why do you cry out to Me? Speak to the Children of Israel." (F.C.O., p. 180)

~~~

"Why do you cry out to Me?"—*Mah titsak eylie?* (Ex. 14:15) The Koznitzer noted that the first letters of the Hebrew words spell out the word *emet*, "truth." Hashem said to Moses, "Why do you cry out to Me?"—you know the truth that I am ready to help. "Speak unto the Children of Israel"—ask them if they are ready to help themselves, and salvation will automatically come to them. (F.C.O., p. 182)

~~~

During a discussion between the Lenchener and one of his Chasidim, the Chasid complained about the difficult conditions of the Jews. He bemoaned the persecutions, the constant expulsion from their homes, and said that the Meshiach should come. "Correct," said the Rebbe, "But, 'Why do you cry out to Me?' Of course it is time for the Meshiach. 'Speak to the Children of Israel.' If they wish with all their heart and all their might to leave the Diaspora, the Meshiach will come." (F.C.O., p. 182)

The Mishmeres Itmar noted that we learn from the *Pasuk* "Speak to the children of Israel and let them go forward" (Ex. 14:15) that one should not remain on one level but must reach for higher goals. (F.C.O., p. 182)

R' Henoch Alexander noted that we can learn from the *Pasuk* "Lift up your staff and stretch out your arm over the sea and split it" (Ex. 14:17) that the Almighty abhors arrogance. The Midrash relates that when Moses and the Israelites came to the sea, Moses asked the sea to split. The sea said with a sense of arrogance, "I am older than you, for I was created before you." At that point, God became annoyed and said to Moses, "Lift your staff and split the sea." (F.C.O., p. 183)

On the *Pasuk* "On that (*hahu*) day, Hashem saved Israel" (Ex. 14:30), the Ropshitzer noted that the letters of the word *hahu* can stand for *hashamayim v'et ha'aretz*—the heavens and the earth. As soon as the heavens and the earth were created, Hashem had already willed to make them better for us and to save us. (*Zerah Kodesh*, p. 45)

On the *Pasuk* "And then they sang" (Ex. 14:31), R' Bunim of Pshys'cha explained that when one makes a wise statement, we do not realize its wisdom until the entire statement is made. However, the wisdom of "The Song," which was said with utmost sincerity and with a holy spirit, was felt as soon as the first word was uttered. That is why the Midrash says in discussing "The Song": "It was opening the mouth with wisdom." (M.T., vol. 1, p. 70)

On the *Pasuk* "And they believed in Hashem and Moses His servant" (Ex. 14:31), R' Tzadok HaKohen commented that just as a person must believe in Hashem, so must he believe in himself. (F.C.O., p. 186)

The Gerer Rebbe based his comment on the *Pasuk* "And the people revered Hashem, and they had faith in Hashem." (Ex. 14:31) He noted that by the division of the waters, the virtues of reverence and true faith in Hashem were instilled into the Israelites. By means of these virtues, they were able to overcome insurmountable obstacles. That is a lesson for all time; namely, that nothing can withstand the unity of genuine reverence and sincere belief. (S.S.K., p. 66)

On the *Pasuk* "Israel saw the great hand . . . and they had faith in Hashem" (Ex. 14:31), the Kotzker noted that at the time of the plagues, the Israelites had doubts. They thought that they were occurring because of magic or chance. It was at the sea that they saw the great power of the Almighty. It was at that point that they started to believe in the greatness of Hashem. A moment of "the fear of Heaven" is more powerful than all the miracles. (F.U.A.O., p. 87)

There are two interpretations of the concept that earning a living is as difficult as the splitting of the Red Sea. R' Bunim of Pshys'cha noted that when the Israelites left Egypt, they noticed that the Egyptians were running after them. They became disheartened, confused, and concerned about how they were going to be saved. That Hashem would save them did not enter their minds. It is the same with earning a living. One can become, after a while, very discouraged when employment is not found. Somehow, it does not occur to him to rely on God. (F.C.O., p. 184)

The Chidushei Harim said that there are two things that people do contrary to what Providence has decided. It is known that how a person will earn a living is in God's hands. Yet, we will go out of our way to pursue employment with every means possible. When it comes to the service of God, which is in the hands of man—"All is in the hands of Heaven except the fear of Heaven"—we do not do everything that is within our power to pursue that goal. There we rely completely on God. We feel that it is enough to move the lips in prayer. (F.C.O., p. 184)

"And they believed in Hashem." (Ex. 14:31) The Chidushei Harim said that even though the Israelites saw all the miracles that God performed, they still needed faith. Faith is on a higher level than witnessing. More is seen through faith than through the eyes. (F.C.O., p. 187)

On the same *Pasuk*, there is a story told that a woman came to the Zanzer crying and bemoaning her miserable plight. The Zanzer consoled her by telling her to have faith in the Almighty, that He would help her. To this, the woman replied that the Torah tells us the opposite, namely: "Hashem saved Israel" and then "they had faith in Hashem." "You are right," answered the Zanzer, and blessed her. (F.U.A.O., vol. 1, p. 86)

"Then Moses and the Children of Israel sang this song to Hashem." (Ex. 15:1) R' Yisroel Riziner was asked if we are to assume that there were no other miracles than that of the Red Sea and that is why we are told that Israel sang at the splitting of the sea. "It was not because of the splitting of the Sea," said the Riziner, "but that the Israelites came to an absolute belief in the Almighty that they burst out in song." (F.C.O., p. 183)

"And the Children of Israel sang this song to Hashem." (Ex. 15:1) The Berditchever commented that the Israelites sang with such deep feeling

and gratitude that they said to God, *Lay'mor*, as if to say "Sing with us."
(F.C.O., p. 187)

～～

There is an interesting story told about the Yid HaKadosh concerning
the significance of song. A Chasid notified the Yid HaKadosh that the
Koznitzer Maggid was ill, so he requested that two of his Chasidim go to
Koznitz for the Shabbat and sing for the Maggid. With every song, he
became better and was on the road to recovery. The Maggid remarked
that the Yid HaKadosh knew that he had walked in all worlds except
the world of music. Therefore, he sent his singers to notify him that he
had another task in life and that was to explore the "world of music."
(*Niflaot Hayehudi*, p. 59)

～～

"For (*ki*) He is exalted above all exaltedness; a horse and its rider He
heaved into the sea." (Ex. 15:1) The Strelisker noted that Rashi translates
the word *ki* as "even though." The meaning of that translation is that if
a person wants to spiritually strengthen himself through prayer and
song, "even though" thoughts of arrogance may enter, Hashem will
"heave the horse and its rider into the sea" and his arrogance will
disappear. (*Imrei Kodesh*, quoted in M.T., vol. 2, p. 132)

～～

R' Meir Primishlaner made the following comment on "This is my God
and I will beautify Him; the God of my father and I will exalt Him."
(Ex. 15:2) He said that the Jew who does not depend on the merits of
"our fathers" nor on the merits of his parents, grandparents, or ancestors, but on his own understanding of the greatness of Hashem, may say,
"This is my God and I will beautify Him." But he who does nothing to
develop his own understanding of the majesty of God, but says the God
of my father and grandfather—who only relies on the merits of his
righteous ancestors—he is an arrogant individual. (F.C.O., p. 187)

On the *Pasuk* "God's strength and power to eradicate has been a salvation for me" (Ex. 15:2), the Skoyler Rebbe, Rabbi Avraham Moshe Rabinowitz, commented that one who has complete faith in Hashem will praise Him and sing to Him in times of joy and, God forbid, in times of trouble. That is the meaning of "God's strength and power"—that the Almighty, Blessed is His name, is my strength and my power, and I will praise and sing unto Him in times of trouble and He will be my salvation; I have faith that He will bring me salvation. (Ch.B., p. 175)

On the *Pasuk* "God is a Man of war" (Ex. 15:3), the Kobriner Rebbe commented that Hashem is with the man who makes war against evil desires, and helps him to overpower them. (*Or Yesharim*, p. 84)

In the *Shirah*, there is a *Pasuk* that says: "Hashem is the Master of war, Hashem is His name." (Ex. 15:3) There is a comment in the *sefer Or HaGanuz* that one who does battle with his evil inclination to attain greater spiritual development can say, "Hashem is His name." (M.D., p. 133)

"Who is like You among the powerful (*ba'elim*), Hashem! Who is like You, mighty in holiness." (Ex. 15:11) The Izbitzer noted the statement in the Talmud (*Gittin* 56b) that changed the vowels of *ba'elim* and formed the word *b'ilmim*, meaning "concealed." He commented that in all human experiences, one should keep in mind that there is a hidden Creator. That is the meaning of "Strength and faithfulness are His Who lives eternally." (Prayerbook) Our trust and faith in God is in knowing that He is in both all that is revealed and all that is hidden. However, that which is obvious does not need as much faith as that which is hidden. Both the hidden and the obvious are in the Almighty. (*Mi HaShaluach*, p. 76)

On the *Pasuk* "You led with Your might to your holy abode" (Ex. 15:13), R' Avraham Meir of Ger noted Rashi's comment that Onkelus rendered "led" as an expression of "bearing and enduring" and did not define the Hebrew term exactly. The Rebbe commented that if the Aramaic translation is "to endure," then it must follow that every leader should have patience. Apparently, the meaning of the word "led" bears a relationship to endurance. (M.T., vol. 2, p. 71)

"And Miriam the prophetess, the sister of Aharon, took the tambourine in her hand." (Ex. 15:20) The S'fas Emes posed the following question: "Where in the desert did Miriam find a tambourine?" He said that when the Egyptians chased the Israelites, they were convinced that they would capture them and return them to Egypt and brought along various musical instruments to celebrate their victory. When they drowned in the sea, Miriam and the other women took the instruments to sing praise to Hashem. (F.C.O., p. 188)

"For I am Hashem your Healer." (Ex. 15:26) The Berditchever commented that just as someone who wishes to improve on an object will first take it apart, then rebuild it and make a better one, so it is with Hashem. There are times when a person finds himself very ill or in dire straits; then his prayers become intense and he tries to improve his behavior. He reaches a higher level in the service of Hashem, and God grants him a full recovery. (F.C.O., p. 188)

The Torah states: "Hashem said to Moses, 'Behold! I shall rain down for you food from Heaven; let the people go out and pick each day's matter on its day, so that I may test him, whether he will follow My Torah or not.'" (Ex. 16:4) The Rimanover commented on the words "That I may test him, whether he will follow my Torah or not." He said that a person may fully believe that Hashem is one and He is the Almighty. However, if he is asked whether he trusts that Hashem will provide all his needs, there will be hesitation, as if to say, "I haven't reached that level yet." One has to realize that belief and trust are linked. He who firmly believes also trusts completely. Anyone who does not have perfect confidence in Hashem, his belief will weaken. That is why Hashem said that He can cause bread to rain from Heaven; so that the one who believes and puts his trust in Him will gather a day's portion and need not worry about tomorrow. (M.T., p. 74)

On the same *Pasuk*, R' Asher Horowitz made the following observation. There are Jews who are poor and always in dire need. Nevertheless, they are believers in God and are observant individuals. However, for some, when their lot in life changes and begins to go well their religious and spiritual lives also change. They begin to become less observant and their spiritual life falters. That is what Hashem meant when He said, "I shall rain down for you food from heaven." He would give abundant sustenance and He would see "whether he will follow My Torah or not." (F.C.O., p. 190)

The Kobriner, on the same *Pasuk*, commented that it means that He would pour down the knowledge that bread, meaning livelihood, comes from Heaven. (F.U.A.O., p. 95)

"And it shall be that on the sixth day when they prepare what they will bring." (Ex. 16:5) The Chidushei Harim noted that the term *v'haya* ("and it shall be") always connotes joy. Therefore, he said that when Friday comes and we begin preparation for the Holy Sabbath, joy is present. (F.C.O., p. 190)

"The Children of Israel saw and said to one another, 'It is manna!'—for they did not know what it was. Moses said to them, 'This is the food that Hashem has given you for eating.'" (Ex. 16:15) The Lubliner commented that the manna was of a spiritual nature because it was the "food that Hashem has given you." The more one ate, the higher he strove spiritually, and his friend could not recognize him as he was before. (M.T., p. 135)

~~~

Eating gives pleasure, but the essence of the Sabbath is the Sabbath itself, noted the Berditchever. That is the meaning of the *Pasuk* "Eat it today, for today is Shabbos for Hashem." (Ex. 16:25) (F.C.O., p. 191)

~~~

The *Pasuk* states: "It happened that when Moses would raise his hand, Israel was stronger, and when he lowered his hand, Amalek was stronger." (Ex. 17:11) The S'fas Emes observed that our Sages commented: "At the time when the eyes of the Jews turned to Hashem, meaning they had faith in God and in Moses, Moses' hands became stronger. If the Jews lost their faith in God and in Moses, then his hands became weaker." (Talmud *Rosh Hashanah* 29) We can learn a lesson from this; namely that when a people have faith and trust in their leader, then he will have the strength to ask for salvation and victory. (M.T., vol. 2, p. 75)

~~~

On the same *Pasuk*, R' Baruch Mezibozer commented that the faith of the Israelites was strong because of the miracles they had seen in Egypt. The Amalekites came to destroy that faith. Moses raised the "hands of faith" to continue to encourage the people, to the extent that "Israel became stronger." (F.C.O., p. 193)

~~~

"Hashem said to Moses, 'Write this as a remembrance in the Book and recite it in the ears of Joshua, because I shall utterly blot out the remembrance of Amalek from under the heavens.'" (Ex. 17:14) The Mezibozer made the comment that God informed Moses of His decree to blot our Amalek in the future. This would occur when Haman, the Amalekite, was slain. However, God did not want to give the exact time for this event for he wanted Mordechai and the Jews of that time to pray for

Haman's extinction. This was based on the concept that if the people were to know the future, there would be no free will in God's service. (H.A., p. 129)

~~~

On the same *Pasuk*, the Lenchener commented that at times hearing may be more significant than learning. Although it would have been enough for Hashem to tell Moses to write the events of the war of Amalek, nevertheless He told him to "recite it in the ears of Joshua." (F.C.O., p. 194)

~~~

In the Torah it is written: "I shall surely wipe out (*moh'cho em'che*) the memory of Amalek." (Ex. 17:14) The Koznitzer asked why there is a double emphasis on the word *mocho*. He answered that at times even a semblance of an erasure may still remain. God said that even the semblance He will destroy. (F.C.O., p. 194)

~~~

Based on the same *Pasuk*, Hashem maintains a war against Amalek from generation to generation. The R' Moshe Teitlebaum commented that because of Amalek, Hashem has to do battle in every generation, as we read in the Haggadah: "For in every generation they arise to annihilate us, but Hashem will save us from their hands." (F.C.O., p. 194)

YITRO
FATHER-IN-LAW OF MOSES

Rabbi Menachem Mendel Schneerson, the Lubavitcher Rebbe, explained the reason the *Sidra* was named after Yitro. He said that Yitro's acknowledgement of God was more than a personal matter. His words of praise brought about the acknowledgment of "the revelation of God in His glory in the higher and lower realms and that He gave the Torah in perfect confirmation of His dominion over all existence," as it says in the Zohar. Yitro's personal recognition of God expressed the purpose of the giving of the Torah. This prepared the world at large for such revelation. (G.O.T., vol. 1, pp. 100–102)

⌒⌒

"What does it mean when the *Pasuk* states, 'And Yitro heard?' (Ex. 18:1) Yitro heard and no one else?" asked R' Dovid Lelever. He said that actually all heard but they remained firm in their own convictions. Yitro, on the other hand, heard and became convinced that "Hashem is greater than all other Gods." (F.C.O., p. 195)

⌒⌒

On the *Pasuk* "Yitro, the father-in-law of Moses, came" (Ex. 18:1), the Belzer Rebbe commented that the Torah usually says "went" and not "came" when discussing going to a destination. In the case of Yitro, it states that Yitro heard and he came. He had made no plans for a journey, but as soon as he heard of the Exodus, he immediately wanted to join

Moses. Had he taken time to consider his decision, he might have hesitated to take his family through the hardships of the desert, and that would have caused him not to join the Israelites in accepting the Torah. The Rebbe advised that from this we learn that when the opportunity arises to perform a mitzvah, we should do so without deliberation. (H.A., p. 436)

On the *Pasuk* "And Yitro heard" (Ex. 18:1), the Lizensker made the following observation concerning the significance of going to the Rebbe to understand serving Hashem when there is so much literature on morality and spiritual behavior. It says in the Torah: "And Yitro heard." Rashi asks, "What did he hear?" Rashi answers, "He heard about the splitting of the Yam Suf and about the war against Amalek." If he heard, why did he have to go to Moses? The Lizensker said that though he heard about the greatness of Hashem, the splitting of the Yam Suf, and the war against Amalek, nevertheless he went to see Moses, who was the Rebbe at that time. It shows the meaning of the statement, "There is no comparison of hearing to seeing." When one goes to the Rebbe, one sees the greatness of Hashem and it remains with the individual forever. Even though we learn and hear and understand the greatness of Hashem, we go to the Rebbe to see from his actions the greatness of Hashem. (F.C.O., p. 195)

On the *Pasuk* "Where he was encamped by the mountain of God" (Ex. 18:5), the Koznitzer remarked that wherever Moses resided, there was God's mountain. There is a saying: "A man honors his place." Therefore the place was honored because of Moses' presence. (F.C.O., p. 196)

On the *Pasuk* "I, your father-in-law Yitro, have come to you" (Ex. 18:6), the Kotzker said that Yitro said to Moses, "Come into my garden; come down from the high rung that you are on. Come down to my level to understand me, then you can raise me to a higher level. Then you can return to your level." This is the attitude that the leaders of a generation should have in order to raise the level of the masses. (F.C.O., p. 196)

⌒⌒

"Yitro rejoiced over all the goodness that Hashem had done for Israel, that He rescued them from the hand of Egypt." (Ex. 18:9) "Yitro said, 'Blessed is Hashem, Who rescued you from the hand of Egypt and from the hand of Pharaoh.'" (Ex. 18:10) The Radamsker said that those few words of Yitro taught us the importance of thanking Hashem for the kindness He show others. Concerning the "Song of the Sea," the Talmud states: "It is a disgrace to Moses and all the people that they did not say 'Blessed' until Yitro came and said, 'Blessed is Hashem.'" (Tractate *Sanhedrin* 94) (F.C.O., p. 196)

⌒⌒

"When they have a matter, one comes to me, and I judge between a man and his fellow." (Ex. 18:16) R' Asher Horowitz said that Moses meant that when a Jew had a problem, a disappointment, or a conflict with someone, Moses wanted him to come because he could feel his pain, and therefore understand the problem. This outlook gave him the ability to judge his people. (F.C.O., p. 197)

⌒⌒

Concerning judging and judgments the Bratzlaver gave the following advice:

1. A true decision stands on its own merits even against the will of the disputants.
2. Good judges cause the Torah to be beloved.
3. Four things bring clemency from the Heavenly tribunal: charity, prayer, a change of conduct, and a change of reputation.
4. He who shows the way to God will be acquitted in the Heavenly tribunal.
5. Knowledge draws God's mercy.
6. Stubborn refusal to repent causes disease. (*Sefer Hamiddot*, pp. 47–54)

The Amshinover interpreted the advice Yitro gave to Moses based on the *Pasuk* "You will not be able to do it alone. Now heed my voice; I shall advise you, and God be with you." (Ex. 18:19) He said that Yitro insisted that Moses have assistants in judging his people because he was over-burdened. However, Yitro was convinced that if Moses asked God's permission, God would not grant it to him, for God might feel that the people's respect for Moses would be diminished. Therefore, Yitro advised Moses to appoint aides on his own. He felt that God would not disagree if Moses did this by himself. (H.A., p. 214)

On the *Pasuk* "And you shall see from among the entire people men of means, God-fearing people, men of truth, and people who despise money and you shall appoint them leaders of thousands" (Ex. 18:21), R' Zusia Hanipoliar commented that the Torah is speaking about the leaders of a people and their conduct. He said that they should be truthful and have the "Fear of Heaven" in them. They must be "people who despise money." If their desire for money is overwhelming and becomes part of them, then it is impossible to eradicate. This desire is so evil that to be rid of it is extremely difficult. (F.C.O., p. 198)

On the same *Pasuk*, the Degel Machnei Ephraim interpreted Yitro's remark to Moses, saying: "When you, Moses, who are the wisest of all and a teacher, will listen to all people, then you will emphasize for all time the statement: 'Who is wise? One who learns from all people.'" (*Ethics of Our Fathers*, ch. 4:1) (*Degel Machnei Ephraim*, p. 99)

On the dictum "Who is wise? One who learns from all people," the Baal Shem Tov remarked that one can learn from all people—even from a wicked person. Even a wicked individual may possess some good quali-ties from which we can learn. (F.C.O., p. 197)

~~~

On the *Pasukim* "And Moses listened to his father-in-law . . ." (Ex. 18:24) and "Moses sent his father-in-law, and he went off to his land" (Ex. 18:27), R' Moshe Kobriner commented that although Moses listened to his father-in-law, he nevertheless was somewhat skeptical. He was concerned that with all the advice Yitro was giving, he might begin to suggest changes in the Torah. Therefore, he listened, but after a while "Moses sent his father-in-law." (F.C.O., p. 200)

~~~

"And Israel encamped (*vayichan*) there, opposite the mountain." (Ex. 19:2) The Vorker said that in the word *vayichan* we can find the word *cheyn*. True unity comes about when one Jew finds *cheyn* (charm) in another Jew. (F.C.O., p. 200)

~~~

On the same *Pasuk*, the Kobriner commented that the word *vayichan* has the word *yachid* in it. The word connotes "single," a sense of oneness. It is only with unity that we can oppose the strong mountain of wickedness that is constantly surrounding us. (F.C.O., p. 201)

~~~

On the *Pasuk* "So shall you say to the House of Jacob and tell to the Sons of Israel" (Ex. 19:3), the Sigheter Rebbe made his comment based on statements from the Talmud (*Baba Basra* 141) and the Zohar. The Talmud states: "Having a daughter (*bat*) first is a good sign for having sons (*banim*)." The Zohar states that *bat* (daughter) symbolizes fear, and *banim* symbolize Torah. He said, "Having a daughter first stands for fear, and sons following stand for Torah, so that Torah will be everlasting." Rashi says, "In this language and in this order: 'House of Jacob'— these are the women; 'House of Israel'—these are the men.' First is fear then is Torah." (M.D., p. 139)

⌒⌒

The Gerer Rebbe commented on Rashi's explanation of the *Pasuk* "You have seen what I did to Egypt, and that I carried you on the wings of eagles and brought you to me." (Ex. 19:4) Rashi said, "The eagle carries his offspring above his wings, as if to say: If an arrow be shot in my direction, let it enter into me, and not into my son." According to the Midrash (*Shemos Rabbah* 21:7), the Attribute of Justice complained that Israel did not merit deliverance at the expense of the Egyptians, since at that time both were pagan. However, the Gerer explained that Hashem responded to the Attribute of Justice, saying, "I have lifted Israel above the wings of strict justice. If you question my act, direct your arrows at Me, not at My children." (S.S.K., 38)

⌒⌒

"If you hearken well to Me (*shamoah tishmeun b'koli*) and keep My Covenant, you will be a treasure to Me from among all the peoples, for all the earth is Mine." (Ex. 19:5) The S'fas Emes commented that the first letters of the words *shamoah tishmeun b'koli* spell out *Shabbat*. It was as though Hashem had said to the Israelites: "If you will listen to Me, obey My Covenant, and observe the Sabbath, you will then be a treasure to Me." (F.C.O., p. 202)

⌒⌒

On the same *Pasuk*, the Alexander Rebbe commented that if the Jews would hearken to God with fervor, longing, and love, then automatically "You will be a treasure to Me" and live in security and quietude, for "All the earth is Mine." (F.C.O., p. 202)

⌒⌒

On the *Pasuk* "You will be a treasure (*s'gulah*)" (Ex. 19:5), the Rebbe of Lvov made a play on the word *s'gulah*, changing it to *segola*, "circle." When one views a circle, no matter from which direction, it always looks the same. The same is true with the Jews: If they obey the Covenant, no matter what other nations try to do to them or what they will do to themselves, they will always remain Jews. (F.C.O., p. 202)

On the *Pasuk* "And you shall be to Me priests and a holy nation. These are the words that you shall speak to the Children of Israel" (Ex. 19:6), R' Moshe Koznitzer noted that "You shall be to Me priests" refers to the *Kohanim* as the teachers of Torah; as it is stated: "In accordance with the instruction that they may instruct you." (Deut. 17:11) "And a holy nation" alludes to faith and awe, which are necessary for the study of Torah. "These are the words that you shall speak" teaches us not to add or detract, as Rashi comments: "These words—no more and no less." (M.D., p. 139)

The *Pasuk* states: "And all the people answered together and said, 'Everything that Hashem has spoken we shall do!'" (Ex. 19:8) R' Meir Simcha D'Vinsker commented that it is impossible for everyone to perform all the *mitzvot*. There are *mitzvot* for the *Kohanim*, some for the Levites, others for the High Priest, and others for owners of fields or private property. That is why the Israelites "answered together"—we are partners in the observance of all the commandments, and not individuals. (F.U.A.O., p. 114)

On the same *Pasuk*, "And all the people answered together," the Mishmeres Itmar said that it meant that one person said to the other, "Let us bond and live in peace and harmony." (F.C.O., p. 203)

The Midrash comments on the *Pasuk* "Moses brought the people forth from the camp toward God." (Ex. 19:17) It says: "On the day of the giving of the Torah, the Israelites were in a deep sleep. Moses had to wake them and bring them to Mount Sinai." The Berditchever Rebbe, known as the defender of the Jewish people, interpreted the Midrash. "God forbid," he said, "that a kingdom of priests and a holy people should fall into a deep sleep because of idleness or laziness on such an eventful day as the time of the acceptance of the Torah. All they did was for the sake of heaven. From the second day of Sivan, they prepared themselves for that important day. They feared that they might be exhausted from all their preparations and that they might not give their full attention to what would be going on. They wanted to have a clear mind at the acceptance of the Torah. They decided to sleep so that they would awaken with a clear mind to accept the Torah." (F.C.O., p. 203)

On the *Pasuk* "Its smoke ascended like the smoke of the kiln" (Ex. 19:18), the Chidushei Harim wondered why the Torah had to be given in a cloud of smoke. He said that it was done to blind the eyes of the jealous people of other nations. (F.C.O., p. 204)

"Moses said to Hashem, 'The people will not be able to ascend Mount Sinai, for You have warned us, saying, "Bound the mountain and sanctify it."' Hashem said to him, 'Go, descend.'" (Ex. 19:23–24) The Kotzker explained that because of his modesty, Moses felt that all Israelites were on his level. He could not understand why anyone would not want to listen to the command of God and ascend the mountain. That is why Hashem told him, "Go, descend." Hashem wanted Moses to be on the same level as the others, so he would see why extra precautions had to be taken. (F.C.O., p. 204)

On the *Pasuk* "God spoke all these words, saying, 'I am Hashem, your God'" (Ex. 20:1), the Linzensker commented that we learn from this *Pasuk* that to accept the sovereignty of Hashem, all the commandments must be performed. The whole Torah was spoken to enable us to say that Hashem is our God. (H.A., p. 480)

R' Tzadok HaKohen noted that "I am" is not a command because those who have no faith have no concern for commandments. (F.C.O., p. 205)

﹌

"I am Hashem, your God, Who brought you out of the land of Egypt, out of the house of slavery." (Ex. 20:2) The Novominsker Rebbe cited the Midrash *Shemot* 29:9, "When Hashem gave the Torah, fowl didn't scream, birds didn't fly . . . the *Seraphim* didn't say, 'Holy, Holy,' the sea didn't move; all of creation was at a standstill. The world was still and only the Voice rang out, 'I am Hashem.'" The Rebbe said that this teaches us that the way mankind can serve Hashem and understand the ways of nature is to "lift up your eyes on high and see Who created these." (Isaiah 40:26) When the Israelites received the Torah, Hashem made all of creation quiet so that the Israelites would not be influenced by natural phenomena and would hear only the voice of Hashem. Hashem quieted the whole world and the world became as naught. The Rebbe further commented that nature should not create a barrier to reach Hashem, for true faith is in "I am Hashem, your God." This is the message of the Midrash: that in the future when the people will err and depend on other nations to redeem them, Hashem will make the world stand still and He will say, "I am He Who consoles you." (Isaiah 51:12) (*Pe'er Nachum*, p. 106)

﹌

On the commandment "Do not make for yourself an idol" (Ex. 20:4), the Kotzker Rebbe warned us not to make an idol out of a mitzvah. We should never have the attitude that a mitzvah has only an outer form and not contemplate its intrinsic meaning. (F.U.A.O., p. 118)

﹌

On the same *Pasuk*, R' Aharon Karliner commented that it meant that one should not consider himself an idol. One should not keep apart from the people, nor desist from communal activities, nor criticize every little incident. (F.C.O., p. 205)

﹌

On the concept of idol worship, there is a story told about the Sochotchover, who was visiting one of his Chasidim and noticed a picture of the

Baal HaTanya on the wall. "You would get a much better picture of who the Rebbe was if you would study his books." (F.U.A.O., p. 118)

〜

"You shall not take the name of Hashem, your God, in vain, for Hashem will not absolve anyone who takes His name in vain." (Ex. 20:7) The Primishlaner Rebbe noted that one cannot repent on every transgression. About swearing falsely, the Torah states: "Hashem will not absolve." The Rebbe explained with the example that when a person eats nonkosher food, the transgression is noted in a book; when the person repents, that transgression is erased. However, when one swears falsely, he does so with God's name; therefore, it is impossible to erase the transgression because God's name cannot be erased. (F.C.O., p. 205)

〜

The Torah tells us: "Remember the Sabbath day." (Ex. 20:8) The Berditchever commented that this means that every day of the week, one should remember the Sabbath day. (F.C.O., p. 206)

〜

On the *Pasuk* "Six days shall you work and do all your work" (Ex. 20:9), Rashi comments: "When Shabbos comes, it should seem to you as if all your work is done." The Chidushei Harim said that the words "all your work" also mean spiritual work, namely, controlling the *yetzer harah*. If, during the week, one does everything properly, one will obtain the peace and quiet symbolic of the Sabbath. That means that doing battle with the *yetzer harah* will have been completed by the Sabbath. (M.T., p. 91)

〜

In the *sefer Divrei Tzaddim*, there is an interesting comment on "Honor your father and your mother." (Ex. 20:12) Observance of this commandment is the barometer of one's character. This is why the Torah states: "So that your days will be lengthened upon the land that Hashem, your God, gives you." (Ex. 20:12) Without this fundamental principle, normal existence in society would be impossible. (F.U.A.O., p. 121)

On the *Pasuk* "You shall not steal" (Ex. 20:13), the Kotzker commented that it means that one should not steal even from one's self. (*Emes V'Emunah*, p. 76)

On the *Pasuk* "You shall not covet" (Ex. 20:14), the Radviller commented that this commandment was put at the end because if one observed this commandment, he most likely would have observed the others. If one does not have the discipline to observe this commandment, he must start again from the first. (H.A., p. 92)

R'Asher Horowitz commented that the letters of *v'chol* in the *Pasuk v'chol asher l'reyecha*, "nor anything that belongs to your neighbors" (Ex. 20:14), stand for *V'ahavta l'reyacha kamocha* — You shall love thy neighbor as thyself. (F.C.O., p. 206)

There are a few interpretations on the *Pasuk* "And all the people could see the sounds and the flames, the sound of the *shofar*, and the smoking mountain; the people saw and they moved and stood from afar." (Ex. 20:15) The Kotzker said that "and they moved" means that they were shaking and trembling and they stood from afar. However, Moses did not have to prepare himself to approach the mist without fear. (F.C.O., p. 206)

R' Zushia Hanipoliar commented on the same *Pasuk*. He said that when the Israelites saw the greatness of the Creator, they stood from afar. They began to realize how far they were from being in the service of Hashem. (F.C.O., p. 207)

〰️

The Kotzker also said that the Israelites saw the outer manifestations of the "sounds and the flames" and nothing further. (F.C.O., p. 207)

〰️

On the same *Pasuk*, R' Yisroel Riziner commented that there are two types of faith. One can obtain faith upon seeing miracles, however this type of faith is not on a high level. The highest level of faith is when one believes in Hashem without seeing miracles. The Israelites saw "the sounds of flames, the sound of the *shofar*, and the smoking mountain," and yet "They stood from afar." They had not reached the highest form of faith. (F.C.O., p. 207)

〰️

The *Pasuk* says: "They said to Moses, 'You speak to us and we shall hear; let God not speak to us lest we die.' Moses said to the people, 'Do not fear, for in order to exalt you God has come; so that you shall not sin.'" (Ex. 20:16–17) The Koretzer commented that the true fear of God is shown through fear of sin and not of punishment. (H.A., p. 141)

〰️

On the same *Pasuk*, the Baal Shem Tov commented that there are two types of fears of Hashem. One is the fear of punishment and the other is not to displease Hashem. If one pleases Hashem by sincere performance of his *mitzvot*, then he has no fear of punishment. (H.A., p. 140)

〰️

The Torah states: "And they stood from afar. . . . And Moses drew near the thick darkness where God was." (Ex. 20:18) The Zakilover commented in his *Likkutei Maharil* that when one observes a great personality, only his outward actions are noted. However, to know greatness, one must recognize the creativeness of his inner spirit. That is the message of the Torah. The Israelites saw the outward manifestations, which is why "They stood from afar," but Moses saw the inner spiritual dimensions and "drew near the thick darkness where God was." (H.A., p. 459)

～

The Kotzker Rebbe made the following comment on the *Pasukim* "You have seen that from the Heavens I have spoken to you. You shall not make [images] with Me; gods of silver and gods of gold, you shall not make for yourselves." (Ex. 20:19–20) It is as though Hashem said to the Jewish people: "We are becoming partners today. Therefore, do not take any other partners. I will request that 'You shall not make with Me'; 'Gods of silver and gods of gold, you shall not make for yourselves.'" (F.C.O., p. 208)

～

"And when you will make an altar of stones for Me, do not build them hewn, lest you wave your sword over it and defile it." (Ex. 20:22) The Noam Elimelech commented that the *sefer Yetzirah* (a Kabbalistic text from the third and fifth centuries C.E.) calls letters "stones." "When you will make an altar of stones for Me" means "When you will sacrifice your evil inclination by occupying yourself in the study of Torah." "Do not build them hewn" means "Do not flaunt your learning through sophistry and hair-splitting arguments, for they become like hewn stones." For you have "waved your sword over it" is showing your sharpness for your own honor and ego, and you will "defile it," God forbid, for you will show your "nakedness" (Ex. 20:23), meaning your arrogance. Your intent should be for the sake of Heaven and to praise Him. (*Noam Elimelech*, p. 33b)

～

"You shall not ascend with steps upon My altar, so that your nakedness will not be uncovered upon it." (Ex. 20:23) the Noam Elimelech explained that the person who has an inflated ego and is boastful will find that all of his personality flaws will reveal themselves. (F.C.O., p. 210)

On the same *Pasuk*, R' Yisroel Riziner commented that during the days of the Temple, when a Jew brought a sacrifice, he confessed to the *Kohen* and regretted his wrongdoing, showing his modesty and humility. Today, we do not have the Temple, the altar, nor sacrifices. We have substituted study and prayer. Therefore, one should have in mind that his studying and prayer must be as pure as the sacrifices of old. "Know before Whom you stand"—do not pray with arrogance. Concern yourself with your wrongdoing, otherwise your pride will be revealed and people will recognize it and that will be your embarrassment. (F.C.O., p. 209)

MISHPATIM
"THESE ARE THE LAWS OF JUSTICE"

On the *Pasuk* "And these are the laws of justice that you shall place before them" (Ex. 21:1), Rabbi Menachem Mendel of Lubavitch made the following observation. He said that the giving of the Torah completes the purpose of Creation. God brought all existence into being because he desired a dwelling place in the lower worlds (noted in Midrash *Tanchumah, Parshas Bechukosai*, sec. 4). The goal of Creation was to have man reveal and disseminate the essence of Hashem through the *mishpatim* of the Torah, for they transmit spirituality into our everyday lives. The understanding and application of these laws create a society that can enable man to achieve spiritual goals and satisfy his material needs in a righteous manner, thereby establishing a "dwelling for God" in the most complete sense. (G.O.T., pp. 108–110)

"And these are the laws of justice. . . ." (Ex. 21:1) Rashi commented: "It adds on to that which has been stated previously; just as those which have been stated previously are from Sinai, so, too, these are from Sinai." The Chidushei Harim commented that there are two types of laws. One group inherently contains logical reasons that can be grasped by man. The other laws are not fathomable to him. Therefore, the Torah tells us that just as all the other laws were given by Hashem, so, too, are the laws that may not be understood given at Sinai, and they are to be obeyed because they were also commanded by Hashem. (F.C.O., p. 211)

~~

"And these are the laws of justice that you shall place before them." (Ex. 21:1) The Sassover noted Rashi's comment that it was "like a table that is set and prepared to be eaten from, that is placed before a person." He said that Rashi implies that a person should make the same concentrated effort to perform *mitzvot* and observe the laws as he does to prepare a table for a meal. (F.C.O., p. 211)

~~

On the same *Pasuk*, the Kotzker Rebbe commented that good manners precede the study of Torah, for good manners are the introduction to learning the Torah. The character of an individual can be told by the way he maintains the Torah. (F.U.A.O., vol. 2, p. 128)

~~

The S'fas Emes noted that even a person who is not involved with the laws must always have the laws in all of his dealings and behavior in front of him "as a table that is always prepared for a meal." (F.C.O., p. 211)

~~

In his *sefer Brit Avram*, R' Yosef Moshe, the Rebbe of Z'barov, explained the connection of the *Pasukim* "And these are the judgments that you shall place before them. When you will buy a Hebrew servant. . . ." (Ex. 21:1–2) He compared the *Pasukim* with a statement in *The Ethics of Our Fathers*, "Know before Whom you stand." He said, "Before you give an accounting to Hashem, consider that you may have to repent." He also said that "These are the judgments" means that one should reflect upon "these judgments" before one is to be judged. "Do the repentance with these judgments in mind when dealing with your servant—namely, the evil inclination that is called "servant"—so that you will *tikneh* ("buy," from *tak'en*, "to purify") the servant and make him a Hebrew servant." (M.D., p. 145)

The Torah states: "If a servant shall say, 'I love my master, my wife, and my children; I shall not go free,' then his master shall bring him to the door or to the doorpost, and his master shall bore through his ear with an awl, and he shall serve him forever." (Ex. 21:6) Rashi asks, "What is it about the ear that it should be bored of all the organs of the body?" The Nikolsberger Rebbe also asked, "Why is the ear more guilty than the hands that steal or the feet that go to steal?" He explained that before the giving of the Torah, thieves were afraid to steal because people protected their possessions. After the giving of the Torah, thieves reasoned that people were going to be dependent on the law "Do not steal," and would not be careful to guard their possessions. Because the thieves forgot what they had heard at Mt. Sinai and started to steal, it was the ear that bore the responsibility. (F.C.O., p. 211)

Interpreting the same *Pasuk*, the Chidushei Harim commented that the ear is punished because if a person chooses not to obey that which he has heard, then it is better not to hear. (F.U.A.O., vol. 2, p. 131)

The Riziner gave the following interpretation of the *Pasuk* "If he gets up (*yakum*) and goes outside on his own power, the one who struck will be absolved; only for his sitting idle shall he pay, and he shall heal." (Ex. 21:19) He said that "If he gets up," meaning when he rises in his economic status, he may think that he has become wealthy on his own. The Midrash explains that one may show his economic status by the way he walks (literally on his feet), meaning his demeanor, "and goes outside on his own power"; if he leaves his people, stops observing the *mitzvot*, and stops believing in God, he will become spiritually bankrupt and go off the path. The cure for "Rock Shivtoe" (only for his sitting idle) is that he must do *teshuvah*. He must repent immediately. Delay would only make matters worse. He should give *tzedakah* and perform acts of righteousness. Then "He shall heal"; he will realize that it was not his power that changed his economic condition. (F.C.O., p. 212)

On the words "He shall heal" (Ex. 21:19), the Vorker commented that when a person becomes ill, first a doctor is called—"He creates medicine." (Prayer Book) If one does not get better then *T'hillim* (Book of Psalms) is said—"How awesome is praise." (Prayer Book) And if the illness continues, then we ask for a miracle from "The Master of miracles." (Prayer Book) (F.C.O., p. 214)

The Torah states: "But if he survives for a day or two days, he will not be avenged, for he is his property." (Ex. 21:21) The Rimanover translated the *Pasuk* literally: "Nevertheless, if he stands up a day or two, the verdict shall not be put into execution, for it is his money." He interpreted the *Pasuk* to mean that if one stands with a sincere heart, full of regret, for one day of Yom Kippur or two days of Rosh Hashanah, but gives no attention to observing the *mitzvot* the remainder of the year, his favorable verdict will be nullified. It is evident that his sincerity was motivated by money and not out of love of God. (H.A., p. 517)

R' Bunim of Pshys'cha, along the same thought, said; "All year we rush our prayers, but if on one day—Yom Kippur—or two days—Rosh Hashanah—we pray slowly and deliberately, that will not suffice, for our concern is really for the money." (F.C.O., p. 214)

The Sassover interpreted the *Pasuk* "But if there be a fatality, then you shall give a life in place of a life." (Ex. 21:23) If a tragedy occurs to a fellow Jew, there is an obligation to do all that is necessary to save that person. (F.C.O., p. 215)

The Torah states: "When a man will open a pit, or when a man will dig a pit and not cover it, and an ox or a donkey fall into it, the owner of the pit shall make restitution; he shall return money (*kesef*, "money," or *kosef,* "longing") to its owner." (Ex. 21:33) The Lizenzker said that if a Tzaddik tries to reach the hard-hearted by "digging" an opening in their hearts, and continues his efforts till they withdraw from materialistic thoughts—*kesef*—then Hashem, who has endowed the Tzaddik with the power to influence, will grant him his reward. Hashem will repay him by increasing his longing—*kosef*—and devotion to God. (H.A., p. 226)

On the *Pasuk* "If the thief will be found in the underground" (Ex. 22:1), the Kotzker commented that if a person digs within himself deeply and finds the wretchedness within him, then Hashem will lengthen his life. (F.C.O., p. 215)

R' Meir Primishlaner commented on the *Pasuk* "Then the householder shall approach the judges." (Ex. 22:7) He said that even an ordinary person can approach Hashem if he has not mixed in his neighbor's business and has not committed any wrongdoing in trade—"He had not laid his hand upon his fellow's property." (Ex. 22:7) (F.C.O., p. 215)

R' Yisroel Modzitzer on the *Pasuk* "That he will say, that it is this" (Ex. 22:8) noted that the essence and basis of all sin is the term "that it is this." When a person says of himself that he is it, he is egotistical and considers himself "this is it." That is the height of arrogance. (F.C.O., p. 216)

On the *Pasukim* "If a man will borrow from his fellow . . . If its owner is with him, he shall not pay" (Ex. 22:13–14), R' Bunim of Pshys'cha commented that every person has a soul on loan on the condition that it is put to good use. We know that a borrower is culpable and must pay even if there is an accident. If this is the case, then how can one be absolved from sin caused by accident or intent. The answer is: "If its owner is with him"—if his Master is with him, as King David prayed: "That I dwell in the House of Hashem all the days of my life." (Ps. 27)

Only if he remembers Hashem and accepts his spiritual responsibilities, then "he shall not pay." (M.T., p. 100)

The Berditchever cried out to Hashem, "It says in the Torah: 'You shall not persecute any widow or orphan.' (Ex. 22:21) You are very careful to obey every letter in the Torah. Then why, Hashem, do You permit the nations to persecute us, for we are like orphans without a father? Why do You not take us out of the Diaspora?" (F.C.O., p. 216)

On the *Pasuk* "When you will lend money to My people, to the poor person who is with you" (Ex. 22:24), the Riziner commented that the word *kesef* (money) can also mean "desire" and the word *talveh* (lend) can mean "to associate." Based on this, he said that the meaning of the *Pasuk* is that it is not enough just to give money to the poor. You must also associate with him and treat him as a human being and not as someone below you. It is true that he is poor, but he is also an associate. (F.C.O., p. 216)

On the same *Pasuk*, R' Yechiel Moshe Koznitzer commented that the mitzvah and acts of righteousness are incumbent on everyone. When those who are poverty-stricken are within your midst, you should try to spare something for them even if you do not have enough for yourself. (F.C.O., p. 216)

"When you will lend money to My people . . . do not act toward him as a creditor." (Ex. 22:24) The Radziminer noted that in the Torah there are instructions applicable to everyone. For example, the lender should obey the dictum to be patient with the borrower—and the borrower must pay back immediately, as it says: "When a man will borrow from his fellow . . . he shall surely pay." (Ex. 22:13) However, it is improper for one to bear in mind the *Pasuk* that is meant for another. For instance, the borrower should not remind the lender that the latter is commanded to be patient. On the other hand, the lender should not remind the borrower that it is wrong not to repay promptly. (S.S.K., p. 101)

~~~

"You shall not curse a leader among your people." (Ex. 22:27) The Torah admonishes us not to besmirch the reputation of a leader. It is in the nature of people, noted the Kosover, to find fault with their leader. For all that occurs and for every negative event, the leader is blamed. The people even accused Moses, our teacher, of negative behavior. They blamed him for all their problems. That is why the Torah admonishes us. (F.C.O., p. 217)

~~~

"Distance yourself from a false word." (Ex. 23:6) The Chidushei Harim notes that nowhere else does the Torah insist on one distancing himself from anything. However, the Sages did "make a fence around the Torah" so that we do not transgress any prohibition. Only when it came to "speaking falsehood" did the Torah demand "distance." (F.C.O., p. 218)

~~~

On the same *Pasuk*, R' Avraham Radamsker said, "One of the reasons that David's son (Meshiach) will come is to bring those who are far closer, and those who are close farther apart." He noted that according to the *aleph bet*, the letters of the word *emes* (truth) are far apart: *aleph* at the beginning, *mem* in the middle, and *sof* at the end. The letters of the word *sheker* (falsehood) are in sequence: *shin-koof-resh*. When the Messiah comes, all will be truth. He will make that which is far close and that which is close far. (F.C.O., p. 219)

~~~

On the same *Pasuk*, the Kosover noted that it is impossible to say that there is someone who speaks the truth at all times. Some are closer to falsehood and others are further away. (F.C.O., p. 218)

The Berditchever noted that man's behavior is very strange. When an individual does not follow the dictum "Distance yourself from a false word," people will not deal with that person. But if an individual does not obey any of the other *mitzvot* or *Halachot,* that does not seem to disturb his dealings with other people. (F.C.O., p. 219)

On the same *Pasuk,* the Rebbe R' Zusia commented that "from a word" means that if you speak one word that is false, you have already distanced yourself from the Almighty, Whose symbol is truth. (F.C.O., p. 219)

The Chidushei Harim commented on the words in Psalms 119:160, "The beginning of your words are truth (*emet*)." He said that the Ten Commandments begin with the letter *aleph* in the word *anochi*, the first Mishnah begins with a *mem* in the word *ma'ey'mati*, and the Talmud begins with a *tof* in the word *tana.* Together the letters *aleph, mem, tof* spell *emet*—truth. That shows that both the written law and the oral law speak the truth. (F.C.O., p. 218)

"Truth sprouts from the ground." (Ps. 85:12) The Berditchever commented that this means that in matters pertaining to this world, we need truth to exist. (F.C.O., p. 218)

The Baal Shem Tov also spoke about the meaning of "And from the earth will spring forth truth." (Psalm 85:12) He said that we learn from this that if a person sees something of worth on the ground, he will pick it up. "But why," he asked, "do not people pick up truth, since it is a worthy commodity. The Baal Shem Tov noted that people are too lazy to bend to pick up truth." (F.C.O., p. 220)

━━

"And on the seventh day you shall desist, so that your ox and donkey shall be at ease." (Ex. 23:12) The Gerer Rebbe referred to the talmudic story of a donkey that refused to work on the Sabbath after a sale by R'Yochanan ben Toratah to show that the observance of the concept of rest on the Sabbath extends to all, even the animals. (M.T., p. 105)

━━

"Three times during the year, all your male (*z'churacha*). . . ." (Ex. 23:17) The Mishmeres Itmar translated *z'churacha* as "your memory" (*zikaron*). Based on this translation, he noted that one should repeat what one learns three times throughout the year, so that whatever one learns will be remembered. (F.C.O., p. 220)

━━

"And you shall worship (*va'a'vad'tem*—plural) Hashem, your God, and He shall bless your bread (*lach'm'cha*—singular) and your water (*mey'mecha*—singular), and I will remove illness from your midst." (Ex. 23:25) The Kotzker noted that when the *Pasuk* speaks about service to Hashem, it speaks in the plural. When it speaks about food, the singular is used. He commented that when we pray, even as individuals, the prayers gather and become a public prayer. However, though many people may eat at one table each person is really eating for himself. (F.C.O., p. 221)

━━

On the same *Pasuk*, the Dzikover noted the connection between bread and water and the cure for sickness. When one gets sick, he will obtain all sorts of medicine or go somewhere for mineral waters. However, what shall a poor person do when an illness strikes? It is to them that Hashem speaks, saying, "Serve Me, and I will cause your bread and water to contain the healing powers of medicines and mineral water." (F.C.O., p. 221)

⌇

R' Tzadok HaKohen commented that one should serve Hashem through the written and the oral law, for they are called bread and water. (F.C.O., p. 221)

⌇

"The appearance of the glory of Hashem was like a consuming fire." (Ex. 24:17) The Berditchever commented that when one feels a burning desire and resolve for serving Hashem, there is reciprocity in attitude. (F.C.O., p. 222)

TERUMAH
"A PORTION"

The Lubavitcher Rebbe, Rabbi Menachem Mendel Schneerson, commented on the *Sidra*. He noted that the word *terumah* may have two meanings. It can mean "lifting up" (based on the Zohar, vol. 2) or "separation" (Rashi, *Targum Onkelos*). Both meanings put the focus on man's attempt to establish a dwelling place for Hashem. Rashi states in Exodus 25:2 that this *terumah* must involve thirteen different articles, such as gold, silver, and copper. This indicates that man's task is to incorporate material existence into God's dwelling. This double interpretation of *terumah* reflects two factors necessary in creating a dwelling for Hashem. First, a person must designate his gift, separating it from his worldly property. Then, through its consecration its nature becomes elevated above the ordinary material plane. This concept has Halachic implications. Once an object is consecrated, it can no longer be used for mundane purposes. So, when a person prepares a dwelling for a King, he must cleanse the place and bring in attractive articles. Similarly, to make our world a dwelling place for Hashem, "separation" is necessary to purge the self attitude encouraged by our worldly existence. Only then is the world "lifted up" to become a medium for God's dwelling. (G.O.T., pp. 115–116)

⌇

There are a number of interpretations on the *Pasuk* "Hashem spoke to Moses, saying, 'Speak to the Children of Israel and they shall take to Me

151

a portion; from every man whose heart will motivate, him you shall take My portion.'" (Ex. 25:2)

~~~

The Rebbe R' Zusia noted that the Torah does not say, "And shall take to me a portion." It does not command that one should give charity with a full heart, for then it would not be remarkable. Therefore, when a poor man takes upon himself the act of charity, even with the understanding that it is not a dictum, that is remarkable. (F.C.O., p. 223)

~~~

The Zanzer commented that the Almighty asks that wherever one goes or whatever one does, let him separate a little bit in his heart for His sake. (F.C.O., p. 223)

~~~

The Degel Machnei Ephraim commented that the world is analogous to a wedding. Some people come for the joy of being at a wedding, which is its essence; others come to eat, drink, and be merry. The Torah comes to tell us not to subordinate the essence. "Take to Me a portion" means take the desires and pleasures of the mundane, which are a momentary aspect, and transform them "for Me," for the soul, for the spiritual life, which is the essence of life. (*Degel Machnei Ephraim*, p. 108)

~~~

R' Sholom Kaminer explains "And they shall take." He says that the takers should be sincere receivers for the sake of Heaven for the performance of the mitzvah. Those who give should give sincerely and for the sake of heaven. (F.C.O., p. 224)

~~~

On the same *Pasuk*, Rashi states: "They should set some of their money aside for Me as a contribution." The Yid Hakadosh commented that Jews should divorce themselves from worldly desires, namely, the desire to accumulate wealth. This desire gives them false goals and drives them off the right path. (F.C.O., p. 224)

R' Schneur Zalman of Liadi commented that just like lightning breaks through heavy clouds and gives light to the earth, so does giving charity give light and understanding to the soul. (F.C.O., p. 225)

"From every man whose heart makes him give shall you take my offering. And this is the offering that you shall take from them: gold, and silver, and copper." (Ex. 25:2–3) The Amshinover said that God said that if there is a man who has sincere piety and worships Hashem from the heart, allow him to continue in that manner by taking away his desire for gold, silver, and copper and bring him to Me as an offering. He will be satisfied to devote his life to Me in security. (H.A., p. 292)

On the same *Pasuk*, the S'fas Emes noted that whatever you give is not really yours, for the Torah says: "to Me." The gold and silver are His and you should give "a portion." (F.C.O., p. 225)

There is a dialogue between the Vorker and the Kotzker. When the Kotzker put himself in isolation, the Vorker was one of the very few people he permitted to visit him. The Vorker asked why he had taken such extreme measures. The Kotzker replied that when a Jew wishes to go on the right path, the path of Hashem, he has no choice but to make an offering "for Me." He must offer up all companionship, not only the evil ones but also the good ones, even "from every man whose heart makes him give" (Ex. 25:2), for only in this manner can one reach the service of Hashem. The Vorker explained that his interpretation was different. He said that when a Jew wishes to make an offering, when he wishes to go on the right path, the path of Hashem, he must take what every man has to offer. He should accept companionship from every man and by associating accept from him whatever is offered for Hashem. There is one exception: From the man whose heart is locked, he will receive nothing at all. Only the man "whose heart makes him give" can give to others. (F.U.A.O., p. 165)

~~~

"They shall make Me a Sanctuary so that I may dwell among them." (Ex. 25:8) Rashi comments: "They will make a house of sanctity dedicated to My name." The Amshinover commented that it is the obligation of the Jew to bring holiness into his home and to develop a sense of holiness in his family. (F.C.O., p. 230)

~~~

"They shall make Me a Sanctuary." The Koznitzer noted that the knowledge that today synagogues have taken the place of the Holy Temple should govern our behavior when we enter them. Just as the *Kohen Hagadol* had to focus all of his thoughts for the sake of Heaven, every Jew upon entering a synagogue or a house of study should concentrate all his thoughts for the sake of the Divine—so that "I shall dwell among them." (F.C.O., p. 230)

~~~

On the same *Pasuk*, the Skoyler Rebbe, R' Avraham Moshe Rabinowitz, noted that it states, "I will dwell among them (*b'so'chom*)." He said that *b'so'chom* shows that there are two ways that the Schechinah dwells within us here on earth. One is through the observance of the Sabbath and the other is through the building of the Sanctuary. Both bring the inspiration of the Divine Presence on earth. (Ch.B., p. 236)

~~~

"So that I may dwell among them." The S'fas Emes commented that Hashem dwells in every Jew because the Sanctuary is in every Jew. (F.C.O., p. 231)

~~~

On the same phrase, the Berditchever noted that one should never think evil thoughts, for in the mind of each individual is the Holy of Holies.

This means that the Ark and the Tablets dwell in it. Any evil or foreign thoughts will contaminate the holiness of the mind. (F.C.O., p. 231)

~~~

"In conformance with all that I show you, the form of the Tabernacle and the form of all its vessels; and so shall you do." (Ex. 25:9) On "so shall you do," Rashi comments that it means "in future generations." The S'fas Emes comments that if the Children of Israel will have an honest desire to build the Temple to reveal the Divine Presence, they will attain that goal. If they do not reach that goal, then it is a sign that their desires are not honest and sincere. Thus our Sages state: "In every generation that the Temple is not built, it is as if it was destroyed in that time." (Talmud Yerushalmi *Yoma* 1:5a) If there is a true willingness to build the Temple, then it will be built in our day. (M.T., p. 117)

~~~

On the *Pausk* "The staves (*badim*) shall remain in the rings (*b'tabot*) of the *Aron*; they shall not be removed from it" (Ex. 25:15), the Koznitzer commented that *tabot* means the ring of marriage (*taba'at kedushin*). When a Jew performs the *mitzvot* and recites the blessing "Who has sanctified us with His Commandments," he betroths himself to the Almighty. *Badim* represent *am l'vadad yishkon* (Num. 23:9), a people separated from others because of their observance of *mitzvot*. "They shall not be removed" means that because of their observance, Hashem will never neglect or leave His people. (F.C.O., p. 232)

~~~

"The rings (*taba'ot*) shall be opposite (*hamisgeret*) the frame." (Ex. 25:27) R' Mordechai Kremnitzer said that the root of *taba'ot* has the letters of the word *teva*, "nature," and *misgeret* has the letters *sagar*, "close." Because desires in a person's nature may become habitual, the Torah tells us that one should lock up his desires and not permit them to get out of bounds. (F.C.O., p. 232)

On the *Pasuk* "And you shall fold (*chalafta*) the sixth panel" (Ex. 26:9), the Ostrovitzer translated the word *chalafta* as *kofel*, "double." He noted that in each morning's reciting of the psalm of the day, the Sabbath is mentioned. On the "sixth" day, one must prepare "double" the amount for the Shabbat. (F.C.O., p. 232)

"There shall be two projections for each board (*keresh*)." (Ex. 26:17) The Noam Elimelech noted that the letters of *keresh* can also spell *sheker*, "falsehood." If you will stay away from falsehood, you will reach a high level of holiness and you will turn *sheker* into *kesher* and become part of the tabernacle. (*Noam Elimelech*, p. 48b)

TETZAVEH
"YOU SHALL COMMAND"

The Lubavitcher Rebbe, Rabbi Menachem Mendel Schneerson, noted that *Parshat Tetzaveh* does not mention the name of Moses; nevertheless, it does communicate an aspect of his being. His association with the *parsha* is revealed through the discussion of leadership and its essence. The word *tzava*, which means "connection," is related to the word *tetzaveh*, "to command." Therefore, the *Pasuk* says that "You command" means your essence should command, and also connect to the people. Moses's essence showed commitment, self-sacrifice, and loyalty. He defended Israel on all occasions—"If You would, forgive their sins; and if not, please obliterate me from the book You have written." (Ex. 32:32) This shows the connection of Moses to the Jewish people. "Moses is Israel, and Israel is Moses." (Rashi, Num. 21:21) It is Moses who enables every Jew to tap his innermost spiritual resources and maintain a constant commitment, as the *Pasuk* states: "And you shall *tetzaveh* (connect) with the Children of Israel that they shall take for you clear olive oil . . . to light a lamp continually." (Ex. 27:20) (G.O.T., pp. 117–119)

❧

"And you shall command the Children of Israel that they take for you clear olive oil, crushed for illumination, to light a lamp continually." (Ex. 27:20) The Koznitzer commented that another definition for *tetzaveh* is "to befriend." Hashem told Moses that though he was on a very

157

high spiritual level, he should not separate himself from the people. To be a source of illumination to others and lift their souls to a higher spiritual level, he had to conduct himself in a becoming manner. (F.C.O., p. 233)

R' Asher Horowitz said that *tetzaveh* is the acronym of *tza'akas hadal takshiv v'toshe'ah*, "The painful cry of the poor will be heard and they will be helped." (Prayer Book, Sfard text, *Nishmat*) Hashem said to Moses, "'Command the Children of Israel' to listen to the cry of the needy and poor." For we are told, "All who have mercy on humanity, Heaven will have mercy on them." (Talmud *Shabbat* 151b) (F.C.O., p. 233)

"Clear (*zach*) olive oil, crushed for illumination, to light a lamp continually." (Ex. 27:20) The Sassover said that *zach* stands for *Zo're'ach kosis*, "It will give light to the crushed." He commented that though the Jews may be crushed while in the Diaspora, eventually the burden will be lightened. (F.C.O., p. 234)

On the same *Pasuk*, R' Yehoshua Dzikover commented that it is possible that as long as a person does not lose himself and become confused when he is crushed, he can in spite of everything reach a higher level. (F.C.O., p. 234)

On the words "to light a lamp continually," Rashi commented: "He would kindle until the flame would rise on its own." The Letchener remarked that in every Jew there is a Divine spark that can never be extinguished. One need only light this spark and it will become a flame on its own. One need only become the one who lights the fire; the rest will follow. (F.C.O., p. 234)

On the words "crushed for illumination," the Sassover commented that it is only after a person crushes his bad habits and desires that he will be able to shine. (F.C.O., p. 234)

"And you, bring near to yourself Aharon, your brother." (Ex. 28:1) The Dinever commented that Hashem requested Moses that he not isolate himself from the people, but bring himself closer to the people, as his brother Aharon, who is a "Pursuer of peace and a lover of Israel." (*Ethics of Our Fathers* 1:12) (F.U.A.O., vol. 2, p. 180)

On the *Pasuk* "It should have two shoulder straps attached to its two ends, and it shall be connected" (Ex. 28:7), R' Zev Tzvi Zbarisher commented that a person's personality is divided into halves: body and soul, the good and bad inclinations. These opposites should be connected and united for the best. (F.C.O., p. 235)

The literal translation of the *Pasuk Safa yih'yeh l'fiv saviv* is "Its opening shall have a border all around." (Ex. 28:32) The Rebbe of Lublin translated the word *safa* as "lips." Based on this, the meaning of the *Pasuk* is that one should put a fence around the lips. Be careful not to malign anyone. Do not go as a talebearer. Do not tell lies. Do not let your lips utter deceit. Above all, do not say one thing and believe something else. (F.C.O., p. 236)

On the same *Pasuk*, the Yid HaKadosh made the following comment based on the talmudic statement "If a barn is found shut, then it is a sign that a human being was there; and if it was left open, then it is a sign that there was no human being." (*Tamid* 26) He said that if a person can contain his speech, by keeping his mouth closed, then he can be considered a human being. If he cannot close his mouth and it is always open, then he cannot be considered a human being. (F.U.A.O., vol. 2, p. 184)

～～

On the *Pasuk* "Its sound shall be heard when he enters the Sanctuary before Hashem" (Ex. 28:38), R' Zusia commented that when a speaker comes to the Sanctuary, a sign that he is being heard is when his words penetrate the depths of the listeners. (F.C.O., p. 236)

～～

On the *Pasuk* "the fat that covers the innards" (Ex. 29:13), R' Bunim of Pshys'cha noted that the person whose intent is to eat and drink to be completely satiated covers his inner essence. Thus, he covers all his ability to behave in a humanitarian manner. (F.C.O., p. 236)

～～

On the *Pasuk* "I shall dwell among the Children of Israel, and I shall be their God (*Elokim*)" (Ex. 29:45), the Alexander Rebbe said that false gods are beautiful and enchanting from afar. However, as one gets closer, he notices that there is nothing to them. With the Almighty, the closer one gets, the more he recognizes His Greatness. (F.C.O., p. 237)

～～

On the same *Pasuk*, the Maggid of Mezritch explained the use of *Elokim*, connoting the attribute of mercy, in the *Pasuk*. He noted that when a father loves his child, he will not only protect him but also wish to punish those who do him harm. Therefore, the Maggid said that the Almighty said, "I shall be your *Elokim* and show you My love and dwell among you, with a sense of mercy to protect you and punish those who wish to harm My children." (F.C.O., p. 237)

～～

On the same *Pasuk*, we are told that when the Ropshitzer Rebbe was a young child, someone said that he would give him a coin if he would tell him where God dwells. He replied, "I will give you two coins if you will tell me where he does not dwell." (F.C.O., p. 237)

When the Kotzker was asked the same question, he answered, "Wherever He is let in." (F.U.A.O., p. 192)

Based on the *Pasuk* "You shall make an altar on which to bring incense up in smoke, of shittimwood shall you make it. . . . You shall cover it with pure gold" (Ex. 30:1,3), the Talmud states: "The fire of *Gehinom* gains no ascendancy over the sinners among Israel. . . . If the golden altar, which was covered by no more than a dinar's thickness of gold, remained intact for many years and the fire that was burnt on it daily had no ascendancy over it to erode it, then the sinners among Israel, who are as full of *mitzvot* as a pomegranate is full of seeds, how much more so are they, the sinners of Israel, immune to fire." (*Chagigah* 27a) The *Avnei Nezer* commented that the Talmud explained that just as the incense placed on the altar of gold by an average person was consumed by fire from above, so too, the sinners of Israel, though they may have sinned and deserved the fire of *Gehinom*. Because of their *mitzvot*, the supernal fire voids the fire of *Gehinom*, making it impossible for it to gain ascendancy. (M.T., p. 138)

"Continual incense before Hashem, for your generations." (Ex. 30:8) In the *sefer Ilana D'Chayeh*, it is noted that the table is considered an altar; therefore, the food that we eat is holy. That means that all our food shall be a "continual incense before Hashem." (M.D., p. 168)

KI SISA
"WHEN YOU WILL TAKE A CENSUS"

"When you will take a census (*ki sisa*) of the Children of Israel according to their counts. . . ." (Ex. 30:12) R' Moshe Leib Sassover translated the words *ki sisa* as "uplifting" to have the *Pasuk* read, "When you will lift up the Children of Israel." He advised the Almighty that "'Every man shall give Hashem an atonement for his soul' (Ex. 30:12), if You, Hashem, uplift the Children of Israel by providing a substantial livelihood. You know that poverty cannot lead one to atone." (F.C.O., p. 238)

The word *v'natnu* (Ex. 30:12) when read both backwards or forwards reads *v'natnu*. The Rimanover said that when one gives charity, it will be returned to him twofold. (F.C.O., p. 238)

On the words "an atonement for his soul" (Ex. 30:12), Moses wanted to know how a coin could be an atonement for the soul. The Kotzker commented that Hashem told Moses that if a coin is given away with happiness then it is for atonement, for when one gives charity with enthusiasm, he is giving with a full heart. (F.C.O., p. 239)

On charity, the Bratzlaver said that one should not be afraid to spend on charity and holy purposes, for God will return your gifts manifold. (L.M., p. 17)

The Torah states: "This is what they shall give." (Ex. 30:13) Rashi commented: "God showed Moses a sort of coin of fire and they should give a coin like this." The Lizensker remarked that when one gives charity, he should look at the coin. This coin is like fire, which can destroy. It can pay for unnecessary desires and can be used for many evil purposes. However, it can warm the heart when the coin is used for charity and spiritual endeavors. (F.C.O., p. 240)

On the same *Pasuk*, the Yid HaKadosh noted that when a flame is burning, it does not remain still. The flame gets bigger and bigger. So it is with a person who does repentance with fervor: It is like the flame that does not rest. Just as the letters of *shekel* (coin) can represent *shachbe'cha* ("while you rest"), *kumecha* ("when you rise up"), *lech't'cha* ("when you walk"); the desire should constantly burn until there is true repentance. (F.C.O., p. 241)

"The wealthy shall not increase and the destitute shall not decrease from half of the *shekel*." (Ex. 30:15) In the *Noam Elimelech*, there is an explanation that one who has accumulated many *mitzvot* should not be overly boastful such that he feels that he has reached the pinnacle of spirituality. He should remember that he has reached only halfway. The one who is poor in accumulating *mitzvot* should not despair and feel that he will not reach high spiritual heights. He should feel that there is still time to give "a portion to Hashem." (*Noam Elimelech*, p. 52b)

On the same *Pasuk*, the Kotzker noted that the poor always direct their hearts heavenward in the performance of *mitzvot*. The wealthy may find it difficult to do the same. That is why the wealthy are also mentioned. The Torah cautions everyone to perform all activities for the sake of Heaven. (F.C.O., p. 242)

"The purpose of the half *shekel*," R' Bunim said, "is 'to atone for your souls.' (Ex. 30:12) Half of a *shekel* is to atone for one's transgressions and the other half is to note that Hashem is somewhat responsible for permitting sin." (F.C.O., p. 242)

On the *Pasuk* "Just observe My Sabbaths, for it is a sign between Me and you for your generations, to know that I am Hashem, Who sanctifies you" (Ex. 31:16), there are many commentaries.

The Kedushas Levi noted that when a person observes the Shabbat properly, it gives him encouragement to serve Hashem the entire week. When the following Shabbat arrives, he finds it easier to appreciate its sanctity. With this approach, it becomes easier to "make the Shabbat an eternal covenant"—for all *Shabbatot*, as the *Pasuk* states: "And the children of Israel will observe the Shabbat." (*Kedushas Levi*, p. 118)

The Nikolsberger commented that Hashem did not give the Sabbath as a mitzvah to observe, but as a gift from His treasure chest. (F.C.O., p. 243)

The Gerer Rebbe noted that for the construction of the Tabernacle, the Talmud (*Sabbath* 73) lists thirty-nine tasks that were needed. He said that we learn from this that just as all the tasks were dedicated for the Tabernacle, so too our weekday activities should emphasize the Sabbath, and therefore all work will have a sanctity. (H.A., 404)

The Lenchener noted that while the Sabbath gives us rest, it is also the easiest mitzvah to perform. Once the Sabbath arrives Friday at sunset, the performance of the mitzvah has begun. It stays every moment and does not leave for even one second until the next night. (F.C.O., p. 247)

~~

R' Bunim asked one of his Chasidim if he was a *Shomer Shabbat*, a Shabbat observer (literally, a "watcher of the Shabbat"). The Chasid, a little surprised at the question, answered in the affirmative. When asked what he does on Friday night, he answered that he learns half the night and sleeps the rest of the time. "You are not a true Shabbat observer," said R' Bunim. "Someone who watches, and takes his job seriously, does not sleep." (F.C.O., p. 244)

~~

The Gerer Rebbe noted that in the *Amidah* (silent prayer) of Sabbath morning, we say: "Moses rejoiced in the gift of his portion." He said that when Moses discovered that Israel appreciated the gift of the Sabbath and the Holy Days, he was joyous. (H.A., p. 404)

~~

"For this Moses, the man who brought us up from the land of Egypt—we do not know what became of him." (Ex. 32:1) The Toldot Yaacov Yosef commented that the Israelites were confused and concerned. Moses was always involved with the people, but after not seeing him for forty days, they feared that he might have separated himself from them. (F.C.O., p. 247)

~~

On the *Pasuk* "And he fashioned it with a tool (*cheret*)" (Ex. 32:4), the Primishlaner noted that when a person repents, a new person is created as though a new child is born. By taking th Hebrew word *cheret*, "tool," and changing its vowels to the word *charata*, "regret," he commented that in having regret (*charata*) to the point of repentance, one fashions it with a tool (*cheret*) to become a new person. (M.D., p. 174)

On the *Pasuk* "I have seen this people, and behold! It is a stiff-necked people" (Ex. 32:9), the Izbitzer commented that it is a statement of praise, as mentioned in the Midrash Rabbah. The fact that they are a stiff-necked people allows them to withstand the persecutions of exile. (*Mi Hashaluach*, p. 65)

On the *Pasuk* "Moses turned and descended from the mountain" (Ex. 32:15), the Ropshitzer noted that this is a lesson for our leaders. While Moses was with Hashem, he was constantly praising the Jews. However, when he came down from the mountain, he admonished them. That shows that a leader should praise his people to others, but when he is talking to them in person, he can enumerate their transgressions. (F.U.A.O., p. 210)

On the *Pasuk* "The Tablets are the work of God" (Ex. 32:16), the S'fas Emes commented that the writing of the Ten Commandments on stone became indelibly inscribed in the hearts of the people forever. That is why it is "the work of God." (F.C.O., p. 247)

On the *Pasuk* "It is not the sound of shouting of might nor the sound of shouting of weakness" (Ex. 32:18), the Midrash comments that Hashem said to Moses, "You are the paradigm of leadership and you cannot distinguish one voice from another?" The Letchener commented that this Midrash tells us that a leader should be able to recognize the needs of the people and the direction they are heading just by the tone of their voices. (F.C.O., p. 247)

On the *Pasuk* "He threw down the Tablets" (Ex. 32:19), R' Yechezkel Kuzmirer noted that when Moses came down from the mountain holding the Torah, he saw the people worshipping the calf. He therefore was like a leader without a people or a teacher without students, so "He threw down the Tablets." (F.U.A.O., p. 211)

～～

On the *Pasuk* "And all the Levites gathered unto him" (Ex. 32:26), the Chidushei Harim commented that there were many Israelites who did not participate in the sin of the golden calf. The reason the Levites were singled out was because they were ready to give their lives to fight against idolatry. Others were either neutral or not willing to get involved. (F.C.O., p. 247)

～～

On the *Pasuk* "I implore! This people has sinned a great sin" (Ex. 32:31), the Kuzmirer Rebbe commented that Moses did not attempt to defend the Israelites, nor did he try to justify their action. He said to God that the mere fact that they recognized their sin meant that they were ready to repent. (F.C.O., p. 248)

～～

On the same *Pasuk*, R' Shmuel Shmayeh Ostrovitzer noted that the word "this" is unnecessary. What Moses was saying was that the people who transgressed were the same people who at the crossing of the Red Sea said, "This is my God and I will praise Him." (F.C.O., p. 248)

～～

"And on a day that I make an accounting, I shall bring their sin to account against them." (Ex. 32:34) The Berditchever, a defender of Israel, commented that Hashem did not mean that further sins would be punished more severely. When they transgressed with the golden calf, it became clear that their submission to authority had not yet become part of their character. Their highbred origin had been destroyed during their servitude in Egypt. Though the Israelites wanted to accept the Commandments through the goodness of their hearts, their obedience had not yet become second nature. However, a person who has conquered his evil habits, implanted by upbringing, and become well-mannered deserves praise. Therefore, Hashem appreciated the greatness of their willingness to accept the Torah. It demonstrated that they had broken the evilness they had acquired in Egypt. Hashem promised to remember this fact always, and to be lenient in all of His future judgments. (H.A., p. 96)

〜〜

On the *Pasuk* "You will see My back, but My face may not be seen" (Ex. 33:23), R' Moshe Sofer of Preshburg, in his *sefer Torat Moshe*, commented that what occurs in one's life is not revealed, nor can it be understood at that moment. Only as time passes, and is seen as historical events, can we grasp the Providential supervision. Thus, says the *Pasuk*, "You will see My back"—only after the occurrence do we realize what Providence had in store for us—"but My face may not be seen," for at first it is impossible to know. (M.T., p. 151)

〜〜

"Carve out (*p'sal*) for yourself two stone Tablets." (Ex. 34:1) There is an interesting story about the Riziner that gives us a lesson in the study of Torah. The Rebbe came to his *bais medrash* (house of study) unexpectedly, and found a few students drinking whiskey. Embarrassed, one of the students explained that the Koretzer Rebbe said that when Chasidim sit in a group and drink, it is the same as if they were studying Torah. "That may be true," said the Riziner, "with one difference. It is written: 'When you carve out (*p'sal*) two tablets' then it is holy. But it also is written: 'Do not make yourself an idol (*pessel*)' (Ex. 24:4), for it now becomes unholy. They are the same letters, but with a different meaning. When Chasidim sit and drink to bring a sense of unity and love for each other to strengthen their service to Hashem, then it is holy. However, if one drinks in the middle of the day for one's own gratification, then it is 'Do not make for yourself an idol.' It is better to learn Torah." (F.C.O., p. 249)

〜〜

"Hashem, Hashem, God, Merciful and Gracious, Slow to Anger, and Abundant in Kindness and Truth." (Ex. 34:6) The Alexander Rebbe was asked why Hashem chose "Truth" to be the last attribute to be mentioned. The Rebbe answered that if the other attributes, such as merciful, long-suffering, and preserver of kindness, were chosen, people would claim that they also possess the attributes that Hashem has. The only attribute that they cannot claim is the attribute of Truth, for only "The One" possesses the truth. (F.C.O., p. 250)

〜〜

On the *Pasuk* "Keeping mercy for two thousand, forgiving iniquity, transgression, and sin, and Who absolves, but does not absolve completely" (Ex. 34:7), R' Shmuel Shmayeh Ostrovitzer commented that a person must serve Hashem by constantly increasing his actions in the service of Hashem, as though he has not amended anything. Therefore, Hashem will absolve the sins of Israel as long as they are constantly increasing their actions. The individual whom "He will not absolve" must learn to scrutinize his actions while serving Hashem. (M.D., p. 176)

〜〜

"For a six-day period you may work, and on the seventh day you shall rest; you shall rest from plowing." (Ex. 34:21) The Koznitzer said that the Hebrew word for plowing is *charish*. The "ch" stands for *Chamishi* (Thursday), the "r" stands for *Revii* (Wednesday), and the "sh" stands for *Sheeshee* (Friday). He explained that this tells us that Wednesday, Thursday, and Friday should be used as days to prepare for the Sabbath. (M.D., p. 176)

〜〜

From the words in the same *Pasuk*, *tishbot* ("you shall rest"), *charish* ("plowing"), and *katzir* ("harvesting"), R' Elazar Halevi Horowitz, in his *sefer Noam Magidim*, noted that on the Sabbath one must not talk about subjects that are of a weekday nature. If we must discuss them, then it should be done in the shortest possible way. (Code of Law, *Orach Chayim* 307) He said that by changing the vowels of the words—*charish* becoming *charash* ("to be quiet") and *katzir* becoming *katzer* ("short")— the *Pasuk* suggests that one should be quiet and short in words so that *tishbot*—you may rest. (M.T., vol. 2, p. 153)

VAYAKHEL
"ASSEMBLED"

" **A** nd Moses assembled the entire assembly of the Children of Israel." (Ex. 35:1) The Lubavitcher Rebbe commented that a group
that gathers together can also move apart, and even while together, their
union may not complete. However, a *kahal* (an assembly) represents an
eternal entity that unites individuals, as is stated in the Talmud: "A
collective can never die." (*Temurah* 15b) The fact that the Sanctuary was
constructed by the Jewish people in a spirit of unity caused the finished
product to be permeated by oneness. This is noted in the fact that its
various components are considered one mitzvah. (Mishnah Torah,
Rambam, *Mitzvah* 20) The Jews are "one nation on earth." (2 Samuel
7:23) The implication is that we are bound through an internal connection enabling us to spread God's oneness throughout the world. The
unity of the Jewish people is an active force rather than a passive one.
Establishing oneness among our people spurs the manifestation of
God's unity in all existence. (G.O.T., pp. 133–135)

"And Moses assembled the Children of Israel and said to them, 'These
are the things that Hashem commanded.'" (Ex. 35:1) The Yid HaKadosh commented that all Jews are commanded to gather in unity and in
peace. (F.C.O., p. 252)

〜〜

On the same *Pasuk*, the Chordkover commented that the Torah discusses the variations that exist among people. Each individual performs the *mitzvot* based on his own understanding and the Torah strength within him. When performing the mitzvah, he endows it with his own uniqueness. However, when "gathering all the Children of Israel," they will be together without differences. (M.T., p. 158)

〜〜

The Lubliner noted that Moses gathered the Israelites to unite them. He said that the first principle for unity is "Love your neighbor as yourself." (F.C.O., p. 252)

〜〜

On the same *Pasuk*, Rebbe Shimon of Yerslov commented that Moses gathered all the Children of Israel and said that this gathering, which is with one heart and one conviction, is what "Hashem commanded." (F.C.O., p. 253)

〜〜

On the words in the same *Pasuk*, "And Moses assembled," Rashi noted that it was "on the day after Yom Kippur." The Kobriner commented that Moses demanded that the Jews behave spiritually and be full of love, one with another, on the Day of Yom Kippur; and even after Yom Kippur, they should assemble and feel the same. (F.C.O., p. 252)

〜〜

On the same *Pasuk*, Rashi noted that Moses gathered the Israelites by his speaking to them. The Sassover commented that the words were "holy words." "It is a known fact," he said, "that words that come from the heart enter the heart." (F.C.O., p. 253)

〜〜

"For a period of six days work may be done, but the seventh day shall be holy for you, a day of complete rest for Hashem." (Ex. 35:2) The

Sassover commented that if during the week we neglect the spiritual aspects of our lives, then we will not experience the complete joy of the holiness of Shabbat. He said that it is like a man who comes out of a dark place and cannot endure the light. (H.A., p. 407)

∽∽

On the eve of Shabbat, we sing *zemirot* (special songs for the Shabbat). "With double loaves and the great *Kiddush*, with abundant delicacies and generous spirit, they will merit much good." The Shinover commented that rich and poor alike are obligated to observe the Shabbat. Though a person of means may observe "with abundant delicacies," the main point is that one should observe with a "generous spirit" so that the pleasure should not be only a physical one. A person who develops such an attitude "will merit much good." (F.C.O., p. 255)

∽∽

On the *Pasuk* "You shall not light fire in any of your dwellings on the Sabbath day" (Ex. 35:3), Rabbi Avraham Moshe Rabinowitz, the Skoyler Rebbe, noted that based on the Zohar, the S'fas Emes said that one is not permitted to get angry on the Sabbath even if it involves a mitzvah. He said that one should not light the fire of anger in his dwelling. The Rambam also noted that one should train himself not to show anger even if he wishes to change someone's attitude for the better. This training is better done during the week. On the Sabbath, when we are enveloped in its holy light and inner sanctity, we are not permitted to show anger. (Ch.B., p. 248)

∽∽

"Take from yourselves a portion for Hashem, everyone who is generous of heart." (Ex. 35:5) The Yaroslover Rebbe said, "One should take from one's inner self all his desires and use them for Hashem's advantage." (F.C.O., p. 256)

∽∽

On the same *Pasuk*, the S'fas Emes commented that every gift should be given out of the generosity of one's heart for it to be "a portion for Hashem." (F.C.O., p. 256)

⚊⚊

"As a gift for Hashem: gold, and silver, and copper." (Ex. 35:5) R' Baruch Mezibozer noted that there are three levels in the giving of charity. The highest level is when one gives while one is able-bodied—that is gold. The next level is when charity is given at critical points in one's life— that is silver. The lowest level is when, during a lifetime, charity is never given. However, when a person leaves money for charity in his will, that is copper. (F.C.O., p. 256)

⚊⚊

"Every wise-hearted person among you shall come and make every- thing that Hashem has commanded." (Ex. 35:10) The Yid HaKadosh commented that the greatest wisdom is not that one should be wise, but that one should "make everything that Hashem has commanded." (F.C.O., p. 257)

⚊⚊

"All the wise people came, that did all the work of the Sanctuary, every man from his work that they were doing. And they said to Moses, as follows, 'The people bring more than is required for the labor of the work that Hashem has commanded to perform.' And Moses com- manded . . . 'Man and woman shall not do any more work for the offering of the Sanctuary.'" (Ex. 36:4–6) The Apter noted that a sense of spirituality awakens holiness. It develops a positive attitude and sparks peak experiences. The Rebbe noted that Moses did not specify that no more materials should be brought, only that no more work should be done. As long as the people were aroused by a sense of holiness and dedication, they could not be restrained from bringing the necessities, while the work was being done. (*Ohev Yisroel*, p. 160)

⚊⚊

On the *Pasuk* "The Cherubim were with wings spread upward shelter- ing the cover with their wings, with their faces toward one another" (Ex. 37:9), the Belzer Rebbe commented that this refers to the concern of Hashem for the service of the Jew. When the prayers ascend upward, they give strength to the Upper Sphere. As the people face each other, they proclaim the equality of righteousness. Their dependence is on the merits of all people and those of our ancestors. Then the Almighty stands on the right side and listens with the attribute of justice. (M.D., p. 184)

~~~

On the *Pasuk* "He made the basin of copper . . . of the mirrors of the assembled" (Ex. 38:8), the Toldot Yaacov Yosef noted that the Maggid of Mezritch said that everyone should consider the other person as a mirror. When one sees the fault of others, then just as a mirror reflects, one can recognize oneself in them and therefore try to rectify one's faults. We learn this from the statement in the *Ethics of Our Fathers*: "Who is wise? He who learns from every person." (4:1) That is why when the *Kohanim* went to wash before they started the service, they had to cleanse themselves spiritually. They had to "wash" away all their blemishes and faults. It was the mirror of the basin that permitted them to reflect upon their faults as well as to see into the mirror of another, for it is very difficult to look at oneself and detect one's own faults. (M.T., vol. 2, p. 168)

PEKUDEI
"ACCOUNTING"

The Lubavitcher Rebbe made the following observation on the *Sidra Pekudei*. He said that the word *pekudei*, which means "accounting" or "reckoning," has significant meaning for the person as an individual and the individual as part of a people. The function of a reckoning is not the totality but the individual parts that make up the whole. The Rebbe commented that any reckoning presumes the existence of many elements, some positive and some negative. This we learn from the tallying of the gold, silver, and brass donated for the Sanctuary and the inventory of its utensils and services. The Sanctuary was dependent on its individual parts. If one part was missing, no matter how seemingly insignificant, the Sanctuary was incomplete, rendering it unfit as a resting place for Hashem. When all the individual parts, having different values, were brought together to form the whole, each fostered the presence of God by being part of the Sanctuary. (G.O.T., pp. 139–140)

⌒⌒

The Baal Shem Tov noted that in the *parsha* of "accounting," as each step in the Tabernacle was executed and as each utensil was made, they were followed by the words "as Hashem commanded Moses." The fact that the Torah does not say after the completion of the Tabernacle "as Hashem commanded Moses" teaches us of the importance of the individual mitzvah. When a mitzvah is performed with sincere intent, respect, and awe, it clothes the soul in the Garden of Eden below and above. As each person performs each and every mitzvah, whether eating during the week or the third meal of the Shabbat, and attaches himself to others in the performance of *mitzvot*, he unites the below with the above and thereby forms a completed task. (*Sefer Baal Shem Tov*, p. 122)

〜

"These are the accountings of the Tabernacle (*Mishkan*) of the Testimony." (Ex. 38:21) R' Yaakov Yitzchak Shapiro, the Rebbe from Blendov, commented that whenever the word "these" is stated in the Torah, it refers to the present and not what has occurred in the past. Therefore, in the *Pasuk* the word "these" refers to the person who has sinned and has repented. This person has chiseled away his earlier behavior and has now sanctified and purified his being. The Rebbe said that *mishkan* can also mean a dwelling within oneself. Therefore, the repentant sinner can become a "*Mishkan* of Testimony," one of those righteous individuals who give testimony to the ways of Hashem. We learn from this that though the Israelites sinned with the golden calf, nevertheless because they repented, they were permitted to build the Tabernacle. (M.D., p. 186)

〜

The Cherneboler Rebbe commented that Hashem has an accounting of Man since the beginning of Creation. However, Man should also give an accounting to himself. There should be a continual introspection. Before one speaks, one should remember that there exists a Divinity within oneself. (M.D., p. 185)

〜

On the same *Pasuk*, the Sochotchover compared the meaning of the statement in the Talmud, "Blessing is only possible in things hidden from sight" (*Taanit* 8b), to the accounting done by Moses. He noted that a blessing has an inner strength of holiness, which prefers modesty and secrecy, while the obvious is generally ruled by evil outwardness. Therefore, when the accounting was done through Moses, whom the Torah described as the most trusted one, outward evilness could not affect the blessing. Evil manifestations can only occur where falsehood is found. (M.T., p. 172)

～

On the phrase "they offered up gold" (Ex. 38:24), the Mezritcher Maggid said that they offered the gold with thankfulness because it was going for a good cause. We learn from this that when we do not do what is worthwhile with our money, our entire value system can be lowered. (F.U.A.O., p. 245)

～

On the words "a hundred sockets" (Ex. 38:27), the Chidushei Harim commented that just as there were a hundred sockets needed to hold up the Tabernacle, so too the hundred blessings that Jews are commanded to make each day hold up the holiness of each individual. (F.C.O., p. 266)

～

In the *sefer Imrey Shefer*, we find the following interpretation on the *Pasuk* "All the work of the Tabernacle, the Tent of Meeting, was completed; the Children of Israel did like all that Hashem commanded Moses, so did they do." (Ex. 39:32) He said that as long as the Israelites worked on the Tabernacle, they did not perform any other mitzvah. That is based on the rabbinic dictum that when one is performing one mitzvah, one is exempt from performing another. Therefore, when they finished the Tabernacle, they then performed the rest "that Hashem commanded Moses." (M.T., p. 177)

～

On the same *Pasuk*, the Dinever commented that the reason it said "did like" and "so did they do" was to teach us that the Tabernacle was built to perform the mitzvah—"All that Hashem had commanded Moses." It was not built to boast of having a beautiful structure. (M.D., p. 190)

～

On the *Pasuk* "Moses erected the *Mishkan*" (Ex. 40:18), the Chernovitzer commented that the knowledgeable people brought the necessary parts for the building of the Tabernacle to Moses. However, they could not bring a sense of holiness to the structure; that only Moses could accomplish. That is why it says: "And Moses erected the Tabernacle." He erected the Tabernacle properly so that it could be called "a *Mishkan*," a dwelling place for Hashem. (M.T., p. 181)

"When the cloud was raised up from upon the Tabernacle, the Children of Israel would journey on all their journeys." (Ex. 40:36) The Radamsker commented that it is imperative that there should be no obstruction between the one who is praying and the wall he is praying against. He said that symbolizes that there should be no partition between the one who prays and the Divine Presence. That is why "the cloud was raised," so that the Children of Israel would be able to go in the service of Hashem. (M.D., p. 192)

"For the cloud of Hashem would be on the Tabernacle by day, and fire would be on it at night, before the eyes of all the House of Israel in all their journeys." (Ex. 40:38) Commenting on this *Pasuk* and the *Pasuk* from *Kohelet*, "One who watches the wind will never sow, and one who keeps his eyes on the clouds will never reap," the Koznitzer Maggid said that the person who waits to pray till he gets into the mood is as "one who watches the wind." He will never sow and be in the service of Hashem. The one who prays but "sees the clouds," his mind is not clear while he is praying; he "will not reap." We must realize that when it comes to prayer and serving Hashem, the "cloud of Hashem" is always on us and the "fire" is always burning within us. Such should be our understanding of prayer and our journeys in the service of Hashem. (M.D., p. 192)

The Tarnigrader Rebbe said that the person who prays but allows his thoughts to stray from Hashem is like one who prepares his home for a banquet for a king and then leaves his home. (H.A., p. 344)

The Kotzker noted that we begin our services with *Adon Olom* and end with *Adon Olom*. He said that we do this to proclaim that we are never finished in praising Hashem. (H.A., p. 325)

WEEKLY PORTIONS OF VAYIKRAH/LEVITICUS

VAYIKRAH
"AND HE CALLED"

The Riziner commented that the reason there is a small *aleph* at the end of the word *Vayikrah* (Lev. 1:1) is to teach us humility. Hashem called to Moses because he was humble even though he was on a high spiritual level. This teaches us that while we are in the midst of prayer or the performance of a mitzvah, though we may be on a high spiritual level, we must still show humility. (F.C.O., p. 267)

The Rimanover also commented on the small *aleph* in the word *Vayikrah*. He said that it teaches us that a wise individual who tries to reach a high spiritual level through his wisdom may develop haughtiness. This may reflect a degrading form of service to Hashem because his ultimate goal is really self-adulation. Rather, one should give thought to the Almighty and reflect on His greatness. This will permit us to come to the conclusion that "Yours, O Hashem, is the righteousness, and ours is the shamefacedness." (Daniel 9:7) This type of humility will lead one to be dissatisfied with his present status of service to Hashem and strive toward a higher spiritual level. Thus, humility will not become a virtue in itself but a driving force to higher levels of service. (T.D.H.T.R., pp. 263–266)

The Cherneboler Rebbe gave a Kabbalistic interpretation as to why there is a small *aleph* at the end of the word *Vayikrah*. An essential aspect of Kabbalah is that while God contracted Himself at the time of Creation, nevertheless He allowed the sparks of His Holiness to penetrate all aspects of life. Therefore, the small *aleph* symbolizes the withdrawal of Hashem, but because it is part of *Vayikrah*, we say that the Almighty "is calling." Not every individual can hear this call or is able to understand it. However, even an evil person possesses this spark. That gives him the inspiration to do repentance. It is when a person hears this call that it becomes "And God spoke to him in the Tabernacle" (Lev. 1:1), which causes the overflowing of Divine Holiness. (M.D., p. 193)

The Belzer noted that the falsely humble believe themselves and all others to be unworthy. The truly humble feels that he is unworthy and everyone else is worthier than himself. (H.A., p. 186)

To understand humility, the Lekhivitzer noted that one must look at the clock. As each hour passes, each one should ask himself, at the hour: Have I accomplished any improvement of my soul? (H.A., p. 189)

The Degel Machnei Ephraim noted that the small *aleph* should teach us that as one learns Torah, he should acquire more humility. There are those who learn and therefore consider themselves greater than others because they think that they know all that is to be known. However, the Chasid understands that the more he learns, the more he is humbled. (*Degel Machnei Ephraim*, p. 136)

R' Bunim of Pshys'cha taught that because the thoughts and actions of the arrogant are filled with selfishness, there is no room for holiness. However, those who are humble and have learned to reject selfishness should strive to fill their minds with holiness; otherwise, of what use is their humility? (H.A., p. 192)

The Torah states: "If any man brings an offering (*korban*) of you to Hashem: from the animals—from the cattle and from the flocks. . . ." (Lev. 1:2). The Lubavitcher Rebbe, Rabbi Menachem Mendel Schneerson, noted that this *Pasuk* is a commentary on the whole nature of sacrifice. Because *korban* can also mean "drawing near" (*korban* and *kiruv* have the same root letters), it shows that when a Jew wishes to draw near to Hashem he must make a sacrifice to Hashem of his very self. It is an inner act of the person; the offering must be the "you," the Godly soul. "From the cattle" refers to the animal soul, which constitutes all physical desires. It is this second offering that is the ultimate aim of sacrifice. It is the sanctification and redirection of the "animal" in man. When an animal was to be sacrificed on the altar, the first thing done was to confirm that it was whole, perfect, and without blemish; only then could it be offered. So it is with man. The "animal" within him must be without blemish before it can be sacrificed. The first step is self-examination. One must search sincerely and without a perfunctory sense of duty. He must search the inner depths of his soul for faults, and once found, he must correct them. His whole spiritual integrity depends on it. Once he realizes what is at stake, he will not cover his faults in self-deception or leave them to fester uncured. Once the blemishes are corrected, the "animal" is sacrificed. The physical drives become spiritual. The Godly and the animal souls are spiritually united. (T.S., pp. 153–158)

"When a person from among you (*mikem*) will bring an offering to Hashem." (Lev. 1:2) The Zanzer Rebbe translated the word *mikem* as "within you." He said that when a person sacrifices himself for something, it should be from "within," that is, with sincerity and devotion of purpose. (F.C.O., p. 268)

On the same *Pasuk*, the Sassover said that when a person does something from the depths of his heart, it means more than any sacrifice. (F.C.O., p. 268)

There are individuals who fast and perform acts of self-castigation as a means of sacrifice. "This is the way of the evil inclination," said the Baal Shem Tov, "to weaken the individual physically so that he will not be able to serve Hashem properly." (F.C.O., p. 269)

The Linzensker noted that Hashem has more satisfaction when one learns two pages of the Talmud than when he spends time fasting. (F.C.O., p. 269)

The Alexander Rebbe noted Rashi's comment on the phrase "You (*atem*) shall bring an offering." (Lev. 1:2) Rashi said: "This teaches that two may donate an *olah* offering in partnership," because the words are written in second person plural. Therefore, the Rebbe remarked that a complete sacrifice can only be offered with a sincere feeling of brotherhood and friendship. One must participate in all communal activities. (M.T., vol. 3, p. 14)

"He shall skin the *olah* offering and cut it into pieces." (Lev. 1:6) The Kremnitzer commented that this means that one should tear away the arrogance from within. One will then notice that he is a person with blemishes to be corrected. (F.C.O., p. 272)

On the same *Pasuk*, in the *sefer Arvei Nachal* we find that the Sochatchover gave advice to the individual who had good qualities but was concerned that he might become arrogant. The Rebbe told him that he should dissect and examine his behavior. If he wished to separate himself from arrogance and strengthen the positive within himself, he should "cut into pieces" his deeds, and give attention to his better qualities. (M.T., vol. 3, p. 17)

The Kotzker noted that a person is born with jealousy. Once it is nourished and it becomes a habit, desires develop. (*Amud HaEmet*, p. 89)

On the phrase "a pleasing fragrance to Hashem" (Lev. 1:13), the Chidushei Harim commented that a pleasing fragrance can be detected from afar. He said that means that a sacrifice must be brought from the best. The person bringing the sacrifice must develop good deeds, which is the fragrance of a sacrifice. That is what Hashem meant by "Why do I need your sacrifices?" (Is. 1:11) Your good deeds should come before you bring the sacrifice. That will bring "a pleasing fragrance to Hashem." (M.T., vol. 3, p. 273)

"It shall be of fine flour mixed with oil." (Lev. 2:7) The Koznitzer Maggid commented that if a person wishes to be like "fine flour," he must divest himself of all wrongdoing. Then he should mix his repentance "with oil," repenting with free will and joy. Repentance with joy is the honest return to a spiritual life. (M.D., p. 198)

"When a person will sin unintentionally against any of the prohibitions of Hashem that may not be done, and he commits any one of them." (Lev. 4:2) The Berditchever asked: If the sin was unintentional then what was the sin that was committed? He said that the sin was that though he performed the *mitzvot*, he did them with arrogance. (F.C.O., p. 273)

On the same *Pasuk*, the Savraner noted that people who inadvertently sin show immediate regret for their action. However, when sins are intentional, such as speaking untruths, they feel no regret but gloss over their prayers concerning their offenses. (H.A., p. 445)

⌐⌐

On the phrase "He commits any one of them," the Kedushas Levi comments that this refers to the person who performs a mitzvah and therefore thinks that he is a servant of Hashem, giving the impression that the performance of the mitzvah puts more clothing on God, which is a sin. (*Kedushas Levi*, p. 129)

⌐⌐

"Thus shall the *Kohen* provide him atonement for his sin, and it shall be forgiven him." (Lev. 4:26) R' Tzadok of Lublin commented that this covers individual sacrifice, public sacrifice, and the sacrifice given by a leader. Everywhere these sacrifices are mentioned, the phrase "It shall be forgiven him" is said. However, when the "anointed *Kohen*" is referred to, these words do not appear, for the *Kohen* himself brings the sacrifice. One can only forgive someone else, not oneself. (F.U.A.O., vol. 3, p. 21)

⌐⌐

On that same thought, the Alexander Rebbe noted that the *Amidah* is said silently by the congregation but the Cantor's repetition is said aloud. The congregation is praying for itself, and that is done quietly; the Cantor is praying on behalf of the congregation, and that must be done aloud. (F.U.A.O., vol. 3, p. 21)

⌐⌐

"But if his means are insufficient for a sheep or goat, then he shall bring as his guilt offering for that which he sinned: two turtledoves or two young doves to Hashem, one for a sin offering and one for an *olah* offering." (Lev. 5:7) The Kuzmirer's concern was that the wealthy brought one lamb for a sin offering while the poor brought two doves, one as a burnt offering and one for a sin offering. He said that the poor bring the dove to blame God for neglecting them, showing that they cannot bring more than the little dove. The Midrash (*Vayikrah Rabbah* 7:3) states that the burnt offering was brought to gain forgiveness for evil thoughts. Therefore, the poor who complain about the ways of Hashem are required to bring the second sacrifice. (H.A., p. 93)

"If a person sins . . . but was unaware and became guilty." (Lev. 5:17) The Kotzker Rebbe said that when a person is not sure if he has transgressed, he must bring a more expensive animal than when he is sure. This means that he is vague about his actions. However, when a person knows that he has transgressed, it is already half of repentance. (F.U.A.O., vol. 3, p. 23)

When the Torah is read in the synagogue, the law is that we are not permitted to end the *parsha* with something on a bad note. Therefore, the Rimanover noted, there was a custom that when the final words of the last sentence of the *Sidra Vayikrah*, *L'ashmah bah* — "for any of all the things he might do to incur guilt" (Lev. 5:26)—were read, the entire congregation would rise and say, using the letters of *L'ashmah bah*, *L'El asher shovas mikol ha'maasim b'yom Hashve'e*—"To the God who rested from all His work on the seventh day." (F.C.O., p. 275)

TZAV
"COMMAND"

On the *Pasuk* "Command Aharon and his sons . . ." (Lev. 6:2), Rashi noted that R' Shimon said, "The Torah must especially urge in a situation where there is loss of money." The *Kohanim* had suffered financial loss because they were not paid for their sacrificial service and had given up their regular means of earning a livelihood. The S'fas Emes noted that therefore the word "command" is stressed and is a lesson for our day as well. In troublesome times when one is concerned with earning a living, it becomes difficult to follow the *mitzvot*. Then our actions become testing grounds for our faith and we must put forth much greater effort. (F.C.O., p. 276)

On the same words, Rashi comments: "Command means to express urging for the immediate moment and for future generations." R' Yaacov Yosef of Polnoye said that "to urge" refers to "future generations," when those who will be our spiritual leaders, based on succession, will have finance as their main concern. It will be impossible to engage these leaders without financial recompense. That is the reason why there must be a command. (F.U.A.O., vol. 3, p. 28)

On the same *Pasuk*, the Lubavitcher Rebbe noted that there are three terms that introduce a commandment: *emor* ("tell"), *dabber* ("speak to"), and *tzav* ("command"). All three terms communicate God's will.

The terms "tell" and "speak to" appear to leave options in the hands of the listener. Obviously, though a directive was given, the words imply that he has a choice. However, where the word *tzav* (command) is used, though there is choice, the command is of such a forceful nature that it pressures one toward the fulfillment of the mitzvah. (G.O.T., pp. 151–154)

~~~

"This is the law of the *olah* offering that stays on the flame . . . all night until the morning." (Lev. 6:2) The Koznitzer commented that the laws of the *olah* cause the offering to rise upward. So, too, learning will reach great heights if done with a burning desire. (F.C.O., p. 276)

~~~

On the same *Pasuk*, Rashi comments: "Every time the term 'Law' is mentioned it is as if to say there should be one law for all offerings that ascend unto the *mizbe'ach* (altar). Even those that are disqualified—if they ascended even though they should not have, they should not descend." The Kobriner noted that this is the greatness of learning Torah. Even when one learns Torah and departs from it, he is not lost. There is still hope that he will see the light and return. (F.U.A.O., vol. 3, p. 31)

~~~

The Kotzker noted that the Hebrew word for flame, *mokdah*, is written with a small *mem* at the beginning of the word. This teaches us that the burning desire the Jew has for observances should be kept subdued because it comes from the depths of his soul. There is no need to be boastful of the observance. (F.C.O., p. 277)

~~~

On the words "all night until the morning" (Lev. 6:2), R' Aharon Karliner commented that when a person feels depressed, he should try to overcome it during the time that it seems dark so that he will see the light at daybreak. (F.C.O., p. 280)

On the *Pasuk* "The *Kohen* shall put on his linen garment, and linen breeches shall he put on his body, and he shall lift up the ashes that the fire has made" (Lev. 6:3), R' Bunim of Pshys'cha commented that the Torah commanded the High Priest that when he entered the Holy of Holies on Yom Kippur, he should change his clothing and remove the ashes. He changes his clothing so that at that moment of intense holiness, when the holiest Jew on the holiest day enters the holiest place, he should not forget the basic mundane situations, such as asking for sustenance for his people. Therefore, he was commanded to change to weekday clothing and begin to consider the weekday necessities of his people. (F.U.A.O., vol. 3, p. 33)

There is an interesting story told about the Baal Shem Tov that emphasizes the significance of sincere intentions. Standing in front of a house of learning, he refused to enter, informing the people that he could not come in because the place was already full of learning and prayer. He explained that when one learns Torah and prays with sincere intent the words go heavenward. However, when the words of Torah are just intellectual gymnastics and the words of prayer are frozen in place, then they fill up the entire house of worship and there is no place to enter. (F.C.O., p. 277)

"And he shall remove the ashes to the outside of the camp, to a pure place." (Lev. 6:4) The Izbitzer commented that even the Jew who has left the camp, the correct path, and whose faults do not have the Divine spark may still have redeeming features. Therefore, one should never give up hope, for he may yet return to the pure path. (F.C.O., p. 281)

"A fire, continually, shall remain aflame on the altar; you shall not extinguish it." (Lev. 6:6) On this *Pasuk*, the Baal Shem Tov said, "Our heart is the altar and no matter what we do, we should let the holy fire remain within us so that we may fan it into a flame." (H.A., p. 173)

~~~

On the same *Pasuk*, in his *sefer B'er Mayim Chayim*, the Chernovitzer Rebbe commented that there should be a continuous fire burning on the altar in one's heart. On this altar one should sacrifice the "ashes"—his evil inclinations—and thereby minimize his desires and subdue them, so that his righteous acts are enhanced. That is what is meant by "continuous fire": to be constantly in the service of Hashem and to understand the spiritual life. Maimonides noted, in the name of our Sages, that of two people who eat from the Paschal offering, one may eat because it is a mitzvah. Of this person it is said: "The righteous do walk in them." (Hos. 14:10) The other one may eat of it because of his appetite. Of this person it is said: "Transgressors do stumble therein." (Hos. 14:10) (M.D., p. 206)

~~~

"This is the law of the sin offering." (Lev. 6:18) The Mishnah (*Zevachim*, ch. 5) states: "Regarding sin offerings of the community and of the individual, the communal sin offerings are the following: he-goats of Rosh Chodesh. . . ." The Riziner commented that we are faced with a dilemma in that the Mishnah enumerates the communal sin offerings but does not mention the sin offering of the individual. Our Sages said that as Hashem commanded us to sacrifice on Rosh Chodesh a communal sin offering—"Bring unto Me an atonement offering for My diminishing the moon" (Talmud *Chulin* 60b)—we derive the meaning that there is a sin offering that the community brings for the individual—"The sin offering of the community and individual . . . the he-goats of Rosh Chodesh." (F.U.A.O., vol. 3, p. 36)

~~~

"In the place where the burnt offering is slaughtered shall the sin offering be slaughtered." (Lev. 6:18) The Rebbe of Satmar commented that the burnt offering was given to ask forgiveness for the reflections of the heart. The sin offering was given to ask forgiveness for transgression of actions. We know that all actions begin with a thought process. Those who stumble in an unintentional transgression have given no reflection to the process of thinking. It is therefore incumbent upon the righteous individual to attach himself to Hashem so that there should be no defect in his thought process. He should start the purification process with thoughts. In this way he will not reach the level of wrongdoing in deeds. That is why the burnt offering and the sin offering were slaughtered in the same place. (M.D., p. 67)

SHEMINI
"EIGHTH DAY"

The Lubavitcher Rebbe noted that in Jewish mystical thinking, numbers signify the spiritual forces. Seven is a fundamental number, symbolic of the seven Divine attributes, which illustrate the different levels of our emotions. The Sabbath, which is the seventh day, represents the highest in our natural order. The seventh then prepares us for the eighth, which is a higher level of holiness, namely the Godly light that transcends the limits of our world. The "Glory of God" is the spiritual peak, above the natural order. Thus, our Sages state that the Era of Redemption will be of eight strands. (Talmud *Archin* 13b) The Era of Redemption will permit all mortals to see the spiritual truth. This was described by the prophet Isaiah, who said, "The Glory of God will be revealed and all flesh will see." (Is. 40:5) (G.O.T., pp. 157–159)

～

"Moses said: This is the thing that Hashem has commanded you to do; then the Glory of Hashem will appear to you." (Lev. 9:6) R' Zusia commented that if a person wishes to know if his action is a mitzvah, "the thing that Hashem has commanded you," first he must examine his actions to see "if the Glory of Hashem will appear to you." (F.C.O., p. 283)

～

On the same *Pasuk*, the Kotzker commented that the Jews were ready to reach higher levels of holiness. Moses said that if you wish to reach the

higher levels, first take care of what is at hand. Remove the evil inclination from you and automatically "the Glory of Hashem will appear to
you" and the holiness will reach its level. (M.T., vol. 3, p. 46)

⌐⌐

On the same *Pasuk*, the Chidushei Harim commented that the words
"This is the thing" are specific. That is why they are preceded with the
"definite hey"—"the thing." This teaches us which of the evil inclinations should be removed. We are requested to remove hatred, dissension, and communal conflict from our hearts. "This is the thing Hashem
commanded us to do." (M.T., vol. 3, p. 46)

⌐⌐

The Bratzlaver noted that one should rejoice so much in the performance of a mitzvah that it should bring a greater desire to perform
another mitzvah. (*Kitzur Likkutei Maharan*, p. 8)

⌐⌐

"And any meal offering that is mixed with oil or that is dry, it shall
belong to all of Aharon's sons, every man alike." (Lev. 7:10) The Vorker
explained that from this *Pasuk* we learn that the observant Jew who
brings a voluntary offering and the sinner who brings a sin offering
should be treated equally with a friendly and brotherly attitude, for it
says: "every man alike." (F.U.A.O., vol. 3, p. 38)

⌐⌐

"Aharon raised his hands toward the people and blessed them; and he
descended from having performed the sin offering, the *olah* offering,
and the peace offering." (Lev. 9:22) The Radamsker commented that
the Talmud states: "One does not bypass a mitzvah." (Talmud *Pesachim*
64b) It is the way of the evil inclination to hold back an individual as he
approaches to serve Hashem, especially as he begins to pray. The inclination asks how a person can approach holiness when he is full of
transgression. That is really not the case, insisted the Radamsker. He
said that Hashem listens to all and has mercy on all. While performing
mitzvot, one does not think of his transgressions. When one is doing

good, the evil that lurks in the heart is removed and he does not think of anything else. That is the meaning of "He descended from having performed the sin offering, the *olah* offering, and the peace offering." While Aharon was blessing Israel, he did not remember any of their transgressions. (M.D., p. 212)

~~~

The Chidushei Harim noted that the error made by Aharon's sons Nadav and Avihu was that though they were righteous people, they did not understand the phrase "that He had not commanded them." (Lev. 10:1) They did not realize that when Hashem commands, they should not interpret the mitzvah through reasoning. That is why we say, "that Hashem has commanded us," before the performance of a commandment. That teaches us that one's performance does not involve one's rationalization. (F.C.O., p. 283)

~~~

"Hashem spoke to Aharon, saying: Do not drink intoxicating wine, you and your sons with you, when you come to the Tent of Meeting, that you not die. This is an eternal decree for your generations—to distinguish between the sacred and profane, and between the impure and the pure, and to teach the Children of Israel." (Lev. 10:8) The Ropshitzer Rebbe commented that this instructs us to when we can drink: "You and your sons with you" means a wedding; "When you come to the Tent of Meeting"—at a dedication of a new structure; "That you not die"—when cured from a sickness; "This is an eternal decree"—at a circumcision celebration; "To distinguish between the sacred and the profane"—when making *Kiddush* and *Havdalah*; "Between pure and impure"—on Purim (pure—Mordechai, and impure—Haman); "To teach the Children of Israel"—at a celebration at the end of Torah learning. (F.C.O., p. 284)

~~~

Concerning the bird "the *chasidah*" (Lev. 11:19), Rashi comments: "Why has its name been designated as, literally, 'kind one'? For its kindness with its companions with food." The Yid HaKadosh wondered why it is

considered a nonkosher bird if it is known for its kindness. He noted
that it is considered nonkosher because its kindness is only for its
companions and nobody else. (F.C.O., p. 286)

～～

"And all that walks on its paws." (Lev. 11:27) R' Bunim of Pshys'cha
noted that this teaches us that a person who performs a mitzvah with his
hands but without thought, or inner intent and feeling, is like one who
does things with his paws. (F.U.A.O., vol. 3, p. 60)

～～

"You are to sanctify yourselves and you shall become holy, for I am
holy." (Lev. 11:44) The Izbitzer noted that the Almighty watches Israel
to make sure that they should become holy. He puts a protective fence
around them with commands concerning forbidden foods, relations,
and other behavior. One who neglects the fences is not purified enough
to follow the will of Hashem. The statement "You shall be holy" is
Hashem's guarantee, for self-purification is a difficult task—therefore
the need for fences. (M.D., p. 212)

～～

"For I am Hashem Who brings you up from the land of Egypt to be a
God unto you; you shall be holy, for I am Holy." (Lev. 11:45) The
Zanzer Rebbe commented that the Torah cautions us that because
we are His people we should be holy, for the Almighty is Holy. But
we are physical beings, and so it may be difficult to approach holiness.
The second part of the *Pasuk* explains the reason why we can reach
holiness. "Who brings you up from the land of Egypt" tells us that while
we were in Egypt, Hashem took it upon Himself to extract the physical
impurities from us. Therefore, we cannot say that the physical impurities stop us from reaching holiness. Hashem brought us out of Egypt "to
be a God unto you; you shall be holy, for I am holy." (M.D., p. 216)

～～

On the *Pasuk* "For distinguishing between the impure and the pure"
(Lev. 11:47), Rashi comments: "Between one that has half of its wind-

pipe slaughtered and one that has most of it slaughtered. . . ." R' Bunim of Pshys'cha noted that it takes very little to go from "half" to "whole"—a little nothing. That is all it takes to go from purity to impurity, from Paradise to *Gehinom*. (F.U.A.O., vol. 3, p. 64)

TAZRIA
"CONCEIVES"

The previous *Sidra* explains the laws of the pure and impure animals. This *Sidra* explains the laws of purity and impurity of the human being. Rashi quotes *Vayikrah Rabbah* (14:1): "That just as the fashioning of man came after all cattle, beasts, and fowl in the Torah account of the act of Creation, so the law of the human being is explained after the law of cattle, beast, and fowl." R' Moshe Sofer of Preshburg, in his *sefer Toras Moshe*, said that the Israelites attained a high spiritual level because of the existence of the *Mishkan*. To prevent them from becoming arrogant and considering themselves higher than the angels, the Torah gave the laws concerning the animals first because the impure among people are worse that the animals. Man has choice and therefore can bring impurity upon himself. (M.T., vol. 3, p. 65)

On the *Pasuk* "When a woman conceives and gives birth to a male, she shall be impure . . ." (Lev. 12:2), the Kotzker commented that impurity reminds one of the removal of holiness. Where purity is removed, impurity replaces it. When a woman gives birth, our Sages tell us that Hashem has the key, as it is written: "And Hashem opened her womb." (Gen. 29:31) At the moment when a woman gives birth, she is at a high degree of holiness. Obviously, after she gives birth, she is in a state of impurity. (M.T., vol. 3, p. 66)

"She may not touch anything sacred and she may not enter the Sanctuary until the completion of her days of purity." (Lev. 12:4) The Noam Elimelech interprets this *Pasuk* as teaching that a person cannot arbitrarily make a connection with anything holy, because it has the Presence of the Divine. The connection can only be made after many years of correction of deeds and purification of soul. Before purity, holiness cannot be reached. (M.T., p. 66)

"When a woman conceives and gives birth to a male." (Lev. 12:2) "She gives birth to a female." (Lev. 12:5) The Lubavitcher Rebbe interpreted these *Pasukim* as corresponding to the planting of seeds and the significance of an intimate relationship. The term *tazria* itself means "gives seed," and *mitzvot* as well are referred to as "seeds," as in Hosea 10:12: "Sow for yourselves charity." The Rebbe said that every mitzvah performed brings with it Divine energy into our material world that will blossom and bear fruit. The description of the relationship between God and the Jewish people is analogous to the love between a man and a woman that is a growing dynamic union, as it states in the Zohar (vol. 3, 73a): "The Holy One and Israel are one." They are joined, as was stated by the prophet Isaiah: "Your Maker is your mate." (G.O.T., pp. 163–165)

"If a person (*adam*) will have on the skin a *s'eis*, or a *sapachas*, or a *baheres* (swelling, rising, bright spot). . . ." (Lev. 13:2) The Izbitzer Rebbe commented that in Hebrew the human being is called by four names: *ish*, *gever*, *enosh*, and *adam*. According to the Zohar, the term *adam* is the highest level. Since the disease is a punishment for speaking evil, it appears that speaking evil is prevalent even among the highest level of human being. (F.U.A.O., vol. 3, p. 72)

~~~

On the same *Pasuk*, R' Moshe Chayim Ephraim of Sadilkov, in his Sefer *Degel Machnei Ephraim*, noted that there are many obstacles that can occur in life—even in the category of *adam*, the highest designation of human qualities. The three obstacles are "swelling" (*s'eis*)—uncalled-for arrogance; "rising" (*sapachas*)—befriending evil people and pursuing the accumulation of wealth; and bright spot (*baheres*)—strange thoughts, or trying to understand logically theories that are contrary to ways of Hashem. (F.C.O., p. 289)

~~~

"And it will become an affliction on the skin of flesh; he shall be brought to Aharon the *Kohen*." (Lev. 13:2) The S'fas Emes commented that at the time of Creation, the Divine Presence shone throughout the natural world. Man was surrounded with such holiness that he was able to feel and understand the spiritual life. The strength of evil was overpowered by Godly power. After the sin of man, the Divine Presence became hidden. The world became polluted with evil and true inner Divinity was hidden from man. That is why the *Pasuk* states: "And Hashem made for Adam and his wife a coat of skin." (*Bereshit* 3:21) Everything was covered with clothing of skin; however, just as the skin has pores, so too does the covering in nature have a slit for the Divine supervision to be seen, so that it will shine through to give light to the world. When we see only the affliction, then we must go to the Spiritual Leader to pierce the Heavenly skin. Therefore, the *Pasuk* states that when there was an affliction of the skin, the *Kohen* was to see how deep the affliction was. (M.T., vol. 3, p. 70)

~~~

"The *Kohen* will look at the affliction. . . . the *Kohen* shall look at it and make him impure." (Lev. 13:3) R' Meir Simcha D'Vinsker noted that the words "the *Kohen* will look" is mentioned twice. He commented that when the affliction, considered impure, occurred on a holiday, the person was set free. The reason is that the afflicted should participate in a joyous occasion. First, the *Kohen* should look at the affliction and then he should consider the situation in which the person finds himself. This teaches us that there should be concern for the person with the affliction and the circumstances at the time. (F.U.A.O., vol. 3, p. 74)

METZORA
"LEPER"

R' Elimelech Grodzenser noted that the Hebrew word *hametzora* (Lev. 14:2), "leper," can be divided into *hamotzey ra*, which means "brings forth evil." He commented that when one speaks evil of another, one becomes a leper. (F.C.O., p. 294)

The Baal Shem Tov noted that when one embarrasses another he really is embarrassing himself. If one praises someone, it is as if he is praising himself. (*Toldot Yaacov Yosef*, vol. 1, p. 318)

The Bratzlaver made the following comments about speech:

1. Poverty befalls one who speaks spitefully.
2. Evil talk creates a belligerent person, bringing with it constant wrongdoing in his actions.
3. Both the speaker and the listener are adversely affected by evil speech.
4. Evil words are wings for impiety and unbelief.
5. The sincere study of Torah, the worship of Hashem from the heart, and the speaking of truth will prevent evil talk. (*Likkutei Eytzus*, pp. 55–56)

~~~

"The man who desires life loves days of seeing good. Guard your tongue from evil and your lips from speaking deceit." (Ps. 34:13–14) R' Shlomo Belzer commented that if a person wishes to acquire a decent home and all the necessities that one needs to lead a good life, then let him "Guard your tongue from evil and your lips from speaking deceit." (F.C.O., p. 294)

~~~

On the saying "The reward is in proportion to the exertion" (*Ethics of Our Fathers* 5:26), the Mezibozer commented that to speak evil of someone begets one much grief. However, when one learns Torah and prays, one receives a reward. (F.C.O., p. 294)

~~~

"And the affliction was healed." (Lev. 14:3) The Oheler Rebbe commented that when the affliction comes from speaking evil about someone, then the only cure is for that person to examine every deed and stop speaking evil. (F.C.O., p. 294)

~~~

On the *Pasuk* "You shall separate (*v'hizartem*) the Children of Israel from their impurity" (Lev. 15:31), R' Uziel Meizlish, in his *sefer Tiferet Uziel*, noted that the word *z'rut*, meaning "odd," is derived from the word *v'hizartem*. Therefore, the meaning of the *Pasuk* is that impurity should be strange to you. (M.D., p. 232)

~~~

On the *Pasuk* "For the person being purified, he should bring cedarwood, a crimson wool (*tola'at*), and hyssop" (Lev. 14:4), Rashi comments that afflictions come because of haughtiness. He said that in order to be cured a person should "lower himself from his arrogance like a worm" (*tola'at* can mean both "dyed wool" and "worm"), "and like hyssop," which does not grow tall. The Sochotchover noted that even if one has repented it does not necessarily bring true humility. That comes only when a person understands the greatness of the Almighty and the "nothingness" of man. Humbleness may come from a broken heart, a serious illness, or extreme poverty, but it is not true humility because once these conditions are gone, there may be a return to haughtiness. A person may be embarrassed because of his *metzora* (being a leper) and therefore repent to be purified. That is why "he must lower himself," so that even when he becomes pure, he must understand that true humility does not come as a result of affliction but through the understanding of the greatness of the Almighty. (M.T., vol. 3, p. 87)

Commenting on Rashi's statement, the Chidushei Harim noted that the "cedarwood" alludes to arrogance and the "hyssop" alludes to humility. Both need atonement, for a person may transgress by being either arrogant or humble. A person may be arrogant and ready to trample anyone who damages his honor, and yet show humility when approached for a favor — declining with the excuse that he has no power to help. (F.C.O., p. 295)

R' Bunim of Pshys'cha commented on "Who humbles the haughty and lifts the lowly" (Prayer Book). He said: "What reason is there to raise the lowly? If they are satisfied to be lowly, isn't that a virtue? However, Hashem raises the truly humble, for He is fully aware that even when they are raised they will not become haughty." (M.T., vol. 3, p. 87)

R' Pinchas Koritzer asked how it is possible to be haughty, for the Torah forbids this attitude, as it says: "Arrogance is an abomination to Hashem." (Prov. 16:5) If one does not fulfill the commands of the Torah, of what does he show his arrogance? (F.C.O., p. 295)

"This is the law (Torah) of one in whom there is an affliction." (Lev. 14:32) The Radamsker taught that when one learns Torah for its own sake that will be the cure for the affliction. (M.D., p. 230)

⌇⌇

"You shall separate the Children of Israel from their impurity; and they shall not die as a result of their impurity." (15:31) In the *sefer Tiferet Uziel*, the author notes that the Hebrew word for "separate" is *zayrut*, which comes from the root word *zarah*, meaning "foreign." This teaches that impurity should be foreign to you. (M.D., p. 232)

⌇⌇

On the same *Pasuk*, the Zighter Rebbe commented that one should not separate himself from impurity because of the fear of punishment of death. The separation should be based on the statement in the *Ethics of Our Fathers*: "Do not be as servants who serve their masters for the sake of receiving a reward. . . . Let the awe of Heaven be upon you." If one loves truth for its own sake, then one should serve Hashem because that is the will of Hashem. One should be concerned with the process rather than the result and be a servant of Hashem to bring purity to the world. (M.D., p. 232)

ACHAREI
"AFTER"

"Hashem spoke to Moses after the death of Aharon's two sons, when they approached before Hashem, and they died." (Lev. 16:1) Based on this *Pasuk*, the Lubavitcher Rebbe commented on the method of serving the Almighty and its consequence. The Rebbe said that Aharon's sons had reached a very high level of bonding to Hashem and yet died because of it. "Chasidic thought develops the concept that our love for God must involve two phases: *ratzu*, a powerful yearning for connection with Him; and *shuv*, a commitment to return and express God's will by making this world a dwelling for Him." Their sin was not the closeness they established with Hashem, but the fact that their connection did not bear fruit. They died without having expressed this bond in the realm of ordinary experience, that is, bringing the Divine into daily activity. Hashem's intention is that the deepest levels of love for Him be demonstrated in an appreciation for the Godliness that inhabits every element of creation. The Divine service and the death of Aharon's sons provide us with two lessons. The first is that every Jew has a potential to draw close to Hashem. The second is that the service should not lack the vital element of *shuv*, to serve Him within the context of our world. The public world of the Jew and his private world of religious experiences should be intrinsically related. (G.O.T., pp. 1–5)

⌒⌒

"Hashem said to Moses, 'Speak to Aharon, your brother—he may not come at all times into the Sanctuary.'" (Lev. 16:2) The Riziner commented that based on *Kohelet*, there are twenty-eight circumstances in life; half are good and the other half negative. We are told to give thanks to the Almighty for the good and not be disappointed when something bad occurs. This is what was told to Aharon. He was told that he should not come to the Sanctuary only when there are bad times, but when there are good times as well. "With this shall Aharon come into the Sanctuary. . . ."(Lev. 16:3) He should come "As we bless for what is good, so must we bless on what is bad." (Talmud *Berachot* 54a) We must accept everything that the Almighty gives. This is based on the principle that whatever happens, happens for the best. (F.C.O., p. 298)

～～

"With this (*b'zot*) shall Aharon come into the Sanctuary (*HaKodesh*)." (Lev. 16:3) R' Dovid Talener commented that the word *b'zot* is numerically equivalent to *shafal*, meaning "humble." One must come to *kedushah* (holiness) with humility. (M.D., p. 234)

～～

At the Passover seder we are told that if one swallows the bitter herb he has not fulfilled the performance of the command to eat of the bitter herb. The Yid HaKadosh taught that conversely if a person goes through bad times he should not constantly mull over it. (F.C.O., p. 298)

～～

The Koznitzer, commenting on the statement "Do not despair of problems" (*Ethics of Our Fathers* 1:7), said that when bad times occur one should not give up hope, for there is mercy. (F.C.O., p. 298)

～～

The Baal Shem Tov said that the *Pasuk* ". . . that dwells with them amid their impurity" (Lev. 16:16) teaches us that Hashem dwells with us even when we are impure through sin. But with the arrogant, the Sages tell us that Hashem says: "He and I cannot dwell together." (Talmud *Sotah* 5a) (F.C.O., p. 301)

〜〜

On the same *Pasuk*, there is an interesting story told about R' Heschel Apter. Upon his arrival in a town, there developed a dispute between two owners of inns. Each wanted the Apter to be a guest at his inn. Each one had a specific failing: One was an observant person but arrogant; the other was a kind-hearted person but not as observant. When the Apter chose the not-as-observant person, he explained that it says that Hashem cannot dwell where an arrogant person is. "If Hashem cannot dwell in that house," said the Apter, "how can I?" (F.C.O., p. 301)

〜〜

"For on this day He shall provide atonement for you to cleanse you; from all your sins before Hashem shall you be cleansed." (Lev. 16:30) R' Avraham Yehoshuah Heschel of Meziboz commented that it is very significant that this *Pasuk* is read during the time that we count the *Omer*. We know that as we count the *Omer*, we must feel as if we were entering the portals of Holiness. This attitude is necessary to cleanse ourselves for the day of receiving the Torah. "For on this day," if we count each day with a sense of purity and holiness, "He shall provide atonement from all your sins." For seven weeks, every Jew should rectify his misdeeds so that he may come in holiness and purity and "before Hashem shall you be cleansed"—you shall be pure before Hashem in the acceptance of the Torah. (M.D., p. 236)

〜〜

"Any person (*nefesh*) who will eat that which died by itself or was mauled. . . ." (Lev. 17:15) The Sochotchover commented that the *Pasuk* does not use the word *ish* for "person" but uses the word *nefesh*, meaning "soul." This shows, as Maimonides declared, that when one eats forbidden food, both his body and soul, his physical and spiritual aspects, are affected. (F.U.A.O., vol. 3, p. 102)

〜〜

"Like the practice of the land of Egypt in which you dwelled do not do; and do not perform the practice of the land of Canaan to which I bring you, and do not follow their statutes." (Lev. 18:3) The S'fas Emes commented that this refers not only to transgressions; it teaches us that even actions that are permitted should not be imitated. We should not eat as they do, we should not drink as they do, and we should not even sleep as they do. (F.C.O., p. 302)

On the *Pasuk* "Carry out My judgments and observe My decrees to follow them . . ." (Lev. 18:4), the Kedushas Levi commented that "decrees" mean *mitzvot* for which reasons are not given and "judgments" are *mitzvot* for which reasons are given. When people perform *mitzvot* that do not have reasons, they are more likely to perform *mitzvot* that do have reasons. Also, it is less likely that when people do not perform *mitzvot* that are decrees, that they will do the *mitzvot* that are judgments. That is what is meant by "My judgments and . . . decrees" should be carried out and observed, for when one performs *mitzvot* without knowing the reason he will observe other *mitzvot*. He knows that both are needed to live. (*Kedushas Levi*, p. 141)

"You shall observe My decrees and My judgments, which man shall carry out and live by them; I am Hashem." (Lev. 18:5) Rabbi Avraham Moshe Rabinowitz, the Skoyler Rebbe, noted that in the Zohar it is stated that a Holy Place is called a private domain. The place of evil (*kelipot*) is in the public domain. The Baal Shem Tov said that the *Pasuk* in Noach 6:16, "You shall make a window (*tzohar*) in the ark (*tevah*)," means that one should bring light (*tzohar*) to each word (*tevah*) while praying. From his words we learn that each word of Torah and prayer should become an integral part of one's being. It should become one's private domain. It should dominate to the extent that it could rule the *kelipot* that are prevalent in the public domain. Therefore, if "You shall carry out My decrees and My judgments . . ." you will then "live by them" because each decree has become individualized and internalized. (Ch.B., p. 282)

~~~

The Kotzker Rebbe taught that "and you should live by them" (Lev. 18:5) means that one should not wait to perform the *mitzvot*, especially when the strength gives way. The *mitzvot* should be performed in the youth of our days so that we may "live by them." (F.U.A.O., vol. 3, p. 105)

~~~

On the same *Pasuk*, the S'fas Emes noted that it means that the performance of the *mitzvot* gives life, vigor, and vitality to the individual. (F.C.O., p. 302)

~~~

The S'fas Emes further commented that by following the laws of the Torah, a person becomes a living being, alive in all aspects beyond the ordinary pleasures usually associated with life. Actions based on Torah and the *mitzvot* commanded by the Almighty give meaning to life in this world. (M.D., p. 140)

~~~

"Any person shall not approach his close relative to uncover nakedness." (Lev. 18:6) The Zanzer Rebbe taught that one should be extremely careful not to permit physical desires to become his master. To permit this will not only lead to embarrassment but will degrade his value as a human being. (F.C.O., p. 302)

~~~

"Let not the land vomit you out for having made it impure, as it vomited out the nation that was before you." (Lev. 18:28) The Izbitzer commented that with these words Hashem promised the Jews that no individual Jew will, God forbid, be lost. (M.D., p. 240)

~~~

"You shall safeguard My charge that these abominable traditions that were done before you not be done, and not make yourselves impure through them; I am Hashem, your God." (Lev. 18:30) The Zolotchover Rebbe, in his *sefer Orach L'Chayim*, commented that to understand the phrase "My charge" in the context of the rest of the *Pasuk*, it is best to do so with a parable. The son of a king had his residence surrounded by enemies and was scared to live there. His father told him not to fear his enemies for he would protect him from harm. The father made one condition for his protection: The son must be careful not to go near their borders, and if he would not be careful, then he would no longer be under his father's protection. This is comparable to the Jewish People, who are regarded as thorns by other nations and whose protector is the Almighty, as it is stated in the Psalms: "Behold, He neither slumbers nor sleeps—the Guardian of Israel." (Ps. 121:4) Hashem will protect Israel as they live among the nations as long as they constrain themselves not to follow their abominations. (M.D., p. 240)

KEDOSHIM
"YOU SHALL BE HOLY"

"You shall be holy, for holy am I, Hashem, your God." (Lev. 19:1) The Lubavitcher Rebbe commented that the *Sidra Kedoshim* highlights living life connected with Hashem amidst the realities of ordinary existence. *Kedushah* refers to a level above material existence, and to the Godly light that by nature is separate and distinct from our human frame of reference. Although this holiness cannot be perceived by our senses, it is not beyond our grasp. To do this, a person must focus on the Divine, which is manifest within the physical elements. That enables one to infuse holiness into every aspect of one's life. (G.O.T., pp. 7–9)

~~~

"Speak to the entire assembly of the Children of Israel and say to them: You shall be holy, for holy am I, Hashem your God. Every man shall revere his mother and his father. . . ." (Lev. 19:2–3) The Yid HaKadosh commented on the connection between these two *Pasukim*. He noted that the Sages said that there are three partners in each person: the Almighty, his father, and his mother. The Almighty gives the person the Soul; his parents give him his body. "You shall be holy" is a statement of assurance. From the Almighty the soul is holy, but awe you must have for the body that was given to you by your parents. (F.C.O., p. 304)

〜

On the same *Pasuķim*, Rashi said that this portion of the Torah was said at a gathering of the entire assembly of Israel. R' Moshe Sofer of Preshburg noted that the concept of holiness does not mean that one should separate himself from the world. On the contrary, he should be part of the mundane and still unite it with holiness. That is why Rashi is very specific in saying "at a gathering." "You shall be holy" because one is a part of everything and everyone. (M.D., p. 142)

〜

"You shall be holy (*ķadosh*). . . ." (Lev. 19:2) Rabbi Shmelke of Nikolsberg gave another definition of the word *ķadosh*, and that is "to be ready." He therefore interpreted the *Pasuķ* to read: "You shall make yourself ready to receive My laws, for I, Hashem, am ready to give it to you." (H.A., p. 170)

〜

The Mogilnitzer noted that a person can perform many *mitzvot* during the day if only he has the will to do so. If he would daily restrain his temper, not gossip nor talk evil about his neighbor, not involve himself in frivolities, and do the opposite of the evil inclination, then these deeds would prepare him to become a *ķadosh*, a holy person. (F.C.O., p. 306)

〜

The Alexander Rebbe said that a son of a wealthy father has no worries because his father will sustain him if he desires. So will Hashem sustain those who desire to become holy. (M.T., vol. 3, p. 110)

〜

R' Tzadok HaKohen commented that the reason we say, "And You made us holy with Your commandments," when we recite a blessing is that it states the essence of each mitzvah. The purpose of the creation of man was that he should be holy—because "I, Your God, am Holy." (F.C.O., p. 305)

~~~

"You shall be holy," noted the Kotzker, means that we should always be ready to accept holiness — "for I am Holy," for I am always ready to aid you in its attainment. (F.C.O., p. 305)

~~~

R' Bunim of Pshys'cha commented that in the Zohar it is noted that when Shimon Bar Yochai reached the words "You shall be Holy, for holy am I, Hashem, your God," he became extremely joyful. He was reminded of the dictum of our Sages that if we will make ourselves holy upon earth, God will make us holy above. When a teacher is able to convey the significance of these words to his student, the teacher will also feel fortunate. (M.T., vol. 3, p. 110)

~~~

"Every man shall revere his mother and his father." (Lev. 19:3) A Chasidic interpretation, anonymously quoted, is that the word "man" is used to show that even though one is a "man" and not being supported by his parents, reverence is still an obligation. (M.T., vol. 3, p. 113)

~~~

"When you slaughter a sacrifice of the peace offering (*shlamim*) to Hashem, you shall slaughter it to appease for you. It must be eaten on your day of slaughter and on the next day . . . shall be burned in fire." (Lev. 19:5–6) The Noam Elimelech commented that "slaughter a sacrifice" means slaughtering one's evil inclination. *Shlamim* is interpreted as meaning "complete," so that the sacrifice should be completely to Hashem. "To appease for you" means that the sacrifice should be done with complete intent to serve Hashem. "Shall be burned in fire" means to serve Hashem with a burning desire and sincere cleaving. (*Noam Elimelech*, p. 61b)

~~~

"For the poor and the proselyte shall you leave them. . . . You shall not steal." (Lev. 19:10,11) The Radamsker, in his *sefer Tiferet Shlomo*, comments that one should have pity on the poor, but do not "steal." Give with your own money and not money obtained through devious means. (F.U.A.O., vol. 3, p. 112)

———

"You shall not lie one to another." (Lev. 19:11) The Kobriner noted that one cannot fool the Almighty and one is not permitted to fool other people. What remains is fooling oneself. (F.U.A.O., vol. 3, p. 114)

———

On the same *Pasuk*, R' Pinchas Koritzer noted that for thirteen years he practiced not to tell a lie and for thirteen years he practiced telling the truth. (F.U.A.O., vol. 3, p. 115)

———

On the same *Pasuk*, the Berditchever made the following observation. He said that it seems that the world is in reverse. There was a time that truth was in the marketplace and falsehood was in the synagogue. Among businessmen a "yes" was a "yes" and a "no" was a "no." When they came to pray and beat their breasts and said, "We have become guilty, we have betrayed, we have robbed" (Prayer Book), this was not true, for they had not robbed nor had they stolen. Now, in our time, it is just the opposite. In the marketplace we tell lies, we swear falsely, we color the truth; but when we enter the synagogue and say, "We have become guilty, we have betrayed, we have robbed," we are telling the truth. (F.C.O., p. 307)

———

In the *Or P'nai Moshe* the following comment is found on the *Pasukim* "You shall not steal, and you shall not deny falsely, and you shall not lie to one another. And you shall not swear falsely by My Name, thereby desecrating the Name of your God; I am Hashem." (Lev. 19:11–12) Among friends the only way to amend a wrongdoing is to return an object or to appease the offended, but to the Almighty one need only repent one's transgressions and the Almighty will forgive, for He is merciful. That is not the way of man; there is no forgiveness unless the other wishes it. (M.D., p. 243)

⸺⸺

On the *Pasuk* "You shall not cheat your friend" (Lev. 19:13), the Izbitzer taught that when one wishes to find a good trait in his friend and says he does not find it, that is considered cheating. When one needs to pray on behalf of his friend and does not do so, that is cheating. This we find when Samuel said, "I also; far be it from me to sin to Hashem in ceasing to pray for you." (1 Samuel 12:23) The Talmud comments that when one is obligated to pray on behalf of a friend and does not he is considered a sinner. (*Berachot* 12b) (*Mi HaShaluach*, p. 118)

⸺⸺

On the *Pasuk* "You shall not do wrong in justice" (Lev. 19:15), the Rebbe from Zolizitz commented that is a very clear statement. It is an iniquity for someone to do something wrong and know that he did wrong and not own up to it. If he waits until he is judged, he will not be able to repent, and then he cannot put blame on justice for his own lack of admitting his wrongdoing. (M.D., p. 244)

⸺⸺

"With righteousness shall you judge your fellow." (Lev. 19:15) The Baal Shem Tov said that the method used in the Heavens to judge an individual's transgression is to show the transgression of someone else. In that way, the judged would become angry and thereby declare his own punishment. To clarify his point, the Baal Shem Tov relayed the example told by Nathan the prophet in Samuel 2:12 to King David to point out his wrongdoing. When the King heard that someone had stolen a sheep from a poor man, he became angry and pronounced the death penalty. The prophet informed the King, "Thou art the man." The Baal Shem Tov commented that that is the reason why our Sages recommended that "One should judge everyone favorably," and "Do not judge your fellow until you have reached his place . . ." (*Ethics of Our Fathers* 1:6, 2:5), because when you judge someone else you are really judging yourself. Therefore, in Psalms 39:9, King David asks of

Hashem, "From all my transgressions rescue me; do not make me a disgrace before the degenerate!" for in this way he would be saved from his own sins. (M.T., vol. 3, p. 114)

⤳

On the *Pasuk* "You shall not go about gossiping among your people" (Lev. 19:16), the Baal Shem Tov taught that we should not seek the faults in our people. (F.U.A.O., vol. 3, p. 118)

⤳

"You shall not hate your brother in your heart; you shall reprove your fellow and you shall not bear a sin because of him." (Lev. 19:17) In the *sefer Toldot Yitzchak*, R' Yitzchak Shapiro of Neshchiz commented that one should not maintain a grudge but should "reprove him" and discuss with him that which bothers one. "Do not bear a sin because of him," for after the discussion you may find out that he is really not guilty of your suspicion. (F.U.A.O., vol. 3, p. 119)

⤳

On the same *Pasuk*, the Baal Shem Tov commented that when one sees faults in another and dislikes him for it, the person probably has these faults himself. If he begins to correct his shortcomings first, he will then be able to correct the other with kindness and not with severity, for he will not hate his brother but will love him. With this approach, he might be receptive to goodness and all his faults might disappear. Thus, through a loving rebuke both will attain improvement. However, if he refuses to listen and admit his faults, he shall not be able to improve. (H.A., p. 390)

⤳

On the same *Pasuk*, the Rimanover commented that every individual possesses some good qualities that are lacking in his neighbor. One should not hate his brother because he does not have the same good quality that he has. On the contrary, admonish yourself by saying that you should possess the good trait that is in him. (T.D.H.T.R., p. 293)

＝＝

On the same *Pasuk*, "You shall reprove your fellow," the S'fas Emes said that when one admonishes someone, he should admonish himself at the same time. That would show that he possesses sins as well as does his neighbor. It would also show that his neighbor does not have all the sins but that each person has a share in them. (F.C.O., p. 308)

＝＝

R' Schneur Zalman of Liadi commented that when you admonish your friend, he will love you for it. If you admonish a stranger, he will probably despise you. (F.C.O., p. 308)

＝＝

The Baal Shem Tov said that one should be careful admonishing others. He based his attitude on the *Pasuk* in Proverbs 3:11, "My son, despise not the chastening of Hashem." Therefore, when one begins reproving with the words of the Almighty, one should be very careful not to despise His children. (F.C.O., p. 309)

＝＝

"You shall not take revenge and you shall not bear a grudge against the members of your people; you shall love your fellow as yourself; I am Hashem." (Lev. 19:18) The Nikolsberger commented that one should not carry a grudge nor be a revengeful person. One should love another as he would love himself, for everyone makes mistakes; everyone gets into difficult situations that are self-inflicted. Would a person want to take revenge on himself? (F.U.A.O., vol. 3, p. 310)

＝＝

The Baal Shem Tov commented that according to the Talmud (*Ethics* 1:6), we must judge our fellows on the scale of merit. However, since one finds excuses for one's own misdeeds, he should make excuses for others as well. (F.C.O., p. 122)

The Sassover taught that when one is in dire straits and shows mercy, that feeling of mercy awakens mercy in the Heavens and Hashem will have mercy on him. (F.U.A.O., vol. 3, p. 310)

The Ohev Yisroel, in discussing the various heights a person may reach, warned that one might fool himself into thinking that he has reached great heights when in reality he is not even on the first rung. If one wishes to know on which level he is, he can measure it by his love of the Jewish people. This can be accomplished by his fulfilling the command of "Love your neighbor as yourself." (Lev. 19:18) This is because love of Hashem and love of the Jewish people are the same. It is impossible to reach any level of loving Hashem if one does not love His people. (F.C.O., p. 310)

In Yiddish *Yid* means "Jew." Based on this, the Ropshitzer noted that when two *yid*s are written together Hashem will reign, because it spells Hashem's name. However, if one *yid* is written above the other, it shows that one is greater than his fellow *yid*, and then Hashem is not among them. (F.U.A.O., vol. 3, p. 124)

"You shall plant any food tree; you shall treat its fruit as uncircumcised; for three years it shall be uncircumcised. In the fourth year, all its fruit shall be sanctified, lauding to Hashem." (Lev. 19:23) R' Avraham Eger commented that though the Pasuk speaks of a tree, we can also obtain a lesson for ourselves. Until a child is three, do not burden the child with too much information. In the fourth year, let every day of his youth be fruitful—"lauding to Hashem." Teach the child Torah, so that he will grow a "tree of life" in Torah and have reverence for Heaven. (F.C.O., p. 315)

"You shall observe My Sabbaths and revere My Sanctuary; I am Hashem." (Lev. 19:30) The Radamsker commented that the prophet says: "Rejoice with her a rejoicing, all who mourn over her." (Is. 66:10) He said that the Radak said that what the prophet meant was that when you witness the rebuilding of the Temple, then just as you mourned over its destruction so will you rejoice over its rebuilding. That teaches us that the one who does not mourn over the destruction will not be privileged to witness and rejoice in its rebuilding. He said that is what the Torah teaches us concerning the beauty of the Sabbath. That is what we pray for: that we should not have any problems nor any worries on the Sabbath. In that way, we will be able to understand the rejoicing over the rebuilding of the Temple. That is the beauty of the Sabbath; the Divine Presence is with us so that we need not be sad about the destruction. The *Pasuk* teaches us that we should rejoice on the Sabbath so that we will be able to witness and rejoice in the building of the Temple. (M.D., p. 247)

"You shall honor (*hadarta*) the presence of an elder." (Lev. 19:32) The Hebrew word *hadar* also means "splendor" or "majesty." In the *sefer Degel Machanei Ephraim*, the Rebbe of Sadilkov interpreted the statement in *Kohelet* (Ecclesiastes) 8:1: "A man's wisdom makes his face shine." He said that an elder is one who has gained wisdom and so acquires a dignified and majestic appearance. (*Degel Machnei Ephraim*, p. 164)

"You shall be holy for Me, for I Hashem am holy; and I have separated you from among the peoples to be Mine." (Lev. 20:26) The Zighter commented that the individual who is constantly thinking of Hashem will be different in his thinking, speaking, and deeds, thereby separating himself from among the people to be with Hashem. He said that if one is careful to separate himself, Hashem will watch over him. (M.D., p. 248)

EMOR
"SAY"

The order of the *Sidrot* are *Acharei* ("after"), *Kedoshim* ("holy"), *Emor* ("say"). R' Asher Horowitz commented that only "after" one has reached the level of "holiness" can one teach others with "words" of reproof. (F.C.O., p. 319)

⁓

"Say to the *Kohanim*, the sons of Aharon, and you shall say to them; to a person you shall not become impure among his people." (Lev. 21:1) The Sassover noted that Rashi stated that the Torah repeats the word "say" to instruct adults with regard to the training of minors. He said that it shows that a leader must be able to reach the level of the masses to help them to reach higher degrees of observance and deportment. However, while he is among the masses, he should not become as they. He must behave in such a manner that would permit the masses to rise to higher levels. (F.C.O., p. 319)

⁓

On the same *Pasuk*, the Berditchever commented that the *Kohanim* should command all future generations that their speech should not be impure so that they will not contaminate others. (F.C.O., p. 319)

⁓

On the same *Pasuk*, in the *sefer Yosher Divrei Emes*, an interesting question is posed. Why does the *Pasuk* refer to "*Kohanim*, the sons of

229

Aharon," rather than "the sons of Aharon, the *Kohanim*?" It is because we are called *Kohanim*, from the word "servant," and we are called "the children of Aharon," for Aharon was the father responsible for tending to the sacrifices. Therefore, the *Pasuk* is alluding to our present-day prayer and service to Hashem, which has replaced the sacrifices. (*Berachot* 26a) We are the children who have replaced prayer for sacrifices. (M.D., p. 249)

On the words "to a person, he shall not become impure among his people," R' Ber of Mezritch said that as sons of Aharon, we are not to consider ourselves on a higher level than others, for that will cause others to become impure. (M.D., p. 249)

On that same *Pasuk*, R' Mordechai of Nadburna commented that "impurity" means the use of logic when it comes to the study of Torah. The Torah warns us not to become impure and to know that the Torah is above logic. (M.D., p. 250)

"To a person (*nefesh*, "body") he [the Kohen] shall not become impure." (Lev. 21:1) The Zanzer commented that when the body becomes impure, one should not say that he is evil. He should not become depressed and lose all hope to improve. One should follow the dictum from the *Ethics of Our Fathers*: "Do not consider yourself wicked." That is, do not feel as if all roads to improvement are closed; seek the correct road and Hashem will assist. (F.C.O., p. 320)

On the same *Pasuk*, R' Nachum Mordechai Perlow, the Novominsker Rebbe, examined the laws of impurity and their relation to the laws of the *Kohanim*. He said that the impurity associated with the dead can have a negative effect on the psyche. When a person dies, the tragedy may possibly bring negative thoughts and thoughts of heresy. Therefore, it is imperative for one not to have tragedy take over one's life.

When we console mourners, we must try to strengthen their faith, for that is the law of mourning. The problem is: Who will do the consoling when, God forbid, all of Jewry is in mourning? The Rebbe quotes a *Pasuk* in Ezekiel: "Say to the family of Israel: 'Thus says my Lord Hashem (Elokim): Behold! I shall profane My Sanctuary, the pride of your strength, the darling of your eyes, and the yearning of your soul. Also your sons and your daughters, whom you have forsaken, will fall by the sword. . . . Do not lament nor weep, pine away because of your sins, and moan toward one another.'" (Ezek. 24:21–23) On this Rashi comments: "Do not observe mourning practices because there are none to comfort you. . . . mourning practices make sense only when there are comforters." Public tragedy is greater than private tragedy, for there is no one to console them. The issue of mourning is based on the premise that there is someone to give consolation, to lift the spirit. That is why the laws of impurity are placed on the *Kohanim*. It is their task to console in times of calamity and so the command is to "not become impure among his people" so that they should not defile themselves so that they can comfort. They should always have the awe of Hashem and the yoke of Heaven upon them so that they may bring solace to the people in times of trouble, when doubt and inner discord develop. (*P'er Nachum*, pp. 155–156)

~~~

Speaking to the youth, the Kotzker said that they should not be concerned with transgressing but should make sure that they do not have the time to transgress. (F.C.O., p. 321)

~~~

R' Meir Primishlaner noted that the way of the wicked is to dislike and look for the faults in the good. They claim that they are the righteous ones, the truth tellers; however, they do not see their own imperfections. When King David said that he preferred evil to good, he was referring to his choice of those who do not assert that they are righteous over those who claim to be perfect. (F.C.O., p. 317)

The Torah states: "A husband (*baal*) among his people shall not make himself impure to defile him." (Lev. 21:4) In his *sefer B'er Mayim Chayim*, the Chernovitzer translated the word *baal* as "master"—one who is master over his behavior. As long as a person is a believer in Hashem and that all will be well, he will constantly try to better himself and all will be well. If difficulties occur, God forbid, and he takes leave of belief, his behavior will also change. However, if he becomes the master of his actions, he would not become impure among his people. On the contrary, he would believe that he is a righteous individual with strong spiritual abilities, able to master his behavior for the benefit of his people. Therefore, he should always be aware of his behavior. (M.D., p. 250)

The Glagover taught that no matter the skill or the profession of a person, he is called a *baal*. Examples are a *baal habayit*, the head of a household; or a *baal simchah*, someone who has a happy occasion. We call the one who leads a prayer service a *baal tefilah*. The Torah tells us that a *baal* "shall not make himself impure," he shall not become arrogant and make himself loathsome "among his people." He should lead the service in a pleasant manner and be concerned with the worshippers and pray on their behalf. (F.C.O., p. 322)

"If a daughter of a man who is a *Kohen* is defiled through having illicit relations, she defiles her father." (Lev. 21:9) The Imrei Shefer comments that there are wicked people whose behavior is inherited and is rooted in them, and there are those who do not walk the correct path through their own evil inclination. It is said by the Sages that the evil inclination does not incite one immediately to perform a severe transgression. It starts with something simple. Today it makes one do this and the next day something else, until it says, "Now become an idol worshipper." However, the person who has inherited his wickedness will immediately perform severe transgressions. That is why the Torah states that if she immediately performed a severe transgression, her evil inclination was inherited. Therefore, "She defiled her father." (M.T., vol. 3, p. 129)

〰

"He shall not come to any souls of the dead." (Lev. 21:11) The Kotzker commented that the High Priest must separate himself from his family and his only concern shall be for his people. (F.U.A.O., vol. 3, p. 137)

〰

"Speak to Aharon and to his sons, that they shall withdraw from that which is holy of the Children of Israel—that which they consecrate to Me—so as not to defile My Holy Name." (Lev. 22:2) The Ohev Yisroel commented that Aharon was commanded to tell his children that though they are of "holy seed," they should not consider themselves greater than the people and not defile themselves by thinking that they are "Holy only unto Me," for all the people are "Holy unto Me." (F.C.O., p. 323)

〰

"And they will cause them to bear the sin of guilt when they eat their holy things." (Lev. 22:16) The Dzikover said in the name of the Noam Elimelech that when one prays or learns Torah, he is reminded of his transgressions. However, when one eats or drinks, he usually will forget his transgressions and give in to all his desires. That is not the way we are commanded to behave. When one eats or drinks he should be reminded of his wrongdoing so that he will "bear the sin of guilt when they eat their holy things." (M.D., p. 252)

〰

On the *Pasuk* "I shall be sanctified among the Children of Israel" (Lev. 22:32), Rashi comments: "Surrender yourself and sanctify My Name . . . on condition to die, for whoever surrenders himself on the condition of a miracle will have no miracle performed for him." The S'fas Emes said that one should not sanctify oneself for the sake of having a miracle performed. He must examine his intentions of surrender so that he is not relying on a miracle. Therefore, one should be very careful that he surrenders himself with the sincere intention to sanctify His name. (M.T., vol. 3, p. 130)

〜〜

"When you slaughter a sacrifice thanksgiving offering to Hashem, you shall slaughter it as an appeasement to you." (Lev. 22:29) The Zanzer commented that when the performance of a mitzvah is enveloped by desires, it is imperative to nullify them until they no longer exist. In "Eight Chapters," the Rambam noted that *mitzvot* that are not based on logic should be performed because they were commanded from above. But for *mitzvot* that are based on logic, such as not to steal or commit adultery, a person must subdue his desires. For these *mitzvot*, logic is necessary to keep one away from such transgressions. Otherwise, the desires will be based on foolishness, as is noted in the Talmud: "A person does not commit a transgression except out of stupidity and one must destroy these impulses until his reason will tell him that the deed is disgusting." (*Sotah* 3a) Therefore, the Torah admonishes us that all desires must be subdued so that the sacrifice or the mitzvah will be performed "as an appeasement." (M.D., p. 252)

〜〜

"It must be eaten on that same day; you shall not leave any of it until morning." (Lev. 22:30) The Oheler commented that this concept is logical and is based on the sayings of our Sages: "Whoever asks, 'What will I eat tomorrow?' has little faith." (M.D., p. 253)

〜〜

"You shall guard My commandments and do them." (Lev. 22:31) The Koznitzer commented that if one waits for an opportunity to perform or observe a mitzvah, he should remember that the Torah says that when we were at Sinai and we heard the words, "I am Hashem," we were ready to perform all *mitzvot*. (M.D., p. 253)

～～

"In the first month, on the fourteenth of the month, toward evening it is a Pesach to Hashem." (Lev. 23:5) The Lizensker commented that this *Pasuk* shows us how one progresses in the service of Hashem. Before the fourteenth of the month, which symbolizes the halfway mark in a person's life, a person cannot accept the light of holiness because his impulses are strong. However, in the evening of his life, he is ready to rectify any wrongdoing. It is time for "Pe-sach" (*pe*, "mouth," plus *sach*, "speak"), time to rectify what had come out of the mouth. It is time for the study of Torah and all rabbinical literature. (*Noam Elimelech*, p. 64b)

～～

On the *Pasuk* "From your settled places you shall bring bread of elevation" (Lev. 23:17), R' Meir Halevi of Apt commented that a person should be in a constant state of repentance. The meaning of "from your settled places" is that repentance should come from one's inner self. This in turn will reach the soul and inspire and influence Israel to a high degree of holiness through "bread of elevation." (M.D., p. 255)

～～

"On the tenth day of this month is the Day of Atonement." (Lev. 23:27) Yehudah Leib, the brother of R' Meir Primishlaner, was very careful in his observance of the Sabbath. In fact, he was known as "Leib Yehudah, the observer of the Sabbath." Every Friday morning he would buy only the very best for the Sabbath. When the Sabbath and the Day of Atonement fell on the same day, he still bought the best necessities for the Sabbath. He would set the table for the Sabbath and after the Kol Nidrei service he would come home, sit down at the table, and say, "Almighty God, I really want to enjoy the Sabbath, but You commanded that on this day we should fast, even if it should come on the Sabbath, so if You are satisfied that I should fast, then I, too, am satisfied." (F.C.O., p. 324)

～～

"And you shall afflict yourselves; on the ninth of the month in the evening." (Lev. 23:32) The Belzer commented on the statement in the Talmud: "Do we fast on the ninth and not on the tenth? But for the one who eats and drinks on the ninth it is as if he fasted on the ninth and the tenth." (*Berachot* 8b) He noted that on every fast day we pray that the fat and the blood we lose should be accepted by the Almighty as if that is the sacrifice that we make on the altar. However, we are not permitted to sacrifice forbidden food. Therefore, the Torah made eating and drinking a mitzvah. Therefore, eating and drinking on the eve of Yom Kippur insures that we are sacrificing permitted food on Yom Kippur. (M.T., vol. 3, p. 135)

On the same *Pasuk*, the Lizensker noted that when we begin to note the day that is coming while we are eating, we find that eating is no longer a pleasure. That is why both days can be considered fast days. (M.T., vol. 3, p. 135)

On the *Pasuk* "You shall take for yourselves on the first day . . ." (Lev. 23:40), the Chidushei Harim is quoted as saying that if one considers the fact that during the High Holy Days we repent out of fear, then when the festival of Sukkot arrives and we become enthusiastic to fulfill the *mitzvot* of the festival for Hashem's sake, we notice that our repentance is now out of love. Our Sages tell us that repenting out of love makes all previous transgressions revert to meritorious acts. (M.T., vol. 3, p. 135)

"And Moses declared the appointed festivals of Hashem to the Children of Israel." (Lev. 23:44) R' Yechiel Meir Gostaniner commented that before the Israelites accepted the Torah, all the *mitzvot* and Holidays were hidden in Hashem's treasure chest. That is why they are called Hashem's Torah and *mitzvot*. After the Israelites said, "We will do and we will hear," Moses transferred what was hidden to the Israelites. (F.C.O., p. 325)

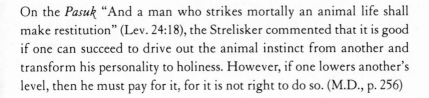

On the *Pasuk* "And a man who strikes mortally an animal life shall make restitution" (Lev. 24:18), the Strelisker commented that it is good if one can succeed to drive out the animal instinct from another and transform his personality to holiness. However, if one lowers another's level, then he must pay for it, for it is not right to do so. (M.D., p. 256)

BEHAR
"ON THE MOUNTAIN"

R abbi Menachem Mendel Schneerson gave the following reason for naming the *Sidra Behar* and not *Behar Sinai*. He said that Mount Sinai exemplifies two aspects of personality. On the one hand, it represents the "lowest of all mountains," a symbol of humility. On the other hand, it is a mountain, showing pride and power. It is a blend of these two opposites. Yet, it is called "the mountain of Hashem" (Ex. 3:1), the place where Hashem chose to make known His presence and transmit His teachings. The title of the *Sidra* emphasizes the pride and not the humility. Once a person understands that he must undertake the mission with which Hashem has entrusted him, there is no need to be reminded to be humble in the face of service to Hashem. This is the intent of the name *Behar*, "on the mountain"—that a servant of Hashem stands proud, invested with strength of purpose. (G.O.T., pp. 23–24)

~~~

"Hashem spoke to Moses on Mount Sinai, saying . . ." (Lev. 25:1) "Speak to the Children of Israel and say to them: When you come into the land that I give you, the land shall observe a Sabbath rest for Hashem." (Lev. 25:2) Rashi questions: "What is the matter of *shemmitah* (sabbatical year) doing next to Mount Sinai?" The *sefer Imrei Shefer* notes that there might be a concern that after the cessation of work on the field for an entire year, there would not be enough food to sustain oneself and one's family. Therefore, the Torah states: "The resting of the land shall be yours to eat, for you, your slave, and for your maidser-

239

vant; and your hired worker and for one who resides with you. And for your animal and for the beast that is in your land shall all its crop be to eat." (Lev. 25:6–7) Although you will not work your field there will be more than enough for you, your household, and even your cattle. More than that, the year of *shemmitah* will bring abundant blessings for the next six years. That is why *shemmitah* is called *Shabbat*, as Rashi notes: "For the sake of Hashem, just as it is said with regard to the Sabbath of Creation, the weekly Shabbat." Just as the Holy Shabbat showers blessings on the entire week, so too will the *shemmitah*, for though we do not work the fields, it is a blessing for the next six years. That is why it is placed near Mount Sinai, for though it is small and with seemingly little significance, it has merited the privilege of showering holiness upon the entire world. (M.T., vol. 3, p. 141)

~~~

"When you come into the land that I give you, the land shall observe a Sabbath rest for Hashem." (Lev. 25:2) The Riziner commented that Hashem is saying to the Israelites that when they plant and sow the fields and are blessed with much produce, they should not begin to think that it was from their work but that it was "I"—"I give you"—Who gave you the land. Since I gave you the land, therefore I command you: "The land shall observe a Sabbath," the same as I commanded you to observe the Sabbath. (F.C.O., p. 326)

~~~

The Bratzlaver noted that whenever the Land of Israel is mentioned, it always is in the present tense, such as: "That I give you." The reason is that when a Jew is in Israel, he should feel as if the land was just given. Every day is a new day and should bring a feeling of freshness and newness. (F.U.A.O., vol. 3, p. 152)

~~~

"And you shall return, each man to his ancestral heritage, and you shall return, each man to his family." (Lev. 25:10) The Radamsker commented that a person is born complete. Each transgression committed puts a blemish on the soul. However, when a person does repentance (*shavtem*, "return") he will be restored to his ancestral home to become complete again. Rearranging the last letters of the Hebrew phrase *U'shavtem ish el achuzato* spells out the word *shalom*, "complete." (M.D., p. 269)

〰️

On the same *Pasuk*, R' Shmuel Mohilever commented that when the Jews return to their ancestral land, then we will regain our families and our children who are prone to be lost in the Diaspora. In our own land, it is easier to bring families closer to Torah. (F.U.A.O., vol. 3, p. 154)

〰️

"When you make a sale to your fellow or when you buy from the hand of your fellow, do not victimize one another." (Lev. 25:14) The Shpolyer Zayde commented that one should not assume that he has a fear of Heaven and at the same time can deceive another. (F.C.O., p. 327)

〰️

On the same *Pasuk*, the Cherneboler commented that if we are honest in our business dealings and are observant of the laws against fraud, interest, and false weight, that in itself is serving Hashem. The Baal Shem Tov noted that when one learns the Mishnah and discusses the laws of "If a man exchanged a cow for an ass" (*Baba Metzia* 100a), he is studying Torah. If he fulfills those laws, he is performing a worthy service to Hashem. (M.T., vol. 3, p. 144)

〰️

On the same *Pasuk*, the Ropshitzer commented that according to strict law one should not deceive another—and by going beyond what the law requires, one does not deceive oneself. (F.U.A.O., vol. 3, p. 155)

〰️

On the same theme, R' Bunim of Pshys'cha taught that to be a Chasid, one should go beyond the letter of the law. Not to deceive another means not to deceive one's own soul. (F.C.O., p. 327)

On the same *Pasuk*, the Kotzker's comment was based on a verse in Proverbs 23:23, which states: "Buy truth and do not sell it." There are people who are seekers of truth—for others! They would turn the whole world for truth, except for themselves. Therefore, the verse in Proverbs teaches us to buy truth for one's own use, and not to use it to sell to someone else. (F.U.A.O., vol. 3, p. 158)

It is related that when the Pshys'cha was going blind, he kept on repeating the phrase "It is better to take my eyes than I should see that which is false." (F.U.A.O., vol. 3, p. 158)

The Lubliner commented that Hashem regarded more highly the wicked person who knows that he is wicked, than the righteous person who thinks that he is righteous. The first one is truthful, and Hashem loves truth. The second one lies, since no human being is exempt from sin; and Hashem despises falsehoods. (H.A., p. 487)

Concerning truth the Bratzlaver taught that:

1. Faith can be attained only through adherence to truth; he who adheres merely to reason has no faith.
2. A man of truth knows no difference between service to Hashem in public or in private. Such a man is not troubled by doubts.
3. One who adds to truth decreases it.
4. Where there is no truth, there is no peace. (H.A., p. 488)

"Do not harass one another, and you shall have fear of your God; for I am Hashem, your God. You shall perform My decrees, and observe My ordinances and perform them." (Lev. 25:17–18) The Ropshitzer commented that if people will not mislead one another, then it is a surety that the rest of the decrees and ordinances will be observed. (F.U.A.O., vol. 3, p. 158)

⌐⌐

"The land will give its fruit and you will eat to satisfaction. . . . If you will say: What will we eat in the seventh year? Behold! We will not sow and we will not gather our crop! I will ordain My blessing in the sixth year and it will yield a crop sufficient for the three years." (Lev. 25:19– 21) The S'fas Emes commented that the question "What will we eat?" is really not the basic issue. Everyone is aware that the One Who gives life will give sustenance, for one should realize that nature and miracles are bound together; nature itself is a miracle. Yet, not all generations deserve to depend on miracles and must obtain their livelihoods in the natural way. The answer is that the blessing will be in the produce itself of the sixth year and it will be clothed in the natural way. Every time there is sustenance it is a great miracle. It really should not matter how a miracle occurs. If one understands this, then there is no room for the question, for the question is really separating nature and the miracle. This should not be done, for what Hashem ordained is attained through natural events. (M.T., vol. 3, p. 146)

⌐⌐

"You are sojourners and residents with me." (Lev. 25:23) In the *sefer Ohel Yaacov*, there is a comment that Hashem says to His people that we are both in the category of sojourner or resident. If you consider yourselves strangers, and you know that this is a temporary abode, then My Presence will be with you. If you consider yourselves as residents, then obviously I will be to you as a stranger. That is why one of us will be either one. (M.T., vol. 3, p. 147)

⌐⌐

On the same *Pasuk*, the Sildokover commented that when two strangers meet in a foreign country, they will discuss matters that disturb them. The Almighty says to the Jews that that are strangers in this world and residents in the World to Come. You are with Me for we are in the same position. I, too, am a sojourner in this world, for I cannot find a place for My Presence. (M.T., vol. 3, p. 260)

～～

On the same *Pasuk*, R' Baruch Mezbitzer commented that the more a person feels himself a sojourner in this world, the more he becomes a resident. (F.U.A.O., vol. 3, p. 160)

～～

"If your brother becomes impoverished and sells of his ancestral heritage. . . ." (Lev. 25:25) In his *Toldot Yaacov Yosef*, the Polnoyer commented that it is known that a small spark from a piece of coal can ignite a flame. It is also known that if the small spark dies out, it is the end of the fire. If an individual leaves his tradition and the spark is gone, there is no hope for his return. However, if there is the tiniest spark left in him, he may return to the fold. (F.C.O., p. 328)

～～

"If your brother becomes impoverished and his hand becomes weak then shall you assist him. . . ." (Lev. 25:35) The Baal Shem Tov commented that when times are bleak and there seems to be no hope, you should not resign yourself to that predicament and state of mind. Become strong and develop a positive attitude. (F.C.O., p. 329)

～～

On the same *Pasuk*, R' Aharon Karliner taught that when someone falls into mud, we must jump into the mud to save him. So is it when your brother stretches out his hand in need, put yourself in his place and save him. (F.C.O., p. 329)

～～

R' Tzadok HaKohen commented that the verse "All is from You" means that even the willingness to give charity is from the Almighty. (F.C.O., p. 330)

"Do not give him your money for interest (*neshech*)." (Lev. 25:37) Based on the Hebrew word *neshech*, which can mean "interest" or "biting," the Kotzker taught that one should not depend on his money earning his food, nor hope that the borrower would work off the debt. He should depend on his own efforts. (H.A., p. 26)

"After he has been sold, he shall have redemption; one of his brothers shall redeem him; or his uncle . . . or a relative may redeem him." (Lev. 25:48–49) The Kobriner commented that we learn from this that if we find ourselves in trouble we should pray to Hashem, Who is our Friend, to aid us. We should also go for help to our Rebbe or to our family and friends within our community. We may receive benefit from all of them. (H.A., p. 484)

BECHUKOSAI
"MY DECREES"

The Chernovitzer in his *sefer B'er Mayim Chayim* emphasized the importance of the observance of the decrees and the *mitzvot*. A person performs a mitzvah correctly when there is a burning desire to do this one and not wait to perform another. When one goes from prayer to learning Torah, and learning Torah to prayer, that is called "fire," as Jeremiah said: "My word is like a fire, and a hammer that shatters rock." (Jer. 23:29) The nature of fire is that as long as it is burning, it continues to flicker and burn more. We find the same with the performance of a mitzvah. If we fulfill them with burning desire and enthusiasm, with the inner sparks of the Divine, there will develop a delight to fulfill all the *mitzvot* of the Almighty. This is the reason the Torah says that Hashem promised as He did: "If you will go in My decrees and observe My commandments and perform them, then I will provide your rains in their time, and the land will give its produce and the tree of the field will give its fruit. . . . I will provide peace in the land and you will lie down and none to frighten you. . . . You will pursue your enemies, and they will fall before you by the sword. . . . I will turn to you; I will make you fruitful and increase you, and establish My covenant with you. . . . I will walk among you; I will be a God to you and you will be a people to Me." (Lev. 26:3–12) All of these blessings, in material and spiritual things, are dependent on the performance of the decrees and *mitzvot* in sincerity and with a deep and abiding heart. (M.D., p. 268)

❧

"If you will go in My decrees and observe My commandments and perform them, then I will provide your rains in their time, and the land will give its produce and the tree of the field will give its fruit." (Lev. 26:3–4) Rashi comments: "These trees, which do not bear fruit, are destined to produce fruit." The Novominsker Rebbe explained that when a person is thorough and pure in his actions and persists in that manner, he is able to influence and improve his environs and intensify their sense of holiness. The *Pasuk* teaches that when we "go in My decrees," when we perform the *mitzvot*, we develop a wholesomeness in ourselves and become righteous in our ways and deeds. This attitude permits us to influence our surroundings, even "the trees that do not bear fruit," so that even the sinners will begin to repent and permit their fruit (offspring) to grow. Then "I will provide peace in the land, and you will lie down with none to frighten you . . . and a sword will not cross your land." (Lev. 26:6) The outcome of such influence will be so powerful that the enemies' sword will not disturb the serving of Hashem and the holiness of the actions. (*Pe'er Nachum*, p. 182)

❧

"If you will go in My decrees and observe My commandments and perform them." (Lev. 26:3) The Riziner commented that if one obeys Hashem's decrees, which are without reason, then the *mitzvot* will definitely be observed. (F.C.O., p. 332)

❧

On the same *Pasuk*, the S'fas Emes taught that one must toil in studying Torah to be considered as one who will "go in My decrees." This means that no matter how much wisdom and knowledge one has accumulated, if there was no effort in learning Torah, then one cannot be regarded as one who has "labored in Torah." (F.C.O., p. 332)

❧

On the same *Pasuk*, Rashi maintained that it meant: "That you should be laboring in the Torah." The Sassover explained it with an analogy.

When someone makes a request of a king, he comes with fear and trepidation. But if someone comes to do work in the palace, he does it without fear; otherwise he would not be able to do his work properly. So too, when one learns Torah he does so feeling at ease, for it is done as the work of Hashem, as our Sages proclaimed: "There is no freer man than one who engages in the study of Torah." (*Ethics of Our Fathers* 6:2) When one engages in worldly affairs, he should be in constant fear that he does not do wrong. One must be aware that all of one's labors should be on the Torah level. (M.T., vol. 3, p. 155)

❧

"Torah study is good together with an occupation." (*Ethics of Our Fathers* 2:2) The Berditchever commented that when one is occupied with worldly matters, he must keep his service to Hashem in mind. Also it is not proper to study Torah and let others worry about worldly matters; likewise, it is not proper to deal with worldly matters and let others worry about the study of Torah. (F.C.O., p. 334)

❧

On the same *Pasuk*, to emphasize the interpretation, the Vorker quoted the Midrash: "I reflected upon my ways and returned to Your congregation. David said that every day, 'I gave thought as to where I was going and my feet always led me to the house of prayer and the house of study.'" The Rebbe taught that even when someone is ready to do a mitzvah, he must give thought as to the method of its performance. He should consider if the mitzvah is for him and if he is properly prepared for its fulfillment. For example: When one rises in the morning and immediately dons *tallit* and *tefillin* without proper preparation, then the mitzvah is not being performed "as was commanded." (M.T., vol. 3, p. 155)

❧

"If you will go," commented R' Bunim, means that one must constantly "go" higher and higher and not stay on one level. (F.C.O., p. 332)

⌇

"If you will go in My decrees and observe My commandments and perform them, then I will provide rains in their time, and the land will give its produce and the tree of the field will give its fruit." (Lev. 26:3–4) The Chernovitzer commented that when a decree is at hand to perform, one should "go" and do it with perfection and in all its beauty. Also, "observe My commandments," so that the love for its performance should grow. This attitude will insure that you will seek to do *mitzvot*. Thus, Hashem says that He will not wait to give His blessings and will give them with abundant love. (M.T., p. 266)

⌇

On the same *Pasukim*, the Koznitzer noted that a field needs plowing, sowing, rain, and warmth to produce fruit. So too does a person need preparation, intention, and fervor to reach the proper service of Hashem. (F.C.O., p. 333)

⌇

The Sassover remarked that he learned seven things about serving Hashem by observing the behavior of a thief. First, he does his work mainly at night. Second, he never goes alone. Third, when he does his work, he takes a lot of risks. Fourth, he will be happy even if he does not get much. Fifth, if he does not succeed today, he will try again tomorrow. Sixth, whatever he stole the day before, he will try again tomorrow. Seventh, he does not consider what he stole the day before enough. (F.C.O., p. 334)

⌇

"And I will turn to you. . . ." (Lev. 26:9) The Chidushei Harim commented that this means that Hashem will always have time for His servants. (F.C.O., p. 335)

⌇

On the *Pasuk* "I led you erect" (Lev. 26:13), the Mezritcher Maggid noted that an animal walks with his head down. If one walks with his head down, it appears that he behaves like an animal. However, if one follows the decrees and observes the commandments, he will automatically walk erect, with his head high. (F.C.O., p. 335)

∽∽

"You will flee but there will be no one pursuing you." (Lev. 26:17) In his *sefer Brit Avraham*, R' Tzvi Melech Moshe Shapiro of Z'barov noted that when one pursues in earnest to be in the service of Hashem, he forgoes his individualism, his ego. (M.D., p. 269)

∽∽

"And I will direct My face against you; you will be afflicted before your enemies." (Lev. 26:17) The Koznitzer, in his *sefer B'er Moshe*, interpreted this *Pasuk* in a positive vein, based on the *Pasuk* "All who see them shall recognize them that they are the seed that Hashem blessed." (Is. 61:9) He commented that when we cleanse ourselves and become holy, everyone will look at us and recognize that we are a righteous people. Even the nations of the world will hold us in awe, for they will recognize that we are the "seed that Hashem blessed." This is confirmed in the Torah in Deuteronomy 25:10: "And all the nations of the earth shall see that you are called by Hashem's name; and they shall be afraid of you." That is what the *Pasuk* meant when it said, "I will direct My face against you." I will put My face, so to speak, into yours, to give you a Divine appearance and then, "you will be afflicted before your enemies." Because of this affliction, your enemies will not be able to approach you. They will fear you, for you will have the image of Hashem upon you. (M.D., p. 269)

∽∽

On the *Pasuk* "Then I, too, will behave toward you with casualness" (Lev. 26:27), R' Tzadok HaKohen commented that all occurrences are with Divine supervision. One should not think that actions occur by accident. This attitude is the basis of faith. Faith is based on an unqualified belief in Divine supervision. That is the reason for observing the *mitzvot* and following the principles of Torah. Losing faith is the curse

of behaving "with casualness," for you will act as if each occurrence is
without Divine supervision. (F.C.O., p. 335)

~~

On the *Pasuk* "I will chastise you, even I" (Lev. 26:28), the Berditchever
commented that Hashem's reaction is the same as the father who is hurt
when he punishes his child. (F.C.O., p. 336)

~~

"I will remember My covenant with Jacob and also My covenant with
Isaac, and also My covenant with Abraham will I remember, and I will
remember the land." (Lev. 26:42) The Shelah HaKadosh wondered
what remembering "My covenant with Jacob and also My covenant
with Isaac, and also My covenant with Abraham" had to do with
reproof. He commented that when one has such ancestry, the transgressions are considered more severely. By way of analogy, he said that when
someone is brought up in a palace and he sins against the king, his
transgression is much greater than someone else's would be. (M.T., vol.
3, p. 161)

~~

On the same *Pasuk*, R' Yaacov Shimshon Shepetivker commented that
the Jews will stop thinking about and then forget the land of their forefathers. Hashem said that only He will remember the land. (F.U.A.O.,
p. 178)

~~

Referring to the *Pasuk* "I will remember for them the covenant of the
forebears, those whom I have taken out of the land of Egypt before
the eyes of the nations, to be God unto them; I am Hashem" (Lev. 26:45),
the Berditchever complained to Hashem: Almighty God, what is Your
complaint about us that we do not follow the ways of the Torah? I want
to remind You that the Israelites that You took out of Egypt were no
better. That is what King David said: "Remember Your congregation,
which You acquired long ago." (Ps. 74:2) In arranging a proposal for
marriage that involves finance, the future in-law has a right to know

that the groom comes from a poor family and to be angry if he was not informed. If it was known beforehand that the groom is poor and the in-law agrees to the proposal, he really has no complaint. Remind Yourself, Almighty God, the circumstances we were in when you took us out of Egypt. We were without anything; we had no Torah, no *mitzvot*, and we did not have any good deeds. Nevertheless, You freed us and consented to the proposal. If this is so, then what is Your complaint against us? We are no different than before. (F.C.O., p. 337)

"These are the decrees, the ordinances, and the Torahs that Hashem gave, between himself and the Children of Israel." (Lev. 26:46) The Ropshitzer, in his *sefer Zera Kodesh*, commented that the *Pasuk* teaches us about the mercy and loving-kindness of Hashem. The entire series of admonitions were given between the Almighty and His people. It is like a father scolding his child. He will tell him how he will be punished unless he amends his ways, but He will not scold him in front of others. In front of others he will praise his child. Based on the *Pasuk* in Numbers 23:19 "Would He say and not do, or speak and not fulfill?" the Sages said that the Blessed One knows the reproof but will have mercy afterwards and not bring the punishment. The good that Hashem has promised, He will keep; but the bad He is ready to retract. The nations know only the reproof but not that the Almighty will have mercy. (*Zera Kodesh*, p. 105b)

WEEKLY PORTIONS OF BAMIDBAR/NUMBERS

BAMIDBAR
"IN THE WILDERNESS"

Rabbi Menachem Mendel Schneerson, the Lubavitcher Rebbe, noted that the *Sidra Bamidbar* is always read before Shavuot. Shavuot, which commemorates Hashem's giving of the Torah to Israel, is called the wedding of Israel to Hashem (Talmud *Taanit* 26b). On the Shabbat before a wedding, the bridegroom is called to the Torah as a preparation for the wedding. Therefore, *Bamidbar* is read as a preparation for the union between Hashem and His people. Another significant aspect is the command to count the Israelites. Rashi comments: "Because they [the Children of Israel] are dear to Him, He counts them all the time: When they went forth from Egypt He counted them; when they fell because of [the sin of] the golden calf, He counted them; when He was about to make His Presence dwell amongst them [i.e., in the Tabernacle] He counted them. For on the first of Nissan the Tabernacle was erected, and on the first of Iyar (the second month) He counted them." (1:1) These three countings were an evolutionary process. In the first, the Jewish soul was awakened by the love of Hashem, in that they followed His commands with complete self-sacrifice, but their emotions were untouched. In the second, the soul began to work its influence on their outward lives in preparation for the building of the Tabernacle for Hashem's Presence. But the impetus still came from the outside rather than from an inner desire. However, by the third counting, because they were now involved with the actual service of the Tabernacle, through their own action they brought Hashem into their midst. That was the testimony to the union of the Jewish soul with Hashem. Therefore, we can see the connection between *Bamidbar*, Shavuot, and the census as a union between Hashem and Israel. (Torah Studies, pp. 222–226)

"Hashem spoke to Moses in the wilderness of Sinai, in the Tent of Meeting (*Ohel Moed*), on the first of the second month." (Num. 1:1) The Noam Elimelech commented that the Torah gives us a lesson in behavior. The Torah was given in the desert of Sinai so that we should maintain a state of humility, for that is the way the Almighty has shown us. He chose the most lowly of mountains in the Sinai desert. (Talmud *Megillah* 29a) Therefore, a person should not become depressed when he feels low. The torah is cautioning us to always be in a joyous state, for the Holy Presence does not dwell in a place of depression. (Talmud *Shabbat* 30b) That is what the Torah means by "the tent of *Moed* (holiday)"—one should enter the tent of holiday in joy. "On the first of the second month" means that if a person says, "How can I be in a state of joy, if I am in a state of sinning?" the Torah says that one should always repent in a state of joy. One should take courage by saying that it is as if he were born that day and he would not return to a state of folly. That is called renewal—to renew to a new being. The Noam Elimelech plays on the word *chodesh* ("month") to mean *chadash* ("new") so that "On the first of the second *chodesh*" means that a person renews himself twice—once when he is born and the second time when he repents and is forgiven. (*Noam Elimelech*, p. 68)

On the same *Pasuk*, the Midrash states that the Torah was given amidst three things: fire, water, and the desert. (Midrash Rabbah) The Lubliner commented that the most significant attribute of the Jewish people is their self-sacrifice for the Torah and faith. They gave their lives on the gallows at the auto-de-fe, stretched out their necks for sacrifice, jumped into the ocean, and became like a desert rather than transgress the principles of the Torah. These characteristics were inherited from their history. Abraham, our father, willingly went into the furnace as punishment when he was accused of preaching our faith and thus implanted the concept of self-sacrifice in his children. That may have been the deed of an individual, but at the splitting of the sea the entire people showed their faith by going into the sea at Hashem's command. And while that may have been only a momentary act, they went through their trek in the desert without sustenance for an extended period of time. All of these tribulations were endured for their love and devotion to the Almighty and His prophet Moses, as we read in Jeremiah: "I remember for your sake the kindness of your youth, the love of your bridal days, your following after Me in the wilderness, in a land not sown." (Jer. 2:2) With these three momentous challenges—fire, water, and the desert—the Torah was given as a perpetual remembrance and guarantee for the everlasting existence of the Jewish people. (M.T., vol. 4, p. 7)

~~~

"In the wilderness of Sinai." (Num. 1:1) The Kotzker, in his *sefer Ohel Torah*, commented that the Midrash stated that the Almighty did not want to have His *Schechinah* (Presence) dwell in a Tabernacle built on the sea, nor on a mountain, but only in the desert. That is why the prophet Isaiah said: "Desert and wasteland shall rejoice over them." (Is. 35:1) The significance of this statement is that Hashem makes His Presence rest on the individual who comports himself like the desert. Just like the desert, which has not been worked on by anyone else, he knows that unless he himself labors to understand, he will not reach the understanding of Torah. Only the individual who understands this and works diligently can reach his integrity in Torah and the service of Hashem. (M.T., vol. 4, p. 8)

~~~

"Take a census of the entire assembly of the Children of Israel." (Num. 1:2) The Chidushei Harim noted that the Torah commanded that the Israelites be counted separately so that they would not become combined with other peoples. As the Halachah (Jewish law) states: "A thing that is counted according to its worth even among a thousand will not become nullified." (M.T., vol. 4, p. 9)

❧❧

On the same *Pasuk,* Rabbi Avraham Moshe Rabinowitz, the Skoyler Rebbe, commented that the essence of our belief and pure faith in Hashem is derived from our holy forefathers. The Torah and the *mitzvot* reveal the inner essence of faith. That is the meaning of "Take a census of the entire assembly *(adas)*." By shifting the letters of *adas* to the word *daas,* the word "assembly" is changed to "knowledge"— knowledge of Torah, signifying that the inner essence of knowledge and thoughts of true and pure faith are derived from our ancestors; therefore we say: "the Children of Israel according to their families." (Ch.D., p. 311)

❧❧

On the *Pasuk* "And with you shall be one man from each tribe; a man who is a prince of his father's house." (Num. 1:4) R' Yaacov Yosef of Ostrow commented that a person should strengthen himself to be an "average" individual. He should not become arrogant, and he should not become overly humble. Neither should he be overcome with bitterness. Sadness is the activity of the evil inclination to the extent that even the good deeds are considered as naught. One must realize that we are human; nevertheless, when we do good deeds we reach a higher level. Though it is imperative that one should be humble, nevertheless one should consider himself "a man who is prince of his father's house," a "man" who is a "prince" in Israel, who merits being on a high plane because he goes in the way of his forefathers. (M.D., p. 276)

❧❧

On the *Pasuk* "As Hashem had commanded Moses, he counted them in the wilderness of Sinai" (Num. 1:19), R' Sholom Belzer commented that this *Pasuk* showed that although there were many tribes, the individual tribes were counted as one. That was because all the tribes were connected and there was one concept. All were as one in the command of Hashem. (M.D., p. 276)

On the same *Pasuk*, the Kedushas Levi commented that the *Pasuk* should have been written in reverse. Moses had counted them in the wilderness of Sinai as Hashem had commanded. However, the Kedushas Levi said that Hashem had given Torah to Israel and that the souls of Israel were the essence of the Torah. Each member of Israel is a letter in the Torah. "There are six hundred thousand letters in the Torah"—*Y'eshnam s'hishim r'ibu o'sios l'Torah*. The first letters of each Hebrew word spell Yisroel—Israel. As there are 600,000 letters in the Torah, there were 600,000 people of Israel at that time. Therefore, when Moses counted the Children of Israel, he was learning Torah with them. That is the meaning of the *Pasuk*: Just as Moses studied Torah to know what Hashem commanded, so did the counting also constitute studying Torah. (*Kedushas Levi*, p. 147)

On the *Pasuk*, "And they shall safeguard all the utensils of the Tabernacle" (Num. 3:8), the Koznitzer remarked that a human being is like Hashem's Tabernacle. Just as the Tabernacle and its utensils had to be guarded so that they would constantly be in a state of holiness and purity, so must the human being be careful of blemish or defect. He must constantly be in a state of holiness and purity. (F.C.O., p. 340)

On the *Pasuk* "Thus they shall do for them so that they shall live and not die: when they approach the Holy of Holies . . . But they shall not come and look as the holy is covered, lest they die" (Num. 4:19, 20), R' Moshe Chayim Ephraim of Sadilkov commented in the name of the Baal Shem Tov that there are times that one may come to his Rebbe to learn from his behavior. However, he might come when the Rebbe is not on a high spiritual level and therefore not able to interpret the behavior correctly. The example he gave was when someone had come to R' Nachman of Horedenko and saw him drinking coffee while wearing his prayer shawl and phylacteries. The man returned to his home and imitated the behavior. That is what the *Pasuk* is warning us not to do. At the time of "approach" the Rebbe's holiness was "covered," meaning that at the moment the holiness was not seen. Thus, one would be accepting his mundane behavior and not his holiness. (M.D., p. 280)

NASSO
"TAKE THE CENSUS"

On the *Pasuk* "They shall send away from the camp everyone with *tzaraas* (leprosy)" (Num. 5:2), R' Yechiel Meir Zlatchever commented that those who speak evil of others and those who are haughty receive the punishment of leprosy. Since they are capable of contaminating others, they are sent out of the camp. (F.C.O., p. 343)

⁓⁓⁓

On the *Pasuk* "Speak to the Children of Israel: A man or woman who commits any of man's sins, by committing a trespass against Hashem . . . and they shall confess their sin that they committed" (Num. 5:6, 7), the Zighter commented that when a person performs a mitzvah while being wicked, he feels no need to bring a sin offering. This behavior adds to his *sitrah acharah* (a Kabbalistic term: "the other side," meaning "evil forces") as it says in Psalms 50:16: "But to the wicked Hashem said, 'To what purpose do you recount My decrees and bear My covenant upon your lips?'" One should first purify oneself from the stain of sin, as it is stated: "Turn from evil and do good." (Ps. 34:15). Cleanse your body and soul; then your performance of the *mitzvot* will rise heavenward "as a sweet savor to God." (Lev. 1:9). That is the meaning of the *Pasuk*, for if one performs one of the *mitzvot* that he really does not want to perform, or if he is unclean, then it is "a trespass against Hashem." That is because he was not purified himself. The only advice is to "confess the sin that was committed"; then there will be reflection about all *mitzvot* performed. (M.D., p. 283)

On the *Pasuk* "And they shall confess their sin that they committed; he shall make restitution" (Num. 5:7), the S'fas Emes quoting the Chidushei Harim commented that he asked why confession is needed when committing the transgression of theft. In essence, he noted that every transgression is in the category of theft. Hashem gives vitality and strength to every person so that he may do the will of the Almighty. However, when one uses this gift of vitality and strength to transgress, then he is taking from Hashem's possessions. That warrants that one should confess his transgression. (M.T., vol. 4, p. 32)

On the same *Pasuk*, the Neshchizer, in his *sefer Rishfei Eish*, noted that the *Pasuk* begins in the plural and ends in the singular. On this he commented that this, unfortunately, is the nature of man. He will beat his breast at the statements of confession and verbally confess all his transgressions; that he is ready to do. However, when "making restitution," changing his behavior, and not committing the transgressions— for this there are very few people, therefore the singular. (F.U.A.O., vol. 4, p. 23)

On the *Pasuk* "And every offering of all the holy things of the Children of Israel" (Num. 5:9), R' Moshele Koznitzer commented that every Jew who distances himself from offensive language, tale-bearing, and telling lies is considered a "holy thing of the Children of Israel." (F.C.O., p. 344)

On the *Pasuk* "And every man's hallowed things shall be his; whatever any man gives to the *Kohen* (priest), it shall be his" (Num. 5:10), R' Avraham Chayim of Zlatshov commented that there are those who serve Hashem out of fear that they will not receive much sustenance. Others serve Him out of love without a need for anything. They have no fears except to serve Him. It states: "Every man's hallowed things." For the fearful man, the "things" represent his fear of many things.

When a "man gives to the *Kohen*," he is in the category of loving-kindness, meaning that he serves Hashem out of love and has no need for anything. That is why Rashi commented that "he will have much wealth"—he will have much goodness. (M.D., p. 284)

⸺

On the *Pasuk* "A man or woman who shall set [himself] apart (*yaphlee*) by taking a nazirite vow to set [himself] apart to Hashem" (Num. 6:2), the Koznitzer Maggid commented that when a person is willing to separate himself from the pleasures of the world he is an extraordinary individual, a *peleh*—a play on the word *yaphlee*. (F.C.O., p. 345)

⸺

On the same *Pasuk*, the Koznitzer viewed the nazirite vow and said that if one should decide to fast and perform afflictions of the body to fool others, then it is better not to fast rather than to ultimately fool oneself. (F.U.A.O., vol. 4, p. 28)

⸺

The Sadigurer noted that just as we will give an accounting of how we treated our souls, so too must we give an accounting on how we misused our bodies with affliction and abuse. (F.U.A.O., vol. 4, p. 28)

⸺

In the same vein, the Zanzer asked one of his Chasidim if he had been given food. The Chasid answered that he did not come to eat, to which the Zanzer replied that the soul, also, did not come to eat—however, if it is not fed, it runs away. (F.U.A.O., vol. 4, p. 29)

⸺

On the *Pasuk* "Anything which grapes have been steeped shall he abstain" (Num. 6:3), the Noam Elimelech commented that there are two interpretations of "Anything which . . . have been steeped." One interpretation is that the taste of something that is forbidden is like the forbidden item itself. The other interpretation is that when a permitted item half the size of an olive is attached to a forbidden item the size of half an olive, then it would be as if one ate the entire piece of a forbidden item. The essence of the taste refers to the transgression that is in the thought of a person, which is like committing the transgression itself. Half of a permitted item attached to a forbidden item is equated with dealing with someone who does not deal honestly. Honest money gets mixed up with dishonest money, and then all the money becomes dishonest. That is why one should be very careful in dealing with another. (*Noam Elimelech*, p. 69)

On the *Pasuk* "Speak to Aharon and his sons, saying: So shall you bless the Children of Israel" (Num. 6:23), the Lubliner noted that Aharon's forte was "Loving peace and pursuing peace." (*Ethics of Our Fathers* 1:12) "So shall you"—with your character—"bless the Children of Israel," that among them there shall be harmony and peace. (F.C.O., p. 346)

"So shall you bless the Children of Israel; say to them: May Hashem bless you and guard you. . . . They shall place My name upon the Children of Israel, and I shall bless them." (Num. 6:23–24, 27) The Primishlaner commented that Hashem told Moses to tell Aharon that it was not through him (Moses) that he was being blessed but that he was only Hashem's messenger. "May Hashem bless you"—for when Hashem will bless you then you will be guarded. "And I shall place My name"— when Aharon and his children speak on My behalf "to the Children of Israel," the *Kohanim* will not bless but "I shall place My name"—I and the *Kohanim* will bless. (F.C.O., p. 346)

The Lenchener noted that the priestly blessing is said in the singular. The greatest blessing that the Jews need is one of unity. (F.C.O., p. 347)

The Ostrovitzer noted that the first letters of *Et B'nai Yisrael*—"the Children of Israel"—add up to thirteen, the same as *echad*, "one."

Because the Jews say *echad* every day, they should be blessed with "May Hashem bless you." (F.C.O., p. 347)

~~~

R' Aharon Karliner asked why it was necessary for the *Kohanim* to bless the people. Why didn't Hashem bless the people? — He, Himself, could give all that is good. His answer was that Hashem, knowing the future, knew that the people would adhere less to the *mitzvot* if wealth were just granted to them. That is why Hashem requested that the *Kohen* or the Tzaddik, who does not know the future, bless the people, for there would be no stumbling block in the blessing. At times, even the Tzaddik may feel that his blessing will have a negative consequence. Therefore we say, "As His will and the will of all of Israel," because the effect of a blessing should be that the will of Hashem and all of Israel would be that they wish to be positive Jews. (M.T., vol. 4, p. 38)

~~~

On the *Pasuk* "May Hashem illuminate His countenance toward you . . ." (Num. 6:25), there is a statement in the Talmud (*Berachot* 20b): "The ministering angels said before the Holy One, Blessed is He: It is written about You in Your Torah that You are He Who does not show favor and Who does not accept a bribe. (Deut. 10:17) But do You not show favor to the Jewish people? It is written, 'May God show you favor.' (Num. 6:26) Hashem replied: And shall I not show favor to Israel? For I have written for them in the Torah: And you shall eat, be satisfied, and bless Hashem, your God. (Deut. 8:10) Yet they are especially exacting upon themselves about this law, and are careful to recite the *Bircat Hamazone* (Grace after meals) for virtually any meal, even to the size of an olive or to the size of an egg!" The Rebbe of Satmar commented that that is the core and essence of Judaism. For everyone else, "You shall eat and be satisfied" represents the necessity to have material gain. If ever there comes a time of difficulty, then, as Isaiah said, "And the one who passes therein shall suffer hardships and hunger, and it shall come to pass, and he is hungry and wroth, that he shall curse his king and his god" (Is. 8:21), for materialism makes him forego his religion "even to the size of an olive and an egg." The goal of the Jew is to "bless Hashem" and not be materialistic even though his satisfaction may not be great. The Jew is ready to resist all odds, even in poverty, and not give up his spiritual attitude. (F.U.A.O., vol. 4, p. 35)

On the *Pasuk* "Because the service of the holy is upon them; they carry on the shoulder" (Num. 7:9), the Kotzker commented that when it comes to holy service, one must put his shoulder to the wheel, as it says: "I didn't seek but I found—do not believe." (Talmud *Megillah* 6b) (F.U.A.O., vol. 4, p. 36)

On the *Pasuk* "The one who brought his offering on the first day was Nachshon, son of Amminadav . . . And his offering was: one silver bowl . . ." (Num. 7:12, 13), R' Kalimus Kalman Epstein of Krakow wondered why the words "his offering" are mentioned twice. Hashem requested that he bring the first sacrifice. Nachshon was very embarrassed. He had a great deal of inner conflict and grief. He did not know why he merited being the first to sacrifice. His grief from embarrassment Hashem considered as self-sacrifice. That is why the *Pasuk* mentions "his offering" twice. The first was his self-sacrifice and the second was "one silver bowl." (M.T., vol. 4, p. 42)

On the *Pasuk* "On the second day, Nesanel son of Zuar . . ." (Num. 7:18), R' Bunim of Pshys'cha wondered why each sacrifice was mentioned separately even though each prince brought the same sacrifice. The reason was that each prince willingly brought his own sacrifice and did not wish to replicate the others. (M.T., vol. 4, p. 43)

BEHA'ALOTCHA
"WHEN YOU ALIGHT"

On the *Pasuk* "When you kindle the lamps, toward the face of the menorah" (Num. 8:2), Rabbi Menachem Mendel Schneerson noted that the menorah symbolizes the Jewish people. The menorah has seven branches, symbolizing the different paths in Divine service, but is made of a single gold piece. The various differences and qualities do not detract from the unity. It means that diversity need not lead to division. Each individual talent should lead to a synthesis of different views and behavior. Each individual should internalize the teachings and he should be able to teach others. (G.O.T., pp. 45–47)

On the *Pasuk* "Aharon did so . . ." (Num. 8:3), R' Bunim of Pshys'cha wondered about the *sifri*'s comment that the *Pasuk* is praising Aharon because he did not change any procedure in lighting the lamp. R' Bunim noted that it is obvious that an individual such as Aharon would not make any changes in Hashem's command. After all, he was chosen by Hashem to perform the priestly duties. What the *sifri* really meant was that Aharon's personality did not change though he was put on a high level. He did not become boastful nor arrogant. He remained the same as always, modest and of a humble nature. (F.C.O., p. 350)

On the same *Pasuk*, the Kosover commented that Aharon's sincere performance of his holy work and his deep feeling for Hashem were not noticeable from the outside. All the emotion about his service to Hashem was within him. His attitude shows us the way one should serve Hashem. (F.C.O., p. 351)

⌐—⌐

"They [the Levites] shall take a young bull and its meal offering (*olah*) . . . and a second young bull shall you take as a sin offering." (Num. 8:8) The Kedushas Levi noted that the *olah* sacrifice is stated before the sin offering. However, in *Pasuk* twelve it states: "You shall make one a sin offering and the *olah* offering to Hashem." The law requires that with all the sacrifices, the sin offering comes before the *olah* offering. We must first ask for forgiveness and then bring a gift. The one exception is asking for forgiveness for idol worship; for that we must first bring the *olah*. The reason is that "a thought accompanies the deed." (Zohar, *Bereshit* 28b) First we bring an *olah*, which forgives the innermost thoughts. The sacrifices of the Levites were brought to earn forgiveness for the sin of the golden calf. Actually, an *olah* sacrifice should have been brought first and then the sin offering, as is the law for idol worship. But the Almighty, Who knows all inner thoughts, knew that the Israelites did not sin because of their thought. All they wanted was a leader. That is why the sin offering came first, as in the case of all others sins. (*Kedushas Levi*, p. 154)

⌐—⌐

R' Aharon Karliner asked why Moses said to the Israelites, "Stand and I will hear what Hashem will command you." (Num. 8:8) The Karliner noted that because of Moses' humility, he insisted that because of the merits of the Israelites they should stand next to him to hear "what Hashem will command." Moses felt that if they were not near him, he did not merit hearing "what Hashem will command you." (F.C.O., p. 352)

⌐—⌐

"There shall not be a plague among the Children of Israel when the Children of Israel approach the Sanctuary." (Num. 8:19) R' Meir Zitkover commented that some approach the Sanctuary when they are in dire straits and need help. Our hope is "there will not be a plague" and "one should approach the Sanctuary" with complete joy. (F.U.A.O., vol. 4, p. 42)

~~

Regarding the *Pasuk* "But a man who is pure and was not on the road" (Num. 9:13), the Ropshitzer explained that it means that if a person remains in one place he will mature and develop a strong personality. If he wanders, then it becomes easier for him to go off the right path. (F.U.A.O., vol. 4, p. 43)

~~

The *Pasuk* "When you gather together the congregation, you shall sound a long blast, but not short blasts" (Num. 10:7) is a lesson in leadership, commented R' Meir Primishlaner. The blasts are like a watch. It is taken apart, cleaned, and then put together again. So it is with the blasts: The long blast is straight and plain, the broken blasts are shattered and crooked, and then there is again a long blast. When one is a leader of a congregation, he should lead like a long blast, plainly, without arrogance. In that way he will bring them together in love and harmony. That is the meaning of "gather together the congregation." However, if he leads with short blasts, with arrogance and haughtiness, then the congregation will leave with a sense of depression and resignation. (F.C.O., p. 353)

~~

On the *Pasuk* "And the wrath of Hashem flared greatly, and in the eyes of Moses it was bad" (Num. 11:10), the Berditchever noted that "the wrath of Hashem flared" because Moses did not defend the Israelites. (F.U.A.O., vol. 4, p. 48)

~~

On the *Pasuk* "Now the man Moses was exceedingly humble" (Num. 12:3), the Mishmeres Itmar noted that Moses stood above all other humble people. (F.C.O., p. 357)

R' Shalom Belzer noted that there are two forms of humility. There are those who feel that they are as nothing and everyone else is also nothing. That is false humility. True humility is when one considers that others may be above him. (F.C.O., p. 357)

SHELACH L'CHA
"SEND FORTH"

This *Sidra* tells of the report made by the spies sent by Moses to scout the promised land of Canaan and its inhabitants. Ten of the twelve spies gave a very negative view of the inhabitants of the land. They said, "We cannot ascend to that people for it is stronger than us (*mimenu*)." (Num. 13:31) The Talmud (*Sotah* 35a) notes that the word *mimenu* can also be read as *mimemno*—"they are stronger than Him," the implication being that the Canaanites were too powerful for Hashem. The Talmud further states that it was as if "the master of the house cannot remove his furniture from it." The Lubavitcher Rebbe gave the following Chasidic explanation of the attitude of the spies. He said that the spies were concerned that the Israelites would be influenced by Canaanite paganism. There were concerned not with physical defeat but with spiritual defeat. Since the land had to be tilled, the Israelites would have no time for sincere service to Hashem and would develop the same attitude toward spirituality as the Canaanites. It was Joshua and Calev who had a positive point of view, for they inspired the people with the statement "We shall surely ascend and conquer it, for we can surely do it." (Num. 13:30) They said: We have overcome all that occurred to us from the time we left Egypt, especially in the wilderness. Our spirituality helped us ascend beyond the concerns of the world. In Canaan, we can again make further spiritual gains and ascend even higher by finding Hashem within the possessions of the land. Let us till the land as a people who inherit the land and not as a people who buy land from a stranger. This narrative is a lesson for the life of a

Jew. We live daily two lives, a life in wilderness and a life in the land of Israel. In the morning, we are in "the wilderness"—learning and prayer. Then we go to the "land of Israel"—to till the soil—the world of livelihood. We must accept the attitude of Joshua and Calev to find within earning a livelihood the spiritual—"ascend and conquer." (Torah Studies, pp. 245–251)

On the *Pasuk* "send forth for yourself men, and let them spy out the Land of Canaan that I give to the Children of Israel." (Num. 13:2) The Ostovitzer noted Rashi's comment, "For yourself (at your discretion), I do not command you; if you wish, send forth." He explained that Rashi's statement meant that Hashem said that I am not commanding you to send spies. But, if you (Moses) are going to send them, then it should be with your sincere feelings toward the land. Instill within them your love and burning desire toward the land, that "I give to the Children of Israel." (F.C.O., p. 363)

On the *Pasuk* "And Moses called Hoshea, son of Nun "Joshua" (Num. 13:16), the Rimanover noted that the Yonatan ben Uziel translation states that when Moses saw that Hoshea was humble, he changed his name to Joshua, for he prayed that Hashem should save him from the plot of the spies. (Rashi 13:16) The Rimanover explained that there are two types of Tzaddikim (righteous people). There are some who will do battle with insincere leaders because they are not concerned for themselves and are not worried that there are many who oppose them. There are those who, due to their humility, do not wish to rock the boat and will step aside and not get involved. Moses was concerned that a moment might arise when Joshua's strength was needed but he would step aside. So Moses prayed that Hashem should save him from being humble. (F.U.A.O., vol. 4, p. 65)

On the same *Pasuk*, the Gerer Rebbe noted that one of the characteristics of a humble person is to be compromising, to be ready to forgo his own views. Moses knew that the spies were people of note. Therefore, he was concerned that Joshua might give in to the views of the others. We find the same with one's religious behavior, for there are times that one must be uncompromising, and the help of the Almighty is needed. (M.T., vol. 4, p. 60)

~~

On the *Pasuk* "See the land . . ." (Num. 13:18), the Kotzker noted that only the inside of an earthenware utensil can become impure. Furthermore, it cannot then be made pure, so the only solution is to destroy the utensil. Because it was made from earth, it had no value until it was made into a utensil and had an inside. That is why when the inside, the part that made it into something, becomes impure, it has no value and therefore it is broken. The same is true with the human being. "The human being is made from earth and returns to earth." (High Holiday Prayer Book) The essence of "the being" is on the inside; that is what makes one human. When what makes one human becomes impure, then only a broken heart can make it pure. (F.C.O., p. 365)

~~

"And how is the land in which it dwells: Is it good or is it bad? . . . You shall strengthen yourselves." (Num. 13:19, 20) The Kotzker noted that Moses requested the spies to report the positive aspects of the land. Even if they detected aspects that were negative, they were to report the positive. If the land looked lean, it was to be seen as fertile. When it comes to the Land of Israel, even if one sees things that are negative, one must strengthen himself and not become depressed. (*Amud Ha'emet*, p. 38)

~~

On the words "You shall strengthen yourselves and take from the fruit of the land . . ." (Num. 13:20), the Bratzlaver noted that the nations have stolen from us the Land of Israel. We must constantly declare, loud and clear, that it is our land and our inheritance, and give notice that they have no right to it even if they have inhabited it for many years. The law is that if one leaves land because it has been taken under protest and by force, the possession by the aggressor is nullified. (F.U.A.O., vol. 4, p. 68)

⌒⌒

On the *Pasuk* "They [the spies] went and came to Moses and to Aharon" (Num. 13:26), Rashi comments: "To compare their going with their coming; just as their coming was with an evil scheme, so, too, their going was with an evil scheme." The Gerer Rebbe asked why Rashi had said earlier in *Pasuk* 3 that they were distinguished men. The Sages note that an evil thought is not considered a deed, but if the thought becomes a deed, then both the thought and the deed are considered as one. (Talmud *Kiddushin* 40a) Although the spies may have gone with evil thoughts, it was not obvious when Moses sent them and they were men of distinction. However, when they returned and gave the evil report, the thought became a deed. Therefore, the deed had become part of the thought and we can now compare their going and their coming. (M.T., vol. 4, p. 64)

⌒⌒

"The cities are fortified and large. . . ." (Num. 13:28) R' Meir Simcha of Dvinsk, though not a Zionist, was a proponent of obtaining land and inhabiting Israel. He became extremely happy with the establishment of each new colony even when made by secularists. He said that though it says, "May His great name grow exalted and sanctified" (Prayer Book), we must first make great and "fortify" and then we will sanctify. (F.U.A.O., vol. 4, p. 71)

⌒⌒

On the *Pasuk* "And Hashem said, 'I have forgiven in accordance with your words'" (Num. 14:20), the Kedushas Levi noted Rashi's statement, "Because of that which you have said, lest they say, 'Lest Hashem lacked the ability.'" He explained that Hashem could have revised the thoughts of the other nations and not let them say that Hashem lacked the ability to bring the Israelites to Canaan. However, Moses already had said, "The nations that heard of Your fame." (Num. 14:15) Therefore, there would have been a desecration of the Name, so Hashem said, "I have forgiven according with your words." (*Kedushas Levi*, p. 157)

⌒⌒

The Berditchever was asked if his constant debate with Hashem, accusing Him of not dealing correctly with His people, was causing him to commit the transgression of *lashon harah* (slander) against Hashem. The Berditchever answered that the spies spoke slander against the Land of Israel and against the Almighty. They said, "We are not able to go up against the people for they are stronger than us." (Num. 13:31) Nevertheless, "Hashem said, 'I have forgiven in accordance with your words.'" (Num. 14:20) In addition, he said that our Sages said the Halachah is that whatever is said before three is not considered slander. (*Eiruchin* 15b) Since "And the glory of Hashem shall fill the world" (Num. 14:21) and Hashem is everywhere, it cannot be considered *lashon harah*. (F.U.A.O., vol. 4, p. 77)

⌒⌒

"And your young children of whom you said they will be taken captive, I shall bring them; they shall know the land that you have despised." (Num. 14:31) R' Mendel Vitebsker wrote a note to his Chasidim concerning the attitude of the youth of his time. Using this *Pasuk*, he noted that though their outlook is easygoing and casual, nevertheless it is they who recognize and have the true love for Israel. (F.U.A.O., vol. 4, p. 79)

⌒⌒

"You shall bear your iniquities—forty years—and you shall experience My withdrawal." (Num. 14:34) In the *sefer Yakar Mipaz*, there is a comment on Rashi's interpretation of this *Pasuk*. Rashi states: "You have removed your hearts from following Me. It is an expression of removal." The author wants us to realize that the spies were not ordinary people. They did not want to leave the desert. They ate food that came from the Heavens, drank from Miriam's well, and were surrounded by Heavenly clouds. It was a spiritual life and now they were asked to do manual labor, namely, to till the soil and other worldly tasks. To them it was as if they were to lower their spiritual standards. Nevertheless, a true servant of Hashem follows His will, as a blind person follows the one who can see. That is the meaning of "You will experience My withdrawal"—though your intentions were good, it was a transgression because you removed yourselves from Me by using your own rationale. That is why the *Pasuk* states: "But My servant Calev, because a different spirit was with him." (Num. 14:24) Though Calev agreed that dwelling in the desert was better for serving Hashem, he nullified his own feelings and performed the will of Hashem. (M.T., vol. 4, p. 72)

"Upon your coming to the land to which I bring you. . . ." (Num. 15:18) The Baal Shem Tov noted that man was created to eat and drink. If the Almighty wanted He could have created man to exist without nourishment. The purpose of eating and drinking is not to satisfy the desire but to remind us that we eat and drink to recall that Hashem created all. When it comes to matters of the earth, "upon your coming to the land," one becomes hungry. Then one should remember: "It shall be that when you eat of the bread of the land" (Num. 15:19), whenever you will eat, "you shall set aside a portion for Hashem," for its purpose is to bring you to recognize the Creator. (F.C.O., p. 369)

"I am Hashem, your God, Who has taken you out of the land of Egypt. . . . I am Hashem, your God." (Num. 15:41) The Kedushas Levi noted that "I am Hashem, your God" is mentioned twice. This is to emphasize that one should remember that all our thoughts and behavior on earth make an impression above. Therefore, we are to be careful in our thinking and actions because of Divine Providence. That is the basis of service to Hashem. (*Kedushas Levi*, p. 158)

KORACH

Rabbi Menachem Mendel Schneerson, the Lubavitcher Rebbe, discussed the reasons Korach, who symbolized dissension, should have a *Sidra* named after him. One explanation was that Korach had good intentions; after all, striving to become the High Priest was a noble goal. That was a goal that Moses also sought, as Rashi states: "Moses said, 'I, too, want this.'" (Num. 16:6) Also, we were told at Sinai that we are a kingdom of priests (Ex. 19:6). Therefore, Korach defended himself by saying, "The entire congregation is holy; Hashem is in their midst." (Num. 16:3) Every Jew has a spark of the Divine within him, and Korach wanted that spark to flourish and was willing to sacrifice his life for that cause. He offered incense even after Moses told him it would mean death, as Rashi states: "And all of you will die." (Num. 16:6) However, the Rebbe said that it is our actions and not our intentions that Hashem judges. Whatever his intentions were, he did create controversy that resulted in the death of thousands of people. Controversy is contrary to the principles of the Torah. However, unity is not absolute; it has limits. Unity comprises many views, each having its own nature. That is the Torah view of unity, as Rashi states: "The Holy One, Blessed is He, divided the world with boundaries. Can you turn morning into evening?" (Num. 16:5) All views, each with its own nature, can merge into harmony. Diversity need not lead to strife. Korach made a wrong choice in using his dissension to cause strife; far worse was that he never admitted his error. However, Korach's children realized that the Torah leads to true unity (Talmud *Sanhedrin* 110a). Therefore, the Levites (Korach's tribe) were elevated to priestly heights. This *Sidra* is a reminder that unity should and can succeed in spite of division. (G.O.T., vol. 2, pp. 55–59)

⮑⮌

The Lubliner noted that right at the beginning of the *Sidra*, we notice the difference between Moses and Korach. Korach did not have any good qualities of his own. He had to depend upon his ancestry, which is why the *Pasuk* states: "Son of Izhar, son of Kohath, son of Levi." (Num. 16:1) The ancestry of Moses is not mentioned. He was able to stand on his own merits. (F.C.O., p. 374)

⮑⮌

"*Vayikach* Korach son of Izhar, son of Kohath, son of Levi. . . ." (Num. 16:1) R' Dovid Talener noted that the *Targum Onkelus* (Aramaic translation) defined the word *vayikach* ("he took") as "he separated himself" from the congregation of Israel. The Talener remarked that the entire world is divided and each individual is in himself divided. (F.C.O., p. 374)

⮑⮌

The Yid HaKadosh noted that Korach had two evil traits, namely, anger and divisiveness. His mistake was that he thought that for the sake of a mitzvah and Heaven, one is permitted to make use of these traits. Therefore the *Onkelus* uses the term "separated"—by using his two evil characteristics, he separated himself from a sense of holiness. (F.C.O., p. 375)

⮑⮌

On the *Pasuk* "Why do you exalt yourselves?" (Num. 16:3), the Kotzker noted that when people look for controversy and wish to find fault with a Tzaddik (righteous one), they look for points that are the opposite of his character. That becomes obvious in Korach's condemnation of Moses: They accused him of being haughty, but the Torah is very clear in declaring Moses a modest individual. (M.T., vol. 4, p. 80)

R' Naftali Ropshitzer gave the following comment on the *Pasuk* in Psalms, "They were jealous of Moses in the camp, of Aharon, Hashem's holy one." (Ps. 106:16) He said that is the method used by those who try to find controversy and seek to divide. They tell the leaders what to do and then criticize them. If he studies all day and is involved with spiritual matters, he is accused of not being concerned with community matters. If he gets concerned with community matters, they prefer that he study and involve himself only with spiritual matters. So it was with Moses and Aharon. Moses left the camp to study Torah and become involved with spiritual matters and was accused of not having concern for the people. Aharon, on the other hand, tried to make peace wherever he could and was concerned with the welfare of the people, but was accused of interfering in matters that were not of his concern, for he was "Hashem's holy one." (M.T., vol. 4, p. 80)

On the same *Pasuk*, the Baal Shem Tov noted the Mishnah in the *Ethics of Our Fathers* (1:1): "Moses (Moshe) received the Torah from Sinai." He stated that the Hebrew letters of Moses' name stand for *Machlokes Shammai Hillel*, which refers to the controversy between Hillel and Shammai, who were two teachers in the Talmud. The disputes of Shammai and Hillel were for the sake of "receiving the Torah" and not for causing conflict. (F.C.O., p. 377)

On the *Pasuk* "And as for Aharon, what is he that you caused protest against him?" (Num. 16:11), the Kotzker commented that Moses was really asking: How well do you know Aharon that you cause protest against him? (*Amud Ha'emet*, p. 39)

The Baal Shem Tov commented that the letters of the Torah are the souls of the Jewish people. When the Torah is divided into fifths then there is no prohibition against erasing a letter. When the Torah is not divided, then one is not permitted to erase a letter. Thus it is with the Jewish people: When there is conflict and disunity then the enemy can do much harm. When there is unity then no harm can come to them. (F.C.O., p. 379)

⌇⌇

On the *Pasuk* "Moses sent forth to summon Datan and Aviram. . . ." (Num. 16:12), Rashi commented that we should not prolong a dispute. R' Yitzchak Vorker noted that in a dispute we are not permitted to say that we have already tried this or that and have given up hope. No matter how long it may take to bring peace between people, we must keep on trying. So it was with Moses; he appealed for peace many times and kept on calling on them. (F.C.O., p. 383)

⌇⌇

On the *Pasuk* "As for the fire-pans of these sinners against their own lives . . ." (Num. 17:3), the Ropshitzer noted that the worst transgression committed by those who are prone to develop conflict is to say that their cause is for the rectification of the soul. In reality their concern is for their own physical needs.(*Otzer Pninim*, vol. 4, p. 276)

⌇⌇

On the *Pasuk* "It shall be that the man whom I choose, his staff will blossom. . . ." (Num. 17:20), the Riziner wondered why all the leaders brought their staffs and put them together with Aharon's staff. The Riziner commented that the Torah shows the righteousness and humility of the other leaders. They deliberately brought their staffs to make known to all the people that only Aharon's staff would blossom, to show that he was the chosen of Hashem to be the High Priest. (F.C.O., p. 384)

⌇⌇

"And I—behold! I have taken your brethren the Levites from among the Children of Israel; to you (*lachem*) they are given a gift for Hashem, to perform the service of the congregation." (Num. 18:6) In his *sefer*

Toldot Yitzchak, R' Yitzchak Shapiro of Neshchiz took the letters of the word *lachem* ("to you") and changed them to the word *melech* ("king") to tell us that the essence of true service is to take on "the kingdom of heaven" and be content to do the will of Hashem. (M.D., p. 310)

CHUKAT
"STATUTES"

R abbi Menachem Mendel Schneerson, the Lubavitcher Rebbe, explained the necessity for the *Chukim*, the *mitzvot* whose rationale
defies human intelligence. To permit everyone to understand the entire
Torah by way of reason would permit man to rely on his own understanding and not allow for the challenge of developing spiritual commitment. There would be a desire to follow one's longing and to
rationalize one's conduct. Specifically, the sacrifice of the red heifer is
unique in that it completely transcends human comprehension, making
the pure impure and the impure pure. In I Kings 5:11 we read that King
Solomon, who was the personification of reason and wisdom, said that
he was able to comprehend every difficult passage in the Torah but that
of the red heifer, which was "far from me." However, to allow for
performing the will of Hashem, the entire Torah could not be written
above human intelligence. We do know that Moses did understand
the laws of the red heifer because Hashem gave him the explanation.
He permitted the rationale for the red heifer to be intertwined with
Divine input. Moses was a medium for the expression of Hashem's
truth. Since in the Torah there are aspects of comprehension and aspects
beyond understanding, one needs both reason and *mesiras nefesh*—self-
sacrifice—to grasp all of Torah. (G.O.T., vol. 2, pp. 61–65)

~~~~~~

The Berditchever noted that Hashem gave us laws that can be understood and laws that are beyond the human ken. That is to show that we

285

should perform all the *mitzvot* because we are commanded to do so. (F.C.O., p. 385)

～

The Kedushas Levi explained that the reason some *mitzvot* of the Torah are hidden from man is that one must perform a mitzvah because it is a command of Hashem. That is why the Torah states that all *mitzvot* are decrees and that we do the *mitzvot* because we are commanded. The soul, which is always with Hashem, wants to do the *mitzvot* constantly and to serve Hashem without hesitation. It is the body that hesitates at times because it may not know the reason. If the reason were known, it too would want to perform the *mitzvot* all the time. For a person who allows his body to dictate the soul, his body is not pure when his soul leaves him. It is the righteous one, whose soul dictates his body, who is always pure. (*Kedushas Levi*, p. 159)

～

On the *Pasuk* "This is the statute of the Torah . . ." (Num. 19:2), Rashi says: "Because the Accuser and the nations of the world aggrieve Israel by saying, 'What is this commandment?' and 'What reason is there to it?' therefore [Torah] wrote it as a 'statute.' It is a decree from before Me: you do not have the right to reflect upon it." The Primishlaner commented that the evil inclination does all it can to dissuade a person who is ready to do a mitzvah and it will taunt the person after the performance of a mitzvah. First it will say that the mitzvah has no meaning. After the mitzvah is done, it will say how deep and significant was its performance. That will bring out the arrogance of the individual. Therefore, one should say before doing a mitzvah that it is a decree from Hashem. After the mitzvah, one should not give it further thought. (M.T., vol. 4, p. 91)

～

R' Moshe Koznitzer noted that true Torah study is for its own sake and not so that one should be called "wise." (F.C.O., p. 385)

⤙⤚

The Bratzlaver explained that one who teaches Torah or expounds it to the public should make sure that his explanation is clear and suitable to the people listening. (F.C.O., p. 385)

⤙⤚

On the words "which has no blemish, upon which a yoke has not come" (Num. 19:2), the Lubliner noted that for one who considers himself without blemish, the yoke of Heaven has not come upon him—for if a person would have the yoke of Heaven upon him, he would know that there is no person who does not have a blemish. (F.C.O., p. 388)

⤙⤚

On the *Pasuk* "He shall purify himself with it [corpse] on the third day, and on the seventh day he shall be pure (Num. 19:12), the S'fas Emes noted that it is known that the transgression committed by Adam and Eve concerning the Tree of Knowledge brought death and the impurity of death to the world. That was because the snake convinced them that if they would eat from the tree "you will be as a god, knowing good and evil." (Gen. 3:5) He convinced them that they must heed their common sense and nullify the sense of the command of Hashem. Therefore, the red heifer, which is a decree without reason, requires that one should nullify his reasoning to the Will of Hashem, a redemption of the transgression of the Tree of Knowledge that therefore purifies the impurity of death. (M.T., vol. 4, p. 95)

⤙⤚

On the words "This is the Torah regarding a man . . ." (Num. 19:14), R' Yaacov Yisroel Cherkaser noted that when a person keeps healthy and holy every part of his body—namely, the two hundred forty-eight organs that are equivalent to the two hundred forty-eight positive commandments, and the three hundred sixty-five blood vessels that are equivalent to the negative commandments—such a person is called "a Torah." (F.C.O., p. 390)

⌒

"They shall take for the impure person some of the ashes of the burnt purification offering, and he shall put on it living water in a vessel." (Num. 19:17) The Gerer Rebbe noted that a person is called *adam* because he was created from *adamah*, earth. He is also compared to *adamah l'elyon*, "the heavenly earth." Though a person should consider himself as humble as the earth, he must also strive by his deeds to emulate the characteristics of Hashem, as our Sages noted: "As He is merciful so shall you be merciful." (Talmud *Shabbat* 133b) He should remember that he has a Divine soul and therefore must constantly say, "Because of me was the world created." (*Sanhedrin* 37) Therefore, we have to purify the impure from the "ashes of the burnt purification" and put "living water" to be humble as dust, but also know that we have a living soul. (M.T., vol. 4, p. 96)

⌒

"And give drink to the assembly and their animals." (Num. 20:8) There is a comment in the *Sefer Chasidim* that according to this *Pasuk* we must first give drink to the assembled and then to the animals. However, we find that our Sages said: "I will provide grass in your field for your cattle and you will eat and be satisfied." (Grace after meals) Therefore, when it comes to eating, we must first feed our animals. (M.T., vol. 4, p. 98)

⌒

"Listen now, rebels (*hamorim*). . . ." (Num. 20:10) R' Heschel said that our Sages noted: "One who comes with anger will make a mistake." (*Sifri Matos* 48) The reason Moses made a mistake and hit the rock was that the spirit of Hashem had left him because he had become angry with the Israelites. (F.C.O., p. 390)

⌒

On the same *Pasuk*, the Gerer Rebbe noted Rashi's comment that in the Greek language *hamorim* means "fools." It intimates that they instruct their teachers because they have no respect for their teachers. However, *morim* may also mean "teachers." The Rebbe said that the reason Rashi equates *morim* with both teachers and fools is because, as it states in Proverbs, "If you see a man wise in his own eyes, there is more hope for the fool than he." (Prov. 26:12) If he teaches his teacher, he apparently considers himself wiser; therefore, he is worse than a fool. (M.T., vol. 4, p. 98)

~~

On the *Pasuk* "Because you did not believe in Me to sanctify Me" (Num. 20:12), the Kedushas Levi notes that there was a difference of opinion between Nachmanides and Rashi as to why Moses was punished. Nachmanides maintained that it was because Moses got angry and insulted the people. Rashi maintained that it was because he hit the stone. The Kedushas Levi said that this points out the two methods of teaching. One Tzaddik may use harsh words to bring people to repentance and another may inspire them so that they do not wish to transgress. The method one uses to teach will apply its use in all his dealings and in turn the universe will react accordingly. Therefore, when Moses spoke harshly to the Israelites and said to them, "Listen now, rebels" (Num. 20:10), the stone also did not listen and he had no choice but to strike the rock. (*Kedushas Levi*, p. 160)

~~

On the *Pasuk* "Edom said to him, 'You shall not pass through me, lest I go forth against you with the sword'" (Num. 20:18), Rashi comments: "You pride yourselves with the voice that your forefather bequeathed you, and say, 'We cried out to Hashem and He heard our voice,' and I go forth against you with that which my forefather bequeathed me." R' Tzvi of Zidichov explained that Jewish prayer is very powerful only when there is no arrogance. Even is there is only a modicum of arrogance, the prayer is not effective. Therefore, Rashi says: If "You pride yourselves with your voice," it shows that you have arrogance in your prayer, and Esav (Edom) will overpower you. When your prayer is honest, then Esav has no power over you; as long as the voice is the voice of Jacob, then the hands are not the hands of Esav. (M.T., vol. 4, p. 100)

On the *Pasuk* "Israel made a vow to Hashem and said, 'If You will deliver this people into my hand . . .'" (Num. 21:2), Rashi commented: "This is Amalek, as it says: 'Amalek dwells in the area of the South.'" (Num. 13:29) Based on Rashi, the Chidushei Harim noted that the Amalekites deliberately changed their language to that of the Canaanites so that the Israelites would think that they were Canaanites. When the Israelites recognized the clothing of the Amalekites but heard the Canaanite language, they became confused and prayed, "Deliver this people into our hands," without mentioning the name of the people. The Chidushei Harim explained that the Amalekites knew that if they had changed their clothing, they would be Amalekites by birth but Canaanites by action and they refused to change their entire national character. From this we learn that one who changes his national language and changes to foreign clothing may be a Jew by birth, but in character he belongs to the people whose language he speaks and clothing he wears. (F.C.O., p. 391)

On the *Pasuk* "God sent snakes, the burning ones, and they bit the people" (Num. 21:6), R' Yaacov Izbitzer commented that Hashem sent people who lacked honesty because they spoke evil, were tale-bearers, and caused dissension among the people. These are snakes in the form of people. In their mouths they have deadly poison that can destroy innocent people and bring disharmony. (F.C.O., p. 392)

"Moses made a snake of copper and placed it on the pole. . . . he would stare at the copper snake and live." (Num. 21:9) On this *Pasuk* Rashi comments: "Could a snake cause death or give life? Rather, at the time that Israel would look upward and subject their hearts to their Father in Heaven, they would be cured." The Ropshitzer explained that a Jew must constantly look Heavenward but not be so completely involved there that he neglects to look at what is happening around him on earth. Therefore, our thoughts should be Heavenward but remain on earth. (F.U.A.O., vol. 4, p. 116)

~~~

"Hashem said to Moses, 'Make yourself a burning one and place it on a pole (*nes*) and it will be that anyone who had been bitten will look at it and live.'" (Num. 21:8) The Koznitzer commented: "Make yourself a burning one" refers to the blessing made over the candles on Chanukah. The Hebrew word *nes* can be translated as "miracle" as well as "pole." Therefore, he interpreted that "place it on a pole (*nes*)" refers to the blessing "That you perform miracles," which is the second blessing over the Chanukah candles. "And live" refers to the blessing "Who has kept us alive." (F.C.O., p. 392)

~~~

"And from the wilderness a gift." (Num. 21:18) On these words our Sages said that when a person makes himself as a desert, he nullifies everything that the Torah has given him as a gift. (Talmud *Nedarim* 55a) R' Bunim of Pshys'cha noted that people are mistaken in their thinking that others and not themselves should give up their needs for the Torah. (F.U.A.O., vol. 4, p. 117)

~~~

"The poets would say, 'Come to Heshbon; let it be built. . . .'" (Num. 21:27) R' Elimelech Lizensker noted that the name "Heshbon" could also be translated to mean "giving an account." He was known for self-affliction for the purpose of ridding himself of bodily desires. He explained why he, a person of high spiritual level, must give such a severe accounting of himself and perform such acts of purification. When an ordinary individual transgresses, the result is not as detrimental as when a righteous person commits the slightest transgression. It is like a knife that penetrates a thick piece but does not go very deep. However, if it penetrates a thin piece it goes right through. (F.C.O., p. 392)

BALAK

The Primishlaner noted that though Balak was not a friend of the Jews, a *Sidra* was named after him. He explained that there are enemies of the Jews who hide their animosity such that the Jews think of them as friends. Balak did not hide his hatred, and for this honesty he merited having his name given to a *Sidra*. (F.C.O., p. 395)

෴

"Moab said to the elders of Midian, 'Now the congregation will chew up our entire surroundings, as an ox chews up the greenery of the field.'" (Num. 22:4) The Kedushas Levi asked why Moab was afraid of the Israelites, for they were told not to bother Moab. However, because Sichon had captured land from Moab and Ammon, Moab feared that others might conquer his land and that therefore the Israelites would be permitted to conquer it. The same is true of food. All food increases in value as a result of human consumption. Grass can be consumed by the human only when one eats the cow; thus grass becomes of value. That is why it says: "Now the congregation will chew up our entire surroundings, as an ox chews up the greenery of the field." In the same manner, the Israelites would be able to conquer Moab by overpowering the other nations that had conquered him. (*Kedushas Levi*, p. 161)

෴

"He sent messengers to Balaam." (Num. 22:5) Rashi said: "So that the nations should not have an excuse by saying, 'Were we to have had prophets we would have repented,' Hashem established prophets for them." R' Bunim of Pshys'cha said that it was not in the nature of the nations to be believers in the Creator, and therefore they should not have an excuse. They say that they cannot believe in something that they cannot see. However, if they are not believers, then why do they believe in Balaam? Why do they believe in witchcraft and other nonsense? (F.U.A.O., p. 119)

〜〜

"Arise and go with them, but the thing that I shall speak to you, that is what you shall do." (Num. 22:20) R' Pinchas Koritzer noted that Hashem said to Balaam that he might go if he wished but nothing would come of his mission. His goal would only be reached based on what Hashem would tell him—that and no more! (F.C.O., p. 395)

〜〜

On the *Pasuk* "Balaam arose in the morning and saddled his she-donkey" (Num. 22:21), the Kotzker explained that Hashem made it clear to Balaam that Abraham had also awakened in the morning to saddle his animal when he went to sacrifice Isaac. However, Isaac was not sacrificed because the Jewish people were to emanate from him. Therefore, it should have been obvious that Balaam's mission would definitely fail because he was seeking the destruction of the Jewish people. (F.C.O., p. 395)

〜〜

"Behold! It is a nation that will dwell in solitude and not be reckoned among the nations." (Num. 23:9) The Rimanover commented that Balaam's curse was that each Jew should be isolated and that there would be no connection, one with the other. It is our task to turn that curse into a blessing and become a thoroughly united people to the extent that there will be no division whatsoever. (*Yalkut Menachem*, p. 183)

〜〜

On the *Pasuk* "You will see its edge but all of it you will not see" (Num. 23:13), the Kotzker Rebbe commented that when one looks at a Jew, one may find fault—however, only at "its edge." If one looks at the nation as a whole, "all of it," there are not faults to be seen because the Jews are a good people. (M.T., vol. 4, p. 111)

***

"He perceived no iniquity in Jacob and saw no perversity in Israel. Hashem, his God, is with him, and the friendship of the King is in him." (Num. 23:21) The Chidushei Harim commented that when "Hashem is with him, and the friendship of the King is in him," then if a person commits a transgression, it is most likely accidental and he will repent immediately, for he is still devoted to the Kingdom of Heaven. (M.T., vol. 4, p. 112)

***

On the same *Pasuk*, the Zanzer said that the one who does not see any "iniquity in Jacob" and "no perversity in Israel" and judges the Jews favorably is a Tzaddik (righteous person) and "Hashem is with him and the friendship of the King is in him." (F.U.A.O., vol. 4, p. 127)

***

On the same *Pasuk*, the Berditchever noted that when a Jew transgresses Hashem does not take notice, so to speak. Therefore, if Hashem, Who knows all inner thoughts, can overlook the transgressions, then without doubt a human being who makes mistakes should not see any "iniquity in Jacob" for he might imagine that another person has committed a sin that in reality might not be a sin. (F.U.A.O., vol. 4, p. 127)

***

"Balaam raised his eyes and saw Israel dwelling according to its tribes, and the spirit of God overcame him." (Num. 24:2) Rashi commented: "He saw that their entrances (*pitcheyhem*) [of their tents] were not aligned opposite each other." The Riziner noted that the word *petach* is also an expression of regret. Therefore, Rashi's comment meant that the regrets and jealousies of the Jewish people are not identical for everyone. Each Jew has a virtue that another does not have. Therefore each Jew is jealous of the other because he regrets that he does not have this particular merit. Balaam saw that in general there are many good qualities that the Jews have, so "the spirit of God overcame him" and he decided not to curse them. (F.C.O., p. 398)

⸺

On the *Pasukim* "The words of Balaam son of Beor, the words of the man with the pierced eye" and "The words of the one who hears the sayings of God, who sees the vision of Shad-ai, while fallen and with covered eyes" (Num. 24:3, 4), the Rebbe of Neshchiz noted that our Sages said that Balaam was blind in one eye (Talmud *Sanhedrin* 105a). He said that every person needs two eyes, for with one he can see the greatness of the Almighty and with the other he should see his own humility. Balaam knew only of the greatness of the Almighty but did not see his own humility, for in fact he was arrogant. (M.T., vol. 4, p. 196)

⸺

On the same *Pasuk*, the Sadigurer explained the words "the words of the man" to mean that the ordinary person maintains that everything is regulated by nature and not by a Higher Power Who takes care of people's actions and behavior. Therefore, when a tragedy befalls him because he is spiritually blind, he does not see the Divinity in the happening; he does not perceive beyond his own ken. He becomes confused, depressed, and resigned to the worst. He does not know on whom he should call for consolation. However, for the one who sees the vision of Shad-ai, the one who is on a higher plane and has complete faith, then when tragedy befalls him, God forbid, he looks at it with open eyes. He does not become depressed because he believes with a perfect faith that all is within the Divine Province. He has hope that "All that Hashem does is for the best." (F.C.O., p. 398)

⸺

"Come, I shall advise you what this people will do to your people in the End of Days." (Num. 24:14). The Kotzker noted that Balaam looked toward the future and saw that as long as the Jews remained strong in their beliefs, refused to become assimilated, and practiced that "they are an isolated people," then no one who wished to destroy them would be able to undo their existence. On the contrary, the more they are pursued the stronger they become. Therefore, Balaam said that the way to break the foundation of the Jews is to destroy the barrier between them and other nations, to try to assimilate them into another way of life, for once they become part of another people they can be subdued. Make the Jews "what this people do to your people," by encouraging the Jews to imitate what your people are doing. This can happen "in the End of Days." (F.C.O., p. 400)

～～

On the same *Pasuk*, R' Bunim of Pshys'cha explained that what is meant by "the End of Days" is that assimilation will occur before the coming of the Redeemer. (F.C.O., p. 400)

～～

"And behold! A man of the Children of Israel came and brought the Midianite woman near to his brothers before the eyes of Moses and before the eyes of the entire assembly of the Children of Israel; and they were weeping at the entrance of the Tent of Meeting. Pinchas son of Elazar, son of Aharon the *Kohen* saw, and he stood up from amid the assembly and he took a spear (*romach*) in his hand." (Num. 25:6–7) Rashi comments that the law (that applied to the situation) was concealed from Moses. The Sassover asked why Moses did not ask Hashem for the law. The Sassover explained that "they were weeping"—everyone had gone into a state of sadness and depression. It is a known fact that Hashem does not dwell in the midst of sadness (Talmud *Shabbat* 30b), so Moses could not ask Hashem. "And Pinchas saw"—he saw that the Israelites were in deep depression, so "he stood up from amid the assembly"—he arose out of the depression that gripped the assembly. "He took the *romach* (its letters numerically representing the 248 organs of the body: r = 200, m = 40, ch = 8) in his hand"—he gathered his entire body to sacrifice himself for the sake of Hashem and that of his teacher. (F.C.O., p. 401)

～～

"And Pinchas son of Elazar, son of Aharon the *Kohen* saw. . . ." (Num. 25:7) On this *Pasuk*, Rashi comments: "He saw the incident [an Israelite bringing a Midianite woman into the camp] and was reminded of the law. He said to Moses, 'I have received from you, that one who has relations with a non-Jewish woman, zealots may kill him.' Moses said to Pinchas, 'The one who reads [in public] the letter, let him be the messenger [to carry out its contents].' Thereupon, he took a spear in hand." The Chidushei Harim asked if the law states that a zealot may kill him. Our Sages say that if one does it alone, without asking at that moment, then it is the law. If one does ask then he cannot do it. The Chidushei Harim explained the difference between the two situations. When a person witnesses a violation and becomes anxious to the extent of trembling so that he cannot control himself and therefore kills the wicked one, the law under these circumstances is that the zealot is correct in his action and cannot be punished. However, if there was time to ask a question of an authority and give it some thought, it shows that there was no zealous feeling, no inner anxiety; then zealous behavior is not permitted. (F.U.A.O., vol. 4, p. 134)

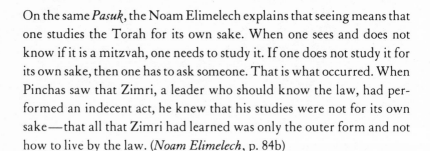

On the same *Pasuk*, the Noam Elimelech explains that seeing means that one studies the Torah for its own sake. When one sees and does not know if it is a mitzvah, one needs to study it. If one does not study it for its own sake, then one has to ask someone. That is what occurred. When Pinchas saw that Zimri, a leader who should know the law, had performed an indecent act, he knew that his studies were not for its own sake—that all that Zimri had learned was only the outer form and not how to live by the law. (*Noam Elimelech*, p. 84b)

PINCHAS

On the *Pasuk* "When he zealously avenged My vengeance among them . . ." (Num. 25:11), the S'fas Emes noted that Pinchas instilled "among them"—within the Jewish people—a sense of zealousness so that the Jews would not be able to tolerate blatant transgressions. (F.C.O., p. 402)

꙳

On the same *Pasuk*, R'Yitzchak Vorker noted that no matter how deep Pinchas's zealousness was, he was still "among them." He did not make himself out to be greater or more religious than the others but remained with everyone. (F.C.O., p. 403)

꙳

"Behold! I give him My covenant of peace (*briti shalom*)." (Num. 25:12) The Degel Machnei Ephraim noted that *shalom* can also mean "complete." He said that since Pinchas was ready to give his entire being for the sanctification of the Name, his reward would be the receiving of the complete covenant. The numerical value of the word *brit* is 612 (b = 2, r = 200, y = 10, t = 400). Not one of the 613 *mitzvot* would be missing. (*Degel Machnei Ephraim*, p. 196)

꙳

"Attack the Midianites and smite them; for they are enemies to you with their deceit." (Num. 25:17) R' Elimelech Lizensker noted that the Almighty requested that the Israelites take revenge on the Midianites for they had deceived them by their evil thoughts and promiscuous behavior. With their idol worship, they confused the Jewish thought. (F.C.O., p. 404)

⌇

"Moses spoke to Hashem, saying, 'May Hashem, God of the spirits of all flesh, appoint a man over the assembly.'" (Num. 27:16) The Kotzker asked why Moses had not, as soon as he had heard that he would not enter the Land of Israel, ask that Hashem appoint a leader "who shall go out before them and come in before them." (Num. 27:17) Before the incident with Zimri, Moses thought that Pinchas would be his successor. When Moses saw how angry and zealous Pinchas had become, he did not want a leader with such a character trait; therefore, he made his request of Hashem. (*Amud Ha'emet*, p. 42)

⌇

"Let the assembly of Hashem not be like sheep that have no shepherd." (Num. 27:17) The S'fas Emes noted that the true shepherd of Israel is Hashem, may He be blessed, as King David said in the Psalms: "Hashem is my shepherd; I shall not lack." (Ps. 23:1) Unfortunately, not everyone recognizes it, nor do many sense it. The function of the Tzaddik or leader is to educate us that there is an Almighty, Who is concerned for the Jew and is His guardian, especially in difficult times. However, when the Jewish people do not have the proper leaders who will reveal that Hashem is there for them, then the people will develop the feeling that Hashem has abandoned them and that there is no Shepherd. That was what Moses was thinking when he said to Hashem, "May Hashem . . . appoint a man over the assembly, who shall go out before them and come in before them. . . ." (Num. 27:16–17) Hashem should appoint a leader who would assist them in knowing that there is a Shepherd and they should not feel as if there is, God forbid, no Shepherd. (M.T., vol. 4, p. 129)

⌇

On the same *Pasuk*, the Berditchever pleaded with Hashem that although we may not be true servants of Hashem and commit transgressions, it is not done deliberately nor to anger Him, but we do need to earn a living, are very busy and therefore neglectful. He said, "You know Hashem, God of the spirits of all flesh, that we are ordinary human beings. Therefore, as the Judge and Leader of mankind, always judge us favorably. I beg of you, Almighty God, whenever it is necessary to appoint a leader "that will go out before them and come in before them," he should lead with the assembly of Hashem, in the same manner as You do, for we are an ordinary people and should be judged favorably. (*Kedushas Levi*, p. 168)

⌒⌒

On the same *Pasuk*, the Koznitzer commented that Moses asked of Hashem that He should appoint a leader "of all flesh"—*basar*. Changing the letters b-s-r around to sh-b-r, which means "broken," the Koznitzer said that the leader should be one with a broken heart, one who is concerned for his people, not arrogant, a person who should feel and understand the needs of the people. (F.C.O., p. 406)

⌒⌒

On the same *Pasuk*, the Sassover pleaded with Hashem that He should not choose a leader who blindly obeys the people. Rather, he should be able to have foresight. He should lead and have the people follow, and he should be able to influence them to go on the right path. (F.C.O. p. 408)

⌒⌒

On the same *Pasuk*, R' Bunim said that Moses pleaded with Hashem that the chosen leader should not be aristocratic but like a shepherd, a plain person. Hashem should choose a leader from the common people. (F.C.O., p. 408)

⌒⌒

"You shall offer as a sacrifice made by fire for a burnt offering to Hashem." (Num. 28:19) The Kedushas Levi explained that if one's sacrifice is offered with "fire," with inner fervor and sincere intentions, then the Almighty becomes elevated, as we read in the Psalms: "May Hashem fulfill all your requests." (Ps. 20:6) The Kedushas Levi explained that "all your requests" should be filled with thoughts of

Hashem—with the intent to elevate the honor of Hashem to the world. (Kedushas Levi, p. 169).

⌒

On the *Pasuk* "This is the fire offering that you are to offer to Hashem: male lambs (*k'vasim*) in their first year, unblemished . . ." (Num. 28:3), the Radamsker commented that the Hebrew word *k'vasim* can come from the word *kovesh*, "to conquer," therefore meaning to conquer one's inclinations. "In their first year" is to be considered as if one is in his first years without sin. "Unblemished" means being pure in one's association with Hashem. That is the essence of sacrifice. (Tiferet Shlomo, p. 210)

MATTOT
"TRIBES"

"Moses spoke to the heads of the tribes of the Children of Israel, saying, 'This is the matter that Hashem has commanded.'" (Num. 30:2) In his *sefer Torat Moshe*, R' Moshe Sofer of Preshburg said that Moses explained to the Children of Israel that they were to value the words of their leaders. It should be clear that the words of the leaders are those that Hashem commanded. The words of our Sages are also the same as Hashem has commanded. (M.T., vol. 4, p. 132)

~~

On the same *Pasuk*, the Lizensker noted that when Tzaddikim speak we must believe that what they say is the Will of Hashem and that they are holy words that will last forever because "that is what Hashem commanded." When the Tzaddik speaks worldly words, he should be aware that what he is saying should be words of holiness so the people will do "what Hashem has commanded." (*Noam Elimelech*, p. 86)

~~

On the *Pasuk* "If a person takes a vow (*yidor neder*) to Hashem or swears an oath to prohibit (*le'sor*) a prohibition upon himself . . ." (Num. 30:3), the Primishlaner played on the word *yidor*, changing it to *hiddur*, meaning "respect." He noted that when a person wishes to respect someone, let him respect Hashem. If he wishes to do someone harm (*soroh*, derived from *le'sor*), then let him do it "upon himself." (F.C.O., p. 411)

~~~

"He shall not profane his word; according to whatever comes from his mouth shall he do." (Num. 30:3) The Koznitzer explained that the person who is careful of what he says and makes sure that none of his words are meaningless, "whatever comes from his mouth shall he do." That is, Hashem will do as he says. His blessings will be fulfilled and his words are like edicts to be implemented. (M.T., vol. 4, p. 135)

~~~

"These are the decrees that Hashem commanded Moses, between a man and his wife, between a father and his daughter in her youth, in her father's house." (Num. 30:17) The Sassover said that when a man and woman live together according to the dictates of the Almighty and His Torah, then they will merit that the Divine Presence will dwell with them; the Almighty will guard them and their home will be blessed. Also, a father should pay attention that his daughter should go on the right path, especially "in her youth," by instructing her in the ways of the Torah while she is in her father's domain. (F.C.O., p. 412)

~~~

"Arm men (*heychaltzu*) from among yourselves for the army . . . to inflict Hashem's vengeance against Midian." (Num. 31:3) The S'fas Emes noted that the word *heychaltzu* can mean "remove," as in *Chaltza et na'alo me'al raglo*—"Remove your shoes from your feet." Moses said that one should remove his own concerns and his honor when he goes to war. His intent should be for the sake of Heaven only. (M.T., vol. 4, p. 137)

~~~

On the same *Pasuk*, the Berditchever noted that when one wages war with pure intent and not for one's own benefit but for the sake of Heaven, he must be successful. (F.C.O., p. 412)

～

"A thousand from a tribe, a thousand from a tribe, for all the tribes of Israel shall you send to the army." (Num. 31:4) Rashi states that this includes the tribe of Levi. The Exegetes point out that if the Levites were included, there would be thirteen thousand from thirteen tribes—so why does it state in the next *Pasuk*: "So there were delivered from the thousands of the Children of Israel, a thousand from each tribe, twelve thousand armed for the army." (Num. 31:5) Rashi states that they had heard that Moses' death was dependent upon vengeance from Midian. Therefore, they were reluctant to go to war and had to be forced, as Rashi says, "against their will." The Gerer Rebbe explained that the strength of the tribe of Levi was that they were able to fulfill the will of Hashem because they were able to disregard their feelings toward their loved ones, as the *Pasuk* states: "Of his father and mother, 'I have not seen him'; his brothers he did not recognize and his children he did not know." (*Devarim* 33:9) Therefore, it states: "Twelve thousand armed for the army," and excludes the thousand that did not have to be forced. (M.T., vol. 4, p. 138)

～

"They (commanders) said to Moses, 'Your servants took a census of the men of war under our command, and not a man of us is missing. So we have brought an offering for Hashem. . . .'" (Num. 31:49–50) The Talmud, in *Shabbat* 64a, noted that Moses said to them, "Why an atonement?" They said, "Though we escaped from sin, yet we did not escape from meditating upon sin." The Chidushei Harim asked why they waited until then to bring the sacrifice rather than immediately after the war. They had thought that a thought without a deed does not constitute a sin; therefore there was no need for atonement. However, when they heard the commandment for the purification of utensils, they became concerned. The law was that though a utensil might be pure, nevertheless because it contains the taste of the forbidden in its walls, it has to be made pure (kosher) for use. From this they learned that even a thought of a transgression, though it may have no substance other than being hidden in the person, is also forbidden and must be purified. If a taste has importance, then a thought becomes as though it was committed and is in need of atonement. (M.T., vol. 4, p. 144)

MASSEI
"JOURNEYS"

On the *Pasukim* "These are the journeys of the Children of Israel, who went forth from the land of Egypt according to their armies, under the guidance of Moses and Aharon. And Moses wrote their departures according to their journeys by the order of Hashem, and these are their journeys according to their departures." (Num. 33:1–2) R' Nachum Perlow, the Novominsker Rebbe, commented that it is significant to know why the Torah mentions the journeys. The importance of the travels was that while the Israelites went farther away from Egypt, the source of evil, and became an army of Hashem resisting the provocations of their enemies and fighting the physical and spiritual battles that ensued, they had to disassemble and reconstruct the Ark as they traveled from place to place: "Aharon and his sons shall come when the camp journeys, and they shall take down the Partition of the Screen and cover the Ark. . . ." (Num. 4:5) "Everyone who comes to the legion to perform the work of the Tent of Meeting." (Num. 4:30) "At the commandment of Hashem they encamped, and at the commandment of Hashem they journeyed." (*Bamidbar* 9:23) The Rebbe interpreted the travels of the Israelites as the destiny of the Jews to be in constant renewal, corresponding to the dismantling and reassembling of the Ark. As cited in the Talmud *Chagigah* 16a, just as the Ark, whether at rest or moving, was considered holy, there was constant support from Hashem while the Israelites were in servitude and in redemption. They too, with the help of Hashem, had to rebuild each time they reached a certain level, so that they could overcome the enemies, as it says: "When the Ark would journey, Moses said, 'Arise, Hashem, and let Your enemies be scattered and let those who hate You flee from before You.'" (Num. 10:35) It is stated in Micah 7:8: "Rejoice not against me, O my enemy; though I am fallen, I shall arise; though I sit in darkness, Hashem is a light unto me." (*Pe'er Nachum*, pp. 224–225)

On the *Pasuk* "These are the journeys of the Children of Israel, who went forth from the land of Egypt" (Num. 33:1), the Lubavitcher Rebbe noted that there are difficulties in the *Pasuk*. He asked why the term "journeys" was used, for only the first of the journeys that was mentioned in the *Sidra*—namely, from Rameses to Succot—constituted "going forth out of the land of Egypt." The others were all made outside of Egypt. The "journeys" refer not only to physical journeys but to spiritual ones as well. Our Sages obligated every Jew "to see himself as if he had traveled out of Egypt that very day" (Talmud *Pesachim* 116b), for it means an exodus from the captivity of the secular world. By not being content with the level that one is on, one strives to higher goals and journeys with conviction toward complete liberation to a bonding with Hashem. (*Torah Studies*, pp. 281–285)

On the words in the *Pasuk* "according to their armies" (Num. 33:1), the Koznitzer commented that there are people who work with persistence at serving Hashem but fail to reach their goals. They would be able to reach that goal if they would first cleanse themselves of impurities and their youthful transgressions. Therefore, it is imperative for one who wishes to serve Hashem to first conquer his evil inclination, cleanse himself, and return with complete repentance by purifying all previous wrong deeds. Only then will he be able to reach the proper service of Hashem. That is the meaning of the words "These are the journeys of the Children of Israel." That is the way one should travel "who went forth from the land of Egypt"—he should leave all the impurities that are called "Egypt." After that, the Zohar says that one could be in the "army" to serve Hashem. (*Avodas Yisroel*, p. 159)

On the *Pasukim* "These are the journeys of the Children of Israel . . . and these were their journeys according to their going forth" (Num. 33: 1, 2), the Riziner noted that the first "these" cancel earlier actions and the second "these" are added to the first. "These" refer to people who find fault with their earlier misdeeds or transgressions and nullify them by correcting them through improving their behavior. "And these" are those who commit transgressions and instead of regretting it add to their misdeeds, so that even "their going forth"—the good deeds that they do unintentionally—is considered evil and unworthy. "These are the journeys of the Children of Israel" describes the way the people behaved. However, because of their improved behavior, their poor earlier actions will in the future be omitted from their accounts. "And Moses wrote their goings forth according to their journeys." (Num. 33:2) (F.C.O., p. 415)

"Moses wrote their departures according to their journeys . . . and these are their journeys according to their departures." (Num. 33:2) R' Moshe Sofer of Preshburg, in his *sefer Torat Moshe*, explained that the Israelites in Egypt believed that by following Moses into the desert they would merit redemption, as is written: "So said Hashem: I remember to you the loving-kindness of your youth . . . your following Me in the desert, in a land not sown." (Jer. 2:1) Therefore, the departure from Egypt was in the merit of "their journeys." Later, when the Israelites transgressed and complained about Hashem, they deserved extinction. But because our teacher Moses pleaded on their behalf, saying, "Why, O Hashem, shall Your wrath burn against Your people, that You have brought out of the land of Egypt?" (Ex. 32:11) and "Why should the Egyptians say thus, for evil did He bring them out?" (Ex. 32:12), their further journeys were permitted because of their exodus from Egypt. (M.T., vol. 4, p. 152)

On the same *Pasuk*, R' Yaacov Yitzchak of Lublin cited a statement in *Chovot L'Vavot* ("Duties of the Heart") that says that there are two exemplary levels that one can reach by fulfilling Torah concepts. One is to reach the high level of attachment to Hashem that the prophets did after the Exodus from Egypt; the other, a higher level, was that of Abraham, who understood the Torah before it was given. "Moses wrote their departures according to their journeys" to show the steps the Israelites had to take to go from strength to strength to develop their attachment. "According to the words of Hashem" meant that they were to accept the oral law, as our Sages said: "Write down these words" (*Shemot* 34:27), for it means the oral law (Talmud *Gittin* 60b). Through these "journeys" the Israelites would be able to reach the exemplary level. (*Divrei Emet*, p. 42b)

On the same *Pasuk*, R' Asher Horowitz noted that there are people who are observant at home, but when they are elsewhere they behave differently. The Torah notes that one should behave the same at all times, when one departs and when one goes on a journey, for it should always be "at the bidding of Hashem." (F.C.O., p. 416)

On the same *Pasuk*, Rashi quotes Rabbi Nanchuma, who gave the following analogy. "This is compared to a king whose son was ill and he took him to a distant place to cure him. When they started back, his father began to count all the journeys. He said, 'Here we slept, here we felt cold, and here you had a headache.'" The Gerer Rebbe noted that the analogy is based on the incidents that occurred to the Jews. "Here we slept" refers to the time that the Israelites went to sleep (according to the Midrash) at the giving of the Torah and Moses had to rouse them. "Here we felt cold" alludes to the time that Amalek chilled them toward idol worship. "Here you had a headache" refers to the episode of the golden calf when the Israelites had doubts concerning the "head," the leader, and doubts concerning their faith. (M.T., vol. 4, p. 151)

〜

"They journeyed from Marah (bitterness) and arrived at Eylimah; in Eylimah were twelve springs of water and seventy date palms, and they encamped there." (Num. 33:9) The Degel Machnei Ephraim observed that there are bitter and sweet wells in the Torah. Sweet waters are the truth and bitter ones are the ways of falsehood. All of our *Tanaaim* (authorities quoted in the Mishnah), *Amoraim* (talmudic sages who interpreted the words of the *Tanaaim*), and Tzaddikim, from Moses till the Messianic Age, drank from the sweet waters of the Torah. The scoffers and their ilk drank from the bitter waters and led a life of falsehood. The *Pasuk* alludes to the Israelites' journey from the "bitterness" of doubting and falsehood and their coming to "Eylim." Eylim signifies a place of truth, for its letters represent the statement *Yaacov Avinu Lo Met*—"Our father Yaacov did not die." Yaacov stands for eternal truth, as it says in the Prayer Book: "Grant truth to Yaacov." At Eylim, there "were twelve springs of water" from which the twelve tribes drew the truth of how to serve Hashem. There the Israelites reached the level of *sod* (hidden meaning of Torah) for there were "seventy date palms," and together *sod* and *temarim* (palms) equal seventy. At this point they rested and received sustenance, thereby strengthening their existence. (*Degel Machnei Ephraim*, p. 203)

〜

"They journeyed from Charadah (*chared*, 'fear') and encamped in Makhelot (*makhel*, 'assembly')." (Num. 33:25) The Yid HaKadosh commented that the Jews went away from fear and anxiety and rested in an atmosphere of togetherness in peace and harmony. (F.C.O., p. 419)

〜

On the *Pasuk* "The six cities of refuge . . . and in addition to them you shall give forty-two cities" (Num. 35:6), the Ohev Yisroel noted that the "six cities of refuge" correspond to the six words of *Shmah Yisroel Hashem Elokeynu, Hashem Echad*—"Hear O Israel, Hashem is our God, Hashem, the One and only." "And in addition to them you shall give forty-two" refers to the forty-two words in the paragraph following the *Shmah*, from "you shall love" to "upon your gates." He said that these words are the "cities of refuge" by which one can protect oneself. By accepting the yoke of Heaven and love of Hashem, he will be protected from those who chase after him and wish to do him harm. (F.C.O., p. 419)

"Cities of refuge shall they be for you." (Num. 35:11) The Chadushei Harim commented that if a person murders another unintentionally, and he is very disturbed by it and his conscience is bothered, the Almighty gives him a place to find some solace. However, when the act is unintentional but the person is not bothered by it and is at peace with himself, then there will be no resting place among the "cities of refuge." (F.C.O., p. 420)

WEEKLY PORTIONS OF
DEVARIM/DEUTERONOMY

DEVARIM
"THESE ARE THE WORDS"

The Lubavitcher Rebbe noted that the *parsha* of *Devarim* is always read on the Shabbat before Tisha B'av, which commemorates the destruction of both Temples and other historical tragedies. The *haftorah* of the *parsha* of *Devarim* is called the "vision" of Isaiah—words of rebuke for a rebellious people. It is part of the *haftorot* of the Three Weeks that contain words of rebuke for the spiritual transgressions that caused the destruction. However, the Berditchever Rebbe saw the "vision" to be the building of the Third Temple even though it was from a great distance. And the *haftorot* after the Three Weeks are words of consolation and hope for the future. The *Chumash Devarim* itself is different from the other *chumashim* in that it gives counsel for future generations. The people who traveled in the desert had immediate knowledge of the Divine, but the succeeding generations, involved with the physical world, heard Hashem but did not see Him. Therefore, they were addressed with the words: "And now, Israel, listen." (Deut. 4:1) Later generations lacked the immediacy of the previous generations but still had to reach what their forebears had. *Devarim* tells us that by living by Hashem's will, our material concerns are transformed to a spiritual level. The highest achievements of the spirit are won in earthly, not heavenly, realms. The Shabbat of "vision" permits us to overcome the sadness of exile and view the joys of redemption. (Torah Studies, pp. 286–289)

Concerning the reading of *parsha Devarim* before Tisha B'av, the Tzemach Tzedek noted that the Shabbatot before Tisha B'av "prepare the
remedy before the blow." (Talmud *Megillah* 13b) When a remedy comes
after a sickness, the effects of the sickness may remain for a period of
time and there may even be traces long afterward. Therefore, a person is
not considered completely well until long after the healing. If the
healing comes before the actual illness, it is as though the illness never
occurred. We read in the Talmud: "A person who is about to be redeemed is considered as if already redeemed" (*Baba Kamma* 77b), for
the remedy is on a higher level and does not allow for the possibility of
damage. That is the intent of the statement that the Shabbatot before
Tisha B'av "prepare the remedy before the blow." The exile and the
mourning prevented the outside influences from having an effect.
Therefore, the Tzemach Tzedek concluded, the *parsha Devarim* is read
on the Shabbat before Tisha B'av because that Shabbat reveals the inner
positive intent within the exile itself. The theme of *Devarim* is Moses
rebuking the Jewish people, which reflects their descent. However, it
concludes with the allusion to the complete redemption. (*Likkutei Sichot*, vol. 5, pp. 6–10)

"These are the words that Moses spoke." (Deut. 1:1) The Koznitzer
Maggid commented that when Hashem commanded Moses to take the
Israelites out of Egypt, Moses wavered and said, "I am not a man of
words." (Ex. 4:10) However, after years of being their leader, dealing
with the people, hearing their constant complaints and disputes, and
withstanding their constant grumbling, he had become a man of words.
(F.C.O., p. 421)

On the same *Pasuk*, the Berditchever commented on Rashi's statement
that these referred to words of rebuke. The Berditchever said that only
when Moses spoke to the Israelites were they words of rebuke. How-

ever, when he spoke to Hashem he always found words of praise and spoke favorably of the Israelites. (F.C.O., p. 421)

⌦

"It was in the fortieth year, in the eleventh month, on the first of the month, when Moses spoke to the Children of Israel. . . ." (Deut. 1:3) Rashi comments: "Moses did not rebuke them except immediately before his death. . . . Because of four things we do not rebuke a person except immediately before death so that he should not rebuke him and then rebuke him again." In his *sefer Torat Moshe*, R' Moshe Sofer of Preshburg noted that the normal behavior of an individual who is being rebuked is to rationalize his behavior. Therefore, the rebuke has to be repeated to show the errors in his reasoning. If the rebuke is not repeated then the one being rebuked will think that his reasoning is correct and will continue to transgress. However, when the rebuke is given before death, the admonishment will not be rejected and the words will enter into the heart and remain there. (M.T., vol. 5, p. 11)

⌦

In the *sefer Yosef Umatz*, the author recalls an historical incident when a decree was issued against the Jews. The Jews examined their behavior and, instead of rationalizing their actions, took it upon themselves to rebuke each other. (M.T., vol. 5, p. 12)

⌦

In his *sefer Maor V'Shemesh*, R' Kalimus Kalman Epstein of Krakow noted that all of his teachers said that the essence of serving Hashem is to reflect on repentance before learning Torah and the performance of a commandment. He said that R' Yaacov Yitzchak of Lublin explained that of a person who does not do so, it is said: "But to the wicked, Hashem said, 'To what purpose do you recount My decrees and bear My covenant upon your lips?'" However, the person who gives thought to repentance before learning is called a Tzaddik. Our Sages noted in the Talmud that if a wicked individual betroths a woman, saying that he is a righteous person, she is betrothed to him, "for it is possible that thoughts of repentance came to him." (*Kedushin* 49b) He may decide to learn Torah to mend his ways. The Torah alludes to this when Moses rebuked the Israelites and recounted the places where they had angered the Almighty and where they had transgressed before they would hear words of Torah. Therefore, the Torah says: "These are the words Moses spoke to all Israel, across the Jordan, in the Plain, opposite the Sea of Reeds, between Paran and Tophel and Laban and Hazerot and Di-zahav" (Deut. 1:1), for these were the places where their behavior warranted rebuke. "Moses began clarifying this Torah." (Deut. 1:5) First he admonished them so they might begin to repent and then he taught Torah. (M.D., p. 355)

On the *Pasuk* "Moses began clarifying this Torah" (Deut. 1:5), R' Chayim Chernovitz noted Rashi's comment that Moses mentioned the places rather than the transgressions themselves "because of the honor of Israel." (Deut. 1:1) R' Chayim explained that Moses did not want the nations to know the transgressions that were committed so that the honor of the Israelites would not be tainted. However, it would have been better to have been specific and given a direct account, for then their transgressions would have been made clear to them. Since the Torah was translated into seventy languages, allowing everyone to know their wrongdoing, the transgressions were hinted at but not enumerated specifically. (M.T., vol. 5, p. 12)

"Hashem, our God, spoke to us in Horev, saying, 'You have dwelled long enough by this mountain.'" (Deut. 1:6) The Cherneboler, in his *sefer Maor V'Shemesh*, commented that the Israelites were told by Hashem that they should not consider every obstacle and hurdle as an unconquerable mountain; rather, they should overcome them and consider them as hair that is easy to handle. The righteous can overcome every obstacle in Judaism even when it is as big as a mountain, for to them it is like a hair. However, the wicked withdraw from the smallest obstacle that is like a hair, because to them it is like a mountain. He cited the statement in the Talmud: "In the future Hashem will show the righteous ones the evil inclination as a mountain, and to the wicked it will appear as a hair—and both will cry. The righteous will say, 'How were we able to conquer such a mountain?' and the wicked will cry, 'Why couldn't we have overcome such a piece of hair?'" (*Succah* 52a) Therefore, in the future it will be measure for measure; the righteous will notice that what they thought was a hair was really as big as a mountain, and the wicked will notice that what they thought was a mountain was really as easy to overcome as a hair. (M.T., vol. 5, p. 15)

On the *Pasuk* "And the matter that is too difficult for you, you shall bring to me and I shall hear it" (Deut. 1:17), the Baal Shem Tov commented that the Rambam taught his son that if one is doubtful about how to do something because it may be done in many ways—whether it is a commandment or one should refrain from doing it—then he should determine if it is for his pleasure or honor. Hashem will let him know the truth and he will be secure in his action. "The matter that is too difficult for you" means that the confusion comes from one's inner self, if one does not know whether to perform it or distance himself from it. "You shall bring to me," for your intention should be for the sake of Heaven without reservation. Then, "I shall hear it"—I will let you understand how to behave. (M.D., p. 357)

On the same *Pasuk*, it is told in the name of the Admur of Ger that he noted that it says, "And I shall hear it," but does not say that He will answer. It seems to imply that there are times that one need only listen and that a reply is not necessary, for listening may be enough. (M.T., vol. 5, p. 21)

On the *Pasuk* "You approached me, all of you" (Deut. 1:22), the S'fas Emes noted that Moses said to the Jewish People that if they found something difficult to understand, such as whether something should be performed, then "approach me," for then you should be able to understand from Hashem's view rather than from your personal reasons. In this way you will know the true path. (F.C.O., p. 425)

On the *Pasuk* "Our brothers have melted our hearts" (Deut. 1:28), the
Chidushei Harim commented that the reaction to the spies recalled an
earlier statement of Rashi: "You approached me as a rabble . . . with
the young pushing the elders and the elders pushing the heads." (Deut.
1:22) Moses admonished the Israelites, who at the time of the giving of
the Torah were complacent when they should have pushed to hear
words of Torah. However, when it came to listen to the spies, they
transgressed, for "the young [were] pushing the elders and the elders
[were] pushing the heads" of the tribes. (F.C.O., p. 425)

VA'ETCHANAN
"I IMPLORED"

The Oheler, in his *sefer Yismach Moshe,* noted the significance of *parsha Va'etchanan* following *parsha Devarim.* In Psalm 34:12 it states: "Go, O sons, heed me, the fear of Hashem I will teach you." The Oheler, in the name of the Nikolsberger, explained that it is not enough to listen to words of admonishment at the time they are being said, but one should "go" to one's dwelling place, then "heed me." The Oheler explained that the Midrash *Yalkut Shimoni,* in the beginning of *Devarim,* quotes the *sifri* that words of admonishment are called *Devarim* — words. He brings proof from the prophet Hosea, who says, "Take with you words and return unto Hashem." (Hos. 14:3) Return is based on reprimand. Therefore, the *parsha Devarim* begins with "words," followed by *parsha Va'etchanan,* which implores the Israelites to heed the words. (M.D., p. 353)

Rabbi Avraham Moshe Rabinowitz, the Skoyler Rebbe, noted Rashi's comment that in all the places the word *va'etchanan* (imploring) is mentioned it means granting a gift for free (*chinam*). The *haftorah* for the *parsha* is *Nachamu nachamu, ami,* "Console, console My people." (Is. 40:1) The Almighty is consoling the Jewish People. The word *chinam* with the added *hey* of the Tetragrammaton (Hashem's name) will form the word *nachamah,* "consolation," which is a gift from Hashem. (Ch.B., p. 373)

⌇⌇

"I implored Hashem at that time, saying. . . ." (Deut. 3:23) The Kotz-ker commented that Moses begged Hashem that "at that time"—at the moment before his death—he should be able to say, "Hashem is God." (M.T., vol. 5, p. 24)

⌇⌇

On the same *Pasuk*, the Ropshitzer noted that the Torah does not mention any specific time. It points out that one should never say that he had no time, patience, or thought at that time, but at another time or when the occasion will arise, he will pray. (*Zera Kodesh*, p. 132)

⌇⌇

The Baal Shem Tov commented that when a person is praying, regard-less of the prayer, his attitude at the time of prayer is what counts. If his prayer is missing the innermost depths of his feelings, it is as though he is not praying. (F.C.O., p. 429)

⌇⌇

The Bratzlaver noted that if a person prays or meditates but feels that Hashem is not responding, God forbid, he should not despair and think that Hashem is not paying attention. He should have complete faith that He is listening to every word of prayer and supplication and no syllable is lost. Each word makes an impression above and evokes Hashem's mercy each time and as long as the individual does not lose his faith under any circumstances. As the intent of his prayers becomes stronger, Hashem will turn to him and will fulfill his needs. (*Likkutei Eytzot*, p. 200)

⌇⌇

The Zanzer said that before he prays, he prays. (F.C.O., p. 436)

⌇⌇

On the same *Pasuk*, the Sassover noted a Midrash that states that when Jacob said, "And my righteousness shall testify for me in time to come"

(Gen. 30:33), Hashem said, "Do not praise the morrow, for tomorrow your daughter Dinah will be violated." We can learn from this that one should pay attention to the present and accomplish what is necessary today, for one does not know what the morrow may bring. "At that time" means that we should merit to say only those things that pertain to the present and not the morrow. (M.T., vol. 5, p. 24)

The Mamshinover commented that Moses prayed for the generations to come. The time will come when the Jews might not be able to pray with proper devotion because of calamity. Therefore it says "saying," so that even though the Jews will be able to pray only with "the mouth," their prayers will be accepted. (M.T., vol. 5, p. 24)

The Berditchever noted that the greatest of pleasures is the Service to Hashem. (*Kedushas Levi*, p. 175)

The Ropshitzer noted that Moses, our teacher, opened the tower of prayer for all time. When he ascended the mountain he requested, "Saying," the prayers that the Jews will pray at all times should be accepted as at this time. All future prayers are bound up in this prayer. (*Zera Kodesh*, p. 132)

"Please let me cross and see the good land." (Deut. 3:25) The Kotzker questioned why the words "and see" were used. It was obvious that if he entered the land he would see. The Rebbe explained that it was his prayer that if he should enter the land that he should "see the good land," not the land that the spies had seen as negative. (F.U.A.O., vol. 4, p. 206)

"Hashem said to me, 'It is much for you (*rav lach*)! Do not continue to speak to Me further about this matter.'" (Deut. 3:26) R' Shalom Belzer noted that Moses was arguing with Hashem that though Hashem had sworn that he would not enter the Land of Israel, nevertheless one can be released from a vow. When Moses had sworn to his father-in-law that he would never return to Egypt, the Almighty released Moses from his vow because Hashem said, "I am your Teacher (*Rav lach*—*rav* meaning "teacher")." However, in this case Hashem said, "I can release you, but who is going to release Me?" Therefore, Hashem said that Moses should not continue to speak on the matter. (F.C.O., p. 437

"But you (*atem*) who cling to Hashem, your God—you are alive today." (Deut. 4:4) R' Moshe Chayim Ephraim of Sadilkov explained that our holy books say that the 248 words that comprise the *Shmah* give sustenance to the 248 organs that are found in the human being. Actually, in the three paragraphs of the *Shmah* there are 247 words, but if we attach the word *emet* (truth), which has the same letters as the word *atem* (you), at the end of the *Shmah*, we then say *Hashem Elokeychem Emet*— "Hashem your God is truth." Then we are able to sustain our bodily organs, for "you are alive today." (*Degel Machnei Ephraim*, p. 209)

On the *Pasuk* "For which is a great nation that has a God Who is close to it" (Deut. 4:7), the S'fas Emes noted a Midrash that says: "May Hashem answer you on the day of distress." (Ps. 20) The Midrash uses the comparison of a woman about to give birth who is comforted by the words, "The One Who answered your mother will also answer you." The S'fas Emes explained that its saying "on the day of distress" bothered the Midrash. "Day" denotes light and is the opposite of "distress." It would have been better to state "in the night of distress." Therefore, the Midrash explains that though unrest may befall the Jews, the goal is a good one. Just as the pain of a woman about to give birth is a preparation for the birth, so are afflictions a preparation for the future salvation. That is why it is said to the woman about to give birth: This is the way of all who give birth; your mother's pangs gave birth to you, so will your pangs bring forth a new life. In the same manner, the Jewish people also have to be assured that their misfortunes will bring the salvation. Therefore, the S'fas Emes said that just as the times of distress for Jacob were for the salvation of Israel, so each new event "born" to Israel will be for a salvation. (*S'fas Emes*, p. 34)

⌥

"Only beware for yourself and greatly beware for your soul, lest you forget the things that your eyes have beheld." (Deut. 4:9) The Lizensker said that a person must be in a constant state of devotion and think of the greatness of Hashem. When one sees the daily miracles and phenomena, and all that occurs from above, he realizes that his being is also from above. As is stated in the Talmud, there are five ways that the human soul is likened to the Creator, blessed be He and blessed is His name. Just as Hashem fills the world, so the soul fills the body; as He observes but is not observed, so it is with the soul; as He nourishes the world, so the soul nourishes the body; as He is pure, so is the soul pure; as He abides in rooms within rooms, so the soul abides in rooms within rooms. (*Berachot* 10a) Thus, if one does not know himself, he will not know Hashem. That is the meaning of "beware of yourself and greatly beware for your soul" for "lest you forget the things that your eyes have beheld." One must be aware of all the physical wonders to remember from where they come. (*Noam Elimelech*, p. 90)

⌥

"And the mountain was burning with fire up to the heart of heaven." (Deut. 4:11) The Chidushei Harim commented that the mountain burned with such a flame that it made the heart of every Jew a heavenly heart. (F.C.O., p. 438)

⌥

"But you should take great care of your souls." (Deut. 4:15) The Baal Shem Tov commented that one should take care of his body, for when the body is sick, the soul also becomes sick. (F.C.O., p. 439)

On the same *Pasuk*, the Berditchever noted that when one torments his body, it is a sign that the evil inclination is weakening the mind so that one can no longer serve Hashem correctly. (F.C.O., p. 439)

"Lest you act corruptly and make yourselves a graven image." (Deut. 4:16) R' Moshe Koznitzer commented that every mitzvah must have a soul, a life, and a vitality. It should not be as a "graven image" made by hand, devoid of life. (F.C.O., p. 439)

"Beware for yourselves lest you forget the covenant of Hashem, your God, that He has sealed with you, and you make yourselves a graven image of a likeness of any thing, which Hashem, your God, has commanded you." (Deut. 4:23) The Kotzker explained that "a graven image" that one makes is not the original; it is an imitation. He said that one should not make from Hashem's commandment an image. One should perform the mitzvah in its original state, not an imitation of it. (M.T., vol. 5, p. 31)

On the same *Pasuk*, the Sassover commented that when one is in the midst of prayer or is involved in the performance of a mitzvah, he should not make pretentious contortions of the body that might make it seem to others that he is behaving with fervor. When praying or performing a mitzvah, the action must be performed in a normal and ordinary manner so that one does not appear to be creating an idol. Its performance must be done as "has been commanded you." (F.C.O., p. 439)

"From there you will seek Hashem, your God, and you will find Him if you search for Him with all your heart and all your soul." (Deut. 4:29)

The Chidushei Harim commented that if you seek Hashem with your heart, you will find Him there. (F.C.O., p. 440

～

On the same *Pasuk*, the Kotzker said that seeking Hashem everywhere, by itself, would be enough. However, once you have found Him, then "you search for Him"—you should continue to search on all levels. (F.U.A.O., vol. 4, pp. 212–213)

～

"When you are in distress and all these things have befallen you, at the end of days, you will return unto Hashem, your God, and listen to His voice." (Deut. 4:30) R' Meir Primishlaner said to the Almighty, "If the Messiah wishes to come nicely, then we will wait for him patiently. However, if he wishes to come with anger, with "pre-Messianic" tribulations, perhaps it would be better if he did not come. (F.U.A.O., vol. 4, p. 213)

～

On the same *Pasuk*, the Skoyler Rebbe noted that if one finds himself in anguish, he should look at it as through a window. He will then notice that the Jews are in the Diaspora and the advice that is given them is: "Return unto Hashem," return with sincere repentance to be saved from all evil. Therefore, he too must "return unto Hashem" and find personal deliverance from affliction. As we read in the Talmud, great is repentance for it will bring the ultimate redemption. (*Yoma* 6b) (Ch.B., p. 374)

～

On the *Pasuk* "You have been shown to know that Hashem, He is your God! There is none beside Him" (Deut. 4:35), R' Yaacov Yisroel Cherkaser commented that there are two ways to reach the level of knowing Hashem. The first is through knowledge and the second is through simple faith that "Hashem, He is God! There is none beside Him." (F.C.O., p. 440)

R' Tzadok HaKohen noted that when we learn Torah, listen to the words of Torah, or sing Shabbat songs at the table, all these become absorbed in our essence, which leads us to the level of knowledge that "there is none beside Him." (F.C.O., p. 440)

On the same *Pasuk*, Rashi quotes a *Pesikta Rabbasi* (20) and says: "He opened seven heavens for them [Israel], and just as He parted the higher realms, so He parted the lower, and they saw that He is unique." On Rashi's statement, the S'fas Emes noted there is no deterring force in nature preventing a Jew who wishes to serve Hashem earnestly from doing so. For this person, the inner secrets within all aspects of nature will be opened and he will know the One and Only Unique One. (M.T., vol. 5, p. 33)

"You shall know this day and take to your heart that Hashem, He is the God—in the heavens above and on earth below, there is none other." (Deut. 4:39) The Yid HaKadosh noted that the only knowledge one must know is that "He is the God—in the heavens above and on earth below, there is none other." (F.C.O., p. 440)

On the same *Pasuk*, it was said in the name of the Chidushei Harim that if the key point is "take to your heart," then we must first cleanse the heart to make room for all necessary information to take root there. (M.T., vol. 5, p. 36)

On the same *Pasuk*, the Kotzker noted that the words "there is no other" refers to the Jew, for no one else believes that "Hashem, He is the God—in the heavens above and on earth below."

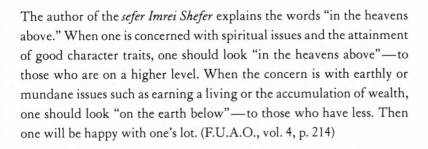

The author of the *sefer Imrei Shefer* explains the words "in the heavens above." When one is concerned with spiritual issues and the attainment of good character traits, one should look "in the heavens above"—to those who are on a higher level. When the concern is with earthly or mundane issues such as earning a living or the accumulation of wealth, one should look "on the earth below"—to those who have less. Then one will be happy with one's lot. (F.U.A.O., vol. 4, p. 214)

"Then Moses set aside three cities on the side of the Jordan, on the east, for a killer to flee there, who will have killed his fellow without knowledge . . . then he shall flee to one of these cities and live." (Deut. 4:41) Rabbi Nachum Mordechai Perlow, the Novominsker Rebbe, explained that when one kills another unwittingly, a part of his soul that makes him an individual has been impaired. He must recognize that because of his action, he has tarnished his soul and has caused himself anguish, at which point he may want to escape to strange ideologies, hoping to find his inner self. Therefore, he may evade his Jewish essence by running away from his inner core. In the same manner, if one attacks his soul unwittingly and thereby loses its divinity, he begins to feel bitterness and wants to leave its holiness and individuality and run to others elsewhere, though he knows that he is not like them. That is what the division of the three cities of refuge teaches us. There are three levels to a person's soul, and it is his inner depth that makes him a unique individual. The Talmud states that the five verses of "Bless, my soul" (Psalms 103 and 104) mention the correlation of Hashem with the human soul. "Just as the Holy One, Blessed is He, fills the world, so too does the human soul fill all the body. Just as the Holy One, Blessed is He, observes but is not observed, so too the soul observes but is not observed." (Talmud *Berachot* 10a) When he begins to realize that the holy soul is his and does not belong to anyone else, he will gain the strength to rectify his behavior and will not need to run away from himself. (*P'er Nachum*, pp. 227–228)

On the *Pasuk* "Honor your father and your mother, as Hashem, your God, commanded you" (Deut. 5:16), the Kedushas Levi noted that the words "as Hashem, your God, commanded you" appear after the commandment here but not in Exodus 20:12. The Kedushas Levi explained that with the first set of commandments the Torah was not yet given. However, with the second set of commandments "honoring your father" was connected to "as Hashem, your God, has commanded you." Therefore, our Sages said that when a father requests that his child transgress a mitzvah, he need not be obeyed because the child, the father, and the mother are bound to "as Hashem, your God, commanded you." (*Kedushas Levi*, p. 177)

"These words Hashem spoke to your entire congregation. . . ." (Deut. 5:19) The S'fas Emes noted that the words contained in the Torah are for all times and all generations, for whenever congregations assemble the Presence will dwell upon them, as our Sages say: "If ten people sit together and engage in Torah study, the Divine Presence rests among them." (*Ethics of Our Fathers* 3:7) (*S'fas Emes*, p. 12)

"Speech," said the Bratzlaver, "has the power to awaken the individual." He said that even though one has no interest in serving Hashem, he should start to speak words of spiritual awakening, requests, and supplication. It will then be revealed to him that his inner self does indeed want to serve Hashem, because the words themselves reveal all that is within him. (*Likkutei Eytzot*, p. 56)

The Baal Shem Tov was asked if it is necessary to repeat the *Shmah* if one did not say it with full devotion. The Baal Shem Tov answered that it is a Chasidic principle that everything in the world, including the words that we speak, has Divine Sparks within it. Therefore, if we repeat the *Shmah* because we prayed without deep feeling and devotion, we deny the basic principle that every word has in it a Divine Spark. (F.C.O., p. 442)

On the same *Pasuk*, the Berditchever explained that "these words Hashem spoke" mean "as Hashem commanded you," and you should not go against His words. (F.C.O., p. 441)

"This day we saw that Hashem will speak to a person and he can live. . . . If we continue to hear the voice of Hashem, our God, any longer, we will die!" (Deut. 5:21, 22) The Kedushas Levi cited *parsha* Pinchas in the Zohar. R' Pinchas, the son of Yair, said that the reason Jews sway while praying is that the Divine Spirit within them awakens and wishes to go to its source. With such an immense burning inner desire, it becomes impossible to "continue to hear the voice of Hashem," and the inner Spirit, wanting to return to its source, cannot stand still while the holy words of prayer are being recited. (*Kedushas Levi*, p. 178)

"Go say to them, 'Return to your tents.'" (Deut. 5:27) The Kotzker said that Hashem told Moses that he should tell the Israelites that He had seen their awe and their devotion at Sinai. However, He wanted to see what happened when they returned home. (M.T., vol. 5, p. 39)

"And you shall love Hashem, your God, with all your heart, with all your soul, and with all your possessions." (Deut. 6:5) The S'fas Emes asked why philosophers cannot comprehend how "to love" can be a command. They say that love is a natural phenomenon and that it cannot be commanded. The S'fas Emes said that it is probably in the nature of the Jew to love Hashem; however, it is necessary to awaken this natural love and cultivate it. That is the mitzvah of "And you shall love"—one should act to awaken the hidden strength to "love Hashem." (*S'fas Emes*, p. 34)

≈

"And these words that I command you today shall be upon your heart." (Deut. 6:6) R' Bunim of Pshys'cha said that the distance from the mouth to the heart is as far as that from the earth to the heaven. (M.T., vol. 5, p. 40)

≈

On the same *Pasuk*, R' Mordechai Cherneboler explained that, first and foremost, "These words that I command you shall be upon your heart" must enter the heart and become an integral part of one's being. Only then can one teach them to others, for words that come from the depths of one's heart will enter the heart of another. (F.C.O., p. 443)

≈

On the same *Pasuk*, the author of *Imrei Shefer* noted that in the *Ethics of Our Fathers* (5:19), it states: "For any love that depends on a specific cause, when that cause is gone, the love is gone; but if it does not depend on a specific cause, it will never cease." "And you shall love . . . with all your heart and with all your soul and with all your possessions"—for such love, which is not dependent on anything, one will give up everything intuitively. "And these words will be upon your heart"—they will always be with you and they will never be nullified. (M.T., vol. 5, p. 40)

≈

On the words "with all your heart and with all your soul," the Chidushei Harim said that our Sages state that even if someone takes your soul and at that moment your heart does not wish or is unable to serve Hashem, the obligation is still there. (M.T., vol. 5, p. 40)

≈

On the *Pasuk* "You shall teach them (*shinantam*, "learn") to your sons" (Deut. 6:7), the Kotzker commented that if you wish your sons to study, then you too must study so that you become a role model. That is why it states *shinantam*; for if you will learn, your son will learn. (F.C.O., p. 444)

EIKEV
"IT WILL BE BECAUSE"

"And it will be because of your listening to these ordinances, and your observing and performing them; then Hashem, your God, will safeguard for you the covenant and the kindness that He swore to your forefathers." (Deut. 7:12) R' Yerachmiel of Pshys'cha said that a person never stays on one spiritual level. However, it is essential that whatever his level, he must be cautious not to transgress nor blemish his soul, God forbid. At the time of being on an elevated level, he should serve Hashem with awe and love. (*Torat Hayehudi Hakadosh*, p. 63)

❦

On the same *Pasuk*, Rashi comments: "If the light commandments that a person tramples with his heels you will listen to, then Hashem, your God, will safeguard for you the covenant; He will keep His promise to you." The author of *Imrei Shefer* says that a person should take preventive measures not to transgress the laws as stated in the Torah. When one will observe "the light commandments, the safeguards, so that one will be able to observe the *mitzvot*," then "Hashem, your God, will safeguard for you the covenant and the kindness"—then Hashem will perform measure for measure. He will give kindness and well-being so that there will be no difficulty in performing the *mitzvot*. Our Sages state: "The reward of a mitzvah is not received in this world." (*Kedushin* 39b) When the Torah mentions a reward to be obtained in this world for material things, the Rambam notes, they are not rewards; they are promises from Hashem so that we will be able to fulfill the conditions of the *mitzvot*. The author of *Imrei Shefer* explained that poverty and pain disturb one from performing the *mitzvot* with a full heart, as our Sages noted that poverty unsettles the mind. Hashem will take away difficulties in life such as poverty and pain, which keep one away from observing the Torah. (M.T., vol. 5, p. 46)

~~~

On the same *Pasuk*, the Kedushas Levi noted that the reward that Hashem grants us for the performance of a mitzvah is only part of the reward for the mitzvah, for the pleasure of a mitzvah is the mitzvah itself. The fact that a person receives satisfaction from performing the will of Hashem is "The reward of the mitzvah is the mitzvah." (*Ethics of Our Fathers* 4:2) As the *Pasuk* states: "It will be"—the result—"because of your listening . . . Hashem, your God, will safeguard for you the covenant and the kindness. . . ." It will be good for you and you will be rewarded, and that is only part of the compensation—for in the last analysis, it is doing the will of Hashem. (*Kedushas Levi*, p. 180)

~~~

On the words "And it will be because of your listening," the Kotzker said that in the end all will have to listen. (F.U.A.O., vol. 4, p. 225)

~~~

On the same words, the Sassover commented that a person must contemplate and give serious thought to every step that he takes. If the step is for the will of Hashem then he should undertake it, and if not then he should not take the step. That is why it says that before you take a step, "you should listen"—one should first listen to see if it is the will of Hashem. (M.T., vol. 5, p. 45)

~~~

The conventional meaning of *v'haya* is "and it will be," and the word *eikev* means "heel" or "step." However, R' Yisroel Riziner noted that the word *v'haya* can also denote joy, and *eikev*, sadness. Old age is the last step in a person's life. In those years, one may fall into melancholy and depression. Looking back at life, one may get a feeling of "Vanity, all is vanity." Therefore, one should listen to the *v'haya* (joy) and be careful that the state of sadness should not become overbearing, for that attitude will bring one to the end. A person in his old age should be hearty of spirit, full of happiness, and serve Hashem with love and joy. (F.C.O., p. 445)

⸻

R' Simcha Bunim noted that a person should always be cheerful and of good spirit, even if he has to pretend, for it is better than being despondent. Sadness itself is definitely a lie. (F.C.O., p. 445)

⸻

"Hashem will remove from you every illness; and all bad maladies of Egypt that you knew, He will not put (*y'simam*) them upon you, but will put (*n'tanam*) them upon your foes. " (Deut. 7:15) The Gerer Rebbe explained that in the Talmud the term *n'tinah* refers to measured giving and *simah* means putting or giving without measure (*Kerisus* 6a). "He will not put them (*y'simam*) upon you"—He will give you the slightest malady—but "will put them (*n'tanam*) upon your foes"—your foes will have it in great measure. (M.T., vol. 5, p. 47)

⸻

"All the commandments that I command you today. . . ." (Deut. 8:1) The Vorker commented that it means today, tomorrow, the day after tomorrow, always, everywhere, in every place, and in every corner. (S.S.K., p. 124)

⸻

"You shall remember the entire road on which Hashem, your God, led you these forty years in the wilderness . . . to test you, to know what is in your heart. . . . He afflicted you and let you hunger, and He fed you the manna. . . ." (Deut. 8:3, 4) The Koznitzer noted that the Mishnah states: "This is the way of Torah: Eat bread with salt. . . ." (*Ethics of Our Fathers* 6:4) It is known that they could have had every pleasurable taste possible in the manna. However, the test was to see if they would be able to be satisfied with the taste of just a piece of bread with salt, so that they would merit receiving the Torah. This means "to know what is in the heart"—to know whether one is looking for the pleasures of having delicacies or a piece of bread in salt, meaning the Torah. (M.T., vol. 5, p. 49)

〜〰〜

"You will eat and you will be satisfied." (Deut. 8:10) R' Ber Mezritch commented that the "Grace after Meals" (benching) needs more feeling than prayer, for prayer is a rabbinical decree but "benching" is a command from the Torah. (F.C.O., p. 449)

〜〰〜

On the same *Pasuk*, the Karliner commented that one should get satisfaction from the blessing after the meal. (F.U.A.O., vol. 4, p. 229)

〜〰〜

On the *Pasuk* "You increase silver and gold for yourselves . . . and your heart will become haughty and you will forget Hashem, your God. . . ." (Deut. 8:13,14), the author of *Binah L'itim* commented that an abundance of money is like having too much blood. Too much blood is detrimental, especially if something impure should enter the bloodstream. With too much money, something impure may also get mixed in, such as fraud, theft, or cheating. The remedy for too much blood is bloodletting. For the overabundance of money, the same remedy is required, such as giving to a needy cause. Without a remedy, "your heart will become haughty and you will forget Hashem, your God." (F.U.A.O., vol. 4, p. 230)

〜〰〜

"It shall be (*v'haya*) that if you forget Hashem, your God, and go after the gods of others . . . I testify against you today that you will surely perish." (Deut. 8:19) R' Baruch Mezbitzer wondered why the word *v'haya*, which denotes joy, is used in this *Pasuk*—for where is the joy in "if you forget Hashem, your God?" R' Baruch noted that there are two ways a person commits transgressions. One may transgress because the evil inclination is too strong to be overcome. The punishment for this is not that severe because it is not a deliberate transgression but one done just to satisfy the desire. However, others transgress deliberately to rebel against the Divine command and to abrogate the Torah. It is about them that the Torah speaks. They are in a state of joy when they "forget Hashem," therefore, "I testify against you today that you will surely perish." (F.C.O., p. 451)

～～

On the same *Pasuk*, the Riziner noted that one should not forget the *v'haya*, the joy and happiness in one's life, and become depressed. If one does forget then he will "forget Hashem, your God." Sadness and depression leads one to forget Hashem. (F.C.O., p. 451)

～～

"They have strayed quickly from the way that I commanded them." (Deut. 9:12) R' Heschel noted that to completely leave the true and right path of Torah, one must commit many transgressions. However, with the transgression of idol worship, one leaves the path of Torah immediately, as our Sages noted: "If one becomes an apostate to idol worship, one becomes an apostate to the entire Torah." (*Chulin* 8a) (F.U.A.O., vol. 4, p. 234)

～～

"I grasped the two tablets and threw them from my two hands, and I shattered them before your eyes." (Deut. 9:17) The Sadigurer noted a Midrash that states that when Moses broke the first tablets all the words flew away except "Remember the Shabbat day to sanctify it." That is why we say in the morning Shabbat prayers, "He brought down two stone tablets in his hand, on which is inscribed the observances of the Shabbat." On the second set of tablets, the mitzvah of the observance of the Shabbat is again written. That is because the words of the observance of the Shabbat remained even after the tablets were shattered. (F.C.O., p. 452)

〜

"And now, Israel, what does Hashem, your God, ask of you but to fear Hashem, your God. . . ." (Deut. 10:12) The Ropshitzer commented that one should constantly be on the level of "what"—who am I, what am I—for humility precedes fear of Hashem, as it states in Proverbs 22:4: "The reward of humility is the fear of Hashem," and as it is written in Psalm 31:20: "How abundant is Your goodness that You have hidden away for those who fear You." Humility is a necessary characteristic for "those who fear You." (*Zera Kodesh*, p. 136b)

〜

On the same *Pasuk*, the Baal Shem Tov commented that one's fear should not be the same as a child's, whose fear is of the punishment. The fear should be that of an adult whose fear is for the consequence of the act upon his soul. (F.C.O., p. 453)

〜

On the same *Pasuk*, the Kotzker noted Rashi's comment: "Our rabbis commented from here that everything is in the hands of Heaven except for fear of Heaven." The Kotzker said that this means there is always doubt if a request will be granted. The one exception is the "fear of Heaven." That request is granted immediately. (*Ohel Torah*, p. 84)

〜

On the same *Pasuk*, the Kedushas Levi noted Rashi's comment on the *Pasuk* in *Shmot* 1:21: "And it came to pass, because the midwives feared Hashem, that He made them houses." Rashi commented that Hashem rewarded the midwives for their devotion. These "houses" were not buildings; they were dynasties. Yocheved, a midwife, became the ances- tor of the *Kohanim* and Levites. Moses and Aharon were her sons in merit of her "awe of Heaven." Moses' humility came naturally to him because he was born as a reward of Yocheved's awe. To Moses, the term "fear" was not a lofty word, for it was not an effort for him to obtain "fear of heaven." (*Kedushas Levi*, p. 182)

On the same *Pasuk*, R' Baruch Mezbitzer commented that it means that Hashem requires of us that whatever He does, we should do. "As He is merciful, you should be merciful; as He is gracious and compassionate, you should be gracious and compassionate." (Talmud *Shabbat* 133b) (F.C.O., p. 453)

"You should cut away the barrier of your heart and no longer stiffen your neck." (Deut. 10:16) R' Moshe Chayim Ephraim of Sadilkov commented that when "you will cut away the barrier of your heart," you will not question Hashem's leadership and therefore you will "no longer stiffen your neck." (*Degel Machnei Ephraim*, p. 221)

On the *Pasuk* "Hashem, your God, you shall fear" (Deut. 10:20), our Sages asserted that it "includes wise men," as it is written in Talmud *Baba Kamma* 41. R' Aharon Karliner said that the *Pasuk* informs us that wise men must also fear Hashem. (F.U.A.O., p. 240)

"And it will be that if listening, you will listen to My commandments that I command you [plural] today. . . . I shall provide grass in your [singular] field for your animal. . . ." (Deut. 11:13,15) The Izbitzer noted that in one *Pasuk* the statement is in the plural and in the second it is written in the singular. In Psalms 134:3 it states: "May Hashem bless you from Zion, Maker of heaven and earth." The Izbitzer, playing on the word "Zion," changed it to *tziyun*, "mark" or "designation." The use of the plural refers to the acceptance of the Torah when all Israel was equal for all Israel wished to serve Hashem. However, the *tziyun*, the mark that each person had in his heart, was different. Therefore, the singular is used to show the individual differences and that each person received a reward according to his mark and wages. (*Mei Hashaluach*, p. 181)

⌒⌒

"You will turn astray and you will serve other gods." (Deut. 11:16) On this *Pasuk*, the Yid Hakadosh said that as soon as one will "turn astray"—abandon the Jewish way of life and turn away from his people—he "will serve others gods." (F.C.O., p. 454)

⌒⌒

"You shall place these words of Mine upon your heart and upon your soul. . . ." (Deut. 11:18) Rashi comments: "Even after you will go into exile, be distinguished through the performance of the command-ments—for example, put on *tefillin* and affix *mezuzot*—so that they should not be new to you when you return." The Yid HaKadosh based his interpretation on the verse in Psalms 139:24: "And see if I have vexing ways; and lead me in the ways of eternity." He said that one should not think that if he becomes depressed, God forbid, and cannot pray with a clear mind that he should not pray, for King David tells us that one should be careful not to have such thoughts, but "lead me in the ways of eternity." One should continue to pray as usual, using the Prayer Book adopted by the Great Assembly, who redacted the words for prayer to enlighten us as to the true ways of the heart. Rashi advises us that when a person's thoughts are in exile and he has lost all desire to perform the *mitzvot* and wishes to refrain from their performance, God forbid, he should nevertheless don the *tefillin* and affix the *mezuzot*, as described in the Torah. That is what is meant by "they should not be new to you when you will return" and "lead me in the ways of eternity." After you come out of depression and despair, and your normal thoughts return, the *mitzvot* should not appear to you as some-thing new, as we read earlier: "And it shall be that if listening, you will listen . . ." (Deut. 11:13). Our Sages interpreted this as: "If you listen to the old, you will listen to the new." (Talmud *Berachot* 40a) (*Torat Hayehudi HaKadosh*, p. 64)

⌒⌒

"And you will perish quickly." (Deut. 11:17) The Baal Shem Tov explained that one should abandon his constant rushing and swift decisions and learn to be deliberate in his thought and conduct himself unhurriedly. (*Sefer of the Baal Shem Tov*, p. 311)

～～

On the *Pasuk* "And you shall bind them for a sign upon your arm and let them be frontlets (*tefillin*) between your eyes" (Deut. 11:18), the Berditchever noted that when our Sages said that they never took their *tefillin* off, it means that they were continually praising and defending the Jewish people, as our Sages observed: "Those *tefillin* of the Master of the Universe, what is written on them? And who is like Your people Israel, one nation in the land?" (Talmud *Berachot* 6a) We deduce from this that Hashem is constantly praising the Jews and also takes pleasure in those who praise them. That means that we can infer that our Sages were constantly wearing their *tefillin*. (F.C.O., p. 455)

～～

"You shall teach them to your children to speak of them." (Deut. 11:19) R' Bunim of Pshys'cha commented on the verse in Proverbs 20:11: "Even a child is known by his doings, whether his work be pure, and whether it be right." While a child is young, his spiritual abilities can be seen. However, it is imperative to be aware of his abilities. If one cannot properly judge the child, besides not helping in the nurturing of the child's spiritual brilliance, the rich spiritual treasures that the child possesses are blunted and uprooted. (F.C.O., p. 456)

～～

"For if observing you will observe all of this commandment that I command you, to perform it, to love Hashem, your God, to go in all His ways and to cleave to Him." (Deut. 11:22) The Baal HaTanya, Rabbi Shneur Zalman of Liadi, explained how necessary it is to understand how "doing" can be applied to love, which is in the heart. "There are two kinds of love of Hashem," explained the Baal HaTanya. "One is the natural yearning of the soul to its Creator," which occurs when the soul masters the desires of the body. Then the love of Hashem "will flare and blaze with a flame that ascends of its own accord, for these are the Tzaddikim, who are in a state of *Ahavah Rabbah* (great love), as it says in

Psalms 97:12: 'Rejoice in Hashem, Tzaddikim.'" It requires a refine-
ment of all bodily desires, a great deal of Torah, and good deeds to attain
this lofty soul. The second form of love can be obtained by every Jew
through contemplation in the depths of his soul. This requires reflection
and meditation to understand the greatness of Hashem in such detail
that the intellect can grasp it. To reflect on Hashem's great love is to
bring us away from the "obscenity of the earth" (*Bereshit* 42:9), and to
understand that He elevated us from defilement to reach holiness.
"Then," the Baal HaTanya continues, "'to do it' is the charge to devote
one's heart and mind to matters that stimulate love." (*Tanya*, vol. 2,
pp. 4–8)

RE'EH
"SEE"

"See, I present before you today a blessing and a curse. The blessing: that you listen to (obey) the commandments of Hashem, your God, that I command you today. And the curse: if you do not listen to the commandments of Hashem, your God, and you stray from the path . . ." (Deut. 11:26–28). The Lubavitcher Rebbe explained the importance of seeing in one's life. He said: "When we see an object or an event, we grasp it in its totality, and only afterwards do we focus on the particulars." As to hearing, the Rebbe explained that we start with the particulars and then develop a picture. Thus, Moses is telling the people that they must be totally aware to make conscious choices. No response to life events should be instant or thoughtless because life consists of challenges to be met. Challenges are given to permit us to face them and overcome them. Once we surmount the obstacles, we can make a contribution of our own. Therefore, we are given the choice to elevate ourselves to a higher spiritual level, for it generates a sense of accomplishment. Evil is given to offer an obstacle to the spiritual life. The power of evil matches the level of holiness. The Rebbe explained: "Man must tap his inner resources to overcome them. . . . God does not want man to fail." Therefore, man must "see" the good and what it can accomplish and "see" evil as a negative choice. When we "see," an impression is made and then we see the wisdom of our choice and we are able to understand the Divine purpose and our objective in Divine service. (G.O.T., pp. 113–116)

⮑⮐

On the same *Pasuk*, the Kotzker noted that the *Pasuk* begins with *re'eh* (see), which is in the singular, and then addresses in the plural. He explained that the Torah was given to all the Jews but not everyone perceives it equally. (*Ohel Torah*, p. 84)

⮑⮐

Our Sages state: "A person should always perceive himself as though he were half guilty and half meritorious. If he performs one mitzvah, he is fortunate, for he has tipped the worldly balance toward merit; however, if he commits one transgression, woe to him, for he has tipped the balance toward guilt." (Talmud *Kedushin* 40b) The Preshburger commented that the Torah first speaks to the individual: "See." He said that for every action that a person performs, the Torah says: "I give you (plural) today a blessing and a curse"—for you bear for everyone. One single action can affect the entire world as a blessing or a curse. (M.T., vol. 5, p. 60)

⮑⮐

On the same *Pasuk*, the Primishlaner said that *Re'eh Anochi* ("See, I") can refer to the "I," or ego, which for every person can be "a blessing and a curse." The "blessing" refers to the "I" that sees that his greatness should be used for the sake of heaven to ascend to higher and more mature spiritual levels as he performs the *mitzvot*. The "curse" of the inner "I" occurs when "you will not listen." When one prides himself on his greatness and becomes egocentric, then that is a real "curse." (F.C.O., p. 457)

⮑⮐

On the same *Pasuk*, the Chernovitzer noted that after the word "blessing" we find the words "that you listen." However, after the word "curse," it states, "if you do not listen," as well as "you stray from the path." The Chernovitzer explained that our Sages said that Hashem attaches good thoughts to deeds. (Talmud *Kedushin* 40a) When one has a good thought even before his action, he receives a blessing. However, when an evil thought is not attached to an action, the curse is not given immediately. Had there been an action, that would have caused "you [to] stray from the path." (M.T., vol. 5, p. 62)

～～

"You shall not do so to Hashem, your God." (Deut. 12:4) The Kotzker said that one should not act perfunctorily or out of habit or because someone else is doing it—do not do so to Hashem. (F.C.O., p. 458)

～～

"Rather, only at a place that Hashem, your God, will choose from all your tribes to place His Name there, you shall seek out (*tidreshu*— plural) His resting place and come (*u'bata*—singular) there." (Deut. 12:5) The Gerer Rebbe noted that our Sages stated: "She is Zion; there is none that inquire after her. From this we gather that she ought to be inquired after." (Talmud *Rosh Hashanah* 30a) The Rebbe explained that "she ought to be inquired after" means that it is imperative that we probe the reasons why the Temples were destroyed and correct them so that there will be a rebuilding. The last destruction came about because of unfounded hatred, which caused a schism among the Jews. The rectification is love and unity. This is what the Torah is asking of us, to "seek out His resting place." When we will inquire why the Tabernacle is no longer in existence, we will understand that we were a multitude and we were splintered into many pieces. We must correct this and become as one, so that when we will "come there" (in the singular) with the strength of unity, so then the plural will become as one. (M.T., vol. 5, p. 64)

～～

"And what is raised of your hand. . . ." (Deut. 12:6) On Rashi's comment, "These are the first fruits," the Chidushei Harim explained that all that we do, all of our actions, must be sanctified for Hashem's sake. That is the meaning of "first fruits." The fruits that grow by means of human intervention we sacrifice unto Hashem. That is why Shavuot is known as the holiday of "the giving of the Torah" and "of the first fruits." It is only by following the Torah that we can reach the level of sanctifying and making holy the actions of the human being. (M.T., vol. 5, p. 65)

‿∾

"You shall not eat it, in order that it be well with you and your children after you, when you do what is right in the eyes of Hashem." (Deut. 12:25) The Satmar Rebbe said that it is the way of the world that when children lead a life of Torah and better their behavior, in turn their parents will improve their ways as well. The opposite, God forbid, is also true; that the parents will also be influenced negatively by their children's actions. Therefore, as we read in Proverbs 22:6: "Train your child in the way he should go, and when he is old, he will not depart from it." A good education is necessary so that "when he is old," the child will not stray from the performance of the *mitzvot*. This is what the *Pasuk* alludes to when it states: "that it be well with you and your children after you." Your training will improve their behavior and their performance of the commandments of Hashem. Thereby, the parents will also have done "what is right in the eyes of Hashem." (M.D., p. 381)

‿∾

"Hashem, your God, shall you follow and Him shall you fear; His commandments shall you keep and to His voice shall you listen; Him shall you serve and to Him shall you cleave." (Deut. 13:5) The Yid HaKadosh commented that if one will follow all that is asked then one will reach the level of "to Him shall you cleave." (F.C.O., p. 458)

‿∾

"If there should stand up in your midst a prophet or a dreamer of a dream, and he will give you a sign or a wonder, and the sign or the wonder comes about, of which he spoke to you, saying, 'Let us follow the gods of others' . . . do not hearken to the words. . . ." (Deut. 13:2–4) The author of *Avnei Nezer* noted that the Torah speaks about three ways people can be influenced to go in the wrong direction. The first way is to be influenced by people whose main goal is to lead people astray to listen to false ideologies. That is what the Torah means when it speaks about false prophets, saying: "Do not hearken to the words of that prophet."

Then there are people who are influenced by relatives or friends to follow a way that will lead them astray. The *Pasuk* states: "If your brother, the son of your mother . . . or your friend who is like your own soul will incite you secretly, saying 'Let us worship the gods of others' . . . you shall not take kindly to him and you shall not listen to him. . . ." (Deut. 13:7–12) Finally, people can be led astray by the latest psychology, street mentality, or fads, as the *Pasuk* states: "Men, sons of lawlessness have emerged from your midst, and they have caused the dwellers of their city to go astray, saying, 'Let us go and worship the gods of others . . .'" (Deut. 13:14) Therefore, the Torah warns, "You shall inquire, search, and investigate and behold, if it is true . . . this abomination was done in your midst" (Deut. 13:15), then, "You shall destroy the evil from your midst.'" (Deut. 13:6) (M.T., vol. 5, p. 66)

～⌒⌒

"You are children to Hashem, your God. You shall not cut yourselves and you shall not make a bald spot between your eyes for a dead person. For you are a holy people to Hashem, your God, and Hashem has chosen you for Himself to be a treasured people, from among all peoples on the face of the earth." (Deut. 14:1–2) R' Nachum Perlow, the Novominsker Rebbe, noted that the Talmud *Shabbat* 88b states: "R' Shmuel the son of Nachmani said in R' Jonathan's name, 'What is meant by "You have ravished my heart, my sister, my bride: You have ravished my heart with one of thine eyes"? (*Song of Songs* 4:9) In the beginning, with one of your eyes; when you fulfill, with both your eyes.'" Rashi commented that at the time of acceptance of the Torah there was one eye and at the performance of the *mitzvot* there were two. Others interpreted that with one eye one introspects and with the second one looks at the perfection of others. At the start we look at ourselves, then at the perfection of others, and then we can work to perfect ourselves, as our Sages say: "First adorn yourself, then adorn others." (Talmud *Baba Metzia* 107b) If a person is blind in one eye, he is absolved from seeing. (Talmud *Chigigah* 2a) Therefore, we are told not to "put a bald spot between your eyes," not to look only at oneself or only on others, but to look with both eyes both ways. The *Pasukim* also teach us that all Jews are responsible for one another because we are all children of Hashem.

Therefore, it says, "You shall not cut yourselves," as it is noted in the Talmud *Yevamot* 14a, that we are not to divide into small groups but become one association. It is stated in *Shemot* 19:2: "And Israel camped opposite the mount." Rashi states that the huge multitude encamped as a single person. The reason we are to work at perfecting others is that we are "a holy people to Hashem." We live a life of holiness, as is stated in the Talmud *Chulin* 89a. As a person makes himself holy he spreads holiness to others, for we are considered as one soul. (*P'er Nachum*, p. 234)

On the same *Pasuk*, "You (*atem*) are children to Hashem, your God," R' Muttel Kazmirer noted another *Pasuk*: "These are the appointed festivals of Hashem, holy convocations, which you (*otam*) are to proclaim in their appointed times." (*Vayikrah* 23:4) Our Sages stated that the use of the word *otam* shows that one may state the appointed time for the festivals even if he errs unwittingly or deliberately or is misled. The Rebbe explained that since our Sages noted that *otam* refers to "unwittingly or deliberately" and is accepted, then in this *Pasuk* where it states specifically *atem*, then people who transgress unwittingly or deliberately are definitely still "children of Hashem." (F.U.A.O., vol. 4, p. 252)

On the *Pasuk* "You shall not eat any abomination" (Deut. 14:3), R' Chayim of Chernovitz noted that the Rambam warned us that we should not be gluttonous. We should eat foods that are healthy for us. We should not eat coarse food nor should we insist on filling our stomachs beyond capacity. There are people who follow the philosophy that they must eat and drink for tomorrow they may die, so they make each meal a festival. "This refers to people who abandon study and spend all their days at feasts." (Talmud *Shabbat* 151) The Rebbe noted that the Torah tells us that this type of eating should be abominable and disgusting to oneself, as if the animal instinct had come to the individual. Therefore, the Torah instructs us, "You shall not eat any abomination." (M.D., p. 383)

⤚⤳

"Tithe, you shall tithe the entire crop of your planting, the produce of the field, year by year." (Deut. 14:22) The Kedushas Levi noted that in the Talmud *Shabbat* 119a, it states that one should tithe in order to become wealthy. To understand this, we should realize that when one gives charity, it ascends to Heaven and is placed before the Almighty. For example, even if one gives a coin or one measure of grain, it ascends upward. The amount does not matter for it is considered as fulfilling one commandment. No matter the amount one gives, it increases the following year. That is what is meant by "the produce of the field, year by year." (*Kedushas Levi*, p. 183)

⤚⤳

On the same *Pasuk*, the Kedushas Levi cited a statement by our Sages: "The reward for a mitzvah is a mitzvah." (*Ethics of Our Fathers* 4:2) Therefore, the Torah states that if you tithe one time, then you will merit tithing many times. When one plants the seed of a mitzvah in holiness, it is planted for eternity. (*Kedushas Levi*, p. 92)

⤚⤳

On the *Pasuk* "And you shall eat before Hashem, your God, in the place that He will choose to rest His Name there . . . so that you will learn to fear Hashem, your God, all the ways" (Deut. 14:23), R' Bunim asked what "eating before Hashem" has to do with "you will learn to fear Hashem." The Rebbe said that the Torah is warning us that when we sit down to eat, we should be careful that we sit with people who will be ready to "learn to fear Hashem." (F.U.A.O., vol. 4, p. 253)

⤚⤳

On the *Pasuk* "So that you will learn to fear Hashem, your God, all the days" (Deut. 14:23), R' Bunim of Pshys'cha commented that the essence of rectification is the learning of Torah. By studying Torah, one learns to understand the "awe of Hashem" and eventually "to fear Hashem, your God, all the days." From this, one also begins to comprehend "The whole world is filled with His glory." (Is. 6:3) There is nothing in the world that does not have a Divine Spark. (F.C.O., p. 459)

～～

On the same *Pasuk*, the Kotzker said that even a busy person, though he may be occupied, should give Torah study some thought, for thought is the same as deed. (F.C.O., p. 459)

～～

On the same *Pasuk*, the Baal Shem Tov commented that one should keep in mind for Whom he is learning. It is possible that even when one is studying, one may distance himself from the Almighty. (F.C.O., p. 460)

～～

On the same *Pasuk*, R' Aharon Karliner noted that fear without love is not wholeness. However, love without fear is nothing. (F.C.O., p. 461)

～～

"You may spend the money for whatever your soul desires—for cattle, or for flock, or for wine, or for strong drink . . . before Hashem, your God, and you shall rejoice—you and your household." (Deut. 14:26) Emphasizing the importance of brotherhood and joy, the Riziner commented that when Jews assemble and toast each other with *L'chayim*, it is serving Hashem. (F.C.O., p. 462)

～～

"If there be a destitute person among you, of one of your brothers . . . you shall not harden your heart nor shall you close your hand against your destitute brother." (Deut. 15:7) The author of the *sefer Imrei Shefer* asks the reason for the statements "one of your brothers" and again "your destitute brother." The normal tendency of people is to readily give money to a poor person of note, rather than any other poor person. The Torah teaches us that when it is "one of your brothers"—one that is known as a worthy person—one's heart does not question the need to give. However, when it comes to "your destitute brother"—a person whom you may not know and so may not want to help—the Torah states, nevertheless, "You shall not harden your heart nor shall you close your hand." (M.T., vol. 5, p. 72)

～～

The words "nor shall you close your hand against your destitute brother" in *Pasuk* 15:7 in Hebrew are *Lo tikpotz et yad'cha Ha'Evyon*. The Riziner noted that rearranging the first letters of the Hebrew words spells *tehilym* (psalms). One may say psalms in times of agony or joy; however, the importance of saying psalms is to help people in need. (F.C.O., p. 463)

～～

The Bratzlaver said that when one sets aside money for charity before one prays, one will be able to pray with deep conviction and avoid all unessential thoughts. (*Sefer Midot*, p. 244)

～～

On the *Pasuk* "Giving, you shall give him, and let your heart not feed bad when you give him, for because of this matter, Hashem, your God, will bless you in all your deeds and in your every undertaking" (Deut. 15:10), R' Shneur Zalman of Liadi commented that the word "give" is mentioned twice for emphasis, because giving charity is in the category of *Avodah*—Service to Hashem. Service applies only to what one does with immense toil, for that is contrary to one's natural inclination. He subdues his nature and will before Hashem, for example, to exhaust himself in Torah and prayer "to the extent of pressing our soul." (*Sifre, Devarim* 32) As the Baal HaTanya says, "And in our case, too, as regards the commandment of charity, he gives exceedingly more than the nature of his compassion and will, and as our Sages, of Blessed Memory, commented on the verse 'Give, you shall give,' 'even a hundred times.'" (*Tanya*, vol. 4, p. 118)

SHOFTIM
"JUDGES"

On the *Pasuk* "Judges and officers shall you appoint for yourself in all your gates, which Hashem, your God, gives you . . . judge the people with righteous judgement" (Deut. 16:18), the Lubavitcher Rebbe explained that ever since man was created there has been a constant search for truth. However, because man is subjective in his thinking, there are limits to its discovery. Therefore, Hashem has given us the Torah, which gives us objective standards that are the guidelines we are to apply under all circumstances. We have to develop a sense of responsibility to scrutinize and judge our surroundings and circumstances. We have to see if our conduct is according to the standards set by the Torah. In this way, one can elevate himself and his environment to a higher level. The words "in all your gates" are interpreted as referring to the body's sensory organs (*Or HaTorah*, p. 822). They serve as the "gates" through which the influences of the environment pass. We are commanded to appoint judges at these gates so that all that pass through will be in conformity with the Torah. The Torah uses the singular form in the pronoun "your" to emphasize that each individual is a "city in microcosm," judging himself to follow the teachings of the Torah. (*In the Garden of the Torah*, pp. 119–121)

❧

On the same *Pasuk*, R' Asher Horowitz commented that when one commits a transgression or performs a tactless act, we should not judge him as guilty immediately. First, judge yourself as to what you would do under the same circumstances, then you will be able to judge "with righteous judgment." (F.C.O., p. 467)

On the same *Pasuk*, R' Baruch Mezbitzer commented that we should appoint judges who will embrace "Hashem, your God," the spiritual aspects of life. (M.T., vol. 5, p. 75)

The Chidushei Harim, based on the statement "Judge everyone favorably" (*Ethics of Our Fathers* 1:6), explained that we should not criticize someone for singular acts of which no person is exempt. Rather one should judge an individual based on his entire persona, for then one would probably judge him favorably. (F.C.O., p. 467)

On the words "for yourself," the Toldot Yaacov Yosef commented that the same judgment you render your friend, you should render "for yourself." Do not judge someone else harshly and yourself leniently. (*Toldot Yaacov Yosef*, vol. 2, p. 652)

On the words "they shall judge the people with righteous judgment," the Kedushas Levi explained that everyone should learn to judge others with "righteous judgment," so that the Judge above will be moved to render a judgment of innocence upon all. With whatever characteristic we judge others below, so will be the judgment from above. (*Kedushas Levi*, p. 183)

On the same *Pasuk*, R' Nachman Bratzlaver commented that if one has the attitude that he can spoil something by his actions, then let him also realize that he can, by his actions, set things straight. (F.C.O., p. 467)

⚬

"You shall not pervert judgment, you shall not take notice of presence, and you shall not take a bribe, for a bribe will blind the eyes of the wise and make righteous words crooked." (Deut. 16:19) It is a sign of a righteous person to always look for what is meritorious among men, as our Sages noted: "If the spirit of one's fellow is pleased with him, the spirit of the Omnipresent is pleased with him; but if the spirit of one's fellow is not pleased with him, the spirit of the Omnipresent is not pleased with him." (*Ethics of Our Fathers* 3:13) Therefore, one might think that it is the will of Hashem for us to behave in this manner even with the enemy—namely, the evil inclination. However, the Toldot Yaacov Yosef cautions us not to apply that thinking to judgment, for the evil inclination may use the belief in the goodness of a man as a bribe. Therefore, the Rebbe of Polnoye cautions us to be aware not to "take notice of [someone's] presence" and thereby "pervert judgment." (*Toldot Yaacov Yosef*, p. 653)

⚬

On the same *Pasuk*, the S'fas Emes noted that an infection can blind the eyes and our Sages state: "A good virtue is greater than severe punishment." (*Sotah* 11a) When one cures his infection and removes his motives and works diligently to achieve righteousness, then his eyes are opened and he will be able to clearly see the truth. (*S'fas Emes*, p. 72)

⚬

On the *Pasuk* "Righteousness, righteousness shall you pursue" (Deut. 16:20), R' Bunim of Pshys'cha noted that to reach the level of "righteousness" we must do battle righteously, with honest means, when we pursue justice. (F.U.A.O., vol. 4, p. 272)

⚬

On the same *Pasuk*, R' Moshe Leib Lechner noted that there is a reason for using "righteous" twice in this *Pasuk*. Based on the *Pasuk*, he admonishes those who hide their lies with the mantle of truth. They swear by the words "We are righteous, but we have sinned," and defend their falsehoods and quote words from the Torah. Therefore, the Torah demands that righteousness and truth must be based on righteousness. (F.C.O., p. 472)

⌁

"You shall not plant for yourself a tree for idol worship, any tree, near the Altar of Hashem, your God, that you shall make for yourself. And you shall not erect for yourself a statue, which Hashem, your God, hates." (Deut. 16:21–22) The *Avnei Nezer* cites Rashi: "This is a negative commandment for one who plants a tree and one who builds a house." The author says that a place that is holy must be proper because of its holiness and not because of outward appearances, such as having pretty plants or an ostentatious building. If one wishes to beautify holiness with outer beauty, then it is a sign that one is hiding under one's own concept of holiness. Instead of the inner beauty of holiness, the outer manifestations are considered. Our Sages note that anyone who appoints a judge who is not proper plants a treat "near the Altar." (Talmud *Sanhedrin* 7a) If a judge is appointed because he speaks well or has a nice personality, though he lacks high spiritual standards, it is as if one "plant(s) any tree near the Altar of Hashem." (M.T., vol. 5, p. 77)

⌁

On the same *Pasuk*, the Koznitzer commented that if one regrets his previous behavior and begins to return to serve Hashem properly by praying correctly, studying Torah, and performing *mitzvot* for its own sake, he may become arrogant. The evil inclination begins to burn within him and because of this attitude his behavior begins to deteriorate and all his good intentions are spoiled. Our Sages state that all who become arrogant are considered as though they are idol worshippers. Therefore, the Torah warns us, "You shall not make for yourself any tree near the Altar of Hashem . . . and you shall not make for yourself a statue." "For yourself" is mentioned twice to emphasize that you should not make yourself as though you are a tree or a pillar—"which Hashem, your God, hates." (*Avodas Yisroel*, p. 183)

On the same *Pasuk*, the Kedushas Levi cited a statement of our Sages: "Prepare yourself in the lobby so that you may enter the banquet hall." (*Ethics of Our Fathers* 4:21) This world is a preparation for the World to Come. Whatever one does to make himself healthy and strengthen himself for the service of Hashem is not completely "for yourself." Our Sages state in the Talmud *Pesachim* 68b that only half is for you. Therefore, the Torah tells us, "Do not erect for yourself a statue," for it is only for the World to Come. (*Kedushas Levi*, p. 183)

On the same *Pasuk*, the Berditchever cautioned that we should not make the pleasures of the body and the pleasures of this world as the essence of life—do not make it a statue (monument) for yourself. (F.C.O., p. 473)

"And it will be told to you and you will hear; and you shall investigate (*v'darashta*) well, and behold! it is true, the matter is well-founded: This abomination was done in Israel." (Deut. 17:4) Based on another meaning of the word *darashta*, "giving a sermon," R' Shalom Belzer commented that when one hears words of Torah and repeats it in one's own name without giving credit to the one who said them first, though "it is true," an "abomination was done in Israel." (F.C.O., p. 473)

On the same *Pasuk*, the Gerer Rebbe cited a passage in Psalms 119:39: "Fulfill Your word to Your servant for the purpose of fearing You." The Rebbe explained that King David requested Hashem that he be given the ability to choose the right words to instill the awe of heaven in each Jew. (M.T., vol. 5, p. 78)

"If a matter of judgment will be hidden from you, between blood and blood, between verdict and verdict, or between affliction and affliction, matters of dispute in your cities—you shall rise and ascend to the place of Hashem, your God, shall choose." (Deut. 17:8) R' Shlomo HaKohen of Radamsk explained that the Torah is teaching us a very important lesson. The lesson becomes obvious when one wishes to attain levels of holiness in each aspect of life, whether in the study of Torah or in learning to serve Hashem. However, when it is "hidden from you," one finds it difficult to do so without the help of a Tzaddik or a wise person. Therefore, one should attach oneself to the Tzaddik from whose words we obtain life and holiness that remains forever. It says in Psalm 16:3: "For the sake of the holy ones who are on earth and for the mighty, all my desires are fulfilled because of them." Many times as we try to attain holiness and it seems as if we are drowning and need help, the Torah advises that we should "ascend to the place that Hashem, your God, shall choose"—go to the Tzaddik whom Hashem has chosen. For every choice is only for His sake, for the Spirit of Hashem is in him. (*Tiferet Shlomoh*, p. 255)

On the words in the *Pasuk* "You shall not turn from the word that they will tell you" (Deut. 17:11), the Maharal, in his *sefer B'er Hagolah*, said that the Torah tells us that all the decrees, edicts, customs, and restrictions that our Sages have ordained are based on the will of Hashem. This will is revealed by the Sages who are the embodiment of the Oral Law. It is the Sages who bring the will of Hashem to reality. (M.T., vol. 5, p. 60)

"You shall surely set over yourself a king whom Hashem, your God, shall choose; from among your brethren shall you set a king over yourself." (Deut. 17:15) R' Asher Horowitz wondered why the Torah had to specify "from among your brethren." The Rebbe said that it should be understood that we would not choose a stranger to rule. The Rebbe explained that the reason for being specific is that we must not choose a ruler who is arrogant and not in touch with his people. Someone who is estranged from his people and lives a daily existence disaffected from the Jewish environment should not rule over his people. (F.C.O., p. 474)

On the same *Pasuk*, R' Yeshaye Ropshitzer commented that one should appoint a King "over yourself." One should be able to rule over one's own actions and be able to take responsibility for all that one does. (F.C.O., p. 474)

"The fire offerings of Hashem and His inheritance shall they eat." (Deut. 18:1) The Sassover commented that this is exactly what we ask of Hashem in the Grace after Meals when we say: "Please make us not needful, Hashem, our God, of the gifts of human hands nor of their loans, but only of Your Hand that is full, open, holy, and generous." (F.C.O., p. 475)

"When the Levite will come from one of your cities, from all of Israel, where he sojourns, and he comes with all longings of his soul to the place that Hashem will choose." (Deut. 18:6) R' Dovid Kotzker explained that the Torah specifically states "with all longings of his soul," that it is only if an individual has a fervent desire to go to Israel shall he settle there. (F.U.A.O., vol. 4, p. 278)

"You shall be wholehearted with Hashem, your God." (Deut. 18:13) R' Avraham Eiger explained that the 613 *mitzvot* that are incumbent upon every Jew to observe are analogous to the organs of the body. Therefore, if a person is missing a part of his body, God forbid, then he is known as a deformed individual. The Torah, therefore, cautions us to perform all the *mitzvot* because one must "be wholehearted," a healthy person, to be "with Hashem." (F.C.O., p. 475)

On the same *Pasuk*, the Kotzker commented that one must "be wholehearted with Hashem" — not one time serving Hashem, and another time oneself. (F.U.A.O., vol. 4, p. 279)

〜

On the same *Pasuk*, R' Bunim noted that the words "be wholehearted with Hashem, your God" appear only with this mitzvah. It is very easy to fool people with the appearance of being wholehearted. Therefore, the Torah finds it necessary to teach us that to be truly wholehearted, one must be honest with Hashem. (F.C.O., p. 476)

〜

On the same *Pasuk*, the Kedushas Levi comments that it is the way of Hashem to improve everything, especially His people, as we are called Children of Hashem. A father fulfills all the needs and wishes of his child before the child is in need. A person who has wholehearted faith in Hashem will have all his needs satisfied and he will know that "Hashem is with him." (*Kedushas Levi*, p. 184)

〜

"For these nations that you are possessing, they listen to astrologers and diviners; but as for you, not so has Hashem, your God, given you." (Deut. 18:14) The Amishover explained that other nations cannot control their desires and bad habits. They surrender to the evil inclination. Therefore, Hashem gave the power of "Not so!" Hashem gave the power of saying "Not so!" to our desires and bad habits and thereby conquering the evil inclination. (M.T., vol. 5, p. 83)

〜

On the same *Pasuk*, R' Bunim said that a Jew should not have only one way in life, by saying that is the way it has to be and there is no other way. When necessary, he should be able to change his habits and nature. "As for you, not so"—you should not always say "so," so is my way. "Not so has Hashem, your God, given you"—that is not the way you should be. (F.C.O., p. 476)

〜

On the *Pasuk* "Lest he die in the war and another man will inaugurate it [a new house]" (Deut. 20:5), Rashi commented: "It is a sorrowful matter." The Gerer Rebbe wondered why Rashi considered inaugurating a new house more of a sorrowful matter than dying in a war. The Rebbe explained that it is a sorrowful matter that a person at the time of death should think about his house rather than repenting. (M.T., vol. 5, p. 86)

~~~

"When you go to battle against your enemy, and you see horse and chariot—a people more numerous than you—you shall not fear them, for Hashem, your God, is with you. . . . And he shall say to them, 'Hear O Israel, you are coming near to battle against your enemies; let your heart not be faint; do not be afraid.'" (Deut. 20:1,3) The Koznitzer said that knowing one's modest worth should not stop one from performing the will of Hashem. Therefore, when one goes to do battle against the evil inclination, which has no mercy on the human being and is the true enemy, one should have no fear. The *Pasuk* states that when one sees the "horse and chariot"—the driving force behind the deed and the shell that covers the deed—one should do battle and "you shall not fear, for Hashem, your God, is with you." As the *Pasuk* continues, "Hear O Israel, you are coming near to battle." Rashi comments: "Even if there is no merit in you but on the recitation of the *Shmah* alone, you are worthy that He should save you." A person should say to himself that as long as the Jewish soul is within him, he should be confident that his repentance will be accepted even if he had committed evil at some time. Hashem's righteousness and mercy will never leave. (*Avodat Yisroel*, p. 183)

~~~

On the *Pasuk* "Who is the man who is fearful and fainthearted? Let him go and return to his house" (Deut. 20:8), the Kotzker said that if one is troubled and depressed, he should not go into any battle, for such a person has no confidence in himself. (F.C.O., p. 476)

KI SEITZEI
"WHEN YOU WILL GO OUT"

"When you will go out to war against your enemies, and Hashem, your God, will deliver him into your hand, and you will capture its captives." (Deut. 21:10) The Lubavitcher Rebbe said that when the soul "descends" from the spiritual world, its natural setting, into the material world, it is confronted with challenges. The Rebbe noted that there are two aspects to one's material existence. On the one hand, the material world was created as a dwelling place for Hashem, as noted in Midrash *Tanchumah* (*parsha Bechukotai*, section 3). However, it is here that His essence is apparent but not revealed, for Holiness in the physical world is not obvious. Therefore, resolving the two facets causes conflict and challenge. The Torah's concept of war is to meet the challenge and transform the physical world into a dwelling place for Hashem. The Rebbe explained that one need not fear undertaking such a battle, for the soul, having descended with spiritual power, compels a person to draw on this inner strength. When this Godly nature is aroused, any challenge can be met, for Hashem "will deliver him into your hand." (*In the Garden of the Torah*, pp. 127–130)

❧

On the same *Pasuk*, R' Ber commented, on "When you will go out," that when one goes away from the awe of Hashem and leaves the path of Judaism, then he will have to "go to war," for there will be constant unrest and inner conflict. One will be in constant battle with himself. (F.C.O., p. 477)

⌐⌐⌐

On the same *Pasuk*, the Lubavitcher Rebbe noted the battle that one has to fight in one's life. The Rebbe cites a verse in Malachai 3:18: "And you shall . . . see the difference between one who serves Hashem and one who does not serve Him." On this verse our Sages in the Talmud *Chagigah* 9b define "one who serves Hashem" as "one who reviews his subject matter one hundred and one times," and "one who does not serve Him" as "one who reviews his subject matter one hundred times." In meeting our personal challenges, it is the 101st time that gives us the opportunity to rise above our natures and challenge ourselves. Serving Hashem means subduing our own natures and committing ourselves to all that is Divine within us. (*In the Garden of the Torah*, pp. 130–131)

⌐⌐⌐

On the same *Pasuk*, the Baal Shem Tov commented that when we continue to battle our constant enemy, the evil inclination, we should take a lesson from it. We should use the same enthusiasm and persistence that it uses to overcome us in order to overcome it. (M.T., vol. 90)

⌐⌐⌐

On the same *Pasuk*, the Kedushas Levi, citing a verse in Psalms 119:98, "Each of your commandments makes me wiser than my enemies, for it is ever with me," gave the following interpretation. He said that from the enemy, the evil inclination, one can learn how to observe the *mitzvot*. It can be noticed that when it is ready to perform a transgression, it is done with much zeal and with a burning desire. Yet, the result is only momentary and does not last forever. Therefore, to perform a mitzvah one must also have the same zeal and fervor. However, its result will last forever. (M.T., vol. 5, p. 90)

⌐⌐⌐

"And you will see among its captivity a woman who is beautiful of form, and you will desire her; you will take her to yourself for a wife." (Deut. 20:11) Rashi comments: "The Torah spoke only against the drive toward evil." R' Meir Primishlaner explained that the nature of the evil inclination is to convince one to do the opposite of the command of the Torah. Therefore, the Torah permitted taking a beautiful woman as a wife so that the evil inclination would persuade one not to do so. (F.C.O., p. 478)

On the same *Pasuk*, the Toldot Yaacov Yosef noted that "take her to yourself for a wife" is the most practical and only solution "against the evil inclination," for when one accepts the responsibility of a family, one cannot be concerned with the desires and foolishness of the evil inclination. (F.U.A.O., p. 286)

On the *Pasukim* "And you will see among its captivity a woman who is beautiful of form, and you will desire her; you will take her to yourself for a wife. . . . And it shall be if you have not desired her, then you shall send her on her own." (Deut. 21:11,14) R' Tzvi Hirsh of Liska, in his *sefer Ach Pri T'vuah*, notes that the Torah is teaching us a lesson in judgment. There are times when it appears to us that a certain action or behavior is appropriate, though in reality it is the evil inclination insisting on the behavior. It is, therefore, imperative that we see the end result. If what was done was positive then it is for a blessing. If the action is regretted, then it was the work of the evil inclination. That is why the Torah says: "And you will see among its captivity a woman who is beautiful of form, and you will desire her; you will take her to yourself for a wife"—then perform the mitzvah. "If you have not desired her"—if you have regret, for it was not a mitzvah—then "you shall send her on her own." (M.D., p. 395)

"If a man will have a wayward and rebellious son. . . ." (Deut. 21:18) Rashi comments that the result of marrying the captive woman for her beauty will cause difficulties and the child of that marriage will be "wayward and rebellious." The author of *Avnei Nezer* noted that if we are to have an impact on our children's upbringing and development, then it is important to be concerned not just with outward appearances.

We can have beautiful buildings, charming teachers, and exquisite uniforms; however, if there is no Torah content and spiritual format, then the result is "a wayward and rebellious son." If the concern is the outer beauty, but no consideration is given to the fact that inwardly there may be a different religious outlook, the result is the rebellious son. (M.T., vol. 4, p. 94)

On the *Pasuk* "You shall destroy the evil from your midst; and all Israel shall hear and they shall fear" (Deut. 21:21), R' Moshe Oheler commented that the person who works at uprooting all the evil within him, "all Israel shall hear and fear." The people will listen to him. Our Sages noted that people will adhere to the words of the one who has the fear of heaven. (F.C.O., p. 478)

The Alter Rebbe, Rabbi Schneur Zalman of Liadi, interpreted the words "You shall destroy out the evil from within you." The Rebbe said that the war one wages against his "animal soul" is not complete because the evil has not been converted to goodness. One may think that the evil has completely disappeared; however, if that were so then it would have been changed to goodness. Based on the talmudic statement "There are righteous people for whom things are bad" (*Berachot* 7a), the Rebbe called them "incompletely righteous," for there still lingers within them a fragment of wickedness. It shows that they do not hate "the other side" with absolute hatred. (*Tanya*, vol. 1, pp. 68–69)

On the *Pasuk* "You shall not see . . . and hide yourself from them; you shall surely return them to your brother" (Deut. 22:1), R' Moshe Koznitzer commented that the Torah teaches us not to neglect the average person. One should not "hide yourself" from those who are rebellious, unresponsive, or withdrawn from our way of life. "Return them"—we have the obligation to teach and to influence them to lift them to the level of "your brother." (F.C.O., p. 481)

⤙⤚

"You shall not see the donkey of your brother or his ox falling on the road and hide yourself from them; you shall surely raise (*ho'keym to'kim*) with him." (Deut. 22:4) R' Moshe Koznitzer, in his *sefer Daat Moshe*, commented that there are times when a person who serves Hashem may fall from his level. In that case, Moshe our teacher requested that one "shall not see" them "falling on the road," the road being the "Kingdom of Heaven." One should not "hide yourself" but "you shall surely raise with him." He noted that R' Aharon Karliner developed this view in another manner. He said that the Torah, by repeating the Hebrew verb "raise" twice—*ho'keym to'kim*—emphasizes the need to raise oneself as well as someone else. Rashi comments: "This is loading—to load up his burden which fell upon it, with its owner." The Koznitzer explained that we should load the yoke of the heavenly Kingdom upon him from whom it fell and do it with him. The Karliner noted the comment of our Sages in Psalms 24:3: "Who may ascend the mountain of Hashem, and who may stand in the place of His sanctity?" He said that one should always stand in "sanctity" so as not to fall from his level. (M.D., p. 396)

⤙⤚

"You shall surely send away the mother and take the young for yourself, so that it will be good for you and you will prolong your days." (Deut. 22:7) The Midrash Rabbah notes that there is a reward for this mitzvah. The reward is that one will beget children and will hasten the coming of the Messiah. The author of *Avnei Nezer* wondered why this mitzvah is so important that it merits such a reward. The *Avnei Nezer* explained that the cause of all problems and every negative situation can be found in the effect of the education of children, in the service of Hashem, interpersonal relationships, and the ego. It is when one cannot forgo his own attitude for the sake of the general good, a higher ideal, or spiritual health that he will find reasons not to give a Torah education and the children will be lost to their parents. The mitzvah of letting the mother bird go is a lesson on how to attain superior ideals when educating our children in spiritual matters. Though a person has the mother bird in hand, and can use it for personal reasons, the Torah, for sake of society, commands us to send it away so that it can give birth to other birds and not permit its annihilation. To perform this mitzvah we learn to give up our own personal needs for the welfare of society. That is why the reward is great for retaining our children in the way of Torah and thereby bringing Elijah the prophet and the Messiah. (M.T., vol. 5, p. 96)

～～

"You shall make a fence upon your roof." (Deut. 22:8) The Savraner said that one should not think evil thoughts in one's head (roof), for our Sages said that evil thoughts are worse than transgressions (*Yoma* 29). (H.A., p. 476)

～～

On the words "You shall guard against anything evil" (Deut. 23:10), the Baal HaTanya explained that a person is called "wicked" when the evil within him prevails. Thought or contemplation of transgression is referred to in *Yoma* 29a, as: "Evil thought is more injurious than sin itself." Speech that is slanderous or scoffing or a deed that violates the caution of the Torah—"You shall guard against anything evil"—must prompt the Divine Soul to assert itself and permit a sense of regret and to seek pardon and forgiveness from Hashem. (*Likkutei Amarim*, part 1, pp. 73–75)

～～

"You shall have a spade in addition to your weaponry, and it will be that when you go outside, you shall dig with it; you shall go back and cover your waste." (Deut. 23:14) The Degel Machnei Ephraim explained that the words of Torah as well as the reproof that a person hears should make an impact upon him and be implanted in his heart as a spade. If "you go outside"—if you should stray from the correct path—then "you shall dig with it"—you should dig out the words of Torah and reproof that you heard. "You shall go back"—you shall repent, and that will cover the transgressions that were performed. (*Degel Machnei Ephraim*, p. 231)

On the same *Pasuk*, the Kedushas Levi commented that if one shields his ears from hearing evil, then he will merit to hear the proclamation from above every day: "Return O evil children." (*Chapters of R' Eliezer* 15) The word "weaponry" in Hebrew is *a'zey'necha* and our Sages commented that it should not be read as *a'zey'necha* but as *oz'necha*, meaning "your ears." (Talmud *Ketubot* 5a). Therefore, whenever he hears the proclamation he will feel embarrassed and say to himself, "How could I have committed a transgression before the Master, for Whom the entire world trembles, and He proclaims, 'Return O evil children.'" Based on this interpretation, the meaning of the *Pasuk* is "You will have a spade" on your ears—you shall watch your ears from hearing evil—and then "you will dig with it" (*chafarta*). You will hear the proclamation and you will always be embarrassed before the Almighty. That is the meaning in Isaiah 24:23: "The moon shall be ashamed (*chafrah*)." "You will sit outside . . . you shall go back and cover your waste"—if you shall at times stop serving Him and transgress, you should immediately return to the Creator because of great embarrassment upon hearing the proclamation. (*Kedushas Levi*, p. 189)

"He shall not see among you a shameful thing." (Deut. 23:15) The S'fas Emes commented that our Sages noted that when the Torah states, "No leavened bread may be seen in your possession" (*Shemot* 13:7), it means that one should nullify it in his heart and it should be of no significance for him. Similarly, the *Pasuk* says that whatever you see that is shameful should be of no import to you and should be offensive to you, and automatically it will be nullified. (*S'fas Emes*, p. 88)

"When you come into the vineyard of your fellow, you may eat grapes as is your desire, your fill, but you may not put it into your vessel." (Deut. 23:25) The Bratzlaver explained that when one eats to excess, the eating is harmful. We obtain nourishment from our foods, for every vegetation has within it some elixir of life and this is the way food has vitality.

However, if one eats more than necessary, then the food loses its vitality. It is like putting it into a pot: Obviously one does not receive any sustenance from that. That is why the Torah tells us: "You may eat grapes as is your desire, your fill, but you may not put it into your vessel." You should not eat more than necessary, for it is like putting it into a basket where it is no longer needed. (*Likkutei MaHaran*, p. 118)

<hr>

"Remember what Amalek did to you, on the way, when you were leaving Egypt . . . when you were faint and exhausted, and he did not fear God." (Deut. 25:17–18) The Kedushas Levi explained that it is imperative for each Jew to eradicate the evil aspect, known as the Amalek, that is hidden within him. As long as the seed of Amalek is everywhere, then the power of evil will arouse an individual to transgress. That is the reason the Torah reminds us that the essence of the Jew is based on the constant burning desire to be with Hashem through prayer and listening to "the voice is the voice of Jacob." (*Bereshit* 27:22) Therefore evil cannot dominate him, for as soon as that inner strength takes over, the fear of Hashem gets hold of him and he does not transgress. That is why the Torah states: "When you were faint and exhausted, and he did not fear God"—the strength of the essence of the Jew leaves and the service of Hashem is weakened and Hashem is no longer feared. Therefore, we must always remember that our strength should not weaken and we should eradicate from our hearts the evil and permit the good to conquer. (*Kedushas Levi*, p. 108)

<hr>

On the same *Pasuk*, the Talmud *Baba Kamma* 82a states that the Israelites went three days without water—that is, without the study of Torah—therefore, the Amalekites came to war with them. The Noam Elimelech explained that the Torah is telling us that a Jew should not let three days go by without the study of Torah, for the evil inclination (Amalek) will be able to overpower. The Torah, therefore, tells us to remember that the temptation to waste time and not study Torah is very powerful, for when we are "faint and exhausted" and do "not fear God," we lose the strength to overcome the evil inclination. We must become strong and study Torah for its sake. (*Noam Elimelech*, p. 40b)

The Yid HaKadosh noted that the intent of the war against Amalek was to destroy the arrogance in oneself. The numerical value of the letters of "Amalek" is equal to the numerical value of the Hebrew word *rom*, which means "haughtiness" (*ayin* = 70, *mem* = 40, *lamed* = 30, and *kuf* = 100, for a total of 240; *resh* = 200 and *mem* = 40, for a total of 240). (*Torat HaYehudi HaKadosh*, p. 252)

On the same *Pasuk*, R' Henoch of Alexander commented that one should "Remember" but he wondered what happens if one forgets. Forgetfulness usually comes from being arrogant, for it is written that when one becomes arrogant he tends to forget. It then becomes a characteristic of the individual. That is why the *Pasuk* says: "Eradicate the memory of Amalek," which numerically is the same as arrogance. Therefore, if you eradicate Amalek, you will not forget. (S.S.K., p. 133)

On the same *Pasuk*, R' Bunim asked why the Torah used the singular when telling the Israelites to "Remember what Amalek did to you (*l'cha*)." Since Amalek wanted to annihilate the entire nation, it should have been written *lachem*, "to you" in the plural. While it is true that Amalek wanted to destroy the entire nation, the Israelites who remained steadfast and united as a people were not harmed. However, the Israelites that split from the camp and went separately were killed. Therefore, the Torah tells us to be as one and "Remember" what Amalek did to you when you split from the rest of the people. (F.C.O., p. 484)

R' Baruch Mezbitzer commented on the dictum of our Sages: "Do not judge yourself to be a wicked person." (*Ethics of Our Fathers* 2:18) He said that every person was created to rectify something in this world.

The world needs each individual and each individual needs the world. Thus, the person who isolates himself and does not participate in communal activities is therefore wicked unto himself. By this behavior, he cannot correct anything and does not fulfill the purpose for which he was created. (F.C.O., p. 484)

"When you were faint and exhausted and he did not fear God." (Deut. 25:18) R' Dov Ber Mezritcher commented that when the time to pray arrives and you are tired, have no time, and rush, it means that you do not fear God. (F.C.O., p. 485)

KI TAVO
"WHEN YOU ENTER"

"That you shall take of the first of every fruit of the ground." (Deut. 26:1) Rashi comments: "A man goes down in his field and sees a field that has begun to ripen. He wraps a reed-grass (*gami*) around the first fruit as a sign, and says, 'This is hereby consecrated as *bikkurim* (first fruits).'" The Sassover asked why it specifies "reed-grass." He then explained that when one sees his field blossoming, he may think that it was of his doing. After all, he planted, sowed, and plowed and therefore feels proud seeing his field producing plenty of crop. That is why our Sages insisted that before he brings the crop to Hashem, he should place a reed-grass around the first fruits. *Gami* is the acronym of *G'dolim Ma'asey Hashem*, "The growth is the work of Hashem." He will then remember that the blessing of a blossoming field is a blessing from Hashem. (F.C.O., p. 486)

❧

On the same *Pasuk*, the Ropshitzer quoted an explanation given by his father, of Blessed Memory. In Psalms 127:2 it states: "It is vain for you who rise early, who sit up late, who eat the bread of sorrows—for He gives His beloved ones restful sleep." The Rebbe explained that before one rests he should remove evil by eliminating his desires. Therefore, the *Pasuk* advises us to remove the evil that one brings "from your land"—from oneself—by "first" obtaining the "fruit" of a mitzvah. In turn, Hashem will bless us with the strength to reach the goal of doing good deeds with sincerity by diverting all evil to good. (*Zera Kodesh*, p. 141)

❧

"Then you shall call out and say before Hashem, your God, 'An Aramean would have destroyed my father; and he descended to Egypt and sojourned there, few in number, and there he became a nation— great, strong, and numerous.'" (Deut. 26:5) The Radamsker interpreted the *Pasuk* to mean that the Hebrew word *v'anita*, meaning "You shall call out," comes from *anah*, "to be humble." The Rebbe said that before one wishes to speak to the Almighty, he should realize his own humility and then "say before Hashem." (*Tiferet Shlomo*, p. 266)

❧

On the *Pasuk*, R' Eliezer Halevi Horowitz noted that "Aramean" de- notes arrogance. Therefore, had our father Jacob chosen to lead a life of arrogance, it "would have destroyed my father." However, he called out to Hashem and was humble. The *Pasuk* teaches that to maintain humil- ity, one must remember our Father and call out and say before Hashem, "An Aramean would have destroyed my father." (*Noam Maggidim*, p. 432)

❧

On the same *Pasuk*, the Izbitzer noted that this *parsha* commences with the laws of the first fruits. Based on those laws the Talmud *Berachot* 34a explains the order of the Eighteen Benedictions. The first three para- graphs deal with praise of Hashem, the middle paragraphs deal with asking for one's needs, and the last three request a reward. If one wishes much wealth from Hashem and is granted abundance, he returns the favor by learning how to apportion each coin according to Hashem's will. When you come to the land and have things in abundance, return it as the laws of the "first fruit." Give of the best and you will know that all is from the Creator. (*Mei Hashaluach*, part 1, p. 192)

~~~~

"You shall rejoice with all the goodness that Hashem, your God, has given to you." (Deut. 26:11) The Radamsker commented that when one receives a gift from a king, he is ecstatic over the fact that he was given a gift and is not concerned with its worth. The significance of who gave the gift is what gives the joy. That is what the Torah teaches: "Rejoice with all the goodness." One should rejoice with that which is good — not only because it is good, but "that Hashem, your God, has given to you." (*Tiferet Shlomo*, p. 268)

~~~~

Concerning "joy," R' Aharon Karliner noted that we do not speak about the joy in the observance of a commandment. That is a level unto itself and we cannot expect every Jew to be on that level. What is meant by "joy" is not being in a state of sadness. (F.C.O., p. 487)

~~~~

The Slonimer Rebbe said that happiness is:

1. studying the Torah and giving satisfaction to the Creator, according to one's ability;
2. constantly searching one's actions and regretting every unworthy act;
3. recognizing the aid one's Master gives him;
4. sanctifying Hashem's name by one's acts and taking care to avoid the opposite;
5. increasing one's devotion in service to Hashem;
6. withstanding temptation;
7. serving Hashem with the whole heart and not considering it out of the ordinary;
8. spending the last days on earth in repentance and having a clear conscience. (H.A., p. 162)

~~~~

The author of *Avnei Nezer* commented on the statement "And make us joyous with Your salvation." (Shabbat *Amidah*) We should derive joy not just from joy itself but because it is from Hashem. (M.T., vol. 5, p. 108)

⌘

"I have eliminated (*bee'arti*) the holy things from the house, and I have also given it to the Levite, to the convert, and to the orphan. . . ." (Deut. 26:13) The Radamsker interpreted the word *bee'arti* to be derived from *bo'er*, "burning." Then the *Pasuk* can be explained as: "I have ignited the holiness of the *mitzvot* that I performed in the house and the holiness became ablaze and spread from the power of the *mitzvot*." (M.T., vol. 5, p. 108)

⌘

"I have not transgressed any of Your commandments, and I have not forgotten." (Deut. 26:13) The S'fas Emes explained that the Torah is saying that one did not transgress, and while performing the mitzvah he did not forget Hashem. (F.C.O., p. 488)

⌘

R' Nachman Bratzlaver explained that there are differences among those who transgress. There are individuals who repent immediately and there are those whose transgressions lead them astray into sinful lives. King David stated: "I have strayed as a lost sheep—seek out Your servant; for I have not forgotten Your commandments." (Ps. 119:176) The Rebbe made an analogy with a sheep who wanders away from the shepherd but is close enough to hear his voice, recognize it, and return. However, if the sheep wanders too far, he no longer hears the voice and continues to wander along winding and twisting paths until the shepherd gives up looking for him. "I have strayed as a lost sheep"—I am as a lost sheep who has not wandered too far from the straight path. You have proof, therefore "seek out Your servant." I am seeking the Shepherd; I want to return to Him "for I have not forgotten Your commandments." I have not forgotten the voice of the Torah and its commandments, and I regret my transgressions and want to return to Hashem. (*Likkutei Maharan*, p. 112)

⌘

On the same *Pasuk*, the S'fas Emes asked the reason for the double language of "I have not transgressed" and "I have not forgotten." It seems that one can perform a mitzvah out of habit, thereby forgetting its significance. Therefore, the Torah teaches us that one should not transgress by forgetting Hashem while performing the mitzvah. (M.T., vol. 5, p. 108)

~~~

"I have listened to the voice of Hashem, my God." (Deut. 26:14) R' Asher Horowitz said that every day in the month of Elul he hears the voice of the shofar. (F.C.O., p. 489)

~~~

"Gaze down from Your holy abode, from the heavens, and bless Your people Israel." (Deut. 26:15) The *sifri* commented that He should bless His people with sons and daughters. The author of *Avnei Nezer* noted that when one fulfills the mitzvah of giving of the first fruits for Hashem's sake, he not only brings the first mature "fruits from the ground," he also brings his own produce—fruit from the womb. We must, during our children's early years, while they are still tender, instill a holiness within them by a thorough Torah education, bringing them closer to Hashem. When this is done we are blessed with sons and daughters who are a blessing to their parents and Israel. (M.T., vol. 5, p. 109)

~~~

On the same *Pasuk*, Rashi comments: "We have done what you have decreed upon us." The Lelever explained that it should not be very difficult to say, "I have heard the voice of Hashem and I performed all that was commanded of me." Such words of self-praise should be wonderful to hear. (F.U.A.O., vol. 4, p. 311)

~~~

"This day, Hashem, God, commands you to perform these statutes." (Deut. 26:16) Rashi comments: "On each day, they should be new in your eyes, as if you were commanded regarding them that day." We find the same in *Pasuk* 27:9, which states: "Be attentive and hear, O Israel: This day you have become a people to Hashem, your God." Again Rashi comments: "Every day [the commandments] shall be in your eyes as if you had entered the covenant with Him that day." An extremely important principle in the performance of the *mitzvot* is that they should be performed with the same diligence as if they were commanded that day and the covenant with Hashem was written on that same day. In this way we will perform the *mitzvot* with zest and joy. To those who do not perform the *mitzvot* in this manner, the Ari HaKadosh noted, the *Pasuk* "Because you did not serve Hashem, your God, with gladness and with goodness of heart, out of an abundance of everything . . ." (Deut. 28:47) cautions us that there should be happiness in the performance of each mitzvah. If there is no joy then the Torah makes note of the consequences. (*Shnei Luchot Habrit*—On the Torah, p. 610)

"You shall inscribe on the stones all the words of this Torah, well clarified." (Deut. 27:8) R' Eliezer Lizensker explained that Hashem said to Moses that he should write the words of admonishment and the curses clearly so that the Tzaddikim of future generations should be able to interpret them for the good. This *Pasuk* teaches us that the righteous have the inner ability to interpret admonishment for the good and change curses into blessings. (M.T., vol. 5, p. 109)

"All these blessings will come upon you and overtake you, if you listen to the voice of Hashem, your God." (Deut. 28:2) The Pshys'cha Rebbe explained that all blessings come from the heavenly source. If a person is not deserving because he does not do good before Hashem, the abundance of blessings will bypass him and go to someone else. Therefore, "if you listen" Hashem will give an abundance of blessing "upon you and overtake you"—specifically you and no one else, for that is a full blessing. (S.S.K., p. 134)

"Then all the peoples of the earth will see that the Name of Hashem is proclaimed over you, and they will be in awe of you." (Deut. 28:10) R' Baruch of Meziboz, in his *sefer Butzino Dinhora*, noted that the nations of the world will revere Hashem because they will see that "you" are proclaiming Hashem's name. (M.T., vol. 5, p. 113)

～～

On the same *Pasuk*, the Talmud states: "The Name of Hashem is proclaimed over you, and they will revere you." R' Eliezer the Great says: "These are the *tefillin* that are worn in the head (*b'rosh*)." (*Berachot* 6a) The Kedushas Levi noted that the wearing of *tefillin* does not make the nations fear us. He explained that it does not say, "*tefillin* that are on the head" but "*tefillin* that are in the head." The concept of *tefillin*, the faith in Hashem, should be internalized so that we constantly think what the *tefillin* are teaching us; then there will be reverence from the nations. (M.T., vol. 5, p. 114)

～～

On the *Pasuk* "Hashem will place you as a head and not as a tail" (Deut. 28:13), the Ohev Yisroel wondered why the Torah states: "Not as a tail." Obviously, if one is the head he will not be "as a tail." The Ohev Yisroel explained that at times it is better to be a tail and not a head, as the Mishnah states: "Be a tail to lions rather than a head to foxes." (*Ethics of Our Fathers* 4:20) The Torah teaches that one should be a head to the "head" and not a head to a tail—a head to lions and not a head to foxes. (*Yalkut Ohev Yisroel*, p. 74)

～～

"But it will be that if you do not listen to the voice of Hashem, your God. . . ." (Deut. 28:15) This section of reproof is read before Rosh Hashanah. The Talmud states: "So that the year should end along with its curses." (*Megillah* 31b) The Radamsker explained that if there is an evil decree from Heaven, God forbid, then it should be carried out only by the reading of the section of reproof and we should begin to receive blessings. (*Tiferet Shlomo*, p. 270)

～～

On the same *Pasuk*, "Because you did not serve Hashem, your God, with gladness . . ." (Deut. 28:47), R' Nachman Bratzlaver commented that joy is the greatest weapon against problems. Against joy the curses enumerated in the section of reproof cannot win. That is why the Torah states: "All these curses will come upon you and pursue you . . ." (Deut. 28:45), for they will come only "because you did not serve Hashem, your God, with gladness." (F.U.A.O., vol. 4, p. 316)

⌐⌐⌐

On the same *Pasuk*, the Pshys'cher found it interesting to note that the Torah, in the section of reproof, does not enumerate the transgressions that precipitate them. The only transgression mentioned is "You did not serve Hashem, your God, with gladness." (F.C.O., p. 491)

⌐⌐⌐

On the same *Pasuk*, R' Yechiel Meir Mogilnitzer noted that just as a person who is hungry eats with zest, so must a person serve Hashem in the same manner. (F.C.O., p. 491)

⌐⌐⌐

"And among those nations you will not be tranquil. . . ." (Deut. 28:65) The Sassover noted that those individuals who assimilate with the hope of finding peace and tranquillity will not find the equality that they are seeking. (F.C.O., p. 492)

⌐⌐⌐

The Torah teaches that the nations will not permit us to "keep (*u'shmartem*) the words of this covenant, and do them, that you may prosper in all that you do." (Deut. 29:8) The Maggid of Koznitz noted that the word *u'shmartem*, which means "to observe" or "to be diligent," is also mentioned in *Bereshit* 37:11: "And his father [Jacob] observed (*shamar*) the matter [in his mind]." The Maggid explained that there are individuals who observe the words of the covenant. They "keep all the words of this covenant" by observation and are thoughtful, but they do not do anything. Therefore, the *Pasuk* states, "Do them." Even though one notes and is diligent in spirit, he must become involved in the doing of the *mitzvot*, "that you may prosper in all that you do." (*Avodat Yisroel*, p. 186)

NITZAVIM
"YOU ARE STANDING"

"You are standing today, all of you, before Hashem, your God: Your heads, your tribes, your elders, and your officers—all the men of Israel . . . from the hewer of your wood to the drawer of your water. . . ." (Deut. 29:9) The Lubavitcher Rebbe noted that this *Sidra* is read on the Shabbat before Rosh Hashanah. The Rebbe pointed out that the *Sidra* begins with the Jews "standing today . . . before Hashem" as an entity, "all of you," and then details the different groups and types of people. Though the Jews are a unit, the individual Jew makes a unique contribution. Each Jew has his mission, which he brings to unite the people. The unity of Israel is created not by every Jew being the same, but by each being himself and fulfilling the directives of "Hashem, your God." (*Torah Studies*, pp. 328–329)

On the same *Pasuk*, the Holy Zohar refers to the *Pasuk* in *Kohelet* 2:14, which states that the eyes of a wise man are in his head. R' Moshe Chayim Ephraim explains that the wise man is always looking at the Divine Presence (*Schechinah*), as it states in the *Ethics of Our Fathers* 2:1: "Know what is above you," for one stands before Hashem. "Your heads" reminds one to remember that Hashem should always be in mind and thoughts. (*Degel Machnei Ephraim*, pp. 236–237)

On the same *Pasuk*, the Letchener noted that by transposing the letters of the word *atem* ("you"), we get the word *emet* ("truth"). When the Jews maintain the way of truth, then they will be able to exist (stand) forever. (F.C.O., p. 493)

On the same *Pasuk*, the Karliner commented that with the truth we will be able to stand before Hashem during the High Holy Days. (F.C.O., p. 493)

On the same *Pasuk*, R' Eliezer Horowitz of Tarnigrad noted that the life of the Jewish people is as the day: "It was evening and it was morning." (*Bereshit* 1:5) First it is night and then comes daylight; first there is the persecution and exile, then comes the redemption and salvation. (*Noam Maggidim*, p. 434)

On the same *Pasuk*, the *Degel Machnei Ephraim* noted that the Jews asked Samuel to anoint a king. "And the thing was displeasing in the eyes of Samuel, when they said, 'Give us a king to judge.'" (1 Samuel 8:6) Samuel informed the Jews that their request was sinful for Hashem is their king. The Torah teaches that when we stand before Hashem in complete honesty and behave properly, there is no need to have an appointed king. (*Degel Machnei Ephraim*, p. 236)

On the same *Pasuk*, R' Baruch of Meziboz noted that the attitude of the general public is that when it is necessary to fulfill the duties of a Jew or to do battle for Hashem's sake, the responsibility is given to the rabbis or to those who are active in communal affairs. This is an error in one's thinking and does much damage. When it is for "before Hashem, your God"—when it pertains to doing honor for the Divine Presence—then it must be "You are standing today, all of you." Everyone must participate—"Your heads, your elders, and your officers," and "the hewer of your wood to the drawer of your waters." Everyone should share in the labor and in the responsibility. (M.T., vol. 5, p. 121)

～～

On the words "your small children, your women" (Deut. 29:10), the Sassover noted that the Torah teaches us that it is the obligation of mothers to train their children to stay on the right path in life. Fathers, though they are obligated to teach Torah to their children, are usually busy earning a living and therefore not at home to supervise the behavior of the children, which is vital for their proper upbringing. (F.C.O., p. 494)

～～

"Perhaps there is among you a root that bears poison and bitterness." (Deut. 29:17) The Yid HaKadosh commented that all bitterness comes from "perhaps." When one wishes to serve Hashem intellectually by analyzing whether "perhaps" this knowledge is correct or this wisdom is better, then this "perhaps," this ambivalence, is the "root that bears poison and bitterness" in serving Hashem. (*Torat Hayehudi HaKadosh*, p. 70)

～～

"The hidden things are for Hashem, our God, but the revealed things are for us and our children forever, to carry out the words of this Torah." (Deut. 29:28) Rabbi Nachum Perlow, the Novominsker Rebbe, explained that the *tefillin* that are on the hand are covered and our Sages say that this implies that the sign shall be for us and not others. (Talmud *Menachot* 37b). The Rebbe further said that the *tefillin* that are on the hand refer to the performance of the *mitzvot*, which the Jewish People accepted when they declared, *Na'aseh v'nishmah*—"We will do and we will listen"—the performance before the tasting. However, the *tefillin* that appear on the head are visible to all, as the *Pasuk* says: "Then all the peoples of the earth will see that the Name of Hashem is proclaimed over you, and they will revere you." (*Devarim* 28:10) The other nations want to know the reason for the mitzvah, as noted by Rashi at the

beginning of *Parshat Chukat* (*Bamidbar* 19:1): 'What is this commandment?' and 'What reason is there to it?'" Therefore, in the future, the
reasons will be revealed and the light of Torah will shine. Then, "the
nations of the world will see that the Name of Hashem is proclaimed
over you, and they will revere you." These are the hidden things that
belong to Hashem, the hidden reasons for the performance of the
mitzvot commanded by Hashem. We do them in spite of what others
may think. The Midrash *Vayikrah* 32 relates that when one was asked
why he was being stoned, he answered that he had circumcised his son.
Another was asked why he was being killed; he answered that it was
because he observed the Shabbat—another because he ate matzah;
another because he built a *sukkah*. When asked the reason for all the
torture, they all answered that they did what was required of them by
Hashem. This will be the status of the performance of the *mitzvot* until
Hashem reveals the reasons for them. Until then they are to be performed for the rectification of the world and future generations. By
teaching Torah to our children, we will bring the revelation of the
reasons of the *mitzvot*. (*Pe'er Nachum*, p. 253)

On the same *Pasuk*, R' Yaacov Yosef of Polnoye, in his *sefer Ben Porat
Yosef*, explained that when one is involved in the material needs that are
"for us and our children," such as earning a living, the physical side of us
is revealed. The hidden refers to the spiritual side when one is attached
to Hashem, our God. (M.T., p. 412)

On the same *Pasuk*, Rabbi Schneur Zalman of Liadi, in his *sefer Likkutei
Amarim*, explained that there are two degrees of love. The "great love" is
the inner desire of the soul to be at one with Hashem, and the "eternal
love" stems from the knowledge and understanding of the greatness of
Hashem. He said: "It is the straining of the intellect that fans the blaze of
the fiery love . . . that rises heavenward so that not even many waters
can extinguish it." These loves are subdivided into many gradations in
each individual according to his capacity. This is made clear in the
interpretation of the verse in Proverbs 31:23: "Her husband is known in

the gates." The Holy Zohar (1, 103b) states that it refers "to the Holy One, Blessed be He, Who makes Himself known and attaches Himself to every one according to the extent that one measures in one's heart." Therefore, the Alter Rebbe said, fear and love are called "the secret things known to Hashem, our God," while the Torah and commandments are those things that are "revealed to us and to our children to do." We all have one Torah and one law, as far as the fulfillment of the commandments is concerned. It is the fear and love that vary according to the knowledge of Hashem in the mind and heart of each individual. There is one love that incorporates something from all gradations of both "great love" and "eternal love," which belongs equally to every Jewish soul, and that is our inheritance from our Patriarchs. (*Tanya*, part 1, p. 282)

~~~

"If your dispersed will be at the ends of the heavens, from there Hashem, your God, will gather you in and from there He will take you." (Deut. 30:4) R' Eliezer Halevi Horowitz of Tarnigrad, in the name of his father, asked why it stated, "at the ends of the heavens," and not "from the ends of the earth." He explained that the Baal Shem Tov tried to find the good in the actions of the Jewish People. Even when he found someone who did not deal properly in business, he tried to find something positive in his behalf. Perhaps he had to pay tuition, wanted to give charity, or needed necessities for the Shabbat. Likewise, when you have transgressed but the end result is for the sake of heaven, "your God will gather you in." "From there Hashem"—from that little spark that might be in the transgression, and from that spark within your thought that was for heaven's sake, you will be saved from going on the wrong path. (*Noam Maggidim*, p. 439)

~~~

On the *Pasuk* "Hashem, your God, will circumcise your heart and the heart of your offspring" (Deut. 30:6), the Kotzker noted that in *Devarim* 10:16 it states: "You shall circumcise the block of your heart." In 10:16 it states: "You shall," and in 30:6 it states: "Hashem will." The Kotzker explained that the individual must make a beginning. He must cut "the block" that is in the heart to accept Hashem's word. However, changing from evil to good the human being cannot do by himself. Only Hashem can help, and that is why it states: "Hashem, your God, will circumcise your heart." (*Ohel Torah*, p. 90)

On the same *Pasuk*, the S'fas Emes wondered why it was necessary for the Torah to state: "the heart of your offspring," for the Torah speaks for all time. He explained that when a person repents, he merits that his children will not have a blockage of the heart. When Hashem "will circumcise your heart," then it automatically includes "your offspring." (*S'fas Emes*, p. 61)

On the words "to love Hashem, your God, with all your heart and with all your soul, that you may live" (Deut. 30:6), R' Tzvi Hirsch of Liska noted that when one reaches the level of knowing that all existence comes from Hashem, may He be blessed, but then separates himself from Him, then he separates himself from all existence. (M.T., p. 415)

On the words "that you may live," The Tarigraner explained that this means that though one leaves this world, if he has decent and honest children, he has not died. Our Sages noted that of David, who left a son as himself, "it cannot be said that he died." (*Baba Batra* 116a) (*Noam Maggidim*, p. 439)

"You shall return and listen to the voice of Hashem, and you shall perform all His commandments that I command you today." (Deut. 30:8) The Radamsker noted that this *Pasuk* repeats the charge to repent that was mentioned in *Pasuk* 30:2, "And you will return unto Hashem." The Radamsker explained that before a person repents he is unaware of the immensity of his transgression, for while he is in the midst of his transgression, he is far removed from Hashem and is completely absorbed in his wrong deed. However, when he begins to repent, he realizes his distance from the Almighty and the depth of the defect in his deed. He should not rely on his initial act of repentance but continue to repent and reflect to develop the understanding that there is a necessity for repentance. (*Tiferet Shlomo*, p. 280)

"Hashem will make you abundant in all your handiwork — in the fruit of your womb, the fruit of your animals, and the fruit of your land — for good, when Hashem will return to rejoice over you for good, as He rejoiced over your forefathers." (Deut. 30:9) The author of *Arvei Nachal* explained that there is a reason a reward is given for each mitzvah. For example: "If in my statutes you walk . . . Then will I give you rains in their due season" (*Vayikrah* 26:3); "And it shall come to pass, if you will listen diligently to My commandments . . . That I will send rain for your land in its time. . . ." (Devarim 11:13,14) Yet there is a statement in the *Ethics of Our Fathers* 1:3: "Be not like servants who serve their master for the sake of receiving a reward." The intention should not be to perform a mitzvah to receive a reward and derive pleasure from the reward. The intent should be to give the Almighty pleasure, for He wishes to give benefits and rewards to His creation. That is the way to receive a reward: to feel that we are doing the will of Hashem. (M.T., vol. 5, p. 131)

"It is not in the heavens to say, 'Who can ascend to the heavens for us and take it for us, and let us hear it, so that we can perform it?' Nor is it across the sea to say, 'Who can cross to the other side of the sea for us and take it for us, and let us hear it, so that we can perform it?' Rather, the matter is very near to you, in your mouth and in your heart, to perform it." (Deut. 30:12–14) The Kotzker Rebbe cited a passage in *Tanna D'vei Eliyahu* that tells of an individual who complained to Eliyahu that heaven did not give him the ability to learn. So Eliyahu said that heaven gave him the ability to obtain flax to make nets and to hunt animals, and as the Torah states, "The matter is near to you." He then asked, "Did not Heaven give you the mind to learn?" He said that an individual is not born a hunter, but the anxiety and the desire to earn a living is so strong that one learns his trade. If one has the same anxiety and desire to study Torah, needs the Torah as much as he needs to earn a living, and wants to succeed, he would be able to study Torah. (*Ohel Torah*, p. 90)

On the same *Pasuk*, the Lubliner commented that any individual can reach a higher and superior level in the Torah if he so desires. All one needs are the "take it for us," the "let us hear it," and then "we can perform it." (F.C.O., p. 496)

On the words "the matter is near to you, in your mouth and in your heart, to perform it," the S'fas Emes commented that for the Torah to be "near to you" is dependent on your mouth and your heart. There are three things that are needed to open the well of wisdom: speech, thought, and action. All of these emanate from the mouth as we related the fervor and desires of the heart. (*S'fas Emes*, p. 63)

On the same words, R' Schneur Zalman of Liadi commented that if something is a matter of the heart then it is not a "very near thing," for our experience tells us that it is difficult to change one's heart from material desires to a sincere love of Hashem. The Talmud *Berachot* 33b states: "Is fear of Heaven a small thing?" The Rebbe observed how much more difficult is love, and that the words "that you may do it" refer to a love that leads to the performance of the commandments. He said, "If one has brains, for his brains are under his control, he is able to concentrate on anything he wishes." He will contemplate the greatness of Hashem and will understand that to love Hashem is to cleave to Him through the performance of the *mitzvot*. That is the essence of man, as it is written: "This day to do them." (*Devarim* 7:11) "This day" refers to the physical world, as is noted in the Talmud *Eruvin* 22a, and tomorrow is the time for reward. (*Likkutei Amarim*, p. 106)

On the same words, the Kotzker said that one should not rely only on talking about it or say that it is in his heart—do it!! (F.U.A.O., vol. 4, p. 336)

On the words "It is not in the heavens," the Chidushei Harim commented that if one truly wishes with all one's heart to attach oneself to the Torah even if it is in heaven or on the other side of the ocean, it is completely dependent on the will. (F.C.O., p. 496)

On the same words, the Toldot Yaacov Yosef commented that one should not say that if he were to reside in a city that is replete with righteous people who are attached to the heavens, he would be able to serve Hashem. The Torah teaches us that it need not be "in the heavens" nor "across the sea" but "the matter is near to you"—on whatever level one has reached one can serve Hashem, for the Divine Presence is on all levels and everywhere. (M.T., p. 415)

"See—I have placed before you today life and good." (Deut. 30:15) The Kotzker commented that the Torah says: "See," life has been given to you to do good. However, if the person is nearsighted and cannot see that he is doing the contrary, rather than living to do good, he does good to live. (F.C.O., p. 496)

VAYEILECH
"AND HE WENT"

"Moses went and spoke these words to all of Israel." (Deut. 31:1) The Mishmeres Itmar commented that Moses' way of life was imparted to all of Israel when he "spoke these words to all of Israel." (F.C.O., p. 498)

On the same *Pasuk*, the Rimanover explained that the Israelites, leaving Egypt and traveling in the desert, had beliefs and attitudes that were faulty. Their inner thoughts were tainted to the extent that even when they were convinced in their belief in Hashem they faltered, as evidenced by the incident of the golden calf. Therefore, he said that Hashem planted Moses in their midst to become "the composite intelligence of Israel." Therefore, it became possible for the "generation of the Exodus" to become known as the "enlightened generation." In this way, they were able to develop the understanding to learn how to lead a proper life. The same occurs in every generation. There arise personalities of stature with the capacity to perform the will of Hashem and the ability to "speak these words to all of Israel" to influence them. (*Torah Discourses of the Holy Tzaddik*, p. 417)

On the same *Pasuk*, the Radamsker noted the interpretation of "Moses went" by our Sages. They said that he went into his own world. However, though Moses was on a high level, he was able to teach Torah to all of Israel, as the Ari, may he be remembered for a blessing, wrote: Whoever studies Torah for its sake is clothed with the soul of Moses (Moshe), for the reward of Moses is the reward for all. It is noted in the *Ethics of Our Fathers* 6:1: "Whoever studies Torah for its own sake (*lishmoh*) merits many things." The Ari said that the word *lishmoh* has the same Hebrew letters as *l'Moshe* ("to Moses"); therefore, whoever studies Torah for its own sake, his merits go to Moses. (*Tiferet Shlomo*, p. 145)

～～

On the *Pasuk* "I am a hundred and twenty years old today; I can no longer go out and come in . . ." (Deut. 31:2), Rashi comments that Moses was saying. "Today my days and years have been filled. On this day I was born, on this day I shall die." R' Moshe Sofer of Preshburg, in his *sefer Torat Moshe*, noted that our Sages said that Haman chose the month of Adar to do harm to the Jews because that was the month that Moses died. He did not realize that he had also been born in that month. If centuries later Haman felt that Moses' death was a bad sign for the Jews, then at the time of Moses' death the Jews must have felt that waging war with the enemy would also be a bad idea. Therefore, Moses told the Jews that he was also born in that month. He said to them, "Be strong and courageous; do not be afraid." (Deut. 31:6) (M.T., vol. 5, p. 135)

～～

On the same *Pasuk*, Rashi comments: "The knowledge handed down and the wellsprings of wisdom had become closed to him." The Gerer Rebbe explained that Moses our teacher, just before his death, reached the highest spiritual level. He had attained the "wellsprings of wisdom" that are "closed" to the ordinary person. That is why Moses said, "I can no longer go out and come in," meaning that he could no longer be a leader, for a leader has the responsibility of removing the secular from the people and instilling holiness. Moses felt that he was no longer close to his people; having attained the highest level possible, he felt that the connection was lost. (M.T., vol. 5, p. 135)

~~~

"And Hashem gave them before you; and you shall do them according to the entire commandment that I have commanded you." (Deut. 31:5) The Radamsker noted that our Sages said that every mitzvah performed for the sake of Heaven will ascend upward, and a mitzvah performed in this manner will lead to the performance of other *mitzvot*. But if one does a mitzvah for one's own purpose, it will not ascend upward. In the wars that the Israelites waged against the seven nations, they made a vow to Hashem "and said, 'If You will deliver this people into my hand, I will segregate their cities.'" (*Bamidbar* 21:2) On this *Pasuk*, Rashi comments: "'I will segregate'—I will consecrate their plunder [the plunder taken from them] to the One on high." Hashem told the Israelites that they should not war with the nations for themselves, for the sake of revenge, but for the sake of Heaven. (*Tiferet Shlomo*, p. 281)

~~~

"You shall read this Torah before all Israel, in their ears. Gather together the people—the men, and the women, and the small children, and the stranger who is in your cities—so that they will hear and so that they will learn, and they shall fear Hashem, your God, and be careful to perform all the words of this Torah." (Deut. 31:11–12) The Gerer Rebbe explained why "Gather together the people" is stated after "You shall read this Torah before all Israel." He said that when Jews are united, that in itself is Torah. (M.T., vol. 5, p. 136)

~~~

On the words "and the small children," Rashi quotes the Talmud *Chagigah* 3a: "And why did they come? To give reward to those who brought them." The S'fas Emes explained that when parents exert themselves to bring their children to the Holy Temple, they show their willingness to maintain their Jewishness and listen to the words of Torah. This action is justification for Hashem to give the reward that their children should be influenced by Torah and grow as productive

Jews. Hashem gives the same proportion of aid in the education of their children as the effort given by the parents. (*S'fas Emes*, p. 132)

~~

On the same *Pasuk*, the Kotzker wondered why it was necessary to state that the children were to go with the parents. He said that it should be obvious that the parents were not going to leave the children by themselves. The Talmud explained that because the parents were told to bring the children, the parents were given a reward. (F.U.A.O., vol. 4, p. 339)

~~

"Hashem spoke to Moses: 'Behold, your days are drawing near to die; summon Joshua, and both of you shall stand in the Tent of Meeting, and I shall command him.'" (Deut. 31:14) There is a Midrash Rabbah that states: "Moses went to Joshua and asked him what Hashem said to him. Joshua answered that when Hashem spoke to you [Moses], I [Joshua] knew all that Hashem told you and you could not tell me. Just like you could not tell me, now I cannot tell you. At that point, Moses cried out that it is better a thousand deaths than to be jealous one time." The Ostrovitzer wondered how it was possible for Moses to have a jealous characteristic. Our Sages taught us that there is no jealousy of a student: "Of everyone a man is jealous, except his son and disciple." (Talmud *Sanhedrin* 105b) The Rebbe explained that Heaven wanted to lighten the pronouncement of Moses' death and thus instilled in him a bit of jealousy. Moses, therefore, became concerned and said, "My entire life I worked on my behavior; now at the end of my life, I notice that I have this terrible characteristic of jealousy; then death is better." (M.T., vol. 5, p. 174)

~~

On the same *Pasuk*, the Gerer Rebbe noted the statement in the Talmud *Sanhedrin* 89b that says that when Hashem, may He be Blessed, speaks to a prophet, all the prophets at that time are aware of what was said. It is based on a statement in Amos 3:7: "For Hashem will do nothing, but He reveals His counsel to His servants the prophets." Joshua told Moses that he did not ask him to repeat anything Hashem told him, though it was told privately, because he knew the prophecy. Joshua said to Moses, "Now that you do not know what Hashem said to me, it must be a sign that Heaven does not want you to know what was said." (M.T., vol. 5, p. 139)

⚬⚬⚬

"It will say on that day, 'Is it not because my God is not in my midst . . .' But I will surely have concealed My face on that day because of all the evil that it did, for it had turned to the gods of others." (Deut. 31:17,18) R' Bunim wondered why it was necessary for Hashem to conceal Himself when one says, "Is it not because my God is not in my midst?" The Rebbe explained that "because my God is not in my midst" is a transgression in itself, because Jews must believe that even in times of much stress and problems Hashem is with them and they will not be forsaken. However, if they will not believe, then it is measure for measure—"I will surely have concealed My face." (M.T., vol. 5, p. 141)

⚬⚬⚬

On the same *Pasuk*, R' Moshe Sofer of Preshburg, in his *sefer Torat Moshe*, explained that though we confess that we committed a transgression, we do not examine what caused the evil act. That is what causes further transgressions. The prime factor in asking for forgiveness is to recognize what caused one to transgress. That is what Hashem is saying: "I will conceal My face . . . for it had turned to the gods of others"—I will not forgive them for the cause of their transgression. (M.T., vol. 5, p. 141)

HA'AZINU
"GIVE EAR"

"Give ear, O heavens, and I will speak; and may the earth hear the words of my mouth. May my teaching drip like rain, may my utterances flow like the dew. . . ." (Deut. 32:1–2) The Radamsker explained that Moses, our teacher, stressed that all the words emanating from his mouth showed the unity of heaven and earth. The Rebbe said that just as the words of the Torah "drip like rain"—influence life and goodness forever—so "may my utterances flow like dew"—so may the heavenly words overflow and the earth listen. (*Tiferet Shlomo*, p. 284)

On the same *Pasuk*, a comment in the *sefer Siach Sarfei Kodesh* explains that Moses taught that every Jewish person should be a witness unto himself before heaven and earth that from that day forward all his words will be words of Torah and not idle ones. The heavens and earth were chosen as witnesses, as in any swearing, to assure that the mitzvah "drip like rain," for Hashem had given the mouth to speak words of Torah. The purpose of the witnesses was to guarantee that the evil inclination would not drive one to use idle words. (S.S.K., p. 139)

On the same *Pasuk*, the Lubavitcher Rebbe noted the comparison the *sifri* had made between Moses' statement with that of the prophet Isaiah. Moses said, "Give ear, O heavens, and I will speak; and earth hear the words of my mouth," for Moses was close to the heavens and far from the earth. Isaiah said, "Hear, O heavens, and give ear, O earth." Despite his personal growth, Isaiah was still "close to the earth, and far from the heavens." The Rebbe explained, in Kabbalistic terms, that there are four spiritual worlds: *Atzilut* (nearness), *Beriah* (creation), *Yetzirah* (formation), and *Asiyah* (completion). *Atzilut*, the highest level, refers to the existence that is at one with Hashem, an extension of Godliness. The other worlds involve personal identity. Therefore, *Atzilut* is referred to as "heavens" and the other worlds as "earth." In the *sefer Likkutei Torah*, Moses is described as *neshamah d'Atzilut*, an individual who, though living in the physical world, saw everything as an extension of Hashem. He felt the directness of Hashem. Therefore, he could speak to the heavens. Isaiah, by contrast, lived in the other worlds, for he had developed a sense of self and thus was closer to the earth. Both addressed heaven and earth, but from their own respective levels. Therefore, the Rebbe explained that it is a fundamental tenet in Judaism that we must relate to both heaven and earth. Material and spiritual entities are interrelated. Judaism involves drawing from the spiritual aspect until it intertwines with the material world (the contribution of Moses). It elevates the material world with the spiritual one (the contribution of Isaiah). By revealing the Torah, "Give ear, O heavens" and "may the earth hear my words," Moses instilled in each Jew the potential to get close to heaven. (*In the Garden of the Torah*, pp. 149–151)

～～

On the words "May my teaching drip like the rain," R' Bunim commented that the words of the Torah are like the rain. While it is raining, we do not see how the produce of the earth grows. It is when the sun shines that we notice the effect of the rain. Likewise, at the time that we hear the words of Torah, we do not notice its effect; it is much later that we recognize its worth. (F.C.O., p. 500)

～～

"When I call out the Name of Hashem, ascribe greatness to our God." (Deut. 32:3) The Chernovitzer Rebbe, in his *sefer B'er Mayim*, noted that in the prayer "Modim of the Rabbis" we say: "For inspiring us to thank You. Blessed is the God of thanksgivings." We give thanks for the privilege of praising Hashem and we bless and praise His great and Holy Name for the beneficence and the goodness He has shown us. That is why "I call out the Name of Hashem" and "ascribe greatness to our God." (M.T., p. 427)

～～

"The Rock, perfect is His work." (Deut. 32:4) The Izbitzer commented that it should be understood that all that one does is from Him, may He be Blessed. One does not move an arm or leg without approval. However, even if one declares that all is in the hands of Heaven, one cannot say that faults are also from Him, God forbid. "Corruption is not His" (Deut. 32:5), for all the good that one does is dependent on Hashem, may He be Blessed, and all faults are ours. "The blemish is His children's"— wherever there are good children, one finds blemished ones also. "A crooked and twisted generation" are twisted because they behave deviously before Hashem. They refuse to do His will because they are drawn toward their own desires, "twisted" because they do the opposite. They fence themselves in places they should not be and afflict themselves. This too is a transgression, as it says in Proverbs 13:17: "A faithful ambassador is health." (*Mei Hashalu'ach*, p. 199)

～～

On the *Pasuk* "Corruption is not His; the blemish is His children's, a crooked and twisted generation" (Deut. 32:5), the Vorker cited the *Pasukim* in Psalms 112:1–2: "Praiseworthy is the man who fears Hashem, who intensely desires His commandments. Mighty in the land will his offspring be, a generation of the upright who shall be blessed." He said that our Sages, in the Talmud *Avodah Zarah* 19a, commented that while one is still young and has the strength to conquer his evil inclination, he is a role model for his children, and his children will grow up as God-fearing Jews. If one repents when he is old, the children will not have seen him as a God-fearing individual and they will be "crooked." The Rebbe said that we praise the one who is a role model when he is young, for his children were able to see the way he conquered his evil inclination; therefore his offspring will be "a generation of the upright who shall be blessed." (M.T., vol. 5, p. 152)

~~~

"A God, faithful, without iniquity." (Deut. 32:4) The Rimanover, in his *sefer Be'eyrot Hamayim*, wrote that this *Pasuk* states the essence of the Holy Torah. However, one may ask what is the necessity for the rest of the Torah. The answer is that it is impossible for one to reach the level of the essence of the Torah without studying and observing the Torah from the beginning till this point. (M.T., p. 427)

~~~

"Remember the days of old; understand the years go generation after generation. Ask your father and he will relate it to you, your elders and they will tell you." (Deut. 32:7) The Noam Elimelech explained that the Torah teaches us how we should conduct ourselves. We are to give thought and remember the greatness of Hashem at all times. We are to remind ourselves of all the miracles and wonders of "the days of old" to instill in our hearts His greatness and majesty. "Understand the years go generation after generation" teaches us to cleave to the behavior of the Tzaddikim, the righteous ones, rather than the opposite, God forbid. If one should ask how it is possible to isolate oneself, constantly think of the greatness of Hashem, separate from worldly issues, and earn a living to support one's family. Then, "ask your father," as the Holy Zohar calls Hashem "your father" (*Ha'azinu* 298b); pray to Hashem, may He be Blessed. The Rebbe said that "he will relate it to you" means that He will extend to you abundance and blessing, and He will sustain you. (*Noam Elimelech* 97b)

~~~

On the words "Remember the days of old," the S'fas Emes commented that when Hashem created the world, "the whole earth was of one language, and one kind of words." (*Bereshit* 11:1) The only language that united the peoples was the Holy Language. When the people at that time transgressed, the language of unity was taken away and given to the Israelites. "Ask your father" and he will relate it to you. "Ask your elders and they will tell you." (F.C.O., p. 502)

On the words "Ask your father and he will relate it to you, your elders and they will tell you," R' Menachem Nachum of Chernoble explained that the Torah is called "father" because Hashem created the world through Torah, with man being the essence of creation. Therefore, every Jew has a part in the Torah, and if he cleaves to and commits himself to the Torah, then it will guide him and teach him how to get closer to Hashem. "Ask your father," the Torah, and it "will relate to you"; in it, one will find everything that one must know. Through all time, even when times and generations change, it will give advice on how to bind oneself to Hashem, may He be Blessed. (*Me'or Einayim*, p. 158)

"Like an eagle arousing his nest hovering over his young, he spreads his wings." (Deut. 32:11) The Rimanover commented that the eagle, before he enters the nest, flutters his wings to awaken the birds. So does Hashem, so to speak, awaken his children to His service through Jacob, the chosen of the forefathers for the category of an "eagle" (Kabbalistic terminology). When some light enters the heart and a great desire to serve Hashem is aroused, it is our father Jacob who is awakening us and giving us this desire. Those that are wise do not become arrogant in thinking that these thoughts come only from their good deeds. (*Yalkut Menachem*, p. 200)

"And you would drink blood of grapes with delicious flavor." (Deut. 32:14) The Izbitzer said that the *Pasuk* informs us that because of the "blood of grapes," one's cry of pain, one will merit to drink with "delicious flavor." When a person makes a cry of pain and complaint, he does battle with the evil inclination because he wants to better his ways and behavior. The Torah says that Hashem will help him to do so— "with delicious flavor." The Izbitzer cited the Aramaic translation, which notes that the angels taste the "blood" as water because they do not merit the flavor since they do not have the evil inclination. (*Mei Hashaluach*, p. 131)

＝＝＞

"You ignored the Rock Who gave birth to you, and forgot Hashem Who brought you forth." (Deut. 32:18) The Kotzker noted that Hashem gave us the capability to forget. So what do we do? We "forget Hashem Who brought you forth." (*Ohel Torah*, p. 94)

＝＝＞

"And He will say, 'I will hide My face from them and see what is their end; for they are a generation of reversals, children without upbringing in them.'" (Deut. 32:20) R' Zusia of Hanipol interpreted this *Pasuk* to mean that Hashem will temporarily hide His face and wait to see what will come later. Since this is a "generation of reversals," they can easily change because of their nature. Therefore, they may reconsider their evil ways and start to behave better. (F.U.A.O., vol. 4, p. 350)

＝＝＞

On the words "see what is their end," the Baal Haflaah, R' Pinchas Horowitz, in his *sefer Panim Yafot*, noted that if the older generation transgresses then one can imagine what the future holds. (F.U.A.O., vol. 4, p. 351)

＝＝＞

"They infuriated Me with a non-god; they angered Me with their vanities; so shall I infuriate them with a non-people; with a vile nation shall I anger them." (Deut. 32:21) The Chernovitzer noted that our Sages opined that the Jews, though they bowed to the idol of Nebuchadnezzar, were saved from Haman's decree of annihilation because they really did not adhere to idol worship; they only pretended to bow to the idol. Therefore, "Hashem also pretended to exterminate them." (Talmud *Megillah* 12a) The Torah tells us: "They infuriated Me with a non-god." They infuriated Hasham with what they themselves did not believe was a god. They behaved foolishly and only pretended. Therefore, "So shall I infuriate them with a non-people; with a vile nation shall

I anger them"—My punishment will also be superficial. The nation that will persecute them will not remain a people; they will become "a non-people" and they will wither. (M.T., vol. 5, p. 158)

~~~

"I shall use up My arrows against them." (Deut. 32:23) On this *Pasuk*, Rashi comments: "My arrows shall be used up, but they [Israel] will not be used up." The Preshburger explained that the nations that persecute Israel use the arrows of Hashem but Israel will not be annihilated. Their arrows will be used up but Israel "will not be used up." The Jewish people will be forever. (M.T., vol. 5, p. 159)

~~~

"When Hashem will have carried out judgment upon His people, and regarding His servants, He shall reconsider. . . ." (Deut. 32:36) R' Elazar Shapira of Lanzhut, in his *sefer Yodei Binah*, explained that though we are called "Children of Hashem," nevertheless King David said, "I am your servant; grant me understanding, so that I may know Your testimonies." (Ps. 119:125) The Rebbe said that King David used the term "servant" wisely. Our Sages said "Whoever buys a servant buys his master." (*Pesachim* 88b) Therefore, it is better to be as servants when Hashem will reveal the profound inner secrets of the Torah to His people. That is why King David said, "I am Your servant"—as Your servant, "I may know Your testimonies"—reveal to me the profound inner secrets of the Torah. The Rebbe further explained that "When Hashem will have carried out His judgment," Hashem will with mercy judge His people in that He revealed His secrets to His people. "Regarding His servants, He shall reconsider"—He will have mercy for we are His servants. "Whoever buys a servant buys his master"—He will reveal the secrets to His servants and His prophets. (M.T., p. 430)

~~~

"See, now, that I, I am He—and no god is with Me. . . ." (Deut. 32:39) The Ropshitzer commented that Hashem is both hidden and revealed. Hashem reveals Himself by saying that He is the One Who speaks, as

Joseph revealed himself to his brothers by saying, "I am Joseph your brother. . . ." (*Bereshit* 45:4) However, every Jew should feel that the Divinity is hidden within the heart. (*Zera Kodesh*, p. 150b)

~~~

On the same *Pasuk*, the Preshburger explained that when the Israelites left Egypt Hashem said, "I will be what I will be" (*Shemot* 3:14)—I will be with the Jewish People during their dispersions. Now, Hashem says to the Jewish People that the time has come that "I am He." Hashem promised that "I will be"; now the time has come and Hashem is here. (M.T., vol. 5, p. 160)

~~~

On the same *Pasuk*, R' Uziel Meisels of Neustadt, in his *sefer Tiferet Uziel*, noted a comment by the Maggid of Mezritch. He said that there is nothing in this world that can call itself "I," for every creation is as nothing facing the Almighty, as Ezra the prophet said: "O my God, I am ashamed and embarrassed to lift up my face to You, my God." (Ezra 9:6) The Rebbe said that the Almighty does not need creation for Himself, though He gives life to everything and He brings forth all. Therefore, "See now," only "I am He,"—only He can be called "I" and no other part of creation, for all is as nought. (M.D., p. 40)

~~~

"Apply your heart to all the words that I testify against you today, so that you may command them to your children, to observe to do all the words of this law . . . for it is your life and through this matter shall you prolong your days. . . ." (Deut. 32:46,47) R' Chayim Tzvi Taub of Seghut, in his *sefer Atzei Chayim*, explained that intention is the most significant factor of a deed and it is not words that express that intention, as the prophet Isaiah said: "With their mouth and with their lips they honor Me, but their heart they draw far away from Me." It is written in our holy books that a mitzvah that is performed without intent or concentration is like a body without a soul, for the intent of the mitzvah is the life of the mitzvah and the performance of it is the body. It is understood that if the body has a deficiency and no vigor, its vital strength and spirit are not in it. That is what the *Pasuk* teaches: "Apply your heart to all the words"—for all the *mitzvot* that you perform, your heart must be in them. "For it is your life"—the life of a mitzvah is in the heart, "and through this matter shall you prolong your days." (M.T., p. 432)

VEZOT HABERACHAH
"AND THIS IS THE BLESSING"

" And this is the blessing with which Moses the man of God blessed the Children of Israel before his death." (Deut. 33:1) The Primishlaner explained that though Moses was a "man of God," it was a blessing for him and for the people that his concern for the Children of Israel was not deflected. Being a "man of God," he was always with the Children of Israel. (F.C.O., p. 506)

On the same *Pasuk*, the Amshinover commented that the essence of the blessing was that a Jew should always be with a "man of God," the Tzaddik of that generation. (F.C.O., p. 505)

On the same *Pasuk*, the Skoyler Rebbe cited Rashi's statement: "Before his death—for if not now, when?" The Rebbe noted that at that point he had no choice but to bless because he was close to death. The question is why did he wait until then to bless the Children of Israel and not before? Though he could have acted as a father to a child and blessed them as is stated in the Talmud, "The father transmits to the son his pleasing appearance, strength, wealth, wisdom, and long life" (*Eduyyot* 2:9), he was a Rebbe teaching the essentials of Torah to his students. While the Rebbe is still teaching the Torah, it is not proper for him to bless them, for they will have not yet reached perfection so that they could transmit the Torah in turn. Therefore, it should be understood that while Moses was teaching, it was not as yet the Israelites' to transmit. At this time it was still "the Torah of Moses," as stated in Malachi 3:22) "Remember the Torah of Moses My servant, which I commanded him in Horeb for all Israel, even statutes and ordinances." He was quiet about this face until before his death, when he had to bless them—"If not now, when?" (Ch.B., p. 427)

The Gerer Rebbe noted that the term "the man of God" is not mentioned till now. The reality is that future generations must know that it was through Moses that the Torah was given. Moses was known as a humble man until, before his death, he had to let it be known that he was "the man of God"—"If not now, when?" (M.T., vol. 5, p. 164)

On the same *Pasuk*, the Baal Haflaah, R' Pinchas Horowitz, commented that Moses was called "the man of God" before his death. It is when Moses concluded his accounting with life, when he no longer had to endure the trials and tribulations of life, that he was called "the man of God." (F.U.A.O., vol. 4, p. 359)

"Hashem came from Sinai . . ." (Deut. 33:2) The Radamsker interpreted those words to have the same meaning as stated in *Shemot* 19:20: "And Hashem came down upon Mt. Sinai." The Rebbe said that the reason for the going down is that Hashem was accepting the fact that when a generation is at a low level in Torah, He will not abandon them. (*Tiferet Shlomo*, p. 300)

On the same *Pasuk*, R' Tzadok commented that "Hashem came from Sinai" is the heart of the acceptance of the Torah for all decisions. He said that "from Sinai" means that the acceptance is based on humility. Our Sages tell us that Sinai was chosen because it was not a towering mountain; therefore, it signified humility. (*Pri Tzaddik*, p. 271)

~~

On the same *Pasuk*, the Berditchever said that when Hashem showed the Torah to the other nations, no one wished to accept the Torah. While unity reigned among the nations there was no animosity, but as soon as the Jewish people accepted the Torah and said, "We will do and we will hear," all of a sudden dreadful hatred descended upon the Jewish People. Our Sages said in Talmud *Shabbat* 89a: "What is the meaning of Mt. Sinai—the mountain whereon there descended hostility (*sin'ah*)?" (F.C.O., p. 506)

~~

"He also showed love to peoples, all the holy ones are in Your hands; and they were brought in at Your feet, He would bear Your utterances. The Torah that Moses commanded us is the heritage of the Congregation of Jacob." (Deut. 33:3–4) One *Simchat Torah*, R' Zusia of Hanipol, upon reading these words began to cry bitter tears. He said, "Almighty God, You show such love to other people that You have dispersed us to be among them in exile. Yet, 'All the holy ones are in Your hands'—Your people do not abandon You and have faith in You. 'And they were brought in at Your feet'—they are constantly being persecuted. Nevertheless, 'He would bear Your utterances' that are constantly proclaiming 'The Torah that Moses commanded us is a heritage of the Congregation of Jacob.'" (F.U.A.O., vol. 4, p. 359)

~~

On the same *Pasuk*, R' Schneur Zalman of Liadi commented that the attainment of true spiritual pleasure can be reached only when one comprehends the esoteric aspects of Torah. (*Likkutei Torah*, p. 96)

~~

"The Torah that Moses commanded us is the heritage of the Congregation of Jacob." (Deut. 33:4) The Kotzker cited the Talmud *Avodah Zarah* 19a, which states that in the beginning the Torah is called by His Name and at the end credit is given to the one who studies it. It says in Psalms 1:2: "But his desire is in the Torah of Hashem, and in his Torah he meditates day and night." Rashi interpreted this to mean that at the outset it is called Hashem's Torah, and then it belongs to the one who labors in it. The Rebbe explained that the Torah can be reached only by toil, and then can one possess it and it will be a strong possession. It will guide one onto the right path on which he will always remain. However, if one does not labor in study, it will not stay with him. That is what the Talmud *Megillah* 6b meant by the statement: "If a may says to you, 'I have labored and found,' you may believe him." (*Ohel Torah*, p. 96)

"When the heads of the nation are gathered, as one, the tribes of Israel. . . ." (Deut. 33:5) The Toldot Yaacov Yosef noted that first there must be unity among "the heads of the people," the leaders, and then the people will be united. (F.U.A.O., vol. 4, p. 360)

"May Reuben live and not die, and may his men be in the count. And this to Judah . . . may his hands fight for him and may You be a helper against his enemies." (Deut. 33:6,7) R' Tzadok HaKohen of Lublin explained that the tribes were blessed individually so that each one would renew the words of the Torah according to its rooting in the Torah. Therefore, because Reuben saved Joseph's life, his blessing was: "May Reuben live"—that his tribe should have abundance of life from the words of the Torah; "May his men be in the count"—may each individual be a part of each letter of the Holy Torah. Our Sages noted that Judah's blessing was based on his confession for his wrongdoing (Talmud *Sotah* 7b): "May his hands fight for him"—that he would be able to handle his problems in this world and Hashem would "be a helper against his enemies." (*Pri Tzaddik*, p. 271)

On the words "And this to Judah," Rashi comments: "Who caused Reuben to confess? Judah." The Gerer Rebbe noted that Reuben confessed by wearing "his sackcloth and with fasting" (*Bereshit* 37:29) and Judah confessed by admitting his wrong deed (38:26). The Torah is telling us that one should not repent just by fasting. What is needed is a confession with the sincere feeling of a broken heart. Our Sages noted: "Neither sackcloth nor fasting are effective but only penitence and good deeds." (Talmud *Taanit* 16a) (M.T., vol. 5, p. 167)

꧁

"May Hashem's beloved dwell securely by Him; He will shield him forever. . . ." (Deut. 33:12) Rav Avraham Yitzchak HaKohen Kook noted that the *Musar* literature suggests that one should not get too involved in friendship for it may end in becoming enemies. However, there is one friend on Whom one can rely and maintain friendship for an entire life: "Hashem's beloved dwell securely by Him; He will shield him forever." (F.U.A.O., vol. 4, p. 362)

꧁

"And through the goodwill of Him that dwells in the thornbush, may it come to (*t'vu'atah*) the head (*l'rosh*) of Joseph." (Deut. 33:16) R' Yosef Moshe of Z'barov, in his *sefer Brit Avraham*, cited *Kohelet* 5:9, which states: "He who loves abundance will have no produce (*t'vuah*)." Rashi noted that it means Talmud and the laws. The Z'barover said that one must study the Talmud and the laws to *la'asot r'tzon avinu shebashamayim* — the first letters of each word spelling *l'rosh* — meaning "to do the will of our Father Who is in Heaven." (M.T., p. 436)

꧁

In the *sefer Siftei Tzaddikim* there is an explanation for the *Pasuk* "For they kept Your words, and Your covenant they would preserve. They shall teach Your laws to Jacob and Your Torah to Israel. . . ." (Deut. 33:9–10) If one is careful of what one says and does not say what is not necessary, then "Your covenant" is preserved, for one is dependent on the other. When both are observed, then we can "teach Your laws to Jacob and Your Torah to Israel," for one acquires the privilege to study and judge the law in accordance with the Torah. (M.T., vol. 5, p. 167)

꧁

"Your locks are iron and copper, and like the days of your prime, so may your old age be." (Deut. 33:25) Rashi comments: "Like your days that are good to you . . . so shall be the days of your old age." The Chidushei Harim explained that if we lock in the strength of our youth with "iron and copper," and not use it up on unnecessary activities, then the strength "your old age will be." (M.T., vol. 170)

~~

"Fortunate are you, O Israel. Who is like you! A people delivered by Hashem, the shield of your help, Who is the sword of your grandeur; and your enemies will lie to you, but you, you will trample their high places." (Deut. 33:29) R' Moshe Kobriner commented that the Jewish People are fortunate to be proud of "Who is like you!" He said that no one can be compared to us for we are of aristocratic descent, children of a King, close to the Kingdom. Therefore, because of persecution by degenerate people and their corrupt behavior, it is not proper to be depressed and walk around bitter and in a state of melancholy and despair. "The sword of your grandeur" is the sword that will be used on your enemies and will be the nullification of arrogance. Have faith in the King of Kings, that Hashem, "the shield of your help," will come to our aid. (F.C.O., p. 507)

~~

In the *sefer Siach Sarfei Kodesh*, the Gerer Rebbe interpreted the *Pasuk* "Joshua son of Nun was filled with a spirit of wisdom." (Deut. 34:9) The Rebbe said that Joshua, the faithful of Moses, was required by Hashem to be strong and unbending in his observance of the Torah (Joshua 1:7). Therefore, we must be on the alert in our piety, or we may succumb to temptations. (H.A., p. 29)

~~

"And Moses, servant of Hashem, died there. . . ." (Deut. 34:5) The Apter noted that even after Moses passed away, he remained the "servant of Hashem, who carried out all that Hashem required of him." As Rashi noted, Moses was told to "say to Abraham, to Isaac, and to Jacob, 'The oath that the Holy One, Blessed be He, swore to you, He has fulfilled.'" (Deut. 34:4) Moses was asked to tell our forefathers that the land Hashem had sworn to give to the Israelites was fulfilled.

"So," the Apter said, "even after death, Moses remained the 'servant of Hashem.'" (M.T., vol. 5, p. 172)

～～

The Lubliner said that the Torah concludes with the letter *lamed* and begins with the letter *bet*. Together they spell *lev*, "heart." Our Sages say, "We must conclude that the Holy One, Blessed be He, desires the heart." (*Sanhedrin* 106b) The Rebbe said that the heart is the entire Torah. (F.C.O., p. 510)

～～

R' Moshe Sofer of Preshburg noted that the Torah concludes with the word *Yisrael* (Israel) and begins with the word *bereshit*. Both words contain the letters that form the word *ashrei*, "praiseworthy." Therefore, the Torah begins and concludes with the concept of being "praiseworthy." Our Sages noted that King David opened the first chapter of Psalms with the word "praiseworthy"—"Praiseworthy is the man"—and concluded with "Praiseworthy are all who trust in Him " (Talmud *Berachot* 10a) When the letters of *ashrei* are removed from *Yisrael* and *bereshit*, there remain the letters *l'v's*. Using *gimatriah* (numerology), we find that two times *yirah* ("fear" or "awe") equal the numerical value of the letters *l'v's*. There are two types of fear: an inner, underlying fear and a fear that uplifts. The last one can be accomplished only through the study of Torah, for it lights the flame of the heart. The Holy One desires the heart. (M.D., p. 440)

～～

"In the sight of all Israel." (Deut. 34:12) The Mezibozer commented that the Torah concludes with these words to indicate that each Jewish person may see into the Torah according to his own ability. (H.A., p. 481)

～～

The Baal Shem Tov noted that Psalms 19:11 describes the words of the Torah by stating: "They are more desirable than gold, even much fine gold; and sweeter than honey, than drippings from the combs." The Besht explained that everyone desires gold, yet no one is content with the amount he possesses. Honey is exceedingly sweet, but is unpleasant to the one who is satisfied. The Torah is both satisfying and pleasant. (H.A., p. 478)

BIOGRAPHIES

Baal Shem Tov: Rabbi Yisroel ben Eliezer (1698?–1760).
Born: Okop, Podolia, South Poland; Died: Medzibosh, South Poland.
Founder of Chasidism.
Known as the Besht, the acronym of Baal Shem Tov.
Seforim about the Besht: *Sefer Baal Shem Tov, Keter Shem Tov.*

Alexander Rebbe: Rabbi Yerachmiel Yisroel Yizchak Danziger (1853–1910).
Born: Turchin, Poland; Died: Alexander, Poland.
Known for his humility and scholarship.
Discourses published under the title *Yismach Yisroel.*

Amshinover: Rabbi Shimon Shalom Kalish of Amshinov (1883–1954).
Born: Amshinov; Died: Brooklyn, New York.
Known for his extreme love of each Jew.
Torah thoughts, Kabbalistic insights, *gimatriahs* published in *Mashmia Shalom.*

Baal Haflaah: Rabbi Pinchas Horowitz (1730–1805).
Born: Chortkov; Died: Frankfort-on-Main.
Known as a *Posek* (leading halachic authority).

415

Halachic responsa published under title of *Teshuvot Givat Pinchas*.
Author of *Haflaah* and *Panim Yafot*.

~~~~

Baal HaTanya: Rabbi Schneur Zalman of Liadi (1745–1813).
Born: Laznia, White Russia; Died: Piena, near Kursk, Russia.
Also known as "the Rav" and the Alter Rebbe.
Disciple of the Maggid of Mezritch.
Founder of Chabad (acronym for *chochmah binah da'at*—wisdom, insight, knowledge)—synthesis between Chasidism and Torah scholarship.
Author of *Likkutei Amarim (Tanya)* and *Shulchan Aruch HaRav*.

~~~~

B'er Mayim Chayim: Rabbi Chayim Tirer of Chernowitz (1760–1816).
Born: near Butchatch; Died: Safed, Israel.
Student of Rabbi Shmelke of Nikolsburg and the Maggid of Mezritch.
Author of *B'er Mayim Chayim*, *Siduro Shel Shabbat*, and *Shaar Ha-Teffilah*.

~~~~

Belzer Rebbe: Rabbi Shalom Rokeach of Belz (1779–1855).
Born: Brody; Died: Belz.
Chasid of Chzeh of Lublin, the Apter, the Maggid of Koznitz.
Known for his blending of excellence in Torah scholarship and the mystical zeal of Chasidut.
His Torah novella were recorded in *Midbar Kadesh*.

~~~~

Berditchever: Rabbi Levi Yitzchak of Berditchev (1740–1810).
Born: Hoshaknov, Galicia; Died: Berditchev, Poland.
Known as the defender of Israel; known to have argued with Hashem, pleading for an end to the Exile.
Author of *Kedushas Levi*.

Bratzlaver: Rabbi Nachman of Bratzlav (1772–1811).
Born: Mizhbozh; Died: Uman, Podolia, Russia.
Great-grandson of the Baal Shem Tov.
Did not leave a successor.
Known for his tales and profound moral messages, which were re-
corded by Rabbi Nathan, his scribe, in *Sippurei Maasiyot*.
His commentaries are published in *Likkutei Maharan*.

Rabbi Simcha Bunim of Pshys'cha (1767–1827).
Born: Voidislav; Died: Pshys'cha.
Chasid of Maggid of Koznitz and the Choze (Seer) of Lublin.
His students were the Kotzker and the Vorker.
Collections of his thoughts on the Torah are found in *Kol Simchah* and
Ramatayim Tzofim.

Chidushei Harim: Rabbi Yizchak Meir Alter of Ger (1799–1866).
Born: Mognuszew; Died: Ger, Poland.
Chasid of Rabbi Simcha Bunim of Pshys'cha and the Kotzker.
Founder of Gerer Chasidut.
Author of *Chidushei Harim*.

Choze: Rabbi Yaacov Yitzchak Halevi Horowitz (1745–1815).
Born: Shbarshin; Died: Lublin, Poland.
Known for his intuitive powers.
Disciple of the Maggid, Rabbi Shmelke of Nikolsburg, and Rabbi
Elimelech of Lizensk.
His disciples were the Yid HaKadosh, Rabbi Simcha Bunim, and Rabbi
Naftali of Ropshitz.
Writings are contained in *Divrei Emet* and *Zot Zikaron*.

Degel Machnei Ephraim: Rabbi Moshe Chayim Ephraim of Sadilkov (1748–1800).
Born: Medzibosh; Died: Medzibosh.
Grandson of the Baal Shem Tov.
Author of *Degel Machnei Ephraim*.

Dinover: Rabbi Tzvi Elimelech Spira of Dinov (1783–1841).
Born: Shklar; Died: Dinov, Galicia.
Also known as the B'nei Yissas'char.
Eminent scholar in Halachah and Kabbalah.
Author of twenty-nine works including *Derech P'kudecha* and *Igra D'Kallah*.

HaShelah HaKadosh: Rabbi Isaiah Horowitz (1556–1630).
Born: Prague; Died: Tiberias, Israel.
Author of *Shnei Luchot Habrit*.

Rabbi Asher Horowitz (1860–1934).
Succeeded father-in-law as Rebbe in Rimanov.
Author of *Maadanei Melech*.

Rabbi Shmuel Shmelke Horowitz of Nikolsburg (1726–1778).
Born: Chortkov; Died: Nikolsburg, Moravia (now Czechoslovakia).
Some of the students in his yeshivah were: Choze of Lublin, Rabbi Mendel of Rimanov, Rabbi Yisroel of Koznitz, and Rabbi Moshe Leib of Sassov.
Author of *Imrei Shmuel* and *Shemen Hatov*.

Izbitzer: Rabbi Mordechai Joseph Leiner (1800–1854).
Born: Tomashov; Died: Izbica.
Believed in uncompromising Divine providence.
Student of Rabbi Simcha Bunim of Pshys'cha and the Kotzker.
Founder of the Izbica-Radzyn dynasty.
Disciples were Rabbi Leibel Eiger and Rabbi Tzadok HaKohen.
Author of *Mei HaShiloah*.

Rabbi Aharon Karliner (1736–1772).
Born: Yanova; Died: Karlin.
Pioneer of Chasidism in Lithuania.

Rabbi Aharon Karliner the Second (1808–1872).
Born: Stolin; Died: Malinov.
Grandson of Rabbi Aharon the great; known as the second Rabbi Aharon.
His Chasidic insights are published in *Beit Aharon*.

Kedushat Yom Tov: Rabbi Hannaniah Yom Tov Lippa of Zighet (1836–1904).
Born: Sztropkov; Died: Zighet.
Author of *Kedushat Yom Tov*.

Kobriner: Rabbi Moshe Polier (1784–1858).
Born: Piesk; Died: unknown.
Known for his extreme modesty.
Teachings published under the title "Amarot Tehorot.

〜〜

Koretzer: Rabbi Pinchas Shapiro (1728–1790).
Born: Shklov, Russia; Died: Shipitovka, Russia.
Anthology of his thoughts are found in *Imrei Pinchas*.

〜〜

Kotzker: Rabbi Menachem Mendel Morgenstern of Kotzk (1787–1859).
Born: Goray, near Lublin, Poland; Died: Kotzk, Poland.
Student of Choze (Seer) of Lublin and Rabbi Simcha Bunim of Pshys'cha.
Uncompromising in the search for truth.
Thoughts collected in *Ohel Torah* and *Emet V'emunah*.

〜〜

Koznitzer Maggid: Rabbi Yisroel Hopstein of Koznitz (1740–1814).
Born: Apta; Died: Koznitz.
Known for his enthusiasm for Chasidut and concern for the needy and sick.
Author of *Avodat Yisrael*, *Nezer Yisrael*, and *Or Yisrael* on the Zohar.

〜〜

Lisker: Rabbi Tzvi Hirsch Friedman of Liska (1798–1874).
Born: Ujhel; Died: Liska.
Author of *Ach Pri Tevunah* and *Hayashar V'Hatov*.

〜〜

Lubavitcher Rebbe: Rabbi Menachem Mendel Schneerson of Lubavitch (1902–1994).
Born: Nikolayev, Russia; Died: Brooklyn, New York.
Launched campaign for intensification of *mitzvot*; revitalized the belief in the coming of Meshiach; followed the tradition of Chabad.
The Rebbe's discourses were published under the title *Likkutei Sichot*.

Maggid of Mezritch: Rabbi Dov Ber (1704–1772).
Born: Lukatch, Volhynia; Died: Hanipol.
Seforim about the Maggid: *Maggid D'varav L'Yaaḳov* and *Or Torah*.
Some of his students were: Rabbi Shmelke of Nikolsburg, Rabbi Zusia of Hanipol, Rabbi Levi Yitzchok of Berditchev, Rabbi Nachum of Chernobyl, Rabbi Schneur Zalman of Liadi, and Rabbi Elimelech of Lizensk.

Maor Vashemesh: Rabbi Klonymos Kalman Halevi Epstein of Krakow (1754–1827).
Born: Galicia, Southeast Poland; Died: Krakow.
Student of Rabbi Elimelech of Lizensk.
Author of *Maor Vashemesh*.

Rabbi Menachem Mendel of Vitebsk (1730–1788).
Born: Vitebsk, Russia; Died: Tiberias, Palestine.
Studied under the Maggid.
Laid foundation for future Chasidic settlements in Israel.
Thoughts published in *Pri Ha'Aretz*.

Modzitzer: Rabbi Yisroel Taub (1849–1921).
Born: Ratzions, Poland; Died: Modzitz.
The Rebbe created hundreds of musical compositions; favorite hymn "Ezkera" composed while undergoing surgery without anesthesia.
Author of *Divrei Yisroel*.

Rabbi Mordechai of Neshchiz (1742–1800).
Born: Neshchiz; Died: Neshchiz.
Commentaries published under title *Rishpei Eish*, bound together with the work of his son Rabbi Yitzchak, entitled *Toldot Yitzchaḳ*.

⟞⟝

Noam Elimelech: R' Elimelech of Lizensk (1717–1786).
Born: Galicia, Southeast Poland; Died: Lizensk.
Some of his students were: Rabbi Avraham Yehoshua Heschel of Apta,
Choze of Lublin, Maggid of Koznitz, Rabbi Menachem Mendel of
Rimanov, and Rabbi Klonymos Kalman Epstein.
Author of *Noam Elimelech*.

⟞⟝

Ohev Yisroel: Rabbi Avraham Yehoshua Heschel of Apta (1755–1825).
Born: Neustadt, Poland; Died: Medzibosh, South Poland.
Also known as the Apter Rav.
Known for his intense love of the Jewish people, hence the title of his
book, *Ohev Yisroel*.

⟞⟝

Novominsker: Rabbi Nachum Mordechai Perlow (1897–1976).
Born: Minsk; Died: Brooklyn, New York.
Known for his scholarship and communal activities.
Member of Mo'etzet Gedolei HaTorah.
Torah discourses, *Pe'er Nachum*, compiled by his son.

⟞⟝

Primishlaner: Rabbi Meir of Primishlan (1780–1850).
Known for his humor and for pointing out the positive aspects of the
Jewish people.
When talking about himself he would start with the words "Meir says."
His sayings are found in *Divrei Meir* and *Or HaMeir*.

⟞⟝

Rabbi Avraham Moshe Rabinowitz—the present Skoyler Rebbe.
Author of *Chacimah Birmizah*.

Radamsker: Rabbi Shlomo HaKohen Rabinowitz (1803–1866).
Born: Wlosziva, Poland; Died: Radamsk, Poland.
Eminent Torah scholar and Kabbalist.
Author of *Tiferet Shlomo*.

Rimanover: Rabbi Menachem Mendel of Rimanov (1755–1815).
Born: Neustadt; Died: Rimanov.
Known for his deep awe of Hashem as seen in his passion when he prayed.
His disciples were Rabbi Naftali of Ropshitz and Rabbi Tzvi Elimelech of Dinov.

Riziner: Rabbi Yisroel Friedman of Rizin (1797–1850).
Born: Pogrobisht, Ukraine; Died: Sadagora, Galicia.
Great-grandson of the Maggid of Mezritch.
Known for conducting his "court" with the trappings of royalty.
Compilations of his commentaries published under titles of *Irin Kadishin* and *Keneset Yisrael*.

Ropshitzer: Rabbi Naftali Tzvi Horowitz (1760–1827).
Born: Linsk, Galicia; Died: Lanzut, Galicia.
Author of *Zera Kodesh*, *Imrei Shefer*.

Sassover: Rabbi Moshe Leib of Sassov (1745–1807).
Born: Brody; Died: Sassov.
Known as "Father of widows and orphans."
Believed in quiet meditations.
Author of *Likkutei Ramal* and *Chidushei Ramal*.

Satmar Rebbe: Rabbi Toel Teitelbaum (1888–1979).
Born: Sighet, Hungary; Died: New York.
Opposed even slight deviation or innovation.
Torah commentaries published under title *Divrei Yoel*.

S'fas Emes: Rabbi Yehudah Aryeh Leib Alter of Ger (1847–1905).
Born: Warsaw, Poland; Died: Ger, Poland.
Author of *S'fas Emes*.

Sochotchover: Rabbi Avraham Borenstein (1839–1910).
Born: Bendin, Poland; Died: Sochotchov, Poland.
Son-in-law of the Kotzker Rebbe.
Chasid of the Chidushei Harim and the Alexander Rebbe.
Author of *Avnei Nezer* and Eglei Tal.

Rabbi Moshe Teitelbaum of Ujhel (1759–1841).
Born: Pshemishl, Galicia; Died: Ujhel, Hungary.
Author of *Yismach Moshe*.

Rabbi Menachem Nachum Twersky of Chernobyl (1730–1797).
Born: Garinsk, Volhynia; Died: Chernobyl, Ukraine.
Known as the student of the Baal Shem Tov and the Maggid of Mezritch.
Author of *Me'or Einayim*.

Rabbi Tzadok HaKohen (1823–1900).
Born: Kreisberg; Died: Lublin.
Chasid of the Izbitzer; became Rebbe of Izbitz.
Author of *Pri Tzaddik*, *Resisei Laylah*, and *Kedushat Shabbat*.

Vorker: Rabbi Yitzchak Kalish of Vorki (1779–1848).
Born: Poland; Died: Vorki.
The Kotzker was his mentor.
Known for his gentleness and his passionate love for every Jew.

Rabbi Zeev Wolf of Zhitomir (?–1798).
Chasid of the Maggid of Mezritch.
Pleaded for high standards in human relations and disapproved of noisy prayers.
Author of *Or HaMeir*.

Rabbi Yaakov Yosef of Polnoye (1710–1784).
Born: unknown; Died: Polnoye, Volhynia, Russia.
Known as the Toldos.
Close disciple of the Besht.
Author of *Toldot Yaakov Yosef*, the first book published in Chasidim; *Ben Porat Yosef*, *Tzofnat Paane'ach*, and *Ketonet Passim*.

Yid HaKadosh: Yaacov Yitzchak of Pshys'cha (1765–1814).
Born: Przedborz; Died: unknown.
Also known as Yid HaKadosh or Yehudi HaKadosh.
Chasid of the Lubliner.
His discourses are found in *Niflaot HaYehudi* and *Torat HaYehudi*.

Zanzer: Rabbi Chayim Halberstam of Zanz (1793–1876).
Born: Tarnograd, Poland; Died: Zanz, Poland.
Torah commentaries published under the title *Divrei Chayim*.

Rabbi Meshulam Zusia of Hanipol (1718–1800).
Born: Galicia, Southeast Poland; Died: Hanipol.
Known as Rebbe Reb Zusia.
Brother of Rabbi Elimelech.
Sefer about Reb Zusia: *Menorat Zahav*.

BIBLIOGRAPHY

Alfasi, Yitzchak. *Toldot HaChasidut*. Tel Aviv: Tzion Publishers, 1959.

Ben-Amos, Dan and Jerome R. Mintz. *In Praise of the Baal Shem Tov*. Bloomington: 1972.

Boim, Yehudah Menachem. *HaRabbe Rebbe Bunim of Pshys'cha*. Bnei Brak, Israel: Torat Moshe Institute, 1996.

Bratzlaver, Nachman. *Likkutei Maharan*. Jerusalem: Menorah Press, 1936.

Bunim, Simcha of Pshys'cha. *Kol Simcha*. Jerusalem: Torat Moshe, 1963 (reprint).

Dov Ber of Mezritch. *Likkutei Amarim: Magid D'varav L'Yaakov*. Brooklyn, New York: Otzer HaChasidim, 1973.

Erlich, Yisroel. *Hamered HaKadosh*. Tel Aviv: Mered Publications, 1988.

Finkel, Avraham Yaakov. *The Great Chasidic Masters*. Northvale, New Jersey: Jason Aronson, 1996.

———. *Contemporary Sages*. Northvale, New Jersey: Jason Aronson, 1994.

M.T.—Friedman, Alexander Z., ed. *M'einah Shel Torah*. 5 vols. Tel Aviv: Pe'er Publishers, 1962.

Gold, Pinchas Mordechai. *Imrei Shefer*. Brooklyn, New York: 1997.

Hager, Yosef Yerucham Fishel, ed. *Torat Hayehudi HaKadosh*. Jerusalem: Me'ein HaChasidut, 1996.

HaKohen, Tzadok. *Pri Tzaddik*. Lublin, Poland: 1933 (reprinted in Israel).

427

Heschel, Avraham Yehoshua. *Ohev Yisroel*. Bnei Brak, Israel: Siftei Tzadikim, 1995 (reprint of the 1865 edition).

Hopstein, Isroel of Koznitz. *Avodat Yisrael*. Bnei Brak, Israel: 1995 (reprint).

Horodensky, Samuel A. *Shivchei HaBesht*. Tel Aviv, Palestine: Dvir Co., 1946.

————. *HaChasidut V' Ha Chasidim*. Tel Aviv: Dvir Publishing, 1953.

Horowitz, Eliezer Halevi. *Noam Maggidim*. Jerusalem: Nofat Tzofim, 1997.

Horowitz, Naftali Tzvi of Ropshitz. *Zera Kodesh*. 2 vols. Jerusalem: 1984.

Horowitz, Shmuel Shmelke of Nikolsburg. *Shemen HaTov*. Pietrokov: 1904.

Izbitzer, Moshe Chayim. *Mei HaShaluach*. Bnei Brak, Israel: Sifrei Kodesh, 1990.

Kasher, Moshe Shlomo. *N'Tivot B'Machshavah HaChasidut*. Jerusalem: Machon Torah Shelomoh, 1964.

————. *Perakim B'Torat HaChasidut*. Jerusalem: Machon Torat Shelomoh, 1967.

Kevalsky, Shalom Dov. *Peninei HaChasidus (Sefer Bereshit)*. Yitzchak HaKohen Feigenbaum, ed. Jerusalem: Agudat Peninei HaChasidut, 1976.

F.C.O.—Kirschenbaum, Dovid. *Fun di Chasidishe Otsros*. New York: Pardes Publishers, 1948.

Levi Yitzchak of Berditchev. *Kedushas Levi*. New York: Pollack Publishers, 1945.

Lizensker. *Noam Elimelech*. Jerusalem: 1947.

Likkutei Eytzot. Brooklyn, New York: Chasidei Bratzlav, 1963.

T.D.H.T.R.—Menachem Mendel of Rimanov. *The Torah Discourses of the Holy Tzaddik*. Trans. Dov Levine. Hoboken, New Jersey: Ktav Publishing Company, 1996.

————. *Menachem Tziyon* and *Yalkut Menachem*. Jerusalem: Siftei Tzaddikim Publication, 1967.

M.D.—*Milei D'Chasida*. Kiryat Yoel. Monroe, New York: Hotza'as Pisgamim Kadishin, 1998.

Mintz, Jerome R. *Legends of the Hasidim*. Chicago: University of Chicago Press, 1968.

Morgenstern, Menachem Mendel of Kotzk. *Amud Haemet*. Tel Aviv: Pe'er Publishing (reprint), 1984.

———. *Ohel Torah*. Jerusalem: Nofat Tzofim, 1996 (reprint).

Moshe Chayim Ephraim of Sadilkov. *Degel Machnei Ephraim*. Jerusalem: Mir Publication, 1994.

H.A.—Newman, Louis I. *Hasidic Anthology*. New York: Bloch Publishing Company, 1944.

Perlow, Aharon, ed. *Imrot Tzaddikim*. Jerusalem: 1993.

Perlow, Nachum Mordechai. *Pe'er Nachum*. Jerusalem: 1994.

Rabinowitsch, Wolf Zeev. *Lithuanian Hasidism*. New York: Schocken Books, 1970.

Ch.B.—Rabinowitz, Avraham Moshe. *Chachimah Birmizah*. Brooklyn, New York: 1994.

T.S.—Rabinowitz, Shlomo HaKohen of Radamsk. *Tiferet Shlomo*. Jerusalem: 1983 (reprint of 1867 edition).

Sacks, Jonathan, ed. *Discourses by the Lubavitcher Rebbe*. Brooklyn, New York: Kehot Publishing Society, 1996.

Schneerson, Menachem M. *On the Essence of Chassidus*. Brooklyn, New York: Kehot Publications, 1978.

Schneur Zalman of Liadi. *Likkutei Amarim (Tanya)*. Brooklyn, New York: Otzer HaChasidim, 1975.

———. *Ma'amorei Admur HaZaken*. Brooklyn, New York: Otzer Ha-Chasidim, 1988.

Shifchei HaRan. New York: 1971.

Schochet, Jacob I. *Tzava'at Harivash*. Brooklyn, New York: Kehot Publishing Society, 1998.

S.S.K.—*Siach Sarfei Kodesh*. 3 vols. B'nei Brak, Israel: Gitler Bros., 1972.

Steinman, A. *Mishnat Chabad*. 2 vols. Tel Aviv: K'neset Publishers.

Stern, Yechiel Michel, ed. *Gedolei Hadorot*. 3 vols. Jerusalem: Minchat Yisroel, 1995.

G.O.T.—Touger, Eliyahu. *In the Garden of the Torah*. 2 vols. Brooklyn, New York: Sichos in English, 1995.

Twersky, Menachem Nachum of Chernobyl. *Me'or Einayim*. Bronx, New York: Twersky Bros.

F.U.A.O.—Yeushson, B. *Fun Unzer Alten Oitzer*. 4 vols. New York: Shengold Publishers, 1956.

INDEX OF REBBES

Author's Note: When an entry appears without a specific rebbe's name and includes the term *admurim*, this indicates that the references are for more than one rebbe from that dynasty or location.

SOURCE INDEX

About the Author

Victor Cohen received his education in *yeshivot* and obtained his Master of Arts degree in Jewish studies from New York University, where he also did his post-graduate work. He taught history in the New Jersey public schools and was an administrator in the field of Jewish education. At present he is an adjunct professor of philosophy at a county college. His grandfather inspired his interest in *Chasidut* at a young age. He has written and lectured on *Chasidut* and Kabbalah. He has three married daughters and is a grandfather. Victor Cohen lives with his wife in New Jersey.

RECOMMENDED RESOURCES

Chasidism: Its Development, Theology, and Practice
by Noson Gurary   0-7657-5960-8

Classic Chassidic Tales
by Meyer Levin   1-56821-911-3

Contemporary Sages: The Great Chasidic Masters of the Twentieth Century
by Avraham Yaakov Finkel   1-56821-155-4

Everyday Miracles: The Healing Wisdom of Hasidic Stories
by Howard W. Polsky and Yaella Wozner   0-87668-880-6

Forests of the Night: The Fear of God in Early Hasidic Thought
by Niles Elliot Goldsteiin   1-56821-945-8

The Great Chasidic Masters
by Avraham Yaakov Finkel   1-56821-939-3

The Hasidic Anthology: Tales and Teaching of the Hasidim
selected, compiled, and arranged by Louis I. Newman   0-87668-698-3

Hasidic Williamsburg: A Contemporary American Hasidic Community
by George Kranzler   1-56821-242-9

Hasidic Wisdom: Sayings from the Jewish Sages
by Simcha Raz, translated by Dov Peretz Elkins,
and Jonathan Elkins   0-7657-9972-3

The Hasidim of Brooklyn: A Photo Essay
by Yale Strom

1-56821-019-1

Hasidism in Israel: A History of the Hasidic Movement
and Its Masters in Israel
by Tzvi Rabinowicz

0-7657-6068-1

The Heschel Tradition: The Life and Teachings of
Rabbi Avraham Joshua Heschel of Apt
by Moshe A. Braun

1-56821-979-2

Legends of the Hasidim: An Introduction to Hasidic Culture
and Oral Tradition in the New World
by Jerome R. Mintz

1-56821-530-4

Nine Gates to the Chasidic Mysteries
by Jiri Langer, translated by Stephen Jolly

0-87668-249-2

The Prince Who Turned into a Rooster:
One Hundred Tales from Hasidic Tradition
by Tzvi Rabinowicz

0-87668-685-4

The Sayings of Menahem Mendel of Kotsk
by Simcha Raz, translated by Edward Levin

1-56821-297-6

Souls and Secrets: Hasidic Stories
by Joseph Patai, translated by Raphael Patai,
illustrated by Miklos Szines-Sternberg

1-56821-355-7

Why the Baal Shem Tov Laughed: Fifty-two Stories
about Our Great Chasidic Rebbe
by Sterna Citron

0-87668-350-2

Wisdom, Understanding, and Knowledge:
Basic Concepts of Hasidic Thought
by Shmuel Boteach

0-87668-557-2